To renew or order library books visit
www.lincolnshire.gov.uk
You will require a Personal Identification Number.
Ask any member of staff for this

WHITE

796.333

In black and white

£12.99

L 5/9

In Black and White

In Black and White

The Jake White Story

WITH CRAIG RAY

ZEBRA

First published in the UK in 2008

Published by Zebra Press
an imprint of Struik Publishers
(a division of New Holland Publishing (South Africa) (Pty) Ltd)
PO Box 1144, Cape Town, 8000
New Holland Publishing is a member of Avusa Ltd

www.zebrapress.co.za

9 10 8

Publication © Zebra Press 2007
Text © Jake White and Craig Ray 2007

Cover photographs © David Rogers/Getty Images/Gallo Images (front);
The Bigger Picture/REUTERS/Bernard Papon/Pool (back)

PUBLISHING MANAGER: Marlene Fryer
MANAGING EDITOR: Robert Plummer
EDITOR: Ronel Richter-Herbert
PROOFREADER: Irma van Wyk
COVER AND TEXT DESIGNER: Natascha Adendorff-Olivier
TYPESETTER: Monique van den Berg
INDEXER: Robert Plummer
PHOTO RESEARCHER: Colette Stott
PRODUCTION MANAGER: Valerie Kömmer

Set in 11 pt on 14.5 pt Adobe Garamond

Reproduction by Hirt & Carter (Cape) (Pty) Ltd
Printed and bound by Athenaeum Press Ltd, Gateshead, United Kingdom

ISBN 978 1 77022 004 1

Contents

FOREWORD by Eddie Jones ix

FOREWORD by Adrian Gore xiii

PREFACE AND ACKNOWLEDGEMENTS xv

AUTHOR'S NOTE xix

PROLOGUE 1

PART I EARLY DAYS 3
1 Childhood 5
2 Jeppe Boys High 10
3 A schoolboy coach 16
4 With a little help from my friend 29
5 On the right track 33

PART II THE MALLETT YEARS: 1997–1999 37
6 First taste of Bok rugby 39
7 The winning habit 46
8 Winning and losing 52

PART III PAYING MY DUES: 1999–2003 61
9 Buenos Aires success 63
10 Hunting with the Sharks 69
11 In green and gold again 74
12 The Baby Boks 82

PART IV RESTORING BOK PRIDE: 2004–2005 95
13 The dream job 97
14 A new beginning 102
15 Tri-Nations glory 110
16 Grand Slam tour 117
17 Car trouble 126

18 Madiba magic   133
19 Trouble with Markgraaff   138
20 Uncharted territory   143
21 World Cup foundations   149

PART V THE YEAR FROM HELL: 2006   157
22 Hung out to dry   159
23 The pressure mounts   165
24 A torturous tour   175
25 In a tight corner   182
26 Knives out in New Zealand   186
27 Os speaks up   194
28 Soul-searching   199
29 Rustenburg redemption   207
30 Selection posers and structural weaknesses   213
31 Managerial merry-go-round   219
32 100 years remembered   225
33 Twickenham heartbreak   232
34 Goodbye Jake?   240
35 Council sessions   250

PART VI THE GUTS AND THE GLORY: 2007   257
36 Welcome back, Jake, we've cleared your desk   259
37 Number 46   263
38 Doing a deal   270
39 A tough week   276
40 The final countdown   283
41 The dream team   292
42 *Bonjour*, Rugby World Cup   298
43 The business end   308
44 Preparing for history   318
45 World champions   325

EPILOGUE   335
INDEX   337

Foreword
by Eddie Jones

I met Jake when he came to Canberra in 2000 as part of Harry Viljoen's Springbok management. They were in town to visit the Brumbies. Jake, Harry and fitness trainer Chris van Loggerenberg wanted to study our approach to the game and exchange ideas. Harry was a forward-thinking coach who arrived with that reputation. I had no background to Jake White, but I was immediately impressed by his hunger to learn and his attitude towards the game. It was the beginning of a very good professional relationship, which has subsequently transformed into a strong friendship.

I'd classify Jake as a real rugby man, steeped in the traditions and ethos of the game. He relates very well to rugby people, which is one of his strengths.

From our first meeting, we clicked and stayed in touch. Whenever I visited South Africa, or if Jake came to Australia, we'd meet for a beer to discuss rugby.

I've long been impressed by his passion for the game and his thirst to become a better coach. He's always favoured a certain style of rugby and was very clear about how South Africa should play, even before he was Springbok coach.

When Jake was appointed South African coach, I was still Wallaby coach. I knew we would have to cross swords on the field, but it never affected our friendship. It may have come across that way in the media because we'd get a little frisky through the press at times, but it was all part of the game of promoting rugby and building interest, particularly in Australia. And Jake entered into the spirit of the jousting. I really enjoyed that, as it was never something we formally discussed.

We'd still meet for the odd beer and chat, although the conversations never centred on the Wallabies' play or on tactics the Springboks employed. We did discuss game plans of other teams such as the All Blacks, and tried to share ideas on mutual opponents. More often than not, I was impressed with Jake's analysis of the opposition.

At the end of 2004, both Australia and South Africa were on an end-of-season tour to Britain. The Boks had lost badly to England, and Jake took a day off to fly to Edinburgh. It was his first northern hemisphere tour and the Boks were up against Scotland the following week. Over breakfast we shared ideas on the strengths and weaknesses of England and Scotland. Jake hasn't always received enough credit for his attention to detail.

After I left the Wallaby job, our friendship grew over numerous phone calls and e-mails. I was due to spend a week or two with the Boks in 2006, but we cancelled it because of bad timing. That's when we first explored the possibility of working together in a more formal capacity. But it took more than a year before it actually happened.

My appointment as technical advisor with the Springboks prior to the World Cup was all because of Jake's insisting and cajoling of his bosses. I felt I had something to offer and he believed I had a role to play. He was determined. That's another example of his determination in difficult odds, because I don't think I was a popular choice with large sections of SA Rugby's administration.

I knew Jake fairly well, but when I worked with the Springboks I realised the extent of his generosity and how much personal time he was prepared to invest in a range of people. Although he's quite young, he's done just about every job in the game and has vast experience, so he goes out of his way to make himself available to his staff and to people in general.

What also impressed me was his sincerity and how he ensured that his players were looked after. Nothing was too much trouble if it benefited the team, and I guess he butted heads with people at times because of that trait.

Those characteristics had a great bearing on how his team gelled, and I don't only mean the players. I'm also referring to the coaching and management staff.

When I entered the Bok set-up, I couldn't help but notice the external pressures Jake had to deal with. It's hard enough being an international coach of one of the top four or five nations. The expectations are massive, especially in a country such as South Africa, where the Springboks are revered.

You're playing with slim margins as a top international coach, so if there is any interference in team selection or any other aspect, it can be destabilising. Jake had those 'normal' pressures as an international coach, and then another layer other coaches I know don't have to endure.

I understand why, in a young democratic country, certain decisions are made for South African rugby, but it makes life incredibly tough for a good coach. And Jake coped amazingly well. I think his record speaks for itself.

Even though there was no direct political interference at the World Cup, when he saw some comments in the papers about how he wasn't meeting political targets, it did have an effect on him. Everyone within the team knew Jake was doing what he could in terms of transformation, while trying to produce a winning team. Negative reports cut him on a personal level. Jake is an emotional bloke who cares a lot about his players and the team, so those aspects got to him on a certain level. Somehow he's come through it all with his sense of humour intact.

I don't know what the future holds for Jake, but I hope we manage to cross swords again at some stage. Until then, I tip my cap to an excellent coach and a great friend.

EDDIE JONES
October 2007

Foreword
by Adrian Gore

'Just be yourself and run like crazy ...'

I recently read these words in a school essay that Jake White had written in 1981 at the age of 17. The essay was found by Jake's English teacher among a pile of old documents and published in the Sunday papers the day after the Springboks won the 2007 Rugby World Cup. In it, he described his life's dream – to play rugby for the Springboks or, better even, to coach the team one day.

The essay is written with sincerity and passion, yet young Jake used words sparingly and wrote in a matter-of-fact style. I found it profoundly moving both in its brevity and its authenticity. It has stayed with me, because it struck me as remarkable that someone so young had such a clear idea of exactly what he wanted to achieve – and how to go about it.

While almost every South African schoolboy may dream of being a great rugby player or soccer star, the essay makes it clear that, even then, Jake's dream was about leading others to greatness. He knew then, as he has proven now, that the key to success is to have an authentic dream true to one's own talents and values (*'Just be yourself'*) – and to invest all one's energy and effort in attaining it (*'... and run like crazy'*).

Reading the essay that Sunday morning, I glimpsed the enormity of his achievement. It took him twenty-six years to realise what he set out to do. I am certain that, in the pages of this book, we will get a clearer sense of the relentless effort, drive and passion it must have required of him.

And this 17-year-old's dream has made an indelible impact on our country. Newspaper reports and passage conversations around the country still speak of the way the 2007 Rugby World Cup victory in France brought our nation's people together. The echoes of the *vuvuzelas* ring in my ears weeks after the event – a reminder of those shared moments of euphoria.

But Jake White's success story is not just one about victory and celebration. It is also a story of challenges, disappointments and misunderstandings. It is littered with hard issues intrinsic to our beautiful yet ever-complex South Africa that affect every sphere of our society. In many respects, it represents a microcosm of our country and the challenges we face not only in our sports, but also in business, politics and our community. However, Jake's story demonstrates that, despite the challenges, if we work together to harness the enormous talents and assets we as South Africans possess, we can overcome them. We undoubtedly have the ability to deal with the issues and to compete and win on any international field. It's an exhilarating thought.

Like Jake, at Discovery we also started small with the simple conviction that we could make a difference. Today that dream is encapsulated in our core purpose of making people healthier and enhancing and protecting their lives. Jake's story has affirmed to me again – in my own life, within Discovery and within the broader context of our nation's future – that as long as our goals are authentic and we 'run' hard to achieve them, they are attainable.

ADRIAN GORE
CEO: Discovery
October 2007

Preface and acknowledgements

When Craig and I discussed writing *In Black and White*, I was adamant that I didn't want to sound like I was whinging. I've always advised the players that they shouldn't take cheap shots at people in a book. The forum for commenting on your teammates or coaches was when you worked with them, and I can honestly say I've done that.

My aim was not to embark on a witch-hunt or to embarrass people, but to tell the truth about my rugby career, from childhood to coaching the Boks. I think Craig and I have achieved our goal.

When we started writing, the story was still unfolding. I was in the midst of a difficult 2006 season, during which the team struggled. At times we weren't sure if there would be a 2007 section to write. It's been a roller-coaster ride, and I've tried to explain the pressures I had to endure.

The following pages contain my account of various incidents and the impact they had on me in my life and career. I make no apologies for that.

There are many people to thank for their help over the past four years. Our team couldn't have achieved what they did without the amazing support of the South African public. Let's start there.

Former Springbok rugby promotions manager Anne-Lee Murray has the knack of popping up in all the right places at all the right times. Sports agent Craig Livingstone has protected my professional welfare. I owe a lot to SA Rugby national teams' manager Andy Marinos, former Bok captain Morné du Plessis, who has been a great inspiration, and my personal assistant Carla van der Merwe. The amazing men and women who comprised the Bok team management from 2004 to 2007 have all done their bit. Springbok selectors

Pieter Jooste and Ian McIntosh always contributed constructive ideas in selection meetings.

Alan Knott-Craig, CEO of Vodacom, has played a huge role as a Bok supporter. Director of sales and marketing Neil Fraser, MD Helder Pereira, John van Rooyen and Hazel Lewis of Southern Sun Hotels have all been unbelievable. Lin Glass of British Airways made sure the Bok team had every type of assistance possible. Charlie Newell of BA, a Jeppe old boy, went out of his way to arrange flights and upgrades. Sasol's Andriessa Singleton, chief executive Pat Davies, former deputy chief executive Trevor Munday, chairman Peter Cox and Richard Hughes have never hesitated to satisfy requests for the good of the team. I've enjoyed the support of Paul Harris, CEO of FirstRand Limited, and Jeppe old boy Nick Dennis of Tiger Brands. Louis von Zeuner of Absa has been good to me.

Tex Texeira and Gert Roets of SuperSport never hesitated to accommodate my requests, and then documented the journey too. Thanks also to Imtiaz Patel, CEO of SuperSport, for pulling me out of a gloomy state with a sobering pep talk in my Sydney hotel during a difficult 2006 Tri-Nations tour.

Professor Tim Noakes, thanks for all the sage medical advice.

In terms of personal benefits, huge thanks go to Paarlberg BMW – Karl Dahl in particular – for ensuring I've driven around the Cape Peninsula in comfort. It seems appropriate that a book documenting the mental and physical struggles of my coaching goals for Bok rugby should have Discovery as a sponsor. CEO Adrian Gore, Sean Hanlon and Suzanne Hanlon all looked out for me over four years.

David Moss and Jenny Moss of Picot & Moss supplied Tag Heuer timepieces. Grant Stevens (we'll forgive him for being a King Edward's boy) ensured I played with Mizuno golfing equipment. Rob Bartrum at Mizuno also did his bit. Callum and Rory Scott provided a good supply of Pringle clothing. Adrian de Souza, Gavin Cowley, Roly Humphrey and Marcello 'March' Fiasconaro kitted me out with Adidas apparel when required.

Butch Watson-Smith, former head of national teams at SA Rugby, has been a close friend. Craig Lardner helped up my game in terms of public speaking and presentations. To Ernie and his father Neels Els, you know I'm a lover of the game. It's helpful to have the backing of fellow South African sporting achievers.

I've had continuous support from Johann Rupert, and my friends Graham George and John Kruger have been at the rugby tournaments that counted. André 'Buda' Badenhorst is another Jeppe mate. Thanks also go to my brother Jon White.

What can I say about John Smit's value to me personally? I have huge respect for him, and there was never any doubt about who led our group. He's matured an amazing amount, and referees talk about how they enjoy working with him on the field. As a captain and a friend, he's been unbelievable.

It's been amazing to bump into Jeppe old boys around the world, and receive messages of support. One old boy sent me our school motto during the World Cup: '*Forti nihil difficilius* – for the brave, nothing is too difficult'. Our Bok slogan during the week of the RWC final was about being brave. It seemed cheesy to recite my school motto to the team, but when I saw Henning Gericke conduct a session with the Boks on being brave, I realised the coincidence was significant.

I'm hoping the joy of victory has outweighed some of the stressful ordeals endured during four years by my wife Debbie and boys Clinton and Wesley. There's no coaching manual for families on how to endure the disappointment of missed birthdays and sporting milestones when your dad travels a lot. Your support has meant the world to me.

JAKE WHITE
October 2007

Author's note

I never imagined that writing a book – especially a book about someone else's life story – would be so all-consuming. For 18 months, *In Black and White* became so much a part of my daily life that it was impossible to neatly lock it away at the end of a day. When we started writing, Jake and the Springboks had embarked on what would become a torrid 2006 international season, and for a while it appeared as if we would have to end the story after the Tri-Nations. A few months later, it looked as if the story might reach its conclusion following a difficult end-of-season tour. Thankfully, 11 months later we found ourselves frantically putting the finishing touches to the manuscript in Paris 20 hours after the Boks had been crowned world champions.

I'd like to thank Jake for taking the chance, firstly in opening himself up in a book, and secondly for backing me to do it. It's been a wonderful ride, full of challenges along the way, which has made it even more rewarding.

To the team at Zebra Press, my sincere thanks: Marlene Fryer for giving the project the green light, and Robert Plummer for his massive input. And a special word of praise to Ronel Richter-Herbert for her patience with my ad hoc delivery of the chapters. We made it in the end.

I'd also like to thank those people who offered their support over the months:

Alex Burger for her legal brains and friendship.

Cecelia Amory of Champion Tours for organising the flights to France and back on Egypt Air, so I could finish the job.

The Hickey clan for opening their family home in Puissalicon, and Ciara especially for her friendship and excellent advice.

My great friend and mentor Andy Colquhoun, who deserves a special mention for always having an ear and a wise word. I hope you enjoy the book.

Stephen Lambrou, the best mate a man could have, and one of the bravest people I know.

And finally the incredible Kim Maxwell, who has all my love and respect. Projects like this can never be successful without support. Kim has been a rock. Her eye for detail has made me look good, and her constant encouragement has been vital.

CRAIG RAY
October 2007

Prologue

Two days before the Rugby World Cup final, the *Sunday Independent* asked for my permission to use extracts from a school essay I'd written as a 17-year-old. I'd forgotten about the assignment in an English class 26 years earlier. Amazingly, Daniela Pitt, my English teacher at Jeppe Boys High at the time, had kept the piece. During the week of the final, she read it out to the Johannesburg school where she teaches now. When the newspaper requested my permission to print the essay, I had no objections. I quipped that if they improved my English, I might get a better mark.

But, when I read what I'd written in 1981, I became a little more sentimental.

Part of the essay read as follows:

I have a big dream and that is rugby. I have felt so much pride wearing the No. 2 Jeppe rugby jersey. I had to work hard to get it and at times my muscles ached and our coach pushed me really hard. He made me feel that I could carry on.

Some of my friends didn't make the team, but I continued. Soon our team started winning, game after game. When I walked on stage to receive my awards, I actually wanted to cry, I felt so fantastic. I saw the Standard 6s looking up at me and I wanted to say 'Hey guys, you can do it too!'

What are my dreams for the future? My greatest dream is to play rugby, especially for the Springboks. But even to become their coach. I have seen how you can make people believe in themselves; how you can show people that every single person can be a winner if you want it.

The secret is not being part of a large pack – just be yourself and run like crazy. That feeling of success is like no other.

So I am going to continue to dream – if I make it, it will make me the happiest in the world. Imagine playing on an international field and winning. That's another essay altogether.

On 20 October 2007, I had had nearly four years of fighting to do things my way, to select the players I'd singled out. But in the dying moments of the final against England, none of that mattered. This match wasn't about saying 'up yours' to anybody. I just wanted to make South Africans and South African rugby proud again. I'd won some battles and lost others, and the Webb Ellis Trophy was within reach: 'South Africa, World Champions 2007.' It had a great ring to it.

I grew up idolising the green and gold and dreamt of playing for the Springboks, but by the end of high school I knew I wasn't good enough to be a Bok. But I loved the game and started coaching. And I found my role – to coach the Springboks.

Now, years of slog and many uphill battles were about to pay off on a cold night in Paris. I had visualised Fourie du Preez kicking the ball into touch in the World Cup final and, as I looked on, that's exactly what happened. Fourie glanced at referee Alain Rolland, who nodded. The ball was booted into Row G as the final whistle sounded.

There was whooping and celebrating. The scene was manic. Fans were ecstatic and relieved players were leaping all over one another, hugging the coaches and back-slapping me. This is what rugby is about – a squad of players sharing a common bond and achieving a goal.

Tears flowed and I sobbed on the shoulders of the brave men who'd done the country proud. Just before we collected our gold medals, SARU president Oregan Hoskins approached me to extend his congratulations.

'Well done,' he said. 'One thing you must know – they can never take this away from you.' I smiled broadly as I replied, 'You're right, Mr President. They can never take this away from me.'

PART I

EARLY DAYS

1

Childhood

Rugby has always been part of my life. Some of my earliest memories involve rugby, and every major decision and aspect of my path is in some way linked to this great game; from moulding me in my youth and providing me with great opportunities and lessons, to meeting my wife, plus the little things in between. It's rugby that's been a constant throughout my life.

I wasn't a great player, but I loved to play, to participate. I was, and still am, acutely aware of the importance of the game, beyond the stratospheric levels that I've occupied for the past four years. There is no greater honour than being part of a Springbok rugby team. That's the reserve of a lucky few. I am one of them, but even if I weren't, rugby would still be an integral part of who I am. It's a game that provides camaraderie and a sense of worth that few other sports can match. I've come to know my best friends through rugby. And all my fondest – and worst – memories are linked to rugby. The personal disappointment of not gaining colours at school to the joy of coaching the Springboks to victory over the All Blacks – they're all part of the roller-coaster ride rugby has afforded me.

I think of years in terms of rugby teams. 'Oh, 1991, that was Brent Moyle's team at Jeppe,' or 'Yes, 2002 was when Clyde Rathbone captained the SA Under-21 side.' Some people relate times and places to music; I attach those memories to rugby teams.

I wanted to be a great player. As a child, I dreamt of running out for the Springboks, as millions of South African boys do. But I eventually realised that my calling was not going to be as a player. I was lucky to meet people honest enough to tell me this at a time when I didn't want to accept it. I'm sure it wasn't easy for them. David Quail, the former headmaster at Jeppe Boys High, my alma mater and the school where I made my first big strides as a coach, perhaps summed up my passion for the game best. When asked by the Transvaal Rugby Union whether I'd be the right man for a coaching job at their organisation, David told them: 'If it's rugby you want him for, then I guarantee you he'll give you 100 per cent and be a wonderful asset. If it's anything else, I wouldn't recommend him.' I got the job.

I'm not someone who can detach himself from the game. I'm always in rugby mode; I think about rugby when I wake up, and I think about it before I fall asleep. Sometimes I dream about it. I don't know what I would've done if I wasn't part of rugby, but I'm sure I would be a miserable person.

My first day of school was in Pretoria at Hatfield Primary, which didn't offer rugby; it was a soccer-playing school. My folks split up at about the same time, and it turned into a very acrimonious divorce. Back in the late 1960s, early 1970s, getting a divorce was legally difficult and socially frowned upon. And my dad and mom went through a very bitter battle, which left an ugly taste for years.

So my mom Rose sent me away to boarding school at Dale College. She initially moved to Queenstown in the Eastern Cape to stay with her parents. The town is about 70 kilometres from King Williams Town, where Dale is situated.

My brother Jon was only four at the time, so he stayed with my mother, but I, as the bigger six-year-old, was packed off to the hostel. Although my mother was reasonably close initially – at least in terms of distance – when you're that small, she might as well have been thousands of miles away. I didn't go through to Queenstown often.

I was sent away and told to get on with it. It was done partly in my interest, as the situation at home had been very unpleasant, but I think my mom just couldn't cope at the time. She stayed in the Eastern Cape for only a few months before moving back to Johannesburg due to circumstances beyond her control.

Those early years were tough. I only went home at the end of each term, and as a six-year-old I had to catch a train from King Williams Town to Johannesburg, which is a journey of nearly 1 000 kilometres. It's a big ask of a young kid, but I guess it taught me a lot of independence as well.

I spent a lot of time in the school hostel over weekends, but occasionally I stayed with families in the town, or I went to farms owned by families whose children attended Dale. I would also be invited to the home of a teacher called Dummy Taylor, who's a legend in education in the Eastern Cape. He ran a small boarding house for a few boys. It was more personal and he was good to me. A lot of the time, though, I remained in the hostel, as people didn't always have time for this little guy from Pretoria with his problems. But while this was going on my father was very unhappy about me being so far away from home.

He told my mother he wanted to come down and steal me out of boarding school. It wasn't fun being caught in the middle, and even as a young child I understood the issues and resented the situation. I look back now and am able to see why my mother sent me away. I can't say I'm happy about it, but she had her reasons and was going through a difficult time.

When I was about nine, my mother met her current husband, Dennis. When he proposed to her, I was removed from Dale and returned to Johannesburg, where I attended school as a dayboy. In Standard 4 (Grade 6), at the age of 12, I went back to boarding school, to Lord Milner near Warmbaths (now Bela Bela). I was happier in boarding school than living at home. And they offered rugby.

Because of the divorce and circumstances that prevailed at the time, I became estranged from my father. It was an unsatisfactory situation for all concerned. Although my dad came to watch me play rugby when I was first-team captain at Lord Milner and was very proud of my achievement, we effectively did not see each other any more. He also came to see me once or twice when I was in matric, but the meetings were fleeting and we had little to say to one another.

A few years after I left school, when I was already married, my wife Debbie and I drove to Pretoria so she could enrol for a university course. She asked me: 'Where did you live?' I told her we were actually very close to my childhood home. She suggested we go and see if my father was still living there. I told her that I thought he'd moved, but that my *ouma* still lived in Church Street, so perhaps we should pay her a visit.

We arrived outside my grandmother's house, and the gardener was tending some plants. I asked him if anyone was in. He said the 'boss' had gone out, but the 'ou missus' was around. As he spoke, my dad drove in. He looked shocked to see me. We hadn't seen each other for five or six years. He invited us in for lunch, and that was the start of us rekindling our relationship. We stayed in touch from that day on. He met my kids, spent time with our family and eventually moved to Cape Town, where he lived with my brother. He died on 25 March 2003. He never saw me become Bok coach, but at least he got to know his grandchildren and we had closure in our relationship.

I was very happy about our reconciliation, as I never really had a father, and having lived away from home from such a young age it was good to have him back in my life.

My first ever rugby game was for Dale. I don't recall the opposition, but I remember the occasion clearly. I went down to the fields in the early morning as a six-year-old, and from that moment rugby became a part of who I am. There was frost on the ground and footprints etched into the field. I remember having numb feet, but above all I remember the joy of playing rugby. The memories down the years are vivid.

I had wonderful coaches at Lord Milner, and they helped shape me into the coach I am today. Jorrie Jordaan was my first coach. He now lives on the South Coast of KwaZulu-Natal, and we are still in touch. The other coach was a guy called Van der Merwe. We played in small, predominantly Afrikaans-speaking towns such as Alma, Naboomspruit and Thabazimbi when I was a prep-school kid. Some of the games took place on dry fields with *dubbeldorings*, a type of thorn that would hurt like hell if it punctured your skin. We played on some grounds that were like concrete; others were lush fields.

Those were unbelievable days. If we won, the coach would let us stop and pick fruit to eat on the way home – lovely ripe marulas to take back to the hostel. We'd fill our jerseys. In a place like Alma we ate a fruit called *klappers*. It's a hard fruit that you have to break open like a coconut. We'd get up at 4 a.m. and drive to play a game against a school in Nylstroom. We'd spend the entire day there, eating *vetkoek* (a savoury doughnut filled with mince) …

The spirit on the drive back to school, stopping for Cokes and sweets and arriving back at the hostel late at night, especially after winning, are happy memories directly linked to rugby. The whole school would go together, from the babies to the netball girls, and as a member of the winning first team, you felt really special. Rugby gave me the stability in my life that I lacked at home.

While attending Lord Milner, I was invited to the Far North Primary School Craven Week Trials in 1976. And although I didn't make the team, it was a vital part of growing up. I was a rare species: an English-speaking boy who made it to Craven Week trials in an Afrikaans-dominated region. Five other boys from my team were also invited. At the trials I saw players who were bigger and better than me, and I realised that I had a long way to go, which prepared me mentally for the more competitive environment of high school.

I'm not exaggerating when I say that rugby saved me. By becoming the

First-XV captain at prep school, I was fully accepted. Boarding school was also a salvation. I became a prefect and head of house, and I owed most of it to my rugby. But heading on to high school, I knew I'd have to start all over again.

2
Jeppe Boys High

Starting over at Jeppe Boys High had special meaning for me, beyond the normal anxiety of going to a new school and making new friends. Several years earlier, my mother had remarried. My stepfather, Dennis White, who was always very good to my brother Jon and me, legally adopted us and, after completing prep school at Lord Milner, he and my mother thought it best if I changed my name to White. I was born Jacob Westerduin, which was my name until I was 13. I'm actually from Dutch descent.

My mother had wanted me to take Dennis's name for some time, but it made sense to wait until high school because of the paperwork involved. I was taken aback, as I hadn't seen it coming, but the matter was not for discussion. I can honestly say that I did not want to change my name. I was angry, upset, scared and shocked in equal measure. Imagine having to change your identity after 13 years. It wasn't easy, but I was left with no choice. Even today, I still sometimes think about it when I sign 'Jake White'. It did affect me for some time. It seemed such a strange thing to do, but I eventually accepted it.

All my application forms to Jeppe bore my new name – the name I still carry today. From day one in Standard 6 (Grade 8) I was 'Jake White'. It took a little getting used to, and I sometimes didn't respond when someone called me or talked to me, because I didn't recognise the name. But I soon grew accustomed to it.

My biological father, Johan, had attended Tukkies (the University of Pretoria), where he studied for a BSc before working for the mining and engineering company AECI. He built homes in and around Pretoria, and was a fanatical Blue Bulls supporter – which is ironic, considering how many people believe I have something against the Bulls.

I have no bad feelings towards my father or about my folks splitting up when I was a kid. Life deals you some tough blows, and I view my circumstances as fortunate in some ways. It happened at an important time in the development of my character. It helped me in the way I do my job today and the way in which I deal with people, as well as the way I manage players and staff. There is a whole trust–value system that I adhere to with the people and players around me, for which I have been heavily criticised. The media has written that I'm too loyal to certain players. But my childhood instilled those values in me, because when you have to survive on your own, your character is perhaps the only thing that you have to rely on.

For my high-school career, I had applied to all the top Johannesburg boys' schools, such as Parktown, King Edward VII School (KES) and Jeppe. I think I actually wanted to go to KES, but Jeppe was the first school to accept my application, and my mother went off to the McCullough and Bothwell shop, stockists of the Jeppe uniform, and bought all my gear. A week later KES also accepted my application, and I told my mother I wanted to go there, figuring they had a better rugby programme. The KES First XV were legendary at the time, and the best marketing tool any school can have is a powerful rugby team. Back then they had more successful rugby teams than just about every school in Johannesburg, including Jeppe.

In 1977, KES were one of the powerhouses of schoolboy rugby, coached by the legendary Norman McFarland. It would have been great to play under him, but I might not have been involved in the game today if I had gone there. By the time I was in matric, I was playing hooker against McFarland's son Steve, who was in the KES first team, so the chances of me making the KES First XV were probably slim. I am not implying that nepotism was involved – Steve ended up playing for the Transvaal Under-21 team, and was definitely a better player than me. The point is, at KES I would not have enjoyed the experience of first-team rugby. And without that enjoyment and achievement, I might not have been as passionate about the game.

My mother simply told me that I wasn't going to KES after she had paid so much money for the Jeppe uniform. I wasn't disappointed, or, if I was, it lasted about five minutes. I was happy because I'd be going to a boys' school where rugby was like a religion.

I was told I'd be a boarder at Tsessebe House, which was traditionally the best sporting house at the school. The hostel was run by some tough housemasters, who demanded high standards, and older boys who wanted Tsessebe to remain the best house in the school. To be really honest, I was scared when I arrived at Jeppe, like any kid would be, even though I had been to boarding school before. I arrived in my khaki uniform with my *trommel* (metal trunk), which contained my life's possessions. I tried to settle in as quickly as possible, which for me meant playing sport.

It was January, cricket season, and I made the Under-13A team. That went well and I made some friends, but what I was most looking forward to was the rugby season. Rugby was everything to me. And by the time I reached Standard 6, it was just about all I cared for. Just to make the Under-13A side was a major achievement, especially in the boarding school pecking order. When someone asked what team you played for and you were able to reply, 'A team', it gave you a little status as a junior.

Out of nearly 100 guys playing rugby in our age group at high school, I was selected for the top team. Only four members of that team were boarders, and I was one of just two from my hostel. It definitely helped when I went back to the boarding house in the evenings. Rugby helped me to become accepted in a hostel environment. If you played rugby, you probably got more food than the guy who didn't play. And if you were good at rugby, you probably got away with a few more things, or had more privileges, than the other guys. Rugby seemed to – and I think still does – establish the hierarchy at boarding school.

My first high-school rugby coach was Bernard Friedman, who would go on to coach me at Under-13, Under-14 and Under-15. Actually, for two weeks at Under-15, I gave up rugby to play hockey, and Bernard persuaded me to come back. I think I gave up the game temporarily because I thought I wasn't going to grow enough, and that I'd get more accolades as a hockey player. I desperately wanted to get full colours, and at that point I believed I wasn't going to make the First XV. Also, my best mate at the time was a guy called Grant Brown, who, along with his brothers Mark and Ryan, would go on to become provincial hockey players.

I spent a lot of time with the Brown family over weekends, and I guess I thought I could be like them and succeed at hockey. But after two games I realised it wasn't for me. I treated the stick like a weapon, and basically wasn't very good at it. My frustration at my lack of skill led to a few unsavoury incidents.

But Bernard Friedman convinced me to return to rugby. He was an amazing guy and a talented sportsman. He came 20th in the Comrades Marathon, fourth in the Iron Man Ultra-Triathlon, and played first-team scrumhalf at Jeppe Old Boys. He was a fanatical sportsman, and went on to lecture at Wits University. He was in the process of moving permanently to Australia when we had lunch together in Sydney in 2006. We reminisced, and it brought back all sorts of memories. As with the coaches I'd had at Lord Milner, he had a profound impact on my life as a person and as a coach.

Bernard showed me how important coaches can be in the life of a young person, and how important developing and maintaining relationships can be. He picked me in the Under-13A and Under-14A teams, and asked me to come back to the team during Under-15. I don't know if I would have gone back had he not been the coach. When he asked me, I couldn't refuse.

The hockey season started a little bit earlier than the rugby season, and that's how I came to play the 'other' winter sport. The rugby team played one game, and the second match of the season was against Marist Brothers in Observatory, which was a crunch game back then. Bernard said to me: 'Jake, you've got to come back.' He put me back in the A team and we won that game, which I guess cemented our relationship.

There was a boy called Clifford Pitt, who was the captain of our Under-13 team. Clifford was an adopted kid, and this story is relevant to why rugby is so important to me. Throughout primary school, rugby was something that gave me status and a place in the social hierarchy of the school. Of course, Standard 6 was a different matter, because all the first-team players were like gods. Clifford, who was a dayboy, and I became best mates soon after starting high school. Clifford's older brother Des was about 26, and he insisted on driving us to every away game, no matter where it was – even Potchefstroom. I didn't have to worry about buses or lifts. In those days, we had to say whether we needed a lift to the away games and pay R1.50 to go on the bus. That was a lot of money for a boarder.

The Pitts lived on a mine on the outskirts of the Johannesburg CBD, which was very convenient. In the 1970s, and even into the late 1980s, the First XV would play at 3:30 p.m. on a Saturday. The junior teams would play in the morning, and throughout Under-13s, -14s and -15s, Des and Clifford would take me to their home after our game. Their mom would always make a great lunch for us, and then we would go to watch the first- and second-team games in the afternoon. It might sound like a trivial thing, but to a boarder it was wonderful. And this whole relationship spawned out of playing sport – in this case, rugby. The Pitts were like a family to me, but they were not the only 'surrogate family' I had during my time at Jeppe. At the end of Standard 9 (Grade 11), I went to stay with the Browns – my hockey pals.

I'd had to leave Jeppe for a while because my brother Jon, who didn't enjoy boarding school, had left. Having two boys at two different schools wasn't ideal for my mom and Dennis. I went to Mondeor High, which was the closest school to our home in the south of Johannesburg. It made sense for my folks to have both of us in one school. I only attended Mondeor for one term, because I disliked it and desperately wanted to go back to Jeppe. I couldn't get back into the hostel, because it was really difficult to secure a place in those days, as there was so much demand.

So, once I'd lost my place in the hostel, it wasn't immediately available when I decided to go back. Luckily the Browns stayed in Ernest Road, which is a couple of streets from Jeppe High, and they offered to take me in. So, for four months, until I went back to Tsessebe, I stayed with them. Through my rugby, I'd developed a relationship with the Brown family, and they were very good to me. I don't think I even paid them board and lodging, although my folks may have given them some money that I didn't know about. I was like one of their sons, and they already had five kids. I shared a room with Grant and became part of the family.

When I think back, it's unbelievable how generous they were to me. You're probably wondering what all this has to do with anything – but the role the Browns and the Pitts played in my life was immense. My bond with these people was formed through rugby.

I hadn't arrived at Jeppe dreaming of colours and honours. I arrived wanting to play rugby, but at first I didn't really have a full appreciation of the history and tradition of the school. It didn't take long for me to be sucked into it, though. To see boys with colours, and the hype surrounding the First XV, with all the old boys attending games, soon made me realise that I wanted to be a part of it. I looked at the white full-colours' blazer and thought it was the best uniform I'd ever seen. I still do. It's a wonderful blazer.

But, as it turned out, as a schoolboy I was never awarded full or even half colours. However, I always tell the headmasters or teachers whom I know that perhaps it had been a blessing, as it made me hungrier to want to achieve after school. A lot of guys who achieved at school didn't do so afterwards, because they'd had their little place in the sun when they played for the first team. I, on the other hand, felt that I had much more to prove, even though I played for the first team in 1981. I was not a 'star' and didn't play every game, so I felt rugby owed me something – and I owed the game something too.

I think I knew as early as Standard 8 (when I went off to play hockey) that I probably was never going to make it as a top rugby player. I still had aspirations, but deep down, and perhaps subconsciously, I knew. I had become aware of my limitations and had begun to realise that I was physically a lot smaller than most of my opponents, especially when I played against Afrikaans schools, which had these huge guys.

You realise then that, to be the best at this game, you have to be something quite special. But despite all of that, I continued to try, because I had such influential people around me. The physical education teacher at Jeppe was a guy called Gerry Wernars, who made me want to become a teacher and coach sport at school.

The only reason I wanted to teach was so that I could be a coach. I was not interested in the academic side, which I guess didn't make me a great teacher in the classroom. In those days, just about all sport was amateur, so being a professional coach was not really an option. I enjoyed sport and wanted to be involved in it. Doing something I loved for a career was important.

All the teachers and coaches I've mentioned had played a part in my life, and I collated their positive influences and thought to myself, 'I think I can do that.'

3

A schoolboy coach

After finishing high school, I attended the Johannesburg College of Education (JCE) to study teaching and, by default, I started coaching. A lot of students at the college had coaching jobs at schools all over Johannesburg. They were involved with cricket and soccer at a primary school, or rugby at a high school, to make extra money. Back then (in the early 1980s) they were earning R30 an afternoon for coaching. By chance I approached Parktown Boys High, which was right across the road from my residence at JCE, and out of all the schools I could have gone to in the whole of Johannesburg, it was the one across the road that had a coaching job for me. It's unbelievable, because if they hadn't had a job for me at the time, I might not have coached rugby at that stage.

I didn't have a car, so I used to run to Parktown after lectures to coach rugby. I got paid for two afternoons a week, but I coached for five. The reason was simply that I was having an influence on some schoolboys in the same way my mentors had had an influence on me. I took some boys who were average and added value to them. I saw the change in them. They had suddenly found a niche, along with confidence and/or acceptance. I'd move a C-team player from centre to flank and he'd make the A team.

Or I'd teach a guy to be a scrumhalf because he was not big or fast enough to play elsewhere, and instead of him being a D-team centre, he'd be a B-team scrumhalf. I had ideas about how I wanted a team to play, and I'd coach them to play like that. The results were good, both personally and for the teams and players, and I realised that this was what I really wanted to do. From the positive results (and I don't only mean victories) I could see that some of those boys were given their place in the hierarchy that I'd also once enjoyed.

I was always a student of the game, even when I was playing at school. I wanted to know how and why we did things, and how a move would work out. I have an excellent retentive memory, almost like a photographic memory, for rugby. I guess that's my passion, so that's just how my mind works. I can recall a move, a pass, a try or an entire game almost exactly as it happened, even if it was years ago. This ability has always helped me, and it certainly helped me when I began to coach, because I'd see a move somewhere and think to myself, 'That could work for us.'

I observe things and see what works and what doesn't. I remember in my early years watching a team doing double switches. They didn't work, and the boys and the coach couldn't figure out why. I could see the problem: the first switch would stop the defender, and the second switch would run back in to where the defender had stopped. I suppose I'm very lucky because I was able to look at the move and see exactly why it failed. I believe I was born with a talent for coaching, and I only discovered that when I was an 18-year-old, playing coach for the first time. If I hadn't realised my potential when I started coaching rugby, I might have moved on to something else. But I got good results and good returns early on. I'd try something, and more often than not it would work. And players would come to me and say, 'Coach, that was great.'

College was not only about rugby, though. I met my future wife, Debbie Potgieter, at JCE. Her cousin is Reg Sutton, who was a Jeppe scrumhalf and a serious bodybuilder. He played Under-20 rugby with me at Jeppe Old Boys, and I met Debbie through him. I'd seen her at JCE, and I'd met her at a social or something, but we had never chatted much. I was definitely keen on her, but I didn't really know how to break the ice properly.

Luckily for me, rugby had a way of intervening in my romantic life. I was a little shy about Debbie, but you know how guys are. I started telling Reg that I fancied this girl at JCE. I mentioned her name and he laughed at me and said, 'She's my cousin.' I wasn't sure whether that was a good or a bad thing, but it did give me an 'in' through Reg. We all met up and he made the formal introductions, which helped my cause. Debbie and I got on well, and a few days later we went on our first date.

I'll never forget, we went to the movies to see *Against All Odds*, which in some ways is quite ironic, given the life we've led in the 25-odd years since then. It was a real 'chick flick', as they call it now, although that term wasn't around then. I didn't care; I was just happy to be going to the movies with this beautiful woman. I don't remember a great deal about the movie itself, but I couldn't have made such a bad impression, because a week or so later she invited me to her 21st birthday party.

That was really the start of our relationship. I was just 20, but we got on brilliantly, and were eventually married after we'd both finished college – I was only 25. It's young by today's standards, but in the 1980s it was quite 'normal' to be married in your mid-twenties. Debbie's father was a long-time Germiston Simmer player and member, and her entire family was mad about rugby – not a bad thing in my eyes.

Her dad was one of 11 kids, and he had five or six brothers who were all involved at the club. Debbie grew up in an Afrikaans-speaking home. She enjoys rugby – another good thing, having ended up with me – and is related to the great Springbok looseforward Hennie Muller. She really understands the game, and it reiterates the point that rugby is huge in every aspect of my life.

While my courtship with Debbie was going well, so was my coaching career. At Parktown I moved up the ranks pretty quickly, after starting with the Under-15s in 1982. By 1983 I was coaching the first team, a job I held until 1985. In 1983, Parktown beat KES for the first time in 20 years; it would also be the last time Parktown would beat KES until the early 1990s, when James Moss (a future provincial player) played for them.

I finished coaching at Parktown after completing my degree, and was then supposed to go to the army. In those days all white South African males were expected to do national service. I wasn't keen, but there was no way around it unless you were a conscientious objector. This was Johannesburg in the 1980s, and South Africa was in a fair amount of political turmoil. But, typically of many young white South Africans at the time, I was not politically active. I just wanted to finish teaching so that I could coach rugby in the afternoons. I remember seeing slogans such as 'Free Mandela', but I had very little clue about what was going on. I'd been through a fairly sheltered school career where sport dominated my life.

Some members of the English department at Jeppe, whom I'd come to know later as a teacher at the school, were very liberal and brave people. Teachers Neil Mitchell and John Broderick were part of various anti-apartheid movements, and occasionally suffered at the hands of the police. They were hugely involved in the End Conscription Campaign, and they slowly opened my eyes.

But, by and large, I went through the 1980s more concerned with rugby than anything else. Luckily for me, I was exempted from national service because I suffer from epilepsy, a result of too many concussions playing rugby as a youngster. The exemption came as a surprise, and suddenly I had to go and teach instead of spending two years in the army. I had applied for a post at Jeppe and was accepted, so I began teaching there in 1986. Then my coaching career really took off.

I was immediately asked to coach the Under-15A team, a talented group of players that included future provincial cricketer Dean Laing, who was a superb sportsman at school. He played SA Schools cricket for two years, and was a final trialist at Craven Week in his matric year. The team also included Dave Morkel, who later played prop for the Sharks, and some other very good players. As Under-15s, we went through the season unbeaten.

At the first training session with assistant coach Mark Grace, we called the boys in, and I told them that I take rugby incredibly seriously. I said I didn't have to coach this team – I could give extra lessons, or I could go and work at the racecourse instead. (In those days, to earn extra money, a lot of teachers did extramural work in corporate hospitality at horse-racing meetings on Wednesdays.) I told the team that I'd rather coach rugby, even though I wasn't going to be paid for it, so they had better take it seriously. They all agreed.

I'll never forget my very first practice. I blew the whistle to call them together, but they carried on kicking the ball and horsing around. They eventually ambled over and gathered round. I was angry, and shouted, 'When I blow the whistle, practice starts!'

A guy called Gunter Kampfmann, who had arrived at practice with a brand new pair of boots, chirped me. I sent the whole group for a run around the field as punishment, and while they were jogging, I thought to myself, 'I don't need this guy in my team.' When they got back, I told Gunter to go back to the hostel – I didn't need him in my rugby team. The boys got such a fright that they quickly fell into line. They thought they were great because they'd had a decent Under-14 season, but I'd coached some good players at Parktown, and I knew they were far from being as good as they could be.

I was very pushy as a coach, because I wanted the First-XV job as soon as I got to Jeppe. The school was always competitive in the junior age groups – even dominant – but for some reason, when the players got to Standard 9 and 10 and had to play for the first team, they lost the ability to win the big games. I could never understand why. It wasn't for lack of talent, yet the same players could not make an impact at first-team level.

While gaining coaching experience, I attended a lot of coaching courses through the Transvaal Rugby Union (now the Golden Lions Rugby Union). Len de Kock and Swys Joubert used to run coaching courses at various schools around Johannesburg. I'd have to travel to Roodepoort or Boksburg or Krugersdorp, because none of the clinics were held at English-speaking schools. Also, most of the lectures were in Afrikaans, because the lecturers were people such as Pa Pelser and Apies du Toit, who were well-known provincial coaches at the time. They taught me about many aspects of the game and, while rugby wasn't professional yet, coaching was still a serious pastime.

The courses were well structured and, in order to move on to level two, you had to coach for at least a year and pass all the exams as a level-one coach, and so on. There were no fast-tracking systems and you had to take it step by step. The guidelines were rigid. I realised I had a calling, because I passed levels one to three *cum laude*.

This was all done on my own time, in the evenings, after performing my coaching duties at the school. Fortunately Jeppe paid for the courses, because I didn't have a lot of spare cash lying around on a teacher's salary. I was then one of the few picked to do a level-four course, which was held in Cape Town. I passed level four *cum laude* as well, so I knew that I had the ability to coach at a higher level. Later on I would do several courses through the International Rugby Board, which I passed well.

But, as a young man, the courses hosted by the Transvaal Rugby Union were my first formal instruction in the art of being a coach. Levels one to four required nearly six years of dedication, because passing the exams was only one aspect; the other was spending a season or two coaching as a level-two or a level-three graduate. It was tough and required commitment, as you'd have to spend about three nights a week on a long drive to Roodepoort Hoërskool.

Some coaches didn't pitch because they had hostel duties or family commitments, but I made sure I never missed one lecture. I would juggle my duty schedule at the hostel (I was a housemaster at Tsessebe House), and later on it required a lot of understanding from Debbie. That's one thing: rugby has never been a debate in our house. There is no argument – we either do it properly, or we don't do it at all.

I obviously had ambition, and having already started the coaching courses – and having got to know some of the Afrikaans school coaches – I was keen to show that Jeppe could play against, and compete with, non-English-speaking schools. I approached Jeppe headmaster David Quail and told him I wanted to take the Under-15A team on a tour. He turned me down, saying that only the first team toured; junior teams did not. I argued that I wanted so see how good we were, having beaten all the best English schools in Johannesburg and Pretoria. He said that if that's what I wanted, I should organise a festival. So I did. That's how the now defunct Jeppe Under-15 Festival at Jeppe Old Boys' Club started. I convinced Paarl Gymnasium, Windhoek Hoërskool and Monument Hoërskool, among others, to come and play. We ended up beating all of them. That's when I received some recognition and where other schools recognised that this English school could play.

That was the start and, as I stayed in the job longer, I came to know more and more coaches from around the country. Neels Bornman (for many years the coach of Monument Hoërskool) and I became friendly rivals. Later it was the same with Neels's replacement Hans Coetzee, and other coaches. Because I stayed at Jeppe a long time and had some success – whether we beat top Afrikaans schools or gave them a good game – it earned the school, and me, some respect. I guess my greatest accolade as Jeppe coach is that, by the time I left, after the 1994 season, we were ranked 12th in the country. Considering where we had been when I took over, it was something of which I was extremely proud.

The last game I ever coached at Jeppe was against Grey PE, traditionally one of the best rugby schools in the country. We won 48-0. That was a measure of how far we had come from my first contact with Jeppe as a schoolboy in 1977. In my Standard 6 year, the Jeppe First XV lost 10 matches out of 14, including a 51-3 hiding by KES, and this in the days of a try being worth four points.

In my first year as a teacher at Jeppe, the First XV lost more than half their games. And in my first year as First-XV coach, we lost 30-3 to Hilton in an early-season tour, but by the end of that year we held Grey PE, who had a particularly strong team that season, to a 12-all draw. By 1994 we were without question the best English-medium rugby school in Johannesburg.

But let's go back slightly. After 1986, the year I had coached the Under-15As with such massive success, I thought I'd stay with the Under-15s for another season. But that didn't happen. In 1987 I actually moved down to coach the Under-14s, because Dave Pitcairn was the Jeppe First-XV coach at the time, and my 1986 Under-15s had moved to Open rugby. Johan van der Merwe, the Under-14 coach from the previous year, had been extremely successful, and moved up to Under-15 with his team. So I was left to take on the slightly younger age group. It wasn't my first choice, but that's where I came into contact with future Springbok James Dalton.

He was a good player, but at that stage he was not exceptional. He would get better and better with each passing year, though. He played flank and stayed in that position until Standard 9 (Grade 11), when I moved him to hooker, which we'll come to shortly. That was a very good age group, and the A to the E sides were unbeaten throughout the year.

I continued to coach the Under-14s the following year (1988), which consisted of another group of talented players, including future Springbok tourist Brent Moyle. We again went through the year unbeaten, and by 1989 I was asked to coach the First XV after Dave Pitcairn left to go to St Stithians College. Although I'd coached a First XV before, at Parktown, this was slightly different. It was my own school, the team that I'd aspired to be a part of as a schoolboy, and I put a lot of pressure on myself to succeed.

There was a lot of expectation because of my connection to the school, and from the network of old boys I knew. It was a lot more challenging than I'd expected, because, as luck would have it, the 1989 matrics were an average side, despite having been good juniors. The first team of 1988 had not been exceptional, but contained only two or three Standard 9s, so by the following year there was hardly any experience to draw on. My Under-14s of 1987 (the James Dalton group) were in Standard 9 and, while there were some good players, they were young.

The first team struggled initially, but improved as the season went on. We beat Pretoria Boys High for the first time in over a decade, and lost a heartbreaker to KES by three points, with a penalty in the final minute. But at the start of the season I was worried. I took the team on a tour to KwaZulu-Natal in the April holidays, where we had lined up three games against Pinetown, Hilton College and Alexandra High.

I knew that Hilton would be tough, but I naively believed that we would comfortably win the other two games. Well, against Pinetown, our first match, I quickly came back to earth. On a sweltering and muggy Durban afternoon, this school with relatively little rugby history beat us 18-0! It was the start of what was a disgusting tour in terms of results. We lost 30-3 to a Hilton side containing future Boks Wayne Fyvie and Hentie Martens, and we managed a scrappy draw with Alexandra.

But in hindsight it was a good experience for me as a coach, and at times I had to draw on the knowledge I'd gained then when the going got tough with the Springboks. Losing helped me see where we needed to improve, and also improved my motivational skills. I was also coaching alone that year, and it made me realise that, in order to be successful, you needed to have someone helping you with the job. It was a tough time, but it stood me in good stead for the rest of my career. The matrics of 1989 were the only age group at the school that I'd not dealt with, so I was also getting to know the individuals.

I had to shake things up after the tour when we got back to school the next term, and I started looking at ways to improve the team. Our scrum-half was a guy called Warren Warner, who had been the Craven Week scrumhalf the year before. But we had another excellent scrummie in Jed van der Wath, so I decided to move Warren to the wing. He was reasonably big and he was also an athlete, which gave us more pace and skill out wide.

It wasn't the most popular move, because Warren's parents wanted him to play scrumhalf, but I had to do what I thought was best for the team at the time. That was the hard part of being a schoolboy coach. At the time it was tough, and leaving boys out, or changing their position, led to some heated confrontations with annoyed parents. But it all helps in the bigger scheme of things when you move up as a coach, because you learn how to manage people.

I was very aware of the prestige and honour that went with making the First XV. I had been in the same boat, so shattering a kid's dream by not selecting him was never easy. But I always tried to let the boy down the same way I would have liked to be let down. I was lucky that I'd been handled properly in my time, as I was massively disappointed when I didn't receive colours for rugby. I had played more first-team games than most of the players who got colours. But the deputy headmaster Warren Boden had called me in and explained why I wasn't getting colours.

I was devastated, but the way in which he'd handled the situation made it more palatable. It was a lesson I had to learn, and it taught me how sensitive you had to be to a young person's feelings. I'd been through it myself, so I understood how a young man felt, and I always tried to be honest and explain my decisions.

I was also aware how important rugby could be to boys who were perhaps going nowhere in life. There was a boy at the school – let's call him 'Attie' – who was huge for his age, but he didn't want to play rugby. He came from a tough home life and had a lot of aggression, but he always had an excuse for why he didn't want to play rugby.

This was before I was first-team coach, and he wasn't one of my players. I asked him why he wasn't playing rugby, and his answer was, 'I don't have any boots, sir.'

'What if I buy you some boots? Will you play then?' I asked him.

He couldn't say no, but he thought I was joking. I bought him a nice pair of boots and, when I gave them to him, he no longer had an excuse. He went on to play first-team rugby for three years and was a superb lock.

Attie is now a qualified accountant and is doing well for himself. I wish I could say I did it for philanthropic reasons – that I wanted to make him a better person. But initially I saw him as a potentially gifted player who could channel all his aggression into something constructive on the rugby field. He's a big guy and, as I am constantly reminded as Bok coach, I have a 'thing' for big players.

Jeppe didn't have the luxury of recruiting all the top primary-school players, unlike Grey College in Bloemfontein or Paul Roos in Stellenbosch. Most of our players came from the suburbs near the school, supplemented by some boarders from further away. Towards the end of my time at Jeppe, I was able to lure some good players to the school because our reputation was very good, but when I first started coaching at the school, it was really a case of having to make do with the raw material you had. That's why I couldn't accept that a guy like Attie didn't want to play rugby.

Another one was Nigel Pickford. He captained the first team in 1992, and was perhaps the best number 8 I ever had. He captained the Transvaal Craven Week side that year, and also became head boy of the school. But in Standard 6 his mother hadn't wanted him to play rugby. She was the school's secretary, and I asked her why she wouldn't allow her son to play. She said she was scared he'd be injured. I nearly fell over. I said, 'He's 6'3 at the age of 13. He's not going to get injured; he's going to injure somebody else.'

I asked her to at least let Nigel try rugby, and he went on to become a great Jeppe player and captain his team. He received a rugby bursary to the Rand Afrikaans University (now University of Johannesburg), and still plays for Pirates Rugby Club in Johannesburg. He also played a few provincial games for Transvaal. Can you imagine what a loss it would have been if he never played rugby?

That sums up how important it was to make the most of the talent we had at the school, because we couldn't afford to lose it. I remember soon after joining Jeppe, I addressed the staff. I gave them a similar speech to the one I would give the Under-15s at their first practice session. I told them that I take rugby seriously, and that we should decide if we wanted to be a rugby school, or just a school that offered rugby as an extramural activity. If we chose to be a rugby school, it meant that the Under-14E-team result would be as important as the first-team result. From 1986 to 1995, Jeppe won about 80 per cent of all its games as a school. As we became more successful, everyone wanted to play rugby, and we had a lot more talent to choose from. I told the boys, 'You play and I'll organise you a game.' So, if we had 100 boys in Standard 6, I would somehow find them a game, even if it meant playing against an older age group from Queens High.

But it required constant pressure from all of us coaches at Jeppe, as not everyone saw rugby as being the most important matter at the school. I spent six years as First-XV coach, during which we had some incredible teams and great seasons. Out of those sides we produced two Springboks and a few provincial players, such as Russell Winter, Grant Hinckley and Sean Raubenheimer.

But, more importantly, it was the 26 Craven Week players we produced that set us apart. Guys such as James Dalton and Justin Mills played for two years, but in all we had 26 caps. I'm disappointed that some of the guys didn't carry on playing seriously after school, while one or two others gave up for valid reasons. But I think that, for most of them, their lives changed in that period because of what they achieved on the rugby field.

I've mentioned Attie and how he'd changed his life through rugby. Russell Winter was a similar case. He came from Sir John Adamson High in the south of Johannesburg, where they had 14 guys at a rugby practice. He came to Jeppe, made the first team, made Craven Week and earned a scholarship to Rand Afrikaans University. From there he made the SA Universities team and was selected for the SA Sevens team, before going on to play provincial and Super 12 rugby. His life changed for the better. Instead of just finishing school and getting an arbitrary job somewhere, rugby allowed him to soar.

The importance of rugby at Jeppe really came to a head in 1990, when the school staged a massive sit-in after James Dalton was handed a one-match suspension – which happened to be Jeppe's centenary celebration game against our old enemies, KES. The week before we'd played Athlone High at Jeppe, which was always a niggly game. This is where the trouble started. We were leading by nearly 40 points, with about 15 minutes to go, when Dalton was tackled into touch, landing among their old boys.

You must understand: Dalton was something of a cult figure in school-boy rugby, because he was known as perhaps the best and toughest schools hooker in the country. As he stood up, someone pushed him, and James being James, he pushed back. Suddenly punches were thrown, and the next thing the Athlone old boys started running from various parts of the field to climb into the fight. The Jeppe old boys joined in, and basically it was a huge free-for-all.

Following the incident, a disciplinary committee decided to suspend James from the team for one game. The timing couldn't have been worse, because we had old boys flying in from all over the world to watch the big match against KES. During the week, many of them pleaded with the head-master to allow Dalton to play, but he said he couldn't change his stance, as it was a matter of principle.

I must have had phone calls from 10 schools, offering to play Jeppe on the Wednesday before the centenary match so that Dalton could serve his suspension. Naturally I was tempted, as KES had a very good team, and my side, while good, relied heavily on Dalton, because he was such a gifted rugby player. It's not every day you have an SA Schools player and future Springbok in your First XV. But the headmaster refused to sanction any midweek game. I accepted the decision and tried to focus on the coming Saturday.

However, when the school assembled for the routine cadet parade on the Wednesday, every pupil sat down on the field and refused to move. When the deputy headmaster arrived to send the boys back to class, one of the youngest kids, a little Standard 6, stood up and said, 'We're not going back to school until James plays rugby again.'

They didn't move, and did not go to class the entire day. The Transvaal Education Department inspector then arrived; I think his name was Liebenberg. He called me in. He was angry and told me that, as the first-team coach, I needed to put an end to the strike. Considering I had nothing to do with it, and that it had been a spontaneous decision by the pupils, I told the inspector that I couldn't put an end to it, and that it was unfair of him to expect that I could.

I was torn, because I knew that discipline was vital to the school, but at the same time I had sympathy for the pupils, who had been looking forward to this game the entire year.

In the end, common sense prevailed when some old boys went to speak to the Dalton family. James addressed the school and asked the pupils to go back to class. I don't think he wanted to, but his parents realised that the incident was bad for the school, and James probably also realised that the situation was stalemate. It looked far more credible for him to give in than for the school to capitulate.

We lost the match in the death, after losing our captain and Craven Week number 8 Dale Ryan in the first minute of the game. We got revenge by beating KES away from home about six weeks later with a full-strength team, but the centenary game had been a huge disappointment. James was a phenomenal player in matric, and I doubt any school had a more influential player than him. He was already practising with the Transvaal men's team a couple of times a week.

Dalton is a tough bloke who has had his fair share of headlines over the years, and not always for the right reasons. But, in his defence, he would never have represented his country as a five-foot-something hooker if he didn't have that mean streak and aggression in his make-up. If he had been Mr Nice Guy, he wouldn't have played for South Africa.

James had played flank from Standard 6 to 8, but by the time he got to Standard 9, I realised that he was too small for the position. At the season's first practice, I told him to wrap his ears because he was going to play hooker. He said, 'I'm playing flank,' and I said, 'You're not.' So we had this Mexican standoff, and he didn't talk to me for two weeks. His father wouldn't talk to me either, and James eventually said he might go to KES. I told him to go, but I wasn't budging – he was going to play hooker. I refused to have a gun held to my head. I told him his career after school was as a hooker, and that he'd never make it as a flank.

He eventually relented, but in the first scrum in the front row he shouted to me, 'I'm uncomfortable, coach.' I told him: 'Well, make your-self comfortable.' So he moved the whole scrum on his own just to make himself more comfortable. I knew at that moment he had it all. He had always been a good cricketer, so he quickly learnt how to throw in at the lineouts. He was also an athlete, and had a great boot on him.

Athletically he had it all to make it as a hooker. I'm sure he'll admit that I was right. I don't take the credit for making James a superb rugby player, because he always had the talent. But I played a role in him finding his place on the field. He went on to be part of the 1995 World Cup–winning squad and South Africa's most capped hooker until John Smit.

4

With a little help from my friend

The sit-in happened in my second year as Jeppe First-XV coach, and while that incident and the subsequent loss to KES left a sour taste, the season was far more successful in terms of results than 1989. There were a few reasons for this: I had a better group of players, for a start; I was improving as a coach; and I had a full-time assistant coach in Noel Shelley – something I didn't have the previous year.

Noel and I had met briefly at the Old Boys' Club, Jeppe Quondam, which I'd played for in the early 1980s. But our friendship was formally struck on the side of the field towards the end of the 1989 season. And nearly 20 years on, he's one of my best friends and godfather to both my sons. As the 1989 season wound down, I'd begun to realise that I needed help. We were preparing for our last game of the year, against Grey High from Port Elizabeth. They were packed with Craven Week players and, if there had been rankings back then, Grey would have been in the top 10 in the country.

I'd seen Noel helping out scrumhalf Jed van der Wath for about two sessions before that game. I knew him, because he'd played First-XV rugby at the Old Boys' Club for years. He was one of the most capped guys who'd ever played at the club, and was a well-respected figure in Jeppe circles. He'd played Craven Week, he was passionate about Jeppe, he was an old boy and he lived across the road from the school. He came to me and said he felt that Jed was only passing the ball and not adding much else to his game. Noel felt Jed wasn't taking any pressure off the flyhalf by kicking or breaking. I was impressed that he was so keen to help and willing to say what was on his mind. So I told him to come down and help Jed.

We drew 13-13 with Grey that day, which was easily our best perform-ance of the season, and Jed had a superb match. Noel enjoyed it so much. A friendship was born, and if you'd lived around the school in the early 1990s, you would have seen Noel walking to practice every afternoon.

We had a pre-season camp in 1990, and Noel immediately made an impact as a coach, mentor and my sounding board. Our first game of the season was away, against old rivals Pretoria Boys High. Our flyhalf, Darryl Weir (who went on to become director of rugby in the United Arab Emirates), scored 20 points as we pukked them. It was our centenary year and it was Pretoria's 75th-year celebration, so it was a huge game.

It was Noel's first 'official' match as a member of the team, and he was more nervous than the players. He phoned me in the morning and babbled away. He wasn't sure if he was part of the team, and asked, 'Am I in or out?' Once I'd assured him that he was 'in', he became even more nervous, and wanted to know what to wear. Should he put on a tracksuit? I was chuckling to myself, and told him to put on a jacket and tie.

In the April holidays, Noel came on his first tour and added huge value to the team. He'd played for the Jeppe First XV in 1970, and was one of four Jeppe 'okes' that year who made the Transvaal schools' team. Peter Brophy, John Hutton and Allan Hall were the others. Noel has always remained a loyal Jeppe supporter and was deeply connected to the Old Boys' Club. He helped me a lot in making sure that the old boys felt part of the first team, and he worked well with the boys. He had his own little electrical business, so he could come and go as he pleased.

I'd learnt in 1989 that I couldn't do this job on my own, even at school-boy level. It was so much easier having someone to help out, as I had in 1990 – and every year after that. Noel's main focus was working with the backs. We worked well together. It was never a case of me trying to overrule him or him trying to take over.

Together we formed a formidable coaching team, and our results were generally superb. By the time I decided to leave, we had taken Jeppe into the top 10 in the country, and it was one of the most respected rugby-playing schools in South Africa.

I could never have done it alone, and when I decided to move on after the 1994 season, Noel also decided to pack it in. He had no real ambition to become the head coach, and he probably felt that working with another coach wouldn't be the same. Also, by then he was considering immigrating to the United States.

Noel left South Africa in the late 1990s and made a new life for himself in America. He's now working at Sea World in Florida. Being an electrician by trade, he services all the back-up electronic systems at the resort.

At our family home we have a spare room, but we don't call it that – we call it 'Noel's room', as he is such a huge part of our family. I've visited him at Sea World, and I know he misses South Africa, rugby and Jeppe – I'm just not sure in what order.

I think he was chuffed to see me carry on coaching and do reasonably well. Noel is a passionate guy who taught me a lot about managing people, and I think he taught many boys the meaning of being a Jeppe boy and a good, honest citizen. It's something he's carried through his life. It's something I'm proud of and something we hopefully gave a few boys, if nothing else.

Rugby is a game that draws interesting personalities and creates legends at every school, club and province in South Africa, and the world. There is hardly a place where rugby is played that won't have tales of legends who graced the game at their club or school.

Guys who were at Jeppe in the late 1980s and early 1990s will probably tell amazing stories about James Dalton. Others from the 1950s might mention Wilf Rosenberg and Des Sinclair with a glint in their eye. As a Jeppe rugby lover, these are all legendary names at the school. But the most recognised and revered name is that of Jack Collard. He's simply an icon, and the man who brought the oval ball game to Jeppe.

Collard started rugby union at Jeppe. When I say started, I mean he was the man who convinced the school to change the winter sport from soccer to rugby in 1935. Rugby wasn't universally popular at the time, but he was successful in convincing the school to change, and I'm sure thousands of Jeppe boys are happy about it – I know this one is.

He was also the man who fought to have the white, full-colours blazer recognised for rugby as well as cricket. The black blazer, which is the half-colours blazer now, was a rugby blazer, and the white blazer was a cricket blazer. Jack and the cricket master, called Beckwith, argued for years about the blazers. Collard wanted rugby players to receive the same level of appreciation as the cricketers, but Beckwith insisted that the white blazer was only for cricket.

Eventually they called a truce after finding some middle ground. The conditions of their agreement were that the white blazer would become the full-colours blazer, and the black blazer would become the half-colours blazer for all sports. In the greater scheme of things it's probably quite trivial, but it was about making rugby the number one sport at Jeppe.

If you look at the history books, it is amazing to see guys like future Springboks Rosenberg and Sinclair appear in the first-team photograph wearing black blazers, because those were full-colours blazers in rugby at the time. Now the white blazer is the full-colours blazer for all sports. This bit of history was important to me, because I believed that if Jack Collard had not fought so hard to make rugby matter at Jeppe, thousands of boys would have missed out on something special. And rugby might never have been played.

To honour Collard, I decided to name the main rugby field after him in my penultimate year as Jeppe coach. I'd learnt the importance of this tradition from other schools in the country. Fields such as Goldstones, the main ground at Maritzburg College, and the Piley Rees field at Bishops, are two great examples of schools honouring coaches. I thought it would be apt if we followed suit. Copying a tradition is not a bad thing if the tradition is worth copying.

I managed to make contact with Jack Collard's daughter, and through her invited him to come and open the field. I also contacted a couple of old boys whom Collard had coached, and who had really strong feelings for the old man, and asked them for their recollections.

Geoff Sprong and Grazer Normand were two of the old boys I called, and they were delighted to help. They told me that Jack used to call everyone 'boneface', although they were never sure why. So that's what we decided to put on the plaque. It reads, 'To all the bonefaces who will grace this field'. I asked him to unveil it.

It was quite an experience, and he died soon afterwards. Often fields are named after guys when they're dead and they don't get to know about it. I didn't want that to happen, and I'm glad we made it just in time. The day we unveiled the plaque, we played against Helpmekaar, which was no coincidence. We had planned it that way, because it was a fixture that Jeppe had regularly filled when Collard was coach. We ended up beating Helpmekaar comfortably, which made it more special for the old man, and even more special for me. He wasn't in great health, but he seemed genuinely moved by the gesture.

About 11 years later, Jeppe named the B-field after me. There's a plaque, which I went to unveil. It's unbelievable; I wasn't expecting it. I'm still a young guy. As an old boy, it's quite amazing to have a field named after you at the oldest school in Johannesburg. It is quite an honour and an achievement, and I rank it right up there with my best in the game.

5

On the right track

I enjoyed a lot of success as a coach at Jeppe, but by 1994 I was becoming restless. I'd helped build Jeppe into a recognised, powerful rugby school, which had been my goal when I took over as First-XV coach. Not only the first team had done well, but all the other age groups also. Although the First XV never managed an undefeated season, Jeppe was the most feared rugby school in Johannesburg by the time I left.

I had grown as a coach as well. I'd not only been involved in the Jeppe set-up, but had been part of the Transvaal Craven Week coaching staff for a few years. By that stage I was also highly qualified due to all the courses I'd attended, so I was starting to see the bigger picture and look beyond schoolboy coaching.

Teaching was not – and still isn't – a highly paid profession, and I was feeling the economic pinch. I'd started building a house in Dower Glen, my son Clinton was a toddler, and after deductions I think I had about R700 a month left to survive on. Fortunately Debbie had a good job as a rep for a paper company, but I started to realise I had to leave teaching. I wanted to be a rugby coach, but not a teacher.

I didn't know what else to do as a career, though. I discussed it with my brother Jon, and he said, 'Come and sell cars with me.' Jon was a top car salesman and had a lot of connections in the business. Initially I was sceptical, and told him he was mad if he thought I was going to be a car salesman. But he kept telling me I could make a lot more money than as a teacher. His company sold Mercedes-Benzes, and he convinced me that he could pull a few strings to land me a job.

I eventually resigned from Jeppe after the 1994 season. I attended the 1994 Craven Week as Transvaal coach, and on my return I started my new job as a car salesman in the East Rand suburb of Boksburg. For the first six months, I was the top salesman in the company. The money was much better – in one month I sometimes made more than in a year of teaching. It was great from a financial point of view, but not very stimulating. Luckily I stayed involved with rugby and still coached at RAU. I'd go down to the club most nights after work – it was what kept me motivated. Selling cars just didn't move me.

At the beginning of 1995, I was headhunted by Sandown Motors to sell cars in the upmarket suburb of Sandton. It was a good career move, because selling Mercedes-Benzes to people in Johannesburg's affluent northern suburbs was a lot easier than in Boksburg's more blue-collar environment.

I'd been in the new job for four days when my phone rang. It was Rudy Joubert from the Transvaal Rugby Union, who simply said, 'Come and work for me.' The TRU wanted me on a full-time basis, and suddenly I wasn't sure if that was what I wanted.

My initial reasoning was, why would I want to coach rugby every day of my life when I was earning great money and coaching rugby in the evenings? Rugby wasn't professional in 1995, and although I would be paid a salary as a TRU employee, it wouldn't be as good as the commissions on selling cars. But it meant full-time involvement with rugby, and that was what niggled at the back of my mind. Rudy had joined the TRU from Tukkies (University of Pretoria) the previous year, and he was battling to fit in, as he was seen as an outsider in some sections.

I didn't know him well, but I had worked at a couple of clinics with him and we both shared a passion for the game. He wanted me on board because I didn't come with the baggage of the other guys who had applied for his position.

Rudy called again, and we eventually met for lunch at Ellis Park, where Avril Malan, a former Springbok captain in charge of the TRU's training and development department, joined us. The restaurant overlooks the field and, sitting there, with Ellis Park below us, I felt something stir inside me. They knew it too, and Avril simply said, 'Think about it. You'll be involved with rugby every day, and you'll be coaching coaches and running coaching courses. This is a chance of a lifetime.'

As it turns out, it probably was. I made up my mind to take the job.

There were a few complications, of course. Johan Engelbrecht, my manager at Sandown Motors, was away on an incentive trip in Egypt. The TRU wanted me to start as soon as possible, which meant I needed to resign quickly. I felt I needed to speak to Johan, as he'd been the guy who had brought me over to that branch.

But Johan couldn't be reached, so one of my colleagues suggested I talk to Roy McAllister, the chairman of the company. I was nervous, as I had only been there a few days, but there was no simple way around the problem.

It was the beginning of 1995, and World Cup fever was starting to grip the country.

I explained the circumstances to Roy, and he hardly hesitated. 'You must go and do it. It's a chance of a lifetime,' he said. 'You can have your job back whenever you want it.' That approach was unheard of in the motor industry. Usually when you leave, your bags are packed that day, so Roy's words were a comfort should matters not work out for me in rugby. I still speak to Roy from time to time.

I worked until the end of the month and delivered all the cars I'd sold before starting at the TRU. I was nervous about changing jobs again. For 10 years I'd been in a fairly safe and conservative teaching environment, and in the space of six months I was about to change jobs for a third time. It was a daunting prospect, but it was about rugby. And that's what mattered most.

My new role was quite flexible, but I spent most of my days attending coaching clinics, from Johannesburg to Wolmaransstad in the North West. I came into contact with many coaches, as well as with promising young players. I was also an unofficial scout, and kept my eyes open for talented youngsters that might be of interest to the union down the line. But mostly I coached coaches who came to the union for rugby courses. Frans Ludeke, a future Cats Super 14 coach, was one of my 'students' in the early days.

Some clinics I hosted weren't at Ellis Park, but in places such as Lichtenburg, in the heartland of South African rugby. The coaches who attended were generally Afrikaans-speaking guys who were suspicious of an Englishman from Joburg trying to tell them how to understand the game.

I didn't have a hugely impressive CV at that stage, and I didn't have cauliflower ears or a Springbok blazer, so my credentials, as far as they were concerned, were flimsy. They would grudgingly attend the first day as I ran through aspects of the scrum or lineout, presenting attacking and defensive scenarios – always speaking in Afrikaans. Almost without exception, by the end of the day I'd have their attention and interest.

I'd show them examples that I'd clipped from match videos, or moves that had worked for me at Jeppe. I'd talk about what selections worked at schoolboy level when options were limited. How would you make a lock? What moves would you use if you only had one quality lock? What about a centre who didn't tackle – how would you cover him in terms of your defensive patterns? I challenged them on options in all areas of play. That changed their perceptions of me, and they softened their approach once they realised I was mad about rugby and that my only goal was to share ideas. My openness allowed me to be successful in my job.

While working as a coach of coaches, I received offers from some of the clubs to come and help out. I slowly realised that I had a small but well-regarded reputation in the game around Johannesburg. I didn't align myself to any single club or school, but as a coaching manager of the union I helped out wherever I was needed.

I came to know a lot of young players, such as Lawrence Sephaka and John Smit, when I helped out at their schools. And when I became the Transvaal Under-20 coach a few years later, I coached or had teams play against many of the players I'd seen in those early days.

In 1996, rugby turned professional. For me it already was, as I was paid a salary to do my job, but the implications of the sport going pro opened many new doors. I was asked to help out with the Golden Lions' (Transvaal changed its name when the sport went professional) Under-21 team, because coach Fanie Bosch was seriously ill with cancer. He obviously went through highs and lows as he bravely battled the illness, and the union knew it would be difficult for him to concentrate fully on the job, so they asked for my assistance. They were incredibly loyal to Fanie, but he needed help and I was given the job.

When Fanie had a good day, he was in charge. When he had a bad day and couldn't get out of bed because of the chemotherapy, I would take over. That lasted for a long time, but in 1997 we made it to the final, where we lost to Natal.

I got to know a lot of young players during that time and built up a reputation as an astute analyst and coach, which, to my surprise, led to the Boks at the end of 1997, when Nick Mallett came knocking.

PART II

THE MALLETT YEARS
1997–1999

6

First taste
of Bok rugby

I'd been building my career through my work with the Golden Lions, but my big break came when I was asked to join the Springboks under Nick Mallett. Ironically, it was André Markgraaff, a former Springbok coach and rugby administrator, who helped me get my first taste of Bok rugby, even though we would later have a falling out.

Towards the end of 1997, Nick was in the running for the Bok job. Being Nick, he left nothing to chance, and started canvassing opinions from people on who his potential coaching and technical staff should be. One of the men he spoke to was Markgraaff, who suggested Mallett should get hold of me.

I wasn't aware that André had such positive views about my abilities, but I think it stemmed from a Craven Week that had taken place in his hometown of Kimberley in 1996. I was very active in assisting all the coaches during the tournament as a technical advisor, even though the Golden Lions had employed me. I felt it was my duty to help out as much as I could where I could. It didn't matter whether I was helping Stellaland on the B field or the Golden Lions on the A field; it was something I loved doing.

I had met some of the coaches who were coaching the provincial sides at the Craven Week during the training courses I had taught over the years. They must have reported back to André about the positive impact I'd had, and André later told Nick.

But this was all going on at a higher level, and I was unaware of Nick's pending appointment to the top job in South African rugby. But I became aware of it soon enough, when respected rugby writer John Dobson called me. Mallett had appointed him to assist him with the media. John's words were: 'Nick might get the Bok job. If he does, would you consider helping him, as a member of his management team?' Do fish swim? Of course I said I would.

It was one of the biggest days of my life. I remember it as if it were yesterday. I was at home when Dobson called, but his intention was to feel me out. It wasn't a done deal. Naturally Nick couldn't commit to anything, because he hadn't yet been officially appointed. But he was already planning in the event of getting the nod.

It was near the end of the 1997 Currie Cup season, and the Boks had an end-of-year tour to Europe and Britain coming up. Carel du Plessis had just been fired as coach after the Boks had suffered a series defeat to the British and Irish Lions, as well as completing an average Tri-Nations. Mallett was still coaching Boland when Dobson called. My excitement took over and I tried to call Nick, but I could only leave messages for him. He couldn't talk to me directly until he was appointed, and was communicating via a third party – Dobson.

I probably phoned Dobson 20 times a day to ask, 'Have you heard from Nick? Has he got the job?' I was still employed by the Golden Lions, who were based at Ellis Park, as was South African rugby boss Louis Luyt. His interview with Nick was to take place at his office.

In hindsight I was a little over the top, but I was dead keen for Nick to get the job. When he arrived at Ellis Park, I stuck to him like glue. He couldn't say much, but I kept in touch with Dobson over the next few days, and I guess I was a little irritating with my incessant nagging.

When Springbok media manager Alex Broun called me to ask for some personal details, which they needed for the end-of-year-tour media guide, I was over the moon. Nothing had been confirmed yet, but it was a pretty good indication that I was a member of the squad, and that Nick had been given the job.

Eventually Dobson called to say that it was official. Mallett had been appointed, and I was part of the management team that was going to Italy and France. I was elated! I was also home alone.

Debbie was working as a teacher, and was away on a school cricket tour to Zimbabwe. I wanted to tell her the good news, but getting hold of her was a problem. This was before everyone had a cellphone. I left a message for her at St John's College in Harare to call home. I was babysitting the boys, so her first reaction when she got the message was that something must have happened to Clinton or Wesley. I'd told the person who took the message to assure Debbie there was no reason to worry, but the message hadn't been correctly conveyed.

When Debbie called back later and I told her the news, she was overjoyed. She and her colleagues popped a bottle of champagne that night. I was sorry that we couldn't be together to share the moment.

While Mallett's appointment was reaching its climax, I had to go to Cape Town with the Lions Under-21 team for a match against Western Province. After the game, I went for a drink with the team doctor, Kevin Scheepers. We ran into Rian Oberholzer, SA Rugby's managing director at the time. He and a friend were also having a drink, having just returned from Wellington, where they'd watched Mallett's Boland team play.

I knew Rian from his days at the Golden Lions, and got on reasonably well with him. About six months earlier, long before Dobson's call, I'd seen Rian and told him he should give me a job at SA Rugby. I was ambitious and not afraid to use my contacts.

A few days after seeing Rian at the bar, I found myself outside his office, waiting to be officially appointed as technical advisor to the Springboks under Nick Mallett. Rian reminded me of our conversation a few months earlier – it was the start of a good relationship.

It had all happened so fast. I was coaching schoolboy rugby in 1994, and three years later I was about to tour with the Boks. Putting the blazer on for that tour with the Springboks was one of the biggest moments of my life.

From the beginning, I realised that the Springbok set-up differed from anything I'd encountered before. Mallett's first squad gathered on a Sunday. A businessman named Tim Southey was brought in to do a presentation about the ethos of teamwork, the meaning of playing for the Bok badge and the importance of the Springbok code of conduct.

He made quite an impact, and I was very impressed. What he said, and how he explained things, were elements I was able to draw on when I became Bok coach seven years later.

The tour itself was tough. We were scheduled to meet Italy and France twice, as well as England and Scotland. But, on the flip side, we had a very good team, which had already embarked on a world-record-winning streak of 17 matches in a row – although we didn't know it at the time.

It had started with coach Carel du Plessis' final match in charge, when the Boks beat Australia 61-22 at Loftus. Italy would be the beginning of 16 straight wins under Mallett. We had players such as James Small, Os du Randt and Mark Andrews in the team. It was a crackerjack side.

I remember Nick asking André Joubert to tour. André was tired, and had been messed around a bit under Du Plessis. After being one of the stars of the 1995 World Cup and being ever present in 1996, he'd played only the first two tests against the Lions in 1997, and had then missed out until the Loftus match against the Wallabies. He was disillusioned.

I think André had decided that he'd had enough, and he declined Nick's offer. That was the end of his test career. It was sad that André never gave it another go, but the nature of sport at the top is that there is always another guy ready to fill the void. Mallett selected Percy Montgomery as fullback for the tour – and he became that guy. It was a controversial decision, as Monty had been one of the scapegoats of the Lions' and Tri-Nations' defeats. But in fairness he had played centre in those games, which wasn't his best position.

Giving Monty another chance was a masterstroke by Mallett. It was essentially the beginning of Monty's career, although he had been a Springbok before. Monty and Western Province's Justin Swart were the two fullbacks for the tour, although Swart initially had the inside edge. But at the captain's practice before the first French test, Swart pulled his hamstring and Monty was given the starting jersey. The Boks won, and a week later he was instrumental in our 52-10 win over the French. A decade later, in 2007, he still held a solid place in the Bok side and was one of the stars in the Rugby World Cup final. He'd outlived five Springbok coaches and broken just about every point-scoring record.

The coaching staff on the end-of-year tour complemented each other well. Nick is a very demonstrative guy, and without question he was the man in charge. He never doubted himself, and was forceful when he needed to be. He was very proud of being the Springbok coach, and it rubbed off on all of us – although, personally, it didn't require Nick's enthusiasm to make me proud of my role as technical advisor.

Nick's assistant was Alan Solomons, who later became the Stormers coach. He was almost the opposite of Nick in personality. Quiet and thoughtful, Solly's greatest asset was his attention to detail. He was meticulous, and spent hours plotting and planning. He wrote everything down, and made sure that we never went into a game without being armed to the teeth with data.

We had a good combination of assets as coaches, and the systems worked well on that tour, and into the following year's Tri-Nations. They only broke down much later. I was the youngster of the coaching staff, having come through the junior ranks. That gave me an advantage, because I knew many of the new young players whom I'd come into contact with at various Under-21 matches and clinics.

I think that was probably my biggest asset. Nick had been coaching in the Boland and, although he kept a close eye on the game nationally, he didn't know all the young players coming through the ranks. Solly was in a similar position. He had been in a university environment, where he was coaching club rugby. Of course he followed the game, but he didn't know the players from Johannesburg, Pretoria and Durban as well as I did. Because I'd been coaching Under-21s, and because I'd been a school-teacher for 10 years, I had the information they needed. I could identify players from certain schools, provide background on what they were like as youngsters, point out their best positions and give insight into the guys who had developed after school. I felt as if I had more than technical analysis to contribute.

And that was important for me, because coming into that particular Bok side was intimidating, as it still comprised many of the 1995 World Cup winners, and I knew that I had to be able to contribute as much as possible. I was extremely confident, and never happier. Mallett was very good to me too. That would change later, but in the beginning it was a comfortable, professional and happy working environment.

We started by winning, and as a consequence the job became easier. The more we won, the easier the job became. After we beat France 52-10 at Parc des Princes – the last match ever played at that stadium – Nick and I had a drink in an Irish pub – a strange thing to do in Paris, I know. He said to me, 'I want you to stay with me until the World Cup.' It was a great moment, because I was dead keen to make an impression. Nick had been sussing me out during my first month in the job. When he said that, it meant I'd passed whatever test he had set for me.

One thing about Mallett: he's rarely insecure. I'm sure many people will agree with me. Although it sometimes comes across as arrogance, Nick is simply a guy who believes in himself completely, which is why he had no problem delegating. He never felt that it undermined his authority, which was something I learnt from him.

Nick encouraged every member of the coaching staff to contribute to team matters. If I approached him with an idea or suggestion, he had enough balls to say, 'Jake, if that's what you think, we'll give it a go.'

Conversely, he wasn't afraid to shoot down an idea or plan if he truly believed it wouldn't work. But he could be convinced if you could back up your thoughts properly.

There were no grey areas with Nick. He knew exactly how he wanted to play, and what he wanted to see. My job was to help him achieve his vision.

Of course, the computer technology for video analysis was a far cry from what it is today. My job as technical advisor meant I had to operate what is now completely antiquated equipment. I had to lug an entire desktop computer around with heavy video recorders and monitors, and make sure that I was ready to answer Nick's queries as he presented them, wherever we were. It was challenging, because I'm more of a rugby man than a computer wiz. I could look at videos, analyse the pictures and come up with a solution in rugby terms. But if the electronic equipment failed me, I was in trouble. The technology we were using at the time had been developed by the Israeli army, which made it super hi-tech, but also impossible to fix if it broke.

Whenever the editing system played up, we had to fly an officer out from the Israeli army to South Africa to fix it. Naturally that was a problem in terms of time – on one occasion the officer was involved in active duty, and we had to wait weeks before he could come to Cape Town to repair the system.

But I think Nick realised that I was happiest on a rugby field, and he went the extra yard to make me feel like part of the coaching staff. I worked out drills and helped implement them. In the training sessions, I would assist individual players on skills drills. I spent hours with Joost van der Westhuizen, helping him sort out the shortcomings in his game that Nick and Solly had identified. Passing off his left hand and kicking with his right foot were two areas we worked on constantly. Passing off the left hand was a problem for Joost, as his reaction time in getting his feet into position was a bit slow. At that stage, Wallaby George Gregan was considered the best passer of the ball off both hands – the role model of the perfect passer off the base of a ruck or scrum. I mucked in and helped wherever I could.

On that first tour to Europe and Britain, we were a happy bunch. We won every test, with record scores against France and Scotland. We beat England, and James Small broke the South African try-scoring record. There were a lot of highlights. After the tour, Nick asked me to join the Boks full time, as I'd only been contracted for the duration of the tour. I was still employed by the Golden Lions Rugby Union at that stage. After Nick told Oberholzer that he wanted me on a permanent basis, I was offered a contract. I moved to Cape Town in 1998, which is where I still live today.

Moving to the Cape was tough, because I'd spent my whole life in and around Bedfordview, Edenvale and Kensington in Johannesburg. My dentist was a Jeppe old boy, my plumber was a Jeppe old boy, and moving to Cape Town felt like I was immigrating to another country. But it was a huge career move to be a full-time employee of SA Rugby.

7

The winning habit

Mallett's first tour was a triumphant success. It was one of the best squads I'd ever been a part of, and that was largely down to Nick and the way he ran the show. He had passion for the game and a strong relationship with the players – most of them seemed to love him. I was like a sponge and absorbed everything I could. One of the things that rubbed off on me – and which I stuck to when I became Bok coach – was consistency in selection. In 1997/98, Mallett knew who his best team was, and he tweaked it only because of injuries or for minor experiments.

The front row of Adrian Garvey, James Dalton and Robbie Kempson started 10 of the 12 tests together. Locks Krynauw Otto and Mark Andrews started every test in 1998. Captain and number 8, Gary Teichmann, played every test. And flank Rassie Erasmus played in 11 tests. Scrumhalf Joost van der Westhuizen started all the games, as did Pieter Rossouw, Percy Montgomery, André Snyman and Stefan Terblanche. Henry Honiball started nine times at flyhalf, after missing the first few tests of the year through injury. And flank André Venter played nine in a row before being dropped (something we'll come to later). The results proved to me that Nick's policy of consistency worked. It was a philosophy I would later follow, although I suffered a lot of criticism for it.

To settle into Cape Town, I immersed myself in what I knew best – coaching rugby. As a full-time employee of the South African Rugby Football Union, which was the name of the union at the time, my defined role was 'technical advisor to the Springboks'. But for the first five months of the year, the Super 12 took precedence, so there was a fair amount of downtime. My job was to study Bok players and their opponents, cut videos and analyse their performances in both the Super 12 and the Five Nations, as it was called then. The objective was to arm Nick and Solly with the maximum information possible before the start of the international season.

I also spent a lot of time coaching at official SA Rugby clinics, on my own, or with Mallett. I coached a bit at schools and clubs as well, where I had contacts from my school and Under-21 coaching years. I loved being near the game.

But the real job was preparing the Boks for the 1998 season, with a longer-term view to the 1999 Rugby World Cup. We had a tricky start to the year, with two tests against Ireland, followed by a one-off against Wales, as well as a test against England.

As it turned out, Ireland were the strongest of the three teams to come to South Africa, as Wales and England both brought depleted squads. The Irish are always great tourists, but they came to fight as much as to play rugby, and both tests were niggly and fractured games. We won 37-13 in Bloemfontein, with Terblanche scoring four tries on debut. A week later we beat them 33-0 in Pretoria, but my lasting memory of the match is that it spiralled into a series of punch-ups – it wasn't pretty, and was hardly a great advert for the game. Professionalism was still new, and the amateur pastime of fighting had yet to be eradicated from rugby. If a match had to be played in that way in 2007, both sides would end the contest with 10 men on the field.

But we were winning, and when Wales arrived at Loftus, we ran them ragged, winning by a record score of 96-13. Wales had already lost to the Emerging Boks, Border, Natal and the Falcons, so by the time they met the Boks, they were completely shattered. It was a great win, but I felt an underlying sense of sadness that Welsh rugby, once the best in the world, had become so poor. Happily they improved over the next decade, and are again a force in the world game.

At that stage, everything the Springbok team tried seemed to work. We were on a high. England arrived after being hammered 76-0 by Australia, and 64-22 and 40-10 by the All Blacks. We were feeling bullish about putting a big score on them. As luck would have it, it poured in Cape Town, and the test became a lottery. We won 18-0, but it was a dire game.

For the 1998 Boks, the real challenge was always going to be the Tri-Nations. Our first two matches were away, which meant our chances of winning were much slimmer. We had the Wallabies in Perth and the All Blacks in Wellington, before return matches in Durban and Johannesburg. The Tri-Nations was very different in 1998 to the previous year. One of Nick's main objectives was to shore up the defence, and in four matches prior to the Tri-Nations we'd kept two clean sheets, and conceded just two tries. But we knew Australia and New Zealand would pose different questions. The 1997 Tri-Nations had seen 52 tries scored in six matches, but in 1998 only 22 tries were scored in all the matches. It was a vastly different competition.

Australia hosted us in Perth, the first time a rugby union international would be played in the city. The week before the test saw a relatively calm build-up, but it rained non-stop the night of the match. It was a tight game, and Matt Burke missed about four kicks, which proved to make the difference on the night. Joost scored a try from a quick-tap penalty, and we won 14-13. It was the first time since our win in Sydney in 1993 that the Springboks had won in either Australia or New Zealand.

What became clear to me in the first few months of the year was that I'd become a conduit between the players and Mallett. They respected him immensely, but he was aloof. I mean that in a good way. He kept his distance to a large extent. He wasn't unfair, but he sometimes wasn't approachable, and I became the middleman. I was only a little older than most of the players, after all.

I knew Pieter Muller had been going through a difficult time at home, and obviously his attention was diverted occasionally. Nick was hard on all of them in training, but I recall Pieter dropping a few passes and Nick really tearing strips off him. I went to Nick and said, 'You must be careful. The oke's going through a bit of a difficult time.' That was also part of my role as technical advisor, although it wasn't part of my job description. It just happened that way. Players would often come to me and ask if I would chat to Nick on their behalf. I had a good relationship with Gary Teichmann, André Venter and Pieter Rossouw. Perhaps they felt more comfortable talking to me.

In some ways my relationships turned out to be my downfall in that squad. We played a bit of golf on the tour. Solly didn't play golf, so Nick, Gary Teichmann, Henry Honiball and I had a standing fourball. Gary and Henry were good mates, so Nick and I would challenge them. Being close to Mallett, and close to the players, put me in a vulnerable position. But that was furthest from my mind as we travelled to Wellington to face the All Blacks. Instead, I was wrapped up in the intensity of a test match against the old enemy, and I loved it.

It poured with rain the entire week leading up to the test. Training was a nightmare, because every field was completely waterlogged. I remember the forwards scrumming against the machine one day, and it literally floated away from them. They fell on their faces and were covered in mud. It was comical, and some of the New Zealand press commented on what a joke we were. The coaching staff did their best, but preparations were hardly ideal under those conditions. The best we could hope for was that the conditions would remain the same that weekend so that New Zealand would also struggle.

The morning of the test suggested a beautiful day ahead. Locals said it was the warmest, finest winter day Wellington had had for 40 years. It was a blow for us, because the All Blacks had Christian Cullen, Jonah Lomu and Jeff Wilson in their backline. Nice, dry conditions suited them perfectly.

If you remember the game, wing Pieter Rossouw scored the try that sealed our victory by coming off his wing. It was a planned move, and one I'd love to take credit for, but the man behind it was Henry Honiball. He drew the movement on a serviette at breakfast. It was a variation of a move we'd worked on. We'd planned for number 8, Teichmann, to pick up the ball and pass to Joost, who would release it to Honiball. He, in turn, would flip it straight back to Joost. But at breakfast Henry said to Joost, 'Why don't you keep running away from me as planned, but I won't give the ball back to you. They'll follow you and I'll run into the flanker, and stop him from going on, as I flip the pass to Pieter. The flank will run into me, and you just make sure the flyhalf keeps following you.'

That's exactly what happened. We won a game in which we'd spent 60 per cent of the time defending. It was our first win in New Zealand since 1981, and again we benefited from poor opposition kicking. Carlos Spencer was the flyhalf, and missed five kicks at goal. A lot of things went in our favour. Wilson dived on a ball and claimed a try – the ref never gave it. With a television match official, that try might have been given today.

Centre André Snyman, who was excellent on defence, was injured before halftime, and Nick put Franco Smith on the field a couple of minutes into the second half. Nick wanted André off when he was injured. I ran onto the field with water bottles during one of the breaks in play, and Pieter Muller came over. 'Tell Nick he must keep André on for as long as he can,' he said. 'He mustn't let him go. André must bite the bullet because, psychologically, these okes are not enjoying having him on the field.'

But André had to come off. Just before Franco went on, Nick said to him: 'I'll put you on, but if you miss one tackle, you will never play for South Africa again.' Franco never missed a tackle, and played very well. Nick knew they were going to target that channel once André was off, but Franco stood up to everything they threw at him.

After the match, Teichmann was in tears. He'd never won in New

Zealand, and it meant so much to him. He gave his match jersey to Nick, and Joost gave his to Solly. It was a 'thank you' to those two coaches.

Henry Honiball probably won that test for us. He was a genius as a player, and a person with unbelievable wisdom. Teammates and opponents respected him hugely, not only for his ability on the field, but also for his humility off it. He never said a bad word about anyone, and would always give someone a chance. He is a farm boy at heart, and still farms in the Drakensberg near Winterton in KwaZulu-Natal.

The respect he commanded had been particularly apparent during the French series the previous year. Henry had asked Nick if he could bring his wife on the tour, as there were lots of violent attacks on farms and farmers at that stage. He didn't feel comfortable leaving his wife home alone. Nick never hesitated, and told him to bring her along. She stayed with Henry, and he went out to dinner with her in Paris. None of the other players ever questioned it. Henry respected Nick for allowing his wife on tour and gave his all for the coach, because the coach had a human side.

In the first test of that tour, Henry hurt his wrist against Italy. He told Nick he didn't think he could play, but Nick said, 'Henry, I need you against France.' So he played and we won, but Henry hurt his neck and knee. He told Nick his knee was sore, and he didn't feel he could play to his full potential. But Nick convinced him to play in the second test, so we could win the series. We won by a record score, and Henry scored his first ever Bok try, and 22 points in all. But he was really in tatters after that game, and asked Nick if he could stand down for the England test. But Mallett said, 'Henry, I need you for England.' Dick Muir, the Bok centre on that tour, went to Nick and said, 'Don't worry, coach, I've got Henry's passport. He can't go anywhere.' Honiball could barely get out of bed in the morning, he was so banged up. But he sucked it up, and gave another great performance against England.

His major problem was a neck injury that wasn't responding to treatment. After the England match, Henry was being held together by sheer willpower. Players receive match fees and win bonuses, and most players would have carried on for the money. But Henry was the one trying to sit out, and it was the coach who kept pleading with him to play. It said a lot about Henry that he wasn't doing it for the money.

By the time we arrived in Edinburgh for the test against Scotland, we were tired as a group, but on an emotional high. The tour had been such a success, both on and off the field. Nick gave the team a lot of time off in Edinburgh. Those who played golf found some lovely links courses to test, while the others wandered around the beautiful city of Edinburgh. We didn't train on the Monday or the Tuesday. At the beginning of the week, Nick told the squad he would announce the team on the Tuesday night. He added, 'Henry will play flyhalf, and he'll have until the end of the week to tell me if he can play.' That was a constant with Nick. He always maintained that he could package the team around Henry, so Henry was picked, and the rest were slotted in around him. Nick said: 'If Henry can't play, then either Jannie de Beer will start, and Franco will be the backup, or the other way around – we'll see.'

But Henry wasn't happy. He went to Nick and said, 'Coach, I'm sore, and I don't think it's fair on the other guys to wait until Thursday or Friday to know if they're playing. I think it's fair that you tell the oke he's in – I'm not playing.'

Henry could have gone onto the field for five minutes, and then come off. He would have earned a match fee and a win bonus, but he didn't think in that way. All he worried about was his teammates, and how unfair it would've been on them. He sat out and Jannie de Beer started, with Franco Smith coming on for his first cap in the match. James Small scored his twentieth test try to break Danie Gerber's record, and Henry enjoyed the occasion almost as much as if he'd played.

As a young coach, observing a guy like Henry rubbed off on me. I saw the value of having senior players with high moral and ethical standards, and how valuable it was to a successful squad. Others, too, such as Gary Teichmann and even James Small, had a huge impact on the tour. But Henry was the most amazing of the lot. And that's why I largely credit Henry for our victory over the All Blacks in Wellington.

We left Wellington brimming with confidence. The All Blacks were shattered at the loss, especially as they'd also lost to Australia in their opening game. They were suddenly under huge pressure, and we had a date with them in Durban a few weeks later. The week after losing at home to the Springboks, they lost to Australia in Christchurch. The All Blacks arrived in South Africa hell-bent on exacting revenge and saving some pride.

8

Winning and losing

There is nothing quite like a Springbok–All Black match. It's the greatest rivalry in rugby. Although there have been times when the contest was uneven, it'll always be the ultimate challenge in this sport. Both countries are mad about the game; boys are raised wanting to be an All Black or a Bok. That intensity is palpable when the two teams play each other. In Durban, it was as intense as ever.

In 1998, we were on the brink of achieving a historic feat by winning the Tri-Nations, but it required an epic clash to pull it off. There were two incidents on that day that stand out for me. The All Blacks picked Isitolo Maka at number 8 for the crunch game at Kings Park. He was a beast of a player, and I doubt we would've won that game if he'd stayed on for 80 minutes. He ran all over us, bullied and smashed us. But, unfortunately for him, he left the field after being injured by his own teammate, and it changed the course of the test.

Early in the second half, the All Blacks had a lineout. When lock Robin Brooke came down, he hit Maka on the head with his elbow. Maka was groggy and couldn't play on. That's when the game turned. There was still a lot of work to do, because we were 5-23 down at that stage, and the game looked to be over. But from that moment, the momentum shifted.

The second incident that changed the course of the match was the result of an earlier development. In the first half, Bok lock Krynauw Otto had been severely rucked, and he was bleeding badly. There was a big hole in his shin, and it looked really ugly. Blood was gushing out, and it seeped through his sock. Team doctor Frans Verster took Otto away for stitches. Back then, you could stay off as long as you liked; there was no 15-minute rule. While he was being stitched up, the halftime whistle went. The guys trooped into the changing room 5-17 down, and they were all pretty glum.

Normally Nick Mallett did most of the talking, as skipper Gary Teichmann wasn't a man of many words. But that changed in Durban. Mallett was giving his halftime talk, which I don't recall well, other than that it consisted of some angry words and expletives. Normally when

Mallett was finished, he'd turn to Teichmann and ask if he wanted to add anything. Gary almost always said no, or merely reiterated Nick's words. But that day it was different.

As the team was about to walk out of the changing room, it fell unusually silent. Normally players would be psyching each other up or slapping one another on the back to fire them up for the second half. That day they were flat and physically looked as if they were being smashed. New Zealand was playing superbly. They were desperate to beat us at home after losing in Wellington. Gary opened the door to lead the team down the tunnel, but without warning he closed it again and turned to the men. He was angry.

'Do me a favour. Look at Krynauw's leg,' he commanded. Everyone stared at Gary as if he were mad. But once they realised he was deadly serious, they all glanced down at Krynauw's gash. Some guys couldn't bear to look, because the doc was still stitching up the wound and it looked terrible. Flesh and blood was hanging off the bone.

Gary said, 'Listen, these Kiwis have been *moering* us, and that's why we're losing. We've been standing back and no one has done anything. Let's sort this out now.'

It was out of character for Gary, but he chose the perfect moment to step forward. The players' mood changed instantly, and you could almost see their chests swell. We took control of the game, and effected one of the greatest comebacks in test-match rugby history. Joost van der Westhuizen started the comeback with a great break in the 68th minute to score. Bob Skinstad scored with about eight minutes to go, which left us four points behind. New Zealand were wilting, and we had the momentum. When hooker James Dalton scored our fourth try in injury time, it sealed a remarkable 24-23 win. And Krynauw played until the 71st minute, despite his injury.

Everyone was emotionally and physically drained after the match, because it had been such a roller coaster. After the formal functions, we returned to the Beverly Hills hotel for the team meeting, and then it was pretty much every man for himself. As you can imagine, Durban was in party mode that night.

Nick and I decided to go out for a beer. Solly wasn't with us; I don't know where he went. We decided to head for the pub up the road from the hotel. But as we walked out of the hotel, we saw that the streets were packed with supporters in good cheer. Nick took one look at the situation and said, 'I don't feel like crowds.' I agreed. At that moment, a bakkie came round the corner with three guys in it.

They obviously recognised Nick, and shouted their congratulations. They didn't know him, but they were elated fans, and they offered us a beer. We happily accepted. They parked, opened a cooler box and handed out the beers. We just sat there around the bakkie and drank with them for a couple of hours.

The next morning I thought to myself: there we were, one of the best moments we'd experienced, and we shared it with some real fans. Those guys would have gone home and said, 'Jeez, you won't believe it, but we had beers with Nick Mallett last night, on the pavement in Umhlanga.' That was memorable. People would've expected us to go to a bar and drink until 4 a.m. or something, but we were too tired for that. I don't even remember the names of those guys. But that was Nick, and I enjoyed the way he got on so easily with people.

On Sunday it was business as usual. Although the victory meant we had one hand on the Tri-Nations trophy for the first time, we needed to finish the job against Australia at Ellis Park.

The Wallaby test was memorable, because by winning the match we also won the Tri-Nations for the first time, and because Gary Teichmann equalled François Pienaar's record of 29 tests as captain. But most people remember it for Bob Skinstad's try. Bob was our super-sub at that stage, and was starting to come through at international level. At Ellis Park he scored one of the cleverest tries I've seen. As a team, things were working well. We were winning and we were happy, because everyone knew they had a role to play. Bob was happy with his as an impact player – the guy who could play anywhere in the back row. He had free rein to play as he wanted, because he was genuinely an unbelievable talent. I'd seen him as a schoolboy at Hilton College, and he was always a special player. At that point, I think Bob was just happy to be part of the Springbok team; part of a winning, happy team. As much as his ambition dictated that it was preferable to be a genuine starting Springbok, he was happy and free of any animosity.

The game was completely different from the one the week before. We were always in control of the match – the Wallabies didn't even score a try. We won 29-15, and the standout feature for me was the defensive play of centre Pieter Muller. In the opening minutes, Muller hammered Australian centre Tim Horan. He then hammered Stephen Larkham, and Joost also got in on the act. They tackled those Aussie players like they'd never been tackled before. Because of the pressure applied by Muller and Joost, the Wallabies began to play deeper and deeper. They never got close to the advantage line. We controlled the match and, when Bob scored, it sealed the win. After the final whistle sounded, Nick, Solly and I went down to the changing room to wait for the players after the trophy presentation ceremony on the field. Someone asked Nick if he was going to join the players on the field, and he declined. That impressed me, because he didn't steal the players' thunder. He allowed them to enjoy the moment.

For the next few months, I continued coaching in and around Cape Town, and preparing for the end-of-year Grand Slam (tests against Ireland, Wales, Scotland and England) tour. At this stage, the team had won 14 tests in a row – 13 under Mallett – and we were confident we could break the world record of 17 consecutive wins on the tour. I spent a lot of time cutting videos from the Five Nations games that year, and from the summer tours of those teams, so that we could be well prepared when we arrived in Britain. Our success as a team was unparalleled at that stage.

But, on the end-of-year tour, some cracks began to appear. And things came to a head for a lot of the people concerned. Although we didn't realise it at the time, one of the problems was our big touring squad. We'd picked 36 players, and basically travelled with two teams, because there were four matches in addition to the four tests. Due to the schedule, more coaches were brought into the mix. Frans Ludeke, who was coaching South Western Districts, was asked to help. And former Bok coach Ian McIntosh came along to add experience. Western Province had won the Currie Cup, and there were a lot of Province players in the squad. Their coach, Harry Viljoen, had resigned, and Alan Solomons was set to take over as Stormers coach in the Super 12 the following year. The tour gave him the perfect opportunity to start bonding with his future players.

At times, it was like having a Stormers squad on tour, although it wasn't anyone's fault. Solly had had meetings with the Stormers players about the coming season, and he'd anointed Bob Skinstad as his captain for the Super 12. Bob was keen to force his way into the starting test XV, and Nick realised that he couldn't be kept out forever. Bob was one of the best players South Africa had ever produced, but at that time he wasn't managed particularly well in my view.

That was another lesson I learnt. I realised that certain players had to be handled differently than others. I've treated Schalk Burger differently, and I've had to handle Bryan Habana in a certain way. Players are all unique, and they need to be treated as individuals. Some guys are easy and follow well, and others don't. It's up to you as the coach to find out what works best.

The dirt-trackers played in Scotland, while the test team prepared in London for the first test of the tour against Wales at Wembley. Cardiff Arms Park had been pulled down, and the Welsh were still building the Millennium Stadium for the 1999 World Cup, so we got to play at Wembley. That was a great occasion, because it was such a wonderful old stadium, with great atmosphere. We struggled in the match, and eventually won 28-20. The whole party then moved on to Scotland for a midweek game. And, of course, the test against the Scots at Murrayfield.

Nick and I were in a pub one evening enjoying a beer, when he turned to me and said, 'I think I'm going to leave André Venter out. I'm going to play Bobby. The more I think about it, the more I believe André is a lock and not a flank. He's a modern-day lock. The sort of guy who can play 80 minutes as a scrummaging tight forward, but someone who can also run around. Using him as a lock could be a bonus, because he's so mobile and so fit.'

He asked what I thought of the idea. I didn't hesitate in my reply: 'I think you're making a hell of a mistake, Nick. I think the team needs Venter. I'm not saying Bob shouldn't be there, but I don't think it's a good call.'

He said something like, 'Rob [Van der Valk – the team logistics manager and a good friend of Nick's] probably agrees with you, Jake. But I know that Rob likes okes that are big.' We left it at that, and I didn't think much more of it.

But a while later, Solly came in for a beer too. Nick said to him, 'I've thought about it. I haven't slept for a couple of nights. I think I'm going to start Bobby at flank, but Jake doesn't think it's a good idea.' I could see Solly was angry about my advice, and his attitude made it clear that he didn't care what I thought. Nick had asked for my opinion and I'd given it. Solly was pissed off because Bobby was one of his favourites, and his Stormers captain-to-be for 1999. It was natural that Solly would be protective of Bob, but things would not be the same after that night. Bob's attitude towards me changed, because he'd been led to believe I was anti-Skinstad and pro-Venter. But I believed the team needed André, and that if he was dropped, the dynamic would change. It did.

André's work ethic and ability were immense. And although he was a man of few words, he was a leader. When Nick dropped him for the Scotland test, there was a lot of angst among the players. They suddenly felt insecure, because if André could be so summarily disposed of (although it hadn't been an easy decision for Mallett), so could they. There was anger as well, and some of it was unfairly directed at Bob. Venter wasn't even selected at lock for the match. He was dropped to the bench, and came on in the 55th minute at lock.

We beat Scotland comfortably (35-10), but the wedge had been driven between members of the squad. And, of course, between Solly and me. Venter was sent off to join the dirt-trackers for a midweek game in Cork against a Combined Provinces team, at lock. He was angry about it. As one of the most capped Boks on the tour, and one of the most respected flanks in the world, the insult of playing lock for the 'B' team was a huge blow.

Almost without realising, I was in the middle of this fallout. Players who were feeling insecure started coming to me, because they didn't feel as comfortable talking to Mallett and Solly. Others, of course, were loyal to Solly, and aligned themselves with him. I became something of a mediator in the camp. It was difficult.

I'd spent a lot of time with Nick over the previous year, both on tour and in Cape Town. We'd played golf together, and we often played against Teichmann and Henry Honiball. I'd also built up relationships with Pieter Rossouw, Pieter Muller and André Venter, so I was trying to be nice to everybody. But at training in Ireland, Solly put me in my place, in no uncertain terms. He took charge of practices, and made sure I held contact sheets and tackle bags. And because he was effectively my superior, I wasn't in a position to tell him to bugger off. I'd have to hold a bag, and he'd make Ollie le Roux charge at me.

The dynamics weren't working, and I'd stopped enjoying the tour, as the mood had changed. The last straw was the video session that took place after the Ireland match, which we won 27-13. With that victory, we equalled the world record of 17 wins in a row. Bob scored a great try, and set up another one with some great individual work. During the game, hooker James Dalton threw a ball into the lineout, which went skew. Teichmann jumped across and took the ball, but the referee blew up the infringement. It was a minor incident, and I decided not to add it to the video I cut for the players. The visuals jumped from the kick to the scrum given for the infringement. When the squad viewed it, Nick asked me where the lineout was. I told him I'd cut it. He lost it completely; you'd have sworn I'd committed mass murder. He went berserk in front of the entire squad, and I was quite shaken by the incident, as it was clear something else was at play.

The tension in the squad had snowballed.

Everyone was under pressure. We were unbeaten on the tour thus far, but it was not all harmony. The midweek team wanted to play a test, and the Venter situation had increased the tension. A day after the video incident, I was having dinner when Gary and Henry joined me at the table. Nick also came over and sat down. After about two minutes, Gary jokingly said, 'By the way, Jake, where's that lineout?' For a second time, Nick went ballistic, and then got up and left. I was flabbergasted, and Gary felt really bad about it. He apologised, because he hadn't realised his remark would set Nick off. I told him to forget about it, but I knew that attitudes towards me had changed. And while I hoped we could sort it out, deep down I probably knew that my time with the Boks was drawing to a close.

We lost 7-13 to England, and that ended the winning streak. The season had come to an end on a disappointing note, in more ways than one.

After we got home, I took a little time off over Christmas before joining the Bulls in the Super 12. SA Rugby, not the Springboks, was employing me. If my assistance was needed somewhere, I would go. The Bulls weren't the force they are now, and started the season badly. I was asked to help out as a technical advisor, and arrived towards the end of March. It was nearly midway through the Super 12 competition.

The first game I was involved in was against the Queensland Reds, which we lost. The next one was against the Sharks in Durban. Again the Bulls lost. The following week, I was called to a Springbok selectors' meeting in Cape Town, as I was secretary of the committee. I had no involvement in team selection, but I attended. I was there on 10 April, the day the Stormers met the Sharks at Newlands. The Stormers were riding high, and Bob Skinstad and Gary Teichmann were about to come up against each other in a clash of the in-form number 8s. The matter was discussed at the selectors' meeting.

When we adjourned for lunch, Nick came over. I hadn't spoken to him in a while. He asked for a word. 'Listen, this is hard for me to tell you, Jake, but Solly is not comfortable with the way things are working, with you in the set-up. Solly's a dogmatic guy, and when he puts his heels in, you're not going to change his mind. Basically, it's you or him. And I've got to make a call to keep the peace,' he said. 'I've decided to use Solly, so I'm going to have to find someone else to fulfil your role.'

I was shocked. Nick had promised that I would go to the World Cup. I asked whether it wouldn't help if I spoke to Solly; I might change his mind. Mallett said there wasn't any point, so I grudgingly accepted the situation.

I was returning to Pretoria the next day, but I went home for the night and told Debbie the awful news. It felt like someone had pulled my heart out. Before I'd left, I asked Nick how I should handle the press, as I knew it would eventually reach the media. He said, 'Just tell the truth.'

When I returned to Pretoria, I was naturally distracted. I thought it best to tell Bulls coach Eugene van Wyk about what had transpired in Cape Town. It's odd what goes through your mind, but I figured that if Eugene heard from someone else that I'd been fired by the Boks, he might think I'd be gunning for his job. I decided I'd let Joost know too, as he was the Bulls captain, and a senior member of the Bok squad. I didn't want him to hear about it from someone else. I confided that I wasn't very happy.

We played the Sharks in Durban, and Joost must have told Gary Teichmann, as he approached me at the function after the game, and was pretty upset. Remember, at that point Gary was also on the verge of losing his Bok place, to Bobby, before the World Cup, and he was starting to feel insecure. He expressed his concerns about possibly being sidelined. The Sharks went on tour the following week, and somebody told journalist Dan Retief that I'd been fired. Dan called and asked if it was true. I couldn't deny it and told him the truth.

It suddenly became a big media thing, even though I was really one of the backroom staff. Dan broke the story, and other journalists followed his lead. Solly referred to me in the press as 'only a video operator', and other stories surfaced that suggested I had been a failure as a technical advisor.

Nick called me in a huff. 'Jake, I'm really annoyed, this is not what I wanted,' he said. I was angry, as he was the one who'd told me to 'tell the truth'. I'd expressly asked him how I should package it. I'd told Dan that it had been a choice between me and Solly, and that Nick had picked Solly. That was the truth. Current Bulls coach Heyneke Meyer replaced me, and also acted as the forwards coach.

I learnt a great deal from that experience. I'd been fired from the Bok set-up, even though we were winning. I thought I'd added value, and some of the players were a little annoyed about what had happened. I'd probably said the wrong thing when Nick asked for my opinion on dropping Venter. But I wouldn't have changed anything, because that had been my viewpoint, which I was surely entitled to.

PART III

PAYING MY DUES
1999–2003

9

Buenos Aires success

I was still struggling to come to terms with being axed from the Bok set-up, but saw out the rest of the Super 12 campaign with the Bulls. Returning to Cape Town, I wasn't sure what the rest of the year would offer in the form of coaching. I was still employed by SA Rugby, and would continue to head up coaching clinics and run courses for coaches, but there was a huge void where I would normally have spent time planning for the Springboks.

I wanted to actually coach a team, and not just act as a technical analyst, advisor or coaching manager at SA Rugby. Rian Oberholzer, knowing my ambitions, was good to me and tried hard to find something else for me to do. As it happened, Willie Hills, a former Springbok hooker, pulled out as assistant coach to the SA Under-21 team that was set to play at the SANZAR/UAR championships. This was an annual tournament co-hosted by Argentina, South Africa, New Zealand and Australia, and was the forerunner to what is the IRB Under-21 World Championships today. It was designed as a competition between the four southern hemisphere nations, but by 1999 it had already expanded to include some northern hemisphere teams.

In 1999, Argentina were the hosts, and Eric Sauls was the Baby Bok coach. With Hills pulling out, Oberholzer asked if I wanted to come in as assistant coach. To be honest, it wasn't my idea of a glamour job – after all, I'd been with the senior Springbok team – so I saw it as a bit of a comedown. I also suspected that I might be being set up to fail. South African Under-21 teams had not performed well in the previous few years, despite a rich talent stream. And since I hadn't been involved in the selection or squad identification, I was a little sceptical.

In 1997 the Baby Boks had lost three out of three matches, with a squad that included Victor Matfield, Bob Skinstad and a very young John Smit. In 1998, South Africa hosted the tournament, but the team only managed to win two of their four matches. So, by 1999, coaching the Under-21s was a potentially career-ending move for any coach. With the talented youngsters we had, there was no reason to believe we shouldn't be competitive. In 1998, Dawie Snyman was a great coach, but he, too, failed to get the desired results.

Eric Sauls had been Dawie's assistant, and he was given the coaching job at the end of 1998. I'd heard grumbles from within the set-up that political selections didn't allow for the best team to be chosen, which was a worry. But I decided to sign up anyway. Most of the flak would fall on Eric's shoulders, but I also knew there would be a lot of expectations from the assistant who'd been part of a successful Springbok squad.

My fears turned out to be unfounded. When I joined the squad, I was welcomed warmly and included in every decision. Team manager Temba Wiso was particularly supportive and made sure I was utilised positively. He was extremely happy that the Under-21s had someone with Springbok coaching experience helping them out. In November the previous year, the Under-21s had gone on a short tour of England, culminating in the main curtain-raiser before the England–South Africa match at Twickenham. Eric was coaching at the time, and Temba was manager. The Baby Boks lost 32-10 with a team that included the likes of John Smit, De Wet Barry, Johan Roets, André Pretorius and Wylie Human. Those players would later form the backbone of the 1999 Under-21s.

All credit should go to Eric as the head coach for the team that subsequently developed, but I think we worked well together because of Temba's attitude. He kept telling the rest of the management: 'You need to listen to what Jake is saying, because he's come with ideas that the Boks have used.' Temba's constant reinforcement of my abilities convinced Eric to utilise me, rather than to see me as a threat. I didn't have to impose my ideas, because the plea to listen came from a man Eric trusted. He therefore gave me a lot of latitude and we formed a good bond.

For the first time SA Rugby took the Under-21s more seriously, which meant a bigger budget for preparation. My motto has always been: 'Fail to prepare and prepare to fail.' During the previous five years, the Under-21s had been an afterthought – a talented group of players thrown together at the last minute. But by 1999 we were well into the professional era, and the importance of having a strong Under-21 squad was becoming apparent.

With the increased budget, we got the players together in a camp a month before the tournament in Buenos Aires. The squad had been selected before I officially joined, but it was a strong team. John Smit and Jaco van der Westhuyzen had both played Super 12 earlier in the year, which was almost unheard of. Oberholzer had given the instruction that we had to do well in the tournament. And to his credit, he gave us everything we needed to achieve that objective.

Many of the players had been involved during the previous year, and they couldn't believe the kind of lead-up we had compared with 1998. We played against a Vodacom All-Stars team, and we beat Namibia's senior World Cup squad in Windhoek. We had the players we wanted, we had the preparation we needed and we had no excuse not to do well. The majority of the team had been on the previous year's tour to Britain, when they had lost heavily to England at Twickenham. About eight players from that tour, who were eligible in 1999, never made the 1999 squad. In the end we showed that our selections were right. In Argentina we were set to face reigning champions Australia, Five Nations champions Wales, and England in Pool A. Given our results over the past few years, we had been drawn in the group of death.

We arrived in Argentina and were written off as tough but ultimately beatable, which was probably a fair assessment, based on our previous results. The squad didn't feel that way, of course, but at the first press conference I fully appreciated how South Africa's Under-21s were regarded. It wasn't flattering.

John Smit, who was captain, sat through the entire press conference with all four SANZAR/UAR skippers and wasn't asked a single question. Aussie captain Nathan Sharpe, Kiwi captain Paul Tito and the Argentinean skipper were all bombarded with questions. John sat there, feeling embarrassed. When he returned to the hotel, he called the squad together and told them nobody thought we could win this thing. The players now had a point to prove.

We took the tournament by storm from the very first game. In our pool games we scored 17 tries and conceded only one. Australia was the next best with six tries, which highlights how good we were. For our opening match against Wales, Eric picked a strong side, and we thumped the Welsh 48-9. We had seven future test players in the starting line-up, including lock Dan Vickerman, who has gone on to be a star with the Wallabies.

In our next game, we faced England – the same team that had thrashed us at Twickenham seven months earlier. I remember the names in the England side – Jamie Noon, Andrew Sheridan, Andy Hazell and Alex Sanderson – who all went on to play full test rugby. It was a very good team, but we blew them away with a 39-5 win.

What stood out for me was how upset our boys were about conceding a try. Centre Barry McDonald had missed a tackle and England scored. The guys were really angry with Barry and he was angry with himself, which highlighted the attitude of the squad.

With Australia as opponents in our final pool match, we needed to win that game to avoid playing New Zealand in the semi-finals. Australia was no match for us, and we won 20-12. Although the score looks tight, we scored three tries while keeping them down to four penalties. They had Steve Kefu, Phil Waugh, Nathan Sharpe, David Pusey, Matt Dunning and David Croft, players that would eventually turn out for the Wallabies.

In our semi, we hammered the French 45-11. Their side included Damien Traille, Cedric Heymans, Elvis Vermeulen, Julien Laharrague, David Skrela and William Servat. It was a testy game, and three French players were red-carded within six minutes of each other in the second half. But when the first red card came out, we were already 28-11 ahead.

As expected, we met New Zealand in the final. It was a hell of a game, and they had a hell of a team. I'll run through more names just to emphasise how important the Under-21 tournament is to a country's rugby future. The Baby Blacks had Ben Blair, Doug Howlett, Rico Gear, Chris Jack, Paul Tito and Carl Hayman, among others who have gone on to play Super 14 rugby.

We could beat them at that level, yet, when our players went on to Super12/14 level and Bok rugby, we were routinely hammered. It's something I've never understood and never accepted, because at that level we were as good as, if not better than, any other nation.

It's one of the reasons I've harped on conditioning for years. Most of the teams at the Under-21 championships had specific programmes to allow their players to develop, with adequate rest and conditioning, when they played less rugby. Overseas the players have a good rest in every four-year cycle, yet in South Africa we choose not to do that. It was something I fought for, with minor success, when I became Bok coach.

That Baby Bok final showed me that we had nothing to fear from New Zealand. We had to give them respect, but didn't need to be in awe of them. We won the match and the title, after a late Frikkie Welsh try to draw the scores level at 25-25. Johan Roets landed a pressure conversion to give us the win. In truth, it should never have been that close in the first place. I always thought we could win, but we let them out of jail.

They scored a try from nowhere. If I remember correctly, it was a forward pass and there was a knock-on as well. We looked like we were dead and buried. Then we spent the last 20 minutes in their 22, and scrummed and scrummed them into the ground. Eventually, we were on their try line, and I remember John looking up and saying, 'What should we do?' I was the closest coach to the action, and I said, 'Scrum again.' When he hesitated, I repeated, 'Scrum!' We eventually scored from a scrum in the last minute. New Zealand didn't like the scrumming, even though they had Hayman and Jack in their tight five.

We had a hell of a pack. We'd brought Hanyani Shimange and Eduard Coetzee on as our impact players. They were really effective, replacing Lawrence Sephaka and Skipper Badenhorst. We simply out-powered New Zealand when the match became trench warfare in the last quarter. Both Shimmy and Coetzee were short and got under their opponents, which really upset the New Zealand pack in those final minutes.

After we scored, it came down to the conversion. Grant Henderson was probably our best goal-kicker, but he wasn't on the field. Roets had been doing all the kicking, even though he wasn't a recognised kicker. His father had come over to Argentina to watch the tournament. The day before, Roets was practising his kicking after training had ended. He missed just about every kick. To help him, I said: 'Your dad's sitting in the stands. He's flown all the way here. You need this kick to win the tournament; let's see how good you are.'

I was playing a mind game with him, putting him in that situation on purpose. Less than 24 hours later he had to do it for real. Just before the conversion, I saw Henderson running onto the field with a kicking tee. I assumed Eric had made a substitution and put Henderson on instead so that he could take the conversion, as he was the most reliable kicker in our team. I thought that it was a great piece of coaching by Eric. But I quickly realised that Hendo was just bringing the tee out and Roets was going to kick. He slotted it.

In the changing room afterwards, Roets's dad asked if he could come in. Actually, quite a few dads were there, and they all joined us in the changing room. It was a hell of a thing for the players to share the moment with their teammates and their fathers. They'd just won the tournament. But they'd also beaten New Zealand. The year before they'd beaten New Zealand with an André Pretorius dropkick, but couldn't win the tournament. Now they'd beaten them again. Winning was starting to become a trend for these players, which was unheard of at junior level. It was a special time.

Afterwards I received a lot of praise, while Eric didn't get as much, which was a little unfair. I had brought some ideas from my time with the Springboks and Eric was big enough to let me do my thing. We won the tournament, which suggests that between us we got something right. Afterwards Eric went overseas to coach and I moved on to other projects for a while, so we never really had the chance to build on our success in Buenos Aires.

10

Hunting with the Sharks

Once the euphoria of winning the Under-21 championships had subsided, I was back in the real world with no coaching post, and it was only July. It was a World Cup year and everything was gearing towards that, which made me feel a little depressed. Less than 12 months earlier I'd been a part of it – and now I was on the outside looking in.

SuperSport asked me to act as a technical analyst on the show *Head to Head* in the second half of 1999, which I slotted in between my daily commitments at SA Rugby. That went pretty well. Towards the end of the year I received a flattering call I didn't expect, from the Natal Sharks, who enquired about my availability to join the coaching staff for the 2000 Super 12 season.

Legendary coach Ian McIntosh had retired after the 1999 Currie Cup final after more than 10 years in charge of the senior team, and the union was set to enter the 21st century with a new approach. I told them I was interested, and applied for the head coaching job. But the Sharks management appointed long-time stalwart and former Bok fullback Hugh Reece-Edwards to that position, offering me the role of assistant coach.

Although the position wasn't my first choice, I was happy to be involved in coaching a team and agreed to their terms. Rian Oberholzer was upset that I wanted to leave SA Rugby, and told me that I was making a mistake. He still holds that view. Although I can't say my time with the Sharks was successful, it wasn't a mistake. Those experiences were useful later in my career.

Looking back now, Reece and I were probably doomed following a legend like Mac. He *was* Natal Sharks rugby in the 1990s, and players such as Gary Teichmann, André Joubert and Henry Honiball had all retired or left at the end of 1999. Quite a few players from the Mac era were coming to the end of their careers, and overall it was a transitional phase, with the two of us at the helm.

We won a dismal one match – against the Waratahs in Sydney – during the entire season. Long before the end of the campaign, we were under pressure; Reece, as the top guy, even more so. We had a decent squad, but we failed to move away from Mac's style of play, which had been so successful. Reece held a lot of sentiment for the senior players who had stayed on after Mac, but I don't think he extracted the same response or got the same output from them. I felt a little awkward, as I had come into the set-up without the baggage of Mac's coaching legacy. I didn't have the same sentiments about the players, that they'd been loyal servants of Sharks rugby.

When I tried to change to a new approach, it was considered anti-establishment, as Natal had been successful for so long under Mac. The hierarchy questioned why we'd want to change things that had worked for over a decade. Publicly I had to appear loyal to Reece, although sometimes I differed with selections. It was a very difficult year.

I must stress that Reece and I never clashed either in private or in public, but privately I didn't feel he was getting the returns from players that he thought he was. It made life difficult, because I'd learnt with Solly in the Bok set-up that opening your mouth was not a good idea if you had long-term aspirations for the job. Nevertheless I ended up in trouble a few times because I voiced my opinions about the contributions of some players. It wasn't wise, but it was the only way I knew how to operate. The Sharks are a close-knit family, and my negative opinions about certain players soon filtered through the union.

I learnt that I had to be very careful about what I said, and how, as everything got back to the players and created negative tension. That was a huge learning curve. I'm not saying that I was blameless and never made a mistake – I did. But so did Reece, the players and the entire Sharks administration. In hindsight, the administration should probably have taken a completely different direction after Mac's retirement.

Although Mac could be spotted around the Absa Stadium almost every week, he never got involved in coaching the team while I was there. But several players who were still loyal to him would phone him and dis-cuss their or the team's problems. He was an ear for them, and this was a natural reaction from the players. But it was intimidating for the new coaching staff.

Rugby politics has always been part of the game in South Africa, and I'd started to experience it during my stint with the Boks. But at the Sharks in 2000 it was elevated to a new level. I was still naive in many ways, and this was the first time I'd been employed by a union as a senior-team coach. I was fast learning that the pressure that came with the expectations was enormous. I quickly learnt about the need to play the political game in South African rugby, and I'm not talking about race. I realised I had to be circumspect about sharing my feelings about specific players with certain people. Or that a successful outcome hinged on choosing my words carefully, depending on whom I was dealing with. I must admit that I haven't been overly successful in that area, because I'm a straightforward guy – which hasn't always been to my advantage. At the Sharks, it certainly wasn't.

In 2000 South Africa was still relatively new to professional rugby, and I don't think players handled criticism as well as they do today. I was of the opinion that a few players were just going through the motions to protect their contracts, so they could renew them for another season or two. I told them so, which didn't go down well at all.

I had worked with a lot of Sharks players in the 1999 SA Under-21 team, and I believed many were good enough to play ahead of some of the more seasoned players. I pushed hard for these hungry 21- and 22-year-olds to start matches. As a result, some of the senior players saw me as a threat to their livelihood. John Smit moved from prop to hooker at the time, but other former Under-21s, such as Shaun Sowerby, weren't given a fair chance.

An incident with captain Wayne Fyvie wasn't my finest diplomatic moment. He was a good player, but in 2000 I thought he was finished because he'd had so many knee operations. I told Reece that we needed someone younger, faster and stronger. It got back to Wayne, who naturally became suspicious of me. I sometimes shoot my mouth off and say the wrong thing, or my intentions don't come out as clearly as I would like. The Fyvie incident was one of those times. I told Reece, 'I think he's finished,' which is not very subtle. Wayne was furious, and I called him to apologise and explain myself properly. The right way to handle the situation would've been to call Wayne into a meeting right from the start and say, 'Listen, this is the way I feel.' As I said, I learnt lessons too.

Now if I have something to say, I meet with the player and tell him my views frankly, so he doesn't hear it from a third party. If he gets a second-hand report, my message might be misinterpreted or misunderstood.

One of the comments made when I joined the Sharks was that a good junior coach doesn't necessarily work well with the senior players, which was true in some respects. It's easier to tell a junior what to do, where to go and how to do something. At the Sharks I was dealing with big stars who were only a few years younger than me: Mark Andrews, Chris Rossouw, Ollie le Roux, John Slade, Wayne Fyvie, Pieter Muller, Joe Gillingham, Stephen Brink and Justin Swart were just some of the guys. It was intimidating, but I gained a lot from the experience.

As mentioned, the Super 12 didn't go well. The board wanted to fire Reece midway through the season, but they decided to hang on until the end of the campaign. As the Super 12 coaches were partly employed by SA Rugby, it wasn't only the Sharks' decision to fire him either. At that point Natal rugby didn't have an academy; they just bought the best junior players from around the country. The Sharks franchise was hugely successful, and it was the leader in creating, branding and marketing a professional union. When results went so poorly, someone had to pay the price. Reece was fired almost immediately after the final game. Although my contract extended into the Currie Cup season, I wasn't sure what the immediate future held.

The politicking reached new levels after Reece left. I thought I might be appointed as coach for the Currie Cup season, although I know that sounds like wishful thinking, considering the Super 12 campaign and our poor results. But I'd pleaded for changes to both players and playing style, and the board had even told me that my chances of coaching the Currie Cup team would not be negatively influenced by the outcome of the Super 12, as I wasn't the man in charge. I thought the union might finally consider my views and give me a chance to prove myself with the ultimate responsibility.

Yet when the time of reckoning came, they opted for Rudolf Straeuli from Border as the new coach. The administrators said I wouldn't be painted with the same brush as Reece, yet I was. As part of the debriefing process following the Super 12, players were asked about my ability. I didn't receive glowing commendations from some senior players whom I'd tried to replace in the preceding months. They got back at me in the best possible way.

In the interim period between the end of the Super 12 and the beginning of the Currie Cup, I had coached the Sharks against Welsh club Newport, who were on a pre-season tour, and we won by 50 points. It wasn't a big game, but I prepared seriously and we won comfortably, using a nice mix of young and old players. This was at the time the board was deciding on a Currie Cup coach. I thought the win might be enough to persuade them that I could do the job, but I was wrong. I was seriously disillusioned. I'd given up everything at SA Rugby to move to the Sharks on the basis that I'd be given a fair opportunity.

But I was still under contract and didn't have too many options at the time, so as a professional I started working with Rudolf. He was a difficult person to work for, because he remained very unemotional. Rugby is a game of passion, and I like to see that come through from time to time.

I tried really hard, but I was angry because I was working as assistant to another head coach. What if it went pear-shaped? Would I be held responsible again? These were constant questions going through my mind while I tried to understand how to work with Rudolf. I was pissed off because he'd come from Border – hardly a world-beating team. And I felt he didn't bring much new to the table. He didn't seem inclined to use me or include me in his thinking. He also didn't stimulate me as a fellow coach, but perhaps that was my anger getting in the way.

At our first meeting, I offered my thoughts on incorporating more young players. They'd done a great job in the match against Newport, and I pointed out some of my concerns about the older guys. Rudolf decided to have a trial match: the *ou manne* against the youngsters. The old boys scored a try in the last minute to draw the game, and Rudolf decided that the result was ample evidence that they were good enough for continued selection. As usual I didn't keep my mouth shut, and at the end of the trial match I told Rudolf: 'You see. That proves my point.' He practically ignored me for the rest of the season.

In hindsight it was probably best for the Sharks that Rudolf was appointed over me, because I would have wielded the axe in a big way. I was unhappy with certain players and their contracting, and would have cut a lot of the dead wood from the squad. That might have ruined the family bond that the union enjoys, so Rudolf, who is far more diplomatic than me, was perhaps the right guy at the time.

He instilled discipline at the beginning of his reign. If he told a player to do something, they would not question him; I sometimes got the feeling it was out of fear. He's not really the sort of bloke who is open to questioning. We reached the Currie Cup final and lost to Western Province at home, which was a huge disappointment.

But by that stage my mind was turning towards the Springboks again.

11

In green and gold again

During the Currie Cup campaign, Harry Viljoen was appointed as Bok coach after Nick Mallett was fired. Unfairly, I might add. In late 2000, Viljoen came to a Sharks practice in Durban, where I was running some complicated phase plays. He stood on the side of the field and watched for some time. At the end of the session, Harry asked if I would come to his hotel that evening, as he wanted to chat.

I had a suspicion that something was brewing, but I wasn't sure. We met, and Harry asked if I would join him for the Springboks' end-of-year tour to Argentina and Britain. I was flattered, but made it clear that if I went it would not be as technical advisor. I wanted to be an official assistant coach. He agreed, and I was appointed as his assistant along with André Markgraaff.

Officially I was the backline coach, which was exciting. At that time the difference between backs and forwards was starting to blur, as centres and wings began to look like flanks. The separate roles of forwards and backs no longer existed. Backs became fetchers and fetchers became backs. The number on the jersey was not relevant any more. If a player was second or third down the line, he had to have enough skill to make a decision and play the play. Harry bought into that because he was a very innovative guy, despite what many think of him. I was very stimulated by Harry and his approach to the game.

There are many perceptions out there about Harry – most of them inaccurate. He was way ahead of his time. He had a picture in his mind about how the game should be played and about how professional rugby should be run. He wanted players to look and feel like the highly paid professionals they were.

I think Harry's biggest fault – and I've said this to him – is that he didn't know how to get his ideas across. He also didn't surround himself with people who sent out the right message. Many of those around him mis-interpreted or misrepresented his intentions. Harry is an entrepreneurial, broad-picture, out-of-the-box kind of guy. But the more he heard negative feedback from his so-called inner circle, the more he retreated into his shell.

I know as much, because I worked with him almost the entire time that he was Bok coach.

You could see how such negativity had affected things by the change that occurred between the beginning of his tenure, when he tried some radical moves in a test match, and the stoic, boring, one-dimensional rugby the Boks played at the end of his stint.

He had the guts to tell the players not to kick the ball in a test match – *ever* – in a soccer stadium in Argentina, which shows how sure he was about how he wanted to play. There was no grey area. Even years later, when I was the Bok coach, it would still have been unthinkable to instruct my players not to kick the ball. It took incredible courage for Harry to do that. It wasn't that he didn't understand how the game should look. He understood clearly – the rest of us just couldn't keep up.

But then, in one of his last test matches as coach, against England, he played two less innovative, kicking players at 10 and 12 in Braam van Straaten and Louis Koen, which just showed how badly he was being influenced. It highlighted the divergence between where he had been at the start and where he eventually ended. Again, this was a lesson for me. I understood how important it was to be clear in your goals and to stick to them despite what other people were saying.

Before I boarded the aeroplane for Buenos Aires, there had been a lot of behind-the-scenes wrangling over my services. The Sharks wanted a transfer fee from SA Rugby, who were reluctant to pay it. The Sharks' attitude was interesting, as a few months earlier they would probably have let me go after the Super 12, but they'd started to appreciate my value in terms of analysis, coaching and talent identification. Suddenly they were reluctant to lose me. I pleaded with chief executive Brian van Zyl and Rudolf Straeuli. 'Guys,' I said, 'you're being helluva unfair. I've been picked to go to the Springbok set-up as assistant coach. This is a chance in a lifetime. You can't withhold that from me. It's not like I'm leaving for another province.'

The discussions went on and on. Harry kept phoning and asking what was happening. And I couldn't give him an answer. I suggested to Harry that he call Rian Oberholzer and put pressure on him to sort it out. But Harry's not that sort of guy. So I had to keep pestering Rian, and eventually the Sharks relented and agreed to release me for the duration of the tour. My long-term appointment, however, was still undecided.

The Bok set-up under Harry was very different to that of Natal under Rudolf, and also different to my time with the Boks under Mallett. Initially every coach understood his job exactly, and there was a lot of innovation and enthusiasm. Many of the players didn't know Harry, but they knew he had a reputation for approaching things differently, which excited them. This made for a happy and potentially groundbreaking tour.

For his first test in charge, against Argentina, Harry instructed the players not to kick the ball. They thought it was a plausible idea, but also figured that by the time they actually took the field, he'd have changed his mind. But in the warm-up the instruction remained the same, and in the tunnel before the team ran out he never altered the plan.

We stuck to it for 73 minutes. By then Argentina were coming back into the game after we'd made a good start. It became like target practice out there, because the Pumas knew the Springboks wouldn't kick. They fanned out and tackled us into the ground. They didn't commit to rucks, and it became too easy for them. I was running on and off the field with water bottles, and with about seven minutes to go, I heard Harry in my earpiece. 'Jake, it's Harry. You can tell them they can kick.' Harry had realised that if we carried on any longer we would end up losing the test. André Markgraaff had been calling for us to kick about ten minutes earlier, as he'd probably read the signs. Harry had held out for as long as he could. In the end we won 37-33.

André had recognised the danger and he let Harry know. That was part of his job. It wasn't a case of undermining the coach, but rather about giving his assistant's opinion on the game playing out in front of him. That was another lesson I learnt. I realised that, as the senior coach, you had to allow your assistant coaches the freedom to express their opinions. That means creating an environment in which differing opinions are not only tolerated, but can flourish. I'd been an assistant coach and knew what it was like thinking you were only making up numbers, and that any opinions you expressed would be ignored.

I had also been a technical advisor, so I knew the importance of that role when I became head coach. I was aware of the late nights and early mornings the technical analysts endured so that coaching staff would have the right information and clips in team meetings. I understood the frustrations when the hours spent cutting clips were wasted if the laptop crashed.

Understanding the pressures and importance of the assistant-coach position was equally important when I later became head coach. While I didn't realise it at the time, I would draw on all of these experiences as a Springbok coach. I learnt from both the strengths and the weaknesses of the head coaches with whom I had worked. André was right to say that we needed to start kicking during that test. Winning the test was the most crucial consideration, and by halftime we'd done enough to win. André only spoke up in the second half, when the kicking issue actually became more important than winning the match. You've got to keep the balance, and perhaps Harry had lost sight of it in trying to do something different. André reminded him of the main objective: to win.

And Harry took the comment as it was intended, because it was best for the team. He made people feel involved and free to question him, perhaps to his own detriment at times, but it was a fresh approach.

The touring party moved on to play Ireland, Wales and England, as well as a series of midweek games. The midweek team was almost travelling in isolation from the test team. They'd beaten Argentina 'A' in Tucuman, where Griquas flank Thando Manana made his Bok debut and famously refused to be initiated. His reasoning was sound, believing that he'd passed through his tribal Xhosa initiation into manhood and that such a ritual should only be endured once in his life. It raised an interesting dynamic in the Bok camp, because it wasn't an issue anybody had ever considered or had had to contend with before. But the team accepted his viewpoint and moved on. The midweek boys then played Ireland 'A', but lost heavily (28-11) after seven players arrived from Argentina only the night before the game. It added pressure to the test team.

We beat Ireland 28-18 in a tight game, after leading comfortably midway through the first half. A young Brian O'Driscoll played superbly for Ireland on that occasion and, although we deserved to win, the Irish made a fight of it. Harry also abandoned the plan of running everything, although he didn't encourage wasteful kicking either.

We travelled to Wales, where Harry and Welsh coach Graham Henry spent the week arguing about whether the Millennium Stadium's roof should be closed to keep out the notorious Welsh weather. Harry was for it, Henry against. The Welsh coach got his way and, although it didn't rain on match day, the field was greasy and the test really didn't live up to any great expectations. Wales had beaten the Boks for the first time a year earlier at the same venue, and we knew they would be up for it again.

We won a reasonably tight game 23-13, after Henry made the odd decision to substitute legendary flyhalf Neil Jenkins when we were only 13-10 ahead midway through the second half. His replacement, Arwel Thomas, known as a more attacking flyhalf, missed an easy penalty opportunity and then slipped a tackle, which enabled us to score the try that sealed the match.

Rudolf Straeuli came over to Cardiff to watch the test, and at the post-match function I saw him chatting to various people. I had a feeling that he would coach the Springboks. I can't explain it, but I knew he would be Harry's successor. I cornered Rudolf and told him that I thought he'd be the next Bok coach. He gave me a bemused look, which was understandable, because it was an odd thing to blurt out.

The tour marched on to England, where we lost at Twickenham against a team that Clive Woodward was moulding into future world champions. But overall the tour had been successful – we had won three out of four tests and brought through some new players, including a test debut for AJ Venter. I'd enjoyed the tour immensely, as I'd learnt many new things. I was inspired by Harry's ideas and his constant search to change the way we thought and operated, as well as the way the Springboks were perceived.

As I was still contracted to the Sharks, my future involvement with the Boks under Harry was not guaranteed. SA Rugby had been reimbursing the Sharks for my salary, which was lower than a Springbok assistant coach would normally have been paid. I was a little annoyed because I could have spent six weeks on holiday and earned the same salary, as it was the off-season for domestic teams. But it wasn't about the money – rather about recognition of my input. However, I was the one who had pushed for the post with the Boks, and the consequences were a negative I had never fully thought through. But I wouldn't have done it differently anyway.

When we got back to South Africa, Harry said he wanted me on board full time, so the negotiations with the Sharks started all over again. Oberholzer was in charge of the talks, but he wasn't impressed with me, as he'd never wanted me to leave SA Rugby to join the Sharks in the first place. Eventually the Sharks relented and I was back on the SA Rugby payroll, but this took months. In the interim, Rudolf employed Kobus van der Merwe as his assistant coach in the Super 12. I was in limbo, still being paid by Natal but sidelined by the coach in favour of someone new.

I just hung around and watched practices while the negotiations over my services continued. Rudolf had to carry on, so he had to bring in new assistant coaches. It felt weird, but that's what happened. I eventually joined up with the Boks in April 2001 after four months of squabbling. I suppose I should have felt flattered that I was in such demand, but instead it was bloody frustrating.

One day, when I was hanging around the practice field, Oregan Hoskins, who was on the Sharks board, told me that he'd voted for me to become Natal coach after Reece-Edwards was fired. Little did we both know then what the future would hold for the two of us in South African rugby!

While I was dragging my heels in Durban, Harry had started a Springbok business unit and, by the time I joined the unit, we had offices in the centre of Cape Town, not at SARFU headquarters in Newlands. If anyone strolled into the office, they would have thought it was a bank or a law firm, because the image was completely corporate. Suits and ties had replaced tracksuits; we had laptops, personal assistants and fancy offices overlooking the city. We had the latest video-editing technology and computer programs to aid us in our jobs. It was unlike any rugby set-up I'd ever seen, and I was impressed.

The programme for the upcoming season was well planned and precise. Harry called on consultants such as Les Kiss, the Waratahs' defensive coach, Frank Ponissi, the coach at Australian rugby league team Manly, and Michael Burn, a New Zealand kicking coach. They were all contacted about providing input, and they joined us at a pre-season Bok training camp in Plettenberg Bay.

It was unbelievable. The amount of knowledge these guys had to pass on was amazing. As a coach it was like being a kid in a candy shop, because sharing ideas with such forward-thinking people was incredible. But there was a downside. There was simply too much information for players to take in at such a short camp. They were bombarded with new techniques and ideas. For a bunch of players with a fairly conservative approach to the game, it was a case of information overload.

In addition, the consultants started competing with each other for player time to get their message across, and the players soon became lost in a minefield of data.

Australian Tim Lane had joined the squad as backline coach, and Markgraaff and I were also on board. With so many consultants around, coaching staff tried to show that they were adding something worthwhile, and thus became a little over-competitive. From being the official backline coach, I became just another management appointment, as there were so many of us jostling for position. After such an exciting start working with Harry, the Plettenberg Bay camp was the beginning of the end of my second stint with the Boks.

Tim had been the backline coach for the Wallabies when they won the 1999 World Cup, so for me to throw my toys out when he joined would have been silly. He had a lot of experience, and I knew I could learn from him. Harry also made it clear that he wanted – and needed – me, but I was starting to wonder how I could benefit the team in such an environment. I was confident in my knowledge and abilities, but Harry obviously wanted Tim to run the backs. So I was inadvertently pushed to the sidelines again.

Initially I spent a lot of time with the backs, with Tim observing and picking up phase calls we had run. He started adding some of the plays that the Wallabies had run, which helped me; it stimulated me. He had new ideas, as well as a clear understanding of what did and didn't work.

By the time the test season started, I was already on the fringes as backline coach. We started poorly, losing 32-23 to France at Ellis Park, before coming back with a 20-15 win in Durban to level the series. But our performance in both matches was fairly dull.

We duly thrashed Italy 60-14 in Port Elizabeth, after an unsettling week in which André Vos had been axed as captain and Bob Skinstad appointed in his place. Markgraaff and Harry had also had a huge fall-out, which led to Markies's resignation a week or so later. I'm still not entirely sure what it was all about, but I think Markgraaff felt he wasn't getting the support he needed as forwards' coach, and that Harry was undermining his decisions. Anyway, the happy, optimistic squad of seven months earlier had started to unravel.

Despite this, results in the Tri-Nations were not terrible and we produced some good moments. We lost a tight kicking contest in the Newlands rain 12-3 against the All Blacks, and beat the Wallabies at Loftus by 20-15. We then managed a 14-all draw against Australia in Perth, before losing 26-15 against New Zealand in Auckland.

In Auckland, Springbok commercial manager Butch Watson-Smith met with me. He said he and Harry felt that I didn't really have a role within the squad any more, and I agreed.

'Butch, you're right,' I responded. 'I'm not enjoying this either. I'm just touring. I'm going from place to place. I don't have any input. I don't have any say in the team. Whether the team wins or loses, I'm still part of it, but I don't contribute really.'

We both knew that I'd been marginalised, though no one was to blame. But admitting it openly was difficult. Up to that point I'd never admitted the way I felt to anyone else, so when Butch put it so bluntly, it hurt. But he was right. I felt like my world was collapsing again, and it was the second time I would be shafted from the Bok squad.

'I've been in this situation before with Nick and Solly,' I said to Butch. 'If I'm not going to add value, it's not right that I'm here.' So, after the Tri-Nations drew to a close, I officially resigned, even though Harry urged me to stay on, promising that he'd find another role for me. I declined, because I didn't want to be a passenger in the Bok set-up. I went to see Rian and said, 'Now what do I do? It's like *déjà vu.*' His response was: 'We'll organise something, Jake.'

So, after the Tri-Nations I was asked to go on the SA 'A' and SA Under-23 tour, with Allister Coetzee as coach. I realised it was the end of my second stint with the Boks. But other challenges lay ahead, and the wheels had been set in motion for me to become SA Under-21 coach.

12

The Baby Boks

I started 2002 in limbo – not unlike I'd begun the year before. Then I hadn't been sure if I'd be with the Boks or the Sharks, and had hung around for four months on the side of the training field, not knowing what to expect. In 1999, it had been the same. It was a frustratingly familiar feeling.

At the end of 2001, I had travelled as an assistant coach on an SA 'A' tour to Georgia and Spain, while at the same time the Springboks toured Italy, France, England and the USA. Ironically, the head coach of the 'A' team was Allister Coetzee, the man who would later become my assistant coach for four years with the Springboks.

It was a great tour, both for the rugby and the experience I gained. We played in exotic locations such as Tbilisi and Seville, and discovered new rugby cultures that, despite years of touring, I'd never encountered. Many of the players in the squad were from the 1999 Under-21s, which made it easy for me, as I had a good relationship with them. Part of my brief was to keep an eye on several players and report on their progress and abilities, as Harry was considering them for the Springbok squad in 2002.

The Boks, meanwhile, endured a terrible tour, of which the lowlight was a 29-9 loss to England at Twickenham. It wasn't the score as much as *how* they played. I felt quite sad, remembering how Harry had started with such enthusiasm to change how South African backline players, in particular, viewed and approached the game. But by then the pressure to win had overridden all his best intentions, and he deviated from his own blueprint.

No one knew it at the time, but Harry had probably decided to quit the Bok coaching job during the year-end tour. Or he seriously considered it. He seemed distant and disinterested, which frustrated me. I was supposed to give him feedback on our tour, but he never seemed keen to hear about it. I took it personally, but in fact it was just Harry knowing that he wasn't going to be the Bok coach much longer.

In 2002, South Africa was set to host the inaugural IRB Under-21 World Cup (it later became known as the World Championships). As hosts,

SA Rugby were adamant that we should have a team capable of putting up a good fight to win the title. After our success in 1999, Under-21 rugby had been taken more seriously, but the 2000 and 2001 teams hadn't achieved the expected results.

After I returned from the 'A' tour, Rian Oberholzer met with me and said, 'You're going to be the Under-21 coach next year. We're going to make you head coach.' It would be the first time since the mid-1990s that I'd be head coach of a team again. But he warned that coaching the Baby Boks could be a potential career-ending appointment. He explained that SA Rugby would support me with all the resources I needed, but, if I failed, he wasn't sure he could find another job for me in the organisation. His words were, 'The noose is around your neck.'

I was excited by the prospect, although it wasn't quite the glamour job of coaching a Super 12 or national team. In fact, when Harry resigned as Bok coach that January, I applied for the Springbok job, even though I was set to coach the Under-21s. But then Rudolf Straeuli was appointed as Bok coach midway through the Super 12. I had known that my chances of becoming Bok coach were slim, but I'd applied because I was confident about my ability. From the outset it was clear that I wasn't seriously in the running, although I was on the final shortlist. I didn't really think about it much and carried on with preparing for the Under-21 World Cup.

Oberholzer was true to his word and gave me everything I needed to mould an Under-21 side with the potential to win the title. I flew all over the country with Professor Derik Coetzee, a world-class sports scientist, testing prospective players and slowly building up a database of their strengths and weaknesses. Although I'd not coached junior rugby for some time, I'd watched enough schoolboy and provincial Under-21 rugby to have an idea whom I rated as players. But we left nothing to chance, and recruited the provinces to start the filtering system for us.

Derik's influence was massive, especially from a conditioning perspective. I met him in 1999, when he was with Free State, but the first time I worked with him was when he came on the SA 'A' tour to Georgia and Spain. I was impressed not only by his knowledge and professionalism, but by what a positive and influential person he was. When I was appointed as Under-21 coach, my first call was to Derik to ask him to be my fitness coach. Free State kindly released him for as long as I would need him.

Budget was approved, and Oberholzer ensured that nothing stood in the way of our pursuit of the title. Professional rugby needs leaders who understand the demands of the job, because if you cut corners, you're destined to fail. Spending millions doesn't guarantee success, of course, because other top teams spend lots of money too. But in a country like South Africa it's easy to rely on talent alone, and that's not enough. In 1999 we had prepared the Under-21s in the most professional way ever, and we won. And in 2002 we took it to another level.

I think it was the most exhaustive selection process in which I've ever been involved. We eventually narrowed it down to 60 players after about four months of searching, and set up a series of trial matches. But we also asked the four Super 12 regions (the sum total then) to enter 60 guys we hadn't chosen. For argument's sake, when I picked Clyde Rathbone and Jean de Villiers for a trial team, then their franchises had to find two guys to replace them. The Sharks therefore had to find another centre to come in for Rathbone, and the Stormers had to pick a centre replacement for De Villiers.

Candidates then played each other on the fields of Johannesburg's Rand Afrikaans University (RAU). Four games took place, one after the other. Each team played twice over a period of four days: the teams we had selected and started coaching versus the teams of the franchises. There was no excuse for players not to emerge, and I doubt any great talents slipped through the cracks. We covered all our bases in that trial process.

Some players from the franchises eventually nudged ahead of some of the guys we'd picked. Hooker Schalk Britz, a current Super 14 player, broke his ankle in the final trial. He'd been close to being my first-choice hooker. However, his misfortune paved the way for Gary Botha, who made the final squad. Prop Pat Barnard and flank Roland Bernard, both from the franchise teams, made it as well.

We whittled the squad down to the final 30 players, although the tournament stipulated a maximum of 26 places. We headed off to a camp in the Mpumalanga bushveld at Sabie River Bungalows. It was no Kamp Staaldraad, but rather a getaway designed to build team spirit through a series of fun exercises interspersed with rugby training. We moved the entire camp down there, which included all our gym equipment. It was the perfect way to prepare for the tournament.

I made only one selection that had little to do with form or trials, and that was wing Ashwin Willemse. He never trained once between January and the tournament's start in June, because of a bad pelvic injury. He never did a thing; he could barely walk. But I knew he was going to offer us value in the tournament, if I could just make sure he was fit enough to play.

I'd seen him as a junior, and I knew he was the kind of guy we needed in our team. Ashwin is a fighter with a huge heart, and if you want to win World Cups, you need players like him in the squad. Still, putting so much faith in him was a risk. But he was a Springbok Sevens player, and he'd also played for the SA Under-21s the previous year. I needed his experience.

The medical team were convinced I'd lost my mind. They kept telling me that Ashwin was going to break down – if he managed to get on the field at all. But I had an unwavering belief that he was going to repay me. Ashwin is a complex person, which stems from a very difficult childhood. He would tell me how unfair he thought rugby was, and how unfairly he was treated because he was black. He felt that white players got away with more and had an easy ride.

At the time he was contracted to Boland, one of the smaller, less wealthy provinces in the country. To attend practices he would have to catch a train to Wellington from his home on the Cape Flats, which was over an hour away. Often he'd arrive late and the coach would tell him to push off and not come back. But he saw white players who drove sponsored cars arriving late and never being chased away. That angered him. Ashwin was an angry young man. He ran with gangs and had done bad things, but deep down he had a sense of righteousness and courage I'd never seen before. In me he found someone he could speak to openly about the unfairness in rugby.

Ashwin was on a Boland contract, which was small. He'd also worked out that, in many cases, contracts for black players were worth much less than those for white players with less ability. He knew it and I knew it, and he couldn't understand why. To him this was unfair, and of course it was.

I kept my faith in him. While he was recuperating, he walked along the side of the field and listened to the calls and watched the plays so that he understood them, even though he couldn't take part. At Sabie I announced the final squad, which included Ashwin. The medical staff rolled their eyes at me, but I was going with my gut.

The day after the team was named, I received a call from team physio Clint Readhead. He told me there was a problem and that Ashwin was going home. I told Clint to keep him there, and I raced downstairs to take Ashwin aside.

'Come and tell me what's going on,' I said. He replied that he didn't feel 100 per cent ready, and he was afraid that he would let the team down. He was also embarrassed because he hadn't contributed much in the build-up, due to his injury. This was all partly true, but he'd had plenty of time with the squad, so I sensed something else was at play. None of the players viewed him as a passenger, as he was a hell of a good squad member, so something else was on his mind. I said, 'You're lying to me. There's another problem here. Tell me what it is.'

He admitted that, because of doubts over his fitness, he was worried he'd break down in the tournament. If that happened, he'd be in big financial trouble. His contract at Boland, although quite small, was up for renewal in October. If he sustained another bad injury, they would cut him loose. He was the sole breadwinner in his family – and I mean his extended family – so the risk of losing his only source of income was a very serious matter.

I understood his problem. 'I will guarantee you a contract for next year, somewhere,' I said to Ashwin. 'And I'm so sure about that, I'll give you the R60 000 your annual contract is worth from my own bank account. I'll write you a cheque. I know that you won't have to cash it, because you'll have a contract. As it stands now, you have a renewal of your R60 000 contract at Boland.' And I wrote out a cheque.

I contacted the Bulls. They were interested, but wanted to contract him on a loan basis to try him out. I told them I couldn't do that, and that I needed some form of commitment. So I called Golden Lions coach Frans Ludeke and asked him if he would consider contracting Ashwin. We arranged a meeting, and within minutes Frans went upstairs to see Lions chief executive Johan Prinsloo. The two of them came down a few minutes later, and Prinsloo said that they would contract Ashwin, but only if they could employ his services for three years. It was even better than we'd hoped for. Ashwin couldn't sign then and there, because he was still under contract to Boland. But he signed a letter of intent to join the Lions once his contract at Boland expired, which was above board and legally binding. In addition, the Lions offered him nearly 10 times his earnings at Boland.

During the brief negotiations, Ashwin asked them what would happen if he broke down in the Under-21 tournament. Would they still honour the contract? Ludeke replied: 'That's why we want to sign you for three years. Our job is to make sure we look after you so that we've got you long term.'

It was an incentive contract that would pay him more money if he played Super 12, and more still if he became a Bok. He did both the following year. In 2003 he was SA Rugby Player of the Year, and he also went to the senior World Cup with the Boks. More immediately, he emerged as one of the best players at the Under-21 World Cup, which started five days after he'd agreed to join the Lions.

At the end of the tournament, Ashwin went straight to Dr Mark Ferguson for an operation. He was out of the game for three months. When he came back the next year, he played in the Super 12 and at the World Cup, as he had had three months to sort himself out. Prinsloo and Ludeke deserve a lot of credit for putting faith in Ashwin and giving him peace of mind. It played to my benefit as well.

Years later, Ashwin told me that after every game at the tournament he could not walk for about an hour. He iced his pelvis without anyone knowing, because he was determined to see the tournament through to the end. That's why I put so much faith in him, and why I always backed him later in his career.

The draw for the tournament was tough, as it was based on the previous year's performance at the SANZAR/UAR tournament. We were seeded seventh, which meant pool games against France and Ireland, and a potential semi-final against either New Zealand or Australia.

We'd obviously prepared well, but we didn't have a great deal of pre-tournament video footage of our opponents, save some snippets of players involved in Super 12 matches. Our secret was to try to get our hands on video footage after each game. I had an advantage through my relationship with SuperSport, fostered when I had given occasional match analyses on the programme *Head to Head*. Gert Roets, the head of SuperSport, and Tex Texeira, a renowned producer, were a great help, as they delivered as much footage as they could of the opposition. They even gave me videos of games that hadn't been televised. Along with technical analyst Timmy Goodwin and assistant coach John Williams, I worked long hours, cutting the footage into neat bundles of information for the players.

And our efforts paid off. We thrashed Romania 135-0 in our opening match, overcame France 28-9 in a niggly game, and beat Ireland 42-22 in a slightly lacklustre performance, to make the semi-finals against old enemies New Zealand. The fact that we had failed to score four-try bonus points against France and Ireland meant that Australia topped our pool (there were cross-section games, which is why we didn't meet). The French game, similar to the one in 1999, was aggressive and included a couple of yellow cards. It included one for hooker Gary Botha. My team manager was Naas Botha, the legendary Bok flyhalf and, at the time, the leading Springbok points-scorer. (Percy Montgomery would later surpass his record.)

Naas, Gary and prop Pat Barnard attended a hearing after the game, as both players had been cited for foul play. We were worried that they could be handed a lengthy ban, but Naas showed his value as an esteemed former international, exercising his managerial role by smoothly handling the hearing.

I had asked to have Naas as a manager for a number of reasons. He is a South African rugby icon. He was respected overseas, which added to the aura of our team, and he was a good disciplinarian. He had a presence, whether it was in conversation with referees before a game, on the side of the field, or even in disciplinary hearings.

Naas addressed the committee, speaking coolly and unemotionally about the importance of the tournament to young players and their careers. He pleaded – without sounding as if he was – that they be given a warning and be allowed to continue. The players were exonerated. I doubt any other manager would have managed to get them off with merely a warning. I can't even remember the details of the alleged crimes, but I'm sure that in most cases they would have received a short suspension.

Although we ended with a comfortable victory over Ireland at Ellis Park to confirm our place in the last four, our performance was poor. With the Baby Blacks looming, the team needed a kick in the pants. And Naas delivered it. The players were extremely happy with themselves for making the last four, and were carrying on as if they'd already won the final. Naas called a meeting at the team hotel and tore strips off them. He didn't scream or shout, but coldly told them that they were nowhere near as good as they thought they were. He informed them that New Zealand would chew them up and spit them out if they delivered a similar performance to the one against Ireland. At one point he even told them they were a disgrace to the jersey. That was a little harsh, but it got their attention. Naas added huge value to the campaign.

Playing New Zealand in the semi was a huge occasion. The legendary Sean Fitzpatrick was the Colts' team manager. Probably the greatest hooker that ever played the game, he was the man that had led the All Blacks to a historic series victory over the Boks in 1996. If Naas was iconic to our boys, Fitzy had the same impact on his team. He hated losing, especially to South Africa, and I knew that New Zealand would be as fired up as ever for the game.

The match was played on a bitterly cold Tuesday evening at RAU. It followed the first semi-final, in which Australia thumped Wales 43-7. That was predictable, but our game against New Zealand was a titanic struggle. When I think back now and compare it with coaching the senior Boks against the senior All Blacks a few years later, that Under-21 semi was as tough and intense as any Bok test. The boys just ripped into one another for 80 minutes – it was a wonderful effort after the performance against Ireland. We won 19-18 with a penalty well into injury time, by the late François 'Swys' Swart.

It was a dramatic finish to the match, which should never have been that close. We were in control for 60 per cent of the game, and at one stage had led 16-6. Victory came down to a last-gasp tackle by Barnard. He snagged one of the Baby Blacks by a fingertip in the last move of the game. Had he missed that tackle, they would have scored and we would have been out. That illustrates how close the match was – it came down to the fingertips.

I later heard from my agent Craig Livingstone, who played golf with Fitzpatrick after the final, that the great All Black had been unsettled by our team's presence before the game. The story goes that Fitzy had happened to be standing in the wrong place when the anthems were sung. He found himself facing the South African team, and saw how ferociously our boys sang and how fired up they were. He turned to his team coach Bryce Woodward and said that he believed they were 'in *kak*'. I suspect he might have used a more forceful, non-Afrikaans word.

Make no mistake – it was a very good New Zealand team. Names such as Dan Carter, Corey Flynn, Jimmy Cowan, Sione Lauaki, Luke McAlister, Joe Rokocoko (he was injured before our game), Sam Tuitupou, Tony Woodcock and Daniel Braid might sound familiar. These were only some of the future stars of New Zealand rugby. The game had been our *real* final.

Australia cruised into the final. I wasn't surprised when, four days later, we struggled in the last 20 minutes of our clash at Ellis Park. We were physically battered after the semi, and luckily made a great start in the final, running into a 24-9 lead early in the second half. Australia came back at us with two tries as the boys wilted in the final quarter, but we hung on to win 24-21. Skipper Clyde Rathbone, who immigrated to Australia a year later, followed John Smit as an Under-21 winning captain.

It was a great effort by the team, as well as certain individuals. Flyhalf Swys Swart, who would tragically die in a car accident a few years later, was the tournament's leading points-scorer, with 107. We didn't finish as top scorers, but we'd only conceded five tries in five matches, and when we had a penalty, Swys usually slotted it. Defence wins World Cups, and we had managed to shut out most teams.

Rathbone played centre. Along with Jean de Villiers, Ashwin Willemse, JP Nel, Fourie du Preez and Ricky Januarie, we had a formidable set of backs. Schalk Burger came into the team as a replacement for lock Gordon Gilfillan, who was concussed in the match against France. I brought in Schalk because Juan Smith, at that stage in his career, was able to play lock, which was where he'd played in the semi against New Zealand. He was outstanding in the second row. Juan was behind Pedrie Wannenburg, Jacques Cronjé and Roland Bernard in the back-row pecking order, so had there been no injury, he wouldn't have started at lock in the semi or the final. He might not even have been on the bench. Competition for places in that team was intense.

Schalk already had all the ingredients that would make him the player he is today, but he was very raw in 2002. He was close to being selected for the original squad, but he lost out because I knew he'd be around in 2003. Also, he'd failed to make the SA Under-19 side in 2002 because of an injury, which he carried into our trials. He didn't play exceptionally well in the trials, which was part of the reason he wasn't picked. But his omission bugged me, because I saw the fury and rage that he brought to the game – aspects that I couldn't coach. So when I needed a replacement for an injury, I called him in, more on a hunch than because of what I'd seen. He delivered two great performances from the bench, and did enough to prove to me that he was the right man to captain the team the following year.

Rian Oberholzer was ecstatic with our victory, especially as he'd warned me that winning the tournament was vital to SA Rugby – as it was to my future prospects as a coach. And the victory put to rest some doubts that may have existed about my credentials. I'd never doubted myself, but a World Cup win, at any age group, was an important addition to my CV. Afterwards, the players drifted off to their various provinces, and I went back to SA Rugby to begin preparing for the defence of our title in Oxfordshire in 2003.

Obviously the players who were eligible that year were all involved in national rugby competitions with their unions, and I could only get them together a few months before the beginning of the tournament. We refined the selection process, re-tested all the players who were still available for 2003, and searched for new players.

The search for talent was as thorough as the previous year, if not more so. But, as is the nature of age-group rugby, we lacked the many high-quality players we'd had in 2002. Still, I was confident, as I'd always maintained that South Africa could produce strong age-group teams because of our natural conveyor belt of talent. We had a few survivors from 2002, such as Jacques Cronjé, Swys Swart, Fourie du Preez, Ricky Januarie and, of course, Schalk Burger. But we were a little thin in some areas.

Schalk was named captain for the tournament in Oxford. We won a tight opening game against Ireland 36-27 at Iffley Road, the venue where Roger Bannister became the first man to break the four-minute mile in 1954. It wasn't a great start, but Ireland was a solid team, and they had beaten South Africa as Under-19s, so it was a decent beginning to the defence of our title.

I started with Swart at flyhalf, as he was the man who had done so well for me the year before. But Derick Hougaard was also in the squad, and at the end of 2002 he'd basically won the Currie Cup final for the Blue Bulls by himself, scoring 26 points against the Lions, and was considered one of the best young talents in the game. Swart hadn't made it at senior provincial level by that stage, despite his heroics for the SA Under-21s the year before. It was difficult to ignore Derick's claim for a place in the team.

In our next match, against Canada, Derick started and scored 26 points as we ran out 102-10 winners. The Canucks were weak, but Derick did enough to usurp Swys as starting flyhalf. In our final pool match against Wales, the Six Nations champions, we produced our best rugby of the tournament, winning 50-21. That left us with a semi-final against New Zealand yet again.

The Kassam Stadium in Oxford is a narrow football pitch, and I believed it would suit us against the Baby Blacks, as it would limit their pace out wide. The day of the semi-final there was a strong wind blowing the length of the field, and my rule of thumb is to always play against the wind in the first half if we win the toss. Before the game I turned to Naas and said, 'What do you think about the wind?' He replied: 'Let's take the wind in the beginning, because you don't know if it's going to stop.'

I listened to him. It was totally contrary to what I believed, which was that if the wind stops, bad luck. Besides, the first 20 minutes of any game are usually even, as the players unleash so much nervous tension and energy it nullifies the wind advantage. But I went against my instinct that day, and I take full responsibility for what turned out to be a bad tactical decision.

We controlled the game with the wind. Derick used his big boot to pin New Zealand back, and we scored a try through flank Bennie Adams, to lead 16-9 at halftime. But, in the second half, Derick couldn't get us into good positions with his boot. And his kicking played into the hands of the Baby Blacks – literally. They ran everything back at us, and we were forced onto the back foot. They ran in four unanswered tries and scored 29 unanswered points to win 38-16. I reckon that it was the worst 40 minutes any team has played under my coaching.

I later found out that former All Black coach Wayne Smith, who had been coach at Northampton, had told the New Zealand management that playing against the wind at Kassam in the first half was the only way to manage those conditions. I don't know whether we would have won had we done it the other way round, but I do know we'd made it tough on ourselves. Some critics said Derick had kicked too much in the game, but I think he just hadn't kicked well. It was disappointing, but you have to move on, and we had a third-place play-off against Argentina to come.

The tournament ended on a low note, as we lost that game too. We should never have lost it, though. Schalk was red-carded early in the second half, after being shown a second yellow. It was a harsh call, because he should never have been yellow-carded in the first half anyway. He was cleared at a hearing after the match, but by then it was too late for us.

Losing that game was even more disappointing than losing the semi-final. I had a great relationship with Argentina, and early in the tournament I had actually helped them at some of their coaching sessions. I was therefore not upset that we lost to them, but because it happened on the wrong end of a bad refereeing decision. We led 13-0 at halftime, but after losing Schalk the wheels came off, and we lost 34-30.

The Under-21 World Cup is one of the hardest tournaments to win. You have five tough games in 16 days. It's brutal on the bodies of the players, and the competition is intense. For me, those two years were important in many ways. The bulk of the players in my Springbok teams came out of the 1999, 2002 and 2003 Under-21 teams that I had helped coach. The quality of the medical staff at those tournaments was vital, which is why Clint Readhead (physio) and Derik Coetzee became part of my management team at Springbok level. I saw the hard work they did to get players on the field during the Under-21 tournaments. I can't praise them enough. Bumps and bruises can be managed for the first and second games, but by the third match you start realising how important medical assessments and medical experts are to a team's success. The way in which medical staff handled players' recuperation was vital to the team's perform-ance in the next match. We won in 1999 and 2002 because we hardly lost players to injury.

I guess it wasn't a bad return for two years in charge of the Under-21s. We'd been world champions, and lost only two out of 10 competitive matches. In all, we probably won 14 out of 16 games, which included our warm-up contests. It laid the platform for my next step – the biggest challenge of my life, and the greatest pleasure. I didn't know it in June 2003 in Oxford, but 12 months later I would be coaching the Boks.

PART IV

RESTORING BOK PRIDE
2004–2005

13

The dream job

Massive life-changing decisions and actions usually follow some sort of message. In early 2004, I was in Canberra with the Brumbies, en route to a conference in Auckland where I was presenting at a seminar on the intricacies of modern defensive patterns and decoy running. While I was there, I received a phone call from SA Rugby board member Arthob Petersen. The message was: 'We want you to apply for the Springbok coaching job.' It was a simple message, but it changed my life forever.

After the 2003 Under-21 World Cup, I hadn't been sure of my future plans. I wasn't that keen on coaching the Under-21s for a further year, but my prospects in South Africa appeared limited. Of course I had ambitions at a higher level, but I'd started to think that coaching overseas might be my only option to further my career. Irish provincial side Munster and English club Sale Sharks had both offered me jobs, but they weren't my preferred choice.

I'd also wanted to show some loyalty to SA Rugby, especially to Rian Oberholzer, as he'd backed me many times. I couldn't face telling him I was leaving again. So I kept my head down and worked at the offices for a few months, deciding where to aim next.

At the end of 2003, the senior Boks endured a torrid World Cup on the back of a race row and the now infamous Kamp Staaldraad. SA Rugby was in turmoil in the fallout of the worst period in Bok history. Rian had to fall on his sword in the aftermath, as he'd backed coach Rudolf Straeuli all the way. When Straeuli's position became untenable, so did Rian's. Oberholzer resigned, and the mood at SA Rugby headquarters was like a funeral parlour. Everyone felt vulnerable. It was a terrible time. But work had to continue, and I was asked to go to Auckland to do the presentation on defensive systems.

SA Rugby, under the new presidency of Brian van Rooyen (there had been a complete clearout after 2003), had started the process of replacing Straeuli. They'd come up with a shortlist of four names for the Bok job. I wasn't on it. The candidates were Heyneke Meyer, André Markgraaff, Chester Williams and the little-known Dumisani Mhani. It was an odd list. Heyneke and André both pulled out for various reasons, which left the potential Bok coaching post to two men with hardly any experience between them. That's when Petersen called me.

I was staying at the home of Clyde Rathbone when the call came through. Clyde, who had been my captain when South Africa won the 2002 Under-21 World Cup, had moved to Brisbane to further his career with the Brumbies and Australia. We remained close after he immigrated.

'I've been asked to ascertain whether you would consider yourself for the job,' Petersen said over the phone. I was considering my future anyway, and the visit to the Brumbies was definitely a way of sizing up coaching options. The visit had been organised by Eddie Jones, then Wallaby coach and a friend. So Petersen's call threw me off balance.

'I'll apply,' I told Petersen. 'But this is the third time I'll be applying for the post. Be straight with me. I don't want to apply if you're leading me up the garden path.' He assured me that all the candidates were starting from the same base, and that we would be required to do a presentation as part of the selection process.

Apparently Morné du Plessis, a legendary Bok and respected rugby man, had asked Van Rooyen why the current Under-21 coach hadn't automatically been added to a shortlist for the job of Bok coach. Van Rooyen didn't have an answer and, when he thought about it, reasoned that it was a logical step up. After the call I went to Auckland, where I presented a case for decoy running, while Clive Woodward, fresh off his success of guiding England to the World Cup, opposed my theories. It was a well-contested debate. The fact that I was respected enough to oppose Woodward at an international conference said something about my status in the rugby community. At home, though, I was an afterthought. Still, I decided to apply on the basis that I would be given a fair shot at making a case for the job.

Petersen was head of the technical committee tasked with appointing the next Bok coach. His assurance that the job was still up for grabs and that I wasn't making up numbers was enough to make me apply. I realised, though, that I needed to make a strong case. My presentation had to be world class. Being at the conference actually helped, because I was able to access a lot of information for my final presentation to the SA Rugby technical committee. I dug out stats that emphasised how the game had changed and where it was going. The International Rugby Board's

Corris Thomas was extremely helpful in finding these stats for me, as well as related video footage.

The theme of my presentation was 'The problems of tomorrow won't be solved by the solutions of today'. I knew I only had one chance to make an impression. I called on my friend Craig Lardner, who had experience in the corporate world. He suggested Rob Nichol, a specialist in presentations for big financial institutions, as the 'guru' for putting together the right information. I looked him up.

Rob and I spent hours and hours putting the presentation together. We changed and tweaked, and Rob also coached me on how to answer questions, the correct body language and the power of using positive phrases when speaking. He anticipated questions they might ask and peppered me with them. My answers were analysed and refined. Even my position in the room and my body language were planned to the tiniest detail. It was like preparing for a big rugby match. The day before my presentation to the technical committee, I did a full presentation to Rob and Craig in the back room of a restaurant – a dry run if you like – and nailed it. That gave me huge confidence.

The presentation was tough. I spoke for about 45 minutes, and then had 90 minutes of answering questions. Because I was so well prepared, I tended to get ahead of myself and started asking the panel questions. Eventually Petersen asked me, 'Who is asking the questions here, you or us?' I was so enthusiastic that I'd use phrases like 'Let me ask you this, gentlemen ...', and while they were amused and perhaps even impressed, they wanted to control the meeting.

I was questioned on the five key areas of the job: transformation, media, selection, tactics and my role as coach. I was on top of every question fired at me, and my answers generally went beyond what their questions required. Makhaya Jack, the man tasked with transformation, actually had no questions for me. When Petersen asked him if he wanted to quiz me, he declined, saying I'd answered all his questions. That told me that I'd nailed the presentation.

During the presentation, they asked me to identify my potential management team and coaching staff. I nominated Gert Smal and Allister Coetzee as my two assistants, although I hadn't approached them yet. In fact, I'd never even met Gert. They were both former Springboks, and Gert had been successful with Western Province, while Allister had impressed me when we worked together with the SA 'A' team. Allister was also a selector at the time, which was a slight complication. Even though I was still at interview stage, they asked if I would consider Chester Williams as my backline coach, rather than Allister. I hadn't even considered Chester, and told them Allister was my preferred choice.

Chester was on the SA Rugby payroll as Cats coach in the Super 12, and they were keen to include him in some way if he wasn't going to get the top job. But I had my doubts about his coaching credentials at the time, and wanted Allister. All this was hypothetical, of course, as I'd not been offered the job.

Markgraaff, who was a member of the committee, called me into an office following my presentation. He asked if I would have a problem with Arthob Petersen as team manager if I got the job as Bok coach. I said no. I was so desperate for the job, I would have agreed to anyone as team manager! I had nothing against Arthob. He'd done the job before when Nick was coach, and I had a reasonable relationship with him. He was also very articulate, which was good for media relations and other official duties.

In the following days, they went through the candidates. They included Rudy Joubert, Chester and Peter de Villiers, among others. Naturally the media got wind of the process and spoke to their contacts. It must have emerged that I was a favourite for the job. Chester was quoted in the newspapers as saying he wouldn't be available as assistant coach if I got the job. I found that presumptuous, as I'd never asked him to be part of my management team.

About a week later, Mr P, as Arthob was known, told me that the technical committee had recommended me for the job of Bok coach. But there was a snag. The President's Council had to sign off on the committee's decision, although it was only a formality. Mr P spoke to me on Wednesday 11 February; the President's Council was only set to meet on Friday 13 February. Mr P asked me to keep their decision to myself, because if there was a hiccup, it would look bad if I'd been going around saying I had the job. It was the longest 48 hours of my life.

SA Rugby had planned a press conference at Santé Winelands Hotel and Wellness Centre that Friday. Mr P said that I should drive out to the hotel, which is about 45 minutes from Cape Town, and wait in one of the chalets they'd booked. Once the council had ratified the decision, I'd receive a call and attend a press conference, which was scheduled for noon at Santé. I just sat there, wringing my hands, pacing the room and waiting for that phone call. It was a strange feeling, because I was about to enjoy a great moment in my life and I was unable to share it with anyone.

As with all meetings, the council meeting was delayed, and 12 noon passed with no phone call. Naturally I started wondering if the council had had a change of heart. But 45 minutes later the phone rang, and I was told to come to the main hotel for my first press conference as Bok coach.

I walked in, and there were dozens of media people and cameras to greet me. I felt like actors must feel when they walk into a hoard of paparazzi. Brian van Rooyen was there, and we held a joint presser. Although I'd done these before, it was the largest gathering of media I'd ever encountered. It was crazy.

There was a dinner at the hotel with the entire council that night. But I wanted to share the moment with my family, so I raced back to Cape Town to see them for an hour or so. My boys were running in an athletics meet that day, so I went to the school and joined Debbie and some friends on the side of the field. Debbie was selling hamburgers behind one of the stands as the boys ran.

Debbie has always been the rock of the family. She's been a rugby widow, but she's done so uncomplainingly and given me total backing. She obviously knew what was happening that day and was excited, nervous and also a little disappointed that she couldn't be there when it was made official. She has been the most supportive person in the world, and has never minded being in the background while I made my career. It was a nice moment, to be there with the people most important to me. I had a few beers at the school clubhouse before heading back to Santé.

A couple of days earlier, when Mr P told me that I had been made coach, I sat down with my family and explained to them that it was going to be a difficult time. I explained to the boys that I'd be away from home for months at a time. I also told them to understand that coaches – especially coaches in South Africa – were often fired. I said I would do the job properly, so if I was fired I could never be accused of not having done my work to the best of my ability. I explained that to the boys especially. I asked my wife and sons whether they wanted me to take the job. Wesley and Clinton were quite young. All three of them agreed.

I had to do the job; it was the chance of a lifetime.

14

A new beginning

Being appointed as Springbok coach was the easy part. Rebuilding the team and its image was going to be a massive challenge. After 2003, the Boks were at their lowest ebb. Players were disillusioned and out of love with the concept of playing for their country. The disastrous World Cup campaign, which had followed a race row and Kamp Staaldraad (where the players were demeaned by being thrown naked into a pit, in the name of World Cup preparation), was going to be difficult to overcome.

Soon after I was appointed, I was invited to the Caltex Masters golf tournament in Singapore. Debbie and I went over for a few days, and I was shocked by what I heard while I was there. I was paired in the pro-am with Sean Fitzpatrick, former All Blacks coach John Hart and former Wimbledon finalist Kevin Curren. There were also a host of other sports stars from various codes. As guests, we visited a variety of sports clubs around Singapore to give talks. Wherever we went, people associated the sports stars with their achievements or the teams for which they played. But when I was introduced, the first comment I heard was more often than not, 'Oh, Kamp Staaldraad.' That concerned me, because if a non-rugby-playing nation's perception of South African rugby was a military boot camp, we had a lot of work to do.

My first business as Bok coach was to visit all the Super 12 regions and speak to both coaches and players about what I wanted from potential Springbok players. Part of my presentation to the players was to show them the type of rugby players – and therefore the type of team – I wanted, and what game plan I believed was best suited to us.

I already had certain players in mind – I was clear in my thinking – which is why 16 players I coached during my first Bok year in 2004 later went to the World Cup in 2007. But in 2004 I wasn't thinking about World Cups and 2007. I was thinking about creating a winning team, and picking the right players to achieve that objective.

Having worked with various Under-21 teams, I already knew what type of players I wanted for certain roles. But I also wanted to recall a few who were based overseas, and to see whether I could lure Os du Randt out of retirement. I wanted Percy Montgomery back from Wales, and to see if Jaco van der Westhuyzen would return to local playing fields. He was playing brilliant rugby for Leicester in England at the time. But Os was particularly important to me, because school rules over the previous decade had de-powered the scrum, placing less emphasis on powerful props. A campaigner like Os was from the old school, and still one of the strongest men in the game. I wanted to reintroduce old-fashioned prop play. Another man I seriously considered was Marius Hurter, who had been around since the mid-1990s. He hadn't come through school in the years when the scrum was a secondary consideration.

My ideas and vision were clear. My first, possibly most important decision (as far as I was concerned) was to name my captain. I had no doubt in my mind that John Smit was the man for the job, and I met with him during the Super 12 campaign. He'd led the Boks in the World Cup against Georgia, had been an SA Under-19 and Under-21 skipper, and had captained the Sharks. He was the logical choice for the job. But, more important than his obvious leadership credentials – I held him in high regard as a person. I still do.

Under Rudolf and Harry, the captaincy had been open to debate. Joost van der Westhuizen, André Vos, Bob Skinstad and Corné Krige had all jostled for the job, which in my opinion was unsettling for the team. I felt that wouldn't work for me. And, while I needed leaders, I wanted one captain. John was the man I chose. When we met and I told him I wanted to make him Springbok captain, I explained that he was an extension of me on the field. But he was also a man I could confide in, and he could question me – but not in front of the team.

He was flattered and definitely keen on the challenge, and his first words in response were simply: 'As long as you believe that I'm the right guy for the job and that I'm good enough to make the team as a player, then I would be honoured.' He had many more questions and practically interviewed me as well. It was exactly the attitude I wanted.

At the end of the meeting I said that as far as I was concerned he had the job, but I had to go back to the board to rubber-stamp my decision. The board unanimously backed John as skipper. I publicly announced that he'd captain the Springboks before the Super 12 had even come to an end, because I wanted to remove all the media speculation about the position before it became front-page news. It also sent a clear message to all the players: John was the captain. There was no more debate, and they would have to get on with it.

My first Springbok squad gathered in Bloemfontein before the Super 12 semi-finals. The city was specifically chosen because our first test of the year, against Ireland, was going to be played at Vodacom Park. Another reason we trained in Bloem was that Derik Coetzee, whom I'd appointed as fitness trainer, was a professor at Free State University. He was able to call on honours students to help test the fitness of players, which cut our costs, and also supplied us with great medical and scientific brains.

The rest of the management squad were the men I'd wanted. Clint Readhead was physio, Gert Smal and Allister Coetzee were my assistant coaches (although Gert only joined after guiding the Stormers to the Super 12 semis), and Mark Steele became my conditioning coach. I employed former South African 1500-metre champion Henning Gericke as my mental and speed coach, and Dr Yusuf Hassan came on board as the team doctor. The management team hardly changed in the four years to the World Cup.

The Stormers were the only South African team to make the semis that year. There were about seven Stormers players in my squad, so it left a hole in the group when we first gathered. But it gave me an extra week to work with most of the squad. The Stormers had only just made the play-offs, while the other teams had endured average to bad campaigns, which high-lighted the problems in South African rugby. It was unacceptable that we could only produce one semi-finalist, with the Bulls and Sharks finishing in mid-table, and the Cats propping up the table with one win.

The bad results – not necessarily only in 2004, but also in previous years – and a culture of losing at Springbok level had had a negative psychological impact on the players. I couldn't do much about Super 12 results, but it was in my power to turn Springbok players' perceptions around, and to try to give them the tools to beat teams from New Zealand and Australia.

I only picked 22 players for my first squad, which was almost unheard of. In retrospect, it was probably too few. André Markgraaff, who was a selector at the time, had suggested the number. He thought a smaller squad would be better. It was strange, coming from a man who'd always picked big squads as a coach. But at least all the players involved knew they would be in the first test against Ireland. Unless they were injured, of course.

In our first 10 days in camp, we lost several players to injury. Ashwin Willemse hurt his knee against the central unions in a warm-up game; De Wet Barry stood on Hanyani Shimange's foot and broke a bone; prop Faan Rautenbach had to go for knee surgery; and Juan Smith pulled a hamstring. It was a difficult time, but at that stage it held no fear for me. I kept saying, 'Fine, we'll bring someone else in.'

I remember lying on my bed and saying to myself, 'I need to be positive; I must remain positive.' And every time I spoke to the players, I would tell them the injuries made no difference. We were still a good side, and were good enough to win every game. I kept reinforcing that mantra, as much to myself as to the players. And despite the injury disruptions, preparations went well.

Early on, I employed a company specialising in team-building techniques to come to the camp for a few days. A woman named Elna van Niekerk facilitated the courses. She was excellent, and her input in those early days played a big role in the team moving forward mentally, after the problems of 2003. One of her exercises was to encourage the players to express their feelings, using colour association. For example, red represented anger, and when she pulled out a red card, the players had to say something about rugby that angered them. They were free to express unhappy feelings about contracts, administration, coaching, selection ... anything. Different colours meant different things. She was trying to draw some emotion out of the players after years of them having to suppress their feelings.

Elna drew up a list of those issues most often raised by the players. From that she was able to find some underlying causes of unhappiness in the squad, and once we had those out in the open, we could address them. Most of their unhappiness, anger, disillusionment and insecurity stemmed from previous associations with the Boks. There were a few laughs and some poignant moments during these sessions. During one meeting, Elna said that purple represented 'the moment'. Players had to say the first thing that came to mind. Faan Rautenbach expressed his bitterness at the hypocrisy he'd experienced with the Bok team in the past.

'Every year we say the right things, like we're not going to fight them [opponents]; we're not going to bicker in the passages; we're going to be supportive and be one team. But the reality is, as soon as the pressure's on, then it is each man for himself. And the true colours of every guy come out. We do this stuff with every coach, and it sounds great, but basically it's a waste of time.' Then he immediately tried to apologise, because he realised he'd verbalised feelings that he'd bottled up for some time. But that's exactly what Elna wanted, and she was quick to reassure him. By telling him that he was entitled, and correct, to speak his mind, she eased the pressure on the rest of the group.

John Smit's answer to the same colour prompt was, 'Excitement, a new coach, new team, new year and a new beginning after the World Cup.' Bakkies Botha was next, and in colourful adjectives in Afrikaans, he spoke from his heart: '*Fokkit tannie, ek kan nie fokken glo dat ...*' Everyone started laughing, and they nervously looked at Elna to assess her reaction to all the cursing. But Elna encouraged him to carry on and get it off his chest. So Bakkies continued. '*Fok ... ek kan nie glo hoe dit nou is nie, dis so fokken positief. En ek kan nie fokken glo ons was so kak gewees nie,*' he said. For the first time, in his own unique way, he was able to express his positive feelings about how the team was emerging from the hole in which they'd been trapped. It was a breakthrough for us all.

Elna then turned to Os du Randt, and asked him to share his feelings. The room fell silent, because Os had only just rejoined the squad after a four-year absence from the Bok team, and most of the players didn't know him. They knew him by reputation as a World Cup winner, but not personally. The room was dead silent as the big man started to speak. Then he stopped as his voice cracked. Elna told him not to worry, but to take a sip of water and compose himself. He was in tears. All the young-sters were wide-eyed, amazed that this great icon of the South African game, representing all the masculinity of Springbok rugby, could be so emotional.

When he eventually found his voice, he said, in Afrikaans: 'I'm sorry ma'am. I just want to say, not only am I happy to be here as a player, because I can play rugby again. But I want to tell this group of players that I'll do anything to stay here.' That was a watershed moment.

Over the previous few years, some players had become jaded about being Springboks. Yet one of the greatest South African players of all time – somebody who'd won a World Cup and achieved almost everything in the game – said he'd do anything to stay there. The importance of being a Bok became apparent to those players. Os's career had nearly ended because of a knee injury. He'd missed four years, and yet he was prepared to give anything to make the most of his second chance. After that I felt a different mood in the camp. The negativity was gone.

I had wanted to change things when I took over, but I can't take credit for the way in which we changed. I think the players had wanted change. And, after 2003, it was a logical time to move forward. We couldn't continue the way we had been, and all the senior players realised that. The new players felt the positive energy, and that set us up for the year.

I'm a traditionalist and I had some ideas I wanted to try out, for example to get the players to understand the history and importance of being a Bok. I spoke to our sponsors and to kit suppliers Canterbury, and asked for a return to a more traditional Springbok jersey – in bottle green, with a gold collar. The skin-tight jersey from the previous World Cup had served its purpose – I wanted to go back in some ways and look to the future in other areas.

Ireland arrived for two tests, and we were as prepared as we could be for our first challenge as a new Bok team. Former flank André Venter presented the players with their jerseys on the eve of the test in Bloemfontein. He was the perfect choice, actually. As a player, André had represented all the traditional values of the Bok jersey, but he'd also been a thoroughly modern player in terms of his athleticism and professionalism.

I was strangely calm on the eve of my first test as coach. The management went out for a sushi dinner, which I guess was slightly unusual for Springboks. After all, most people think we only eat red meat and starch. When I returned to the hotel, I saw Brent Russell and his girlfriend walking towards his room. He saw me out of the corner of his eye and walked faster down the corridor to get away from me. When I got to my door, he was a few metres ahead, and I said: 'Brent, how's it going?' He mumbled a reply, and then started explaining that his girlfriend was only visiting, that she wasn't going to spend the night in our hotel. I stopped him mid-sentence and said: 'It doesn't make a difference where she's staying, my friend. You're a professional rugby player, and you have enough responsibility to know that tomorrow you've got to perform. Don't chase your girlfriend away; make sure she's fine and that she's looked after.' I could see that he was amazed at my attitude, because previously he might have had to make her wait in the lobby until I was out of the corridor.

Alone in my room, I prepared my first pre-test speech for the following day. I thought I'd talk about how it felt to be afraid, and about fear in general. I had a feeling that, despite our preparation, the players feared they might let each other down. So I wrote notes to each player, which

I handed to the guys during the team warm-up at the walk-through in the morning. The note told the individual player what I thought, what I expected of him, what his role was and what I wanted him to do for the team.

My speech was inspired by something I had read in Rod McQueen's book. It was about a young soldier during World War I. He was 18, a machine-gunner on the Western Front, and under instruction to guard his post no matter what happened. He was ordered not to leave his position, even if it meant certain death. What I was trying to impress on the team was that the French soldier had gone through real fear. However, as rugby players, they needn't be scared. The test match was important, but it wasn't about life and death. I told them to play and have no fear. I assured them that I had faith in their ability, and that I would protect them from the media and any negativity that might come their way. All I wanted was for them to play without fear. And they did.

Of course it wasn't a perfect performance, but we did some very good things against one of the best teams in Europe at the time. Ireland had won the Triple Crown during the Six Nations that year, and came to South Africa fully expecting to beat us in at least one of the two tests. We had a total of about 175 caps in our team, while they had triple that, if not more. The media had been writing us off, predicting the Irish would enjoy their first victory in South Africa. But we won 31-17, scoring four tries in the process. However, Gaffie du Toit missed four kicks at goal, which in a tighter game could have cost us victory. I was relieved when Percy Montgomery joined the squad for the second test in Cape Town a week later, having recovered from a hand injury.

Bakkies Botha scored two tries in the first test, and was man of the match. Little things stand out in your coaching career and that was one of them, because his second try was scored based on something I'd told him. He scored from a lineout. At halftime I'd told him that if they called a two-man lineout, he should hang back. Victor Matfield would challenge at the front and, if they overthrew it, Bakkies should be there to catch the ball, with the instruction to charge straight ahead. They called a two-man lineout near their tryline, and promptly over-cooked the put-in. Bakkies grabbed the ball and barged his way over the line. Afterwards he told me that he couldn't believe I'd predicted it.

The second test was closer, as you'd expect. Cape Town was wet and greasy, but in the end we still won comfortably (26-17), with Percy scoring 16 points and landing six out of seven kicks at goal. Had he not played, it might have been a different result.

We then beat Wales 53-18 in Pretoria, to set ourselves up nicely for the Tri-Nations. The media had written us off against Ireland and we'd won. They then said Wales were poor, and this was the team that would go on to win the Six Nations the following year. I quickly realised what I was up against with the press every week, no matter what we did.

After the first test against Ireland, someone said to me, 'Now the honeymoon's over.' And after the second test I was told the same thing. After we beat Wales, I was informed that the honeymoon was now 'really' over, as the next challenge would be the Tri-Nations. I got the feeling that I was to be judged on every single Saturday we played. I've said it to Gert Smal and to Allister Coetzee on many occasions: South Africa is the only country in the world where coaches have to coach every week to prove people wrong, not to prove people right. Critics are very clever in hindsight, but the reality was that I had to back the instincts I felt on a Friday, which was more important.

It had been a good start to my test-coaching career, although I knew tougher challenges lay ahead.

15

Tri-Nations glory

Honeymoon or no honeymoon, we'd made a very positive start to the 2004 season. And while the Tri-Nations draw was tough, with away games against Australia and the All Blacks in the beginning, I was confident that we were mentally prepared to gain our first away Tri-Nations victory in six years.

The way we played, especially against Wales, suggested that our curve was moving upwards. We'd been lucky with injuries and were an increasingly happy group of players. But before the business of the Tri-Nations began, we had another assignment to deal with.

The IRB had scheduled a test against the Pacific Islands in the Australian city of Gosford. It was a combination of players from Tonga, Fiji and Samoa. We knew most of them from the Super 12 and, while I expected that they'd lack a little cohesion as a team, I was under no illusion that the game wouldn't be fast and physical, which it was. The Islanders, particularly the Tongans and Samoans, have a reputation for being bruising defenders, and it's a reputation well earned. Playing the match before the main course of the Tri-Nations was a concern for me in some ways, but I also saw it as a great opportunity for us.

South Africa hadn't done well on the road in the professional era and, with the exception of Nick Mallett's Boks in 1998, we hadn't won in Australia or New Zealand since the game went professional, except some 'soft' games in the World Cup. Victory over the Islanders would improve that statistic, even though it wasn't against the Wallabies or the All Blacks.

The Islanders had played against Australia and New Zealand the previous two weeks and lost both matches by 29-14 and 41-26 respectively. It suggested that they were not going to be pushovers – and they weren't.

The match actually had another edge to it; something unforeseen that I never anticipated. The South African players had embarked on industrial action. They wore white armbands in the match as a symbol of their dissatisfaction about the fact that they didn't have contracts with SA Rugby. They'd been negotiating for months through the players' union and had been constantly fobbed off by SA Rugby. They were the only top rugby players in the world who didn't have national contracts. They were at the end of their tether and decided to take drastic action.

It caught me by surprise, as I didn't know that they were going to strike at all. To be clear, a handful of players who'd been around the previous year had contracts, but the rest were only paid match fees. It was an unhappy situation for the players. It put John Smit in a tough position, because he did have a contract. So if he rocked the boat and demonstrated, then SA Rugby would see him as greedy and unreasonable. But if he stayed out of it, the players would view him as disloyal.

He handled it very well. The team had obviously decided on their course of action, but John instructed them not to tell anyone, including management. As the warm-up for the game came to an end, John asked me if the team could go into the changing room on their own, without the coaches. I didn't think much about it and agreed. I thought that, as it was their first away game as a team, John might want a quiet moment before I came in. But the real reason was so that they could put on the white armbands without me seeing. They'd put their tracksuit tops on over their jerseys by the time I entered, so I was still unaware of what was about to happen.

I gave my pre-match talk and, as the team walked out to take the field, John passed me a piece of paper. I didn't open it immediately, but ran up to the coach's box to sing the anthem. After the anthems, I opened the note. It said that the players were going to be wearing white armbands in protest, and that what was about to happen had nothing to do with me as a coach. The protest wasn't aimed at me or at anyone in particular; it was a show of solidarity for the players without contracts. The last line read: 'Please bear with us.'

I was surprised and turned to Gert and Allister. 'You won't believe what's about to happen,' I said. They looked at me and, as I was about to explain, the players took their tracksuit tops off and Gert and Allister saw the white armbands. We knew what they signified, although the media thought the gesture was a sign of respect for Thabu van Rooyen, a stalwart coach and administrator at Free State who had died earlier in the week. Only afterwards did the full story emerge.

After the match, SARU president Brian van Rooyen summoned me, along with Mr P, back to the hotel for an emergency meeting about the armbands. Van Rooyen demanded to know if I'd known anything about it beforehand. I honestly hadn't, and Mr P backed me, explaining that neither of us had been in the changing room when the players made the decision to wear the armbands. Van Rooyen was angry, but the players had made their point, and none of them were punished. In the end they got their contracts.

The game itself went well. We raced into a 33-0 lead; Percy scored 18 points and moved to 313 points in test rugby to break Naas Botha's long-standing Springbok record. We also came through with only minor niggles. It was a hugely significant victory, as it was the first time since the Boks beat the USA in 2001 that South Africa had won away from home, outside of the World Cup. In the changing room afterwards, the team was jubilant. More than ever before. This took me by surprise, until I realised the significance of the win. It put things in perspective for me. We had played so poorly for so long that some players who had worn the Springbok jersey on an away leg of a tour had never felt what it was like to win. It was a big step.

Despite the controversy over the armbands, we left for Christchurch full of confidence that we could upset the All Blacks in their own backyard. The protest incident had only served to galvanise the team even more, and John's brave stance had further endeared him to the rest of the team.

Heading to New Zealand, I had a big decision to make over Victor Matfield. He'd hurt his knee in training before the Islanders match and didn't play in the test. We were based in Sydney, but were due to fly out to New Zealand. There was a possibility he'd be fit for the test against the All Blacks, but I needed to make a call before we left Australia. If he failed a fitness test in Christchurch in the middle of the week, it would have been too late to fly another player out to New Zealand. It's a 24-hour trip with stopovers in Australia. I agonised over that, but in the end I decided I couldn't risk it. I needed to bring someone else in.

The story broke that Victor and I had had a fallout and that he'd been sent home for that reason. It was all rubbish. He had a knee strain and I wasn't prepared to take the risk.

I admit that the two of us were still learning about each other. Victor can be a difficult guy because he's a born leader, so we occasionally bumped heads. At that stage he might have been in a slight comfort zone, which probably supported my decision not to give him every chance to prove his fitness in New Zealand. Today I would give him the benefit of the doubt, but I didn't then. Some people think we dislike each other, but it's not true. Victor played in every important test while I was Bok coach, and was only left out when he was rested or injured.

We had a selectors' meeting with André Markgraaff to decide on Victor's replacement. I wanted to call Sharks lock Albert van den Berg, but SA Rugby said no. The Sharks weren't happy because he wasn't a first choice at their union, and they believed I'd be sending out the wrong message by choosing him for the Boks. They thought I was undermining their selection policy. But he was the obvious replacement for Victor as the middle-of-the-lineout jumper. We had several other locks, such as Hottie Louw, Jannes Labuschagne and Quinton Davids who could jump at the front of the lineout, but very few specialist middle-of-the-lineout jumpers. I was adamant that Albert should come. Markgraaff also didn't like it, but Albert came and remained a member of my squad for four years.

Playing the All Blacks is a great occasion for a South African. They remain the ultimate test in rugby. For as long as both countries have played the game, we've been arch-rivals. There was a time, a few years before I took over, that we'd lost their respect slightly, after being beaten convincingly so many times. In the build-up to the test I was determined that we were going to push them all the way. We did, and for 79½ minutes we led, before Doug Howlett scored the try that broke our hearts.

Losing 23-21 to New Zealand was crushing, but in amongst the wreckage there were a lot of positives. Even though we didn't win, it was the game that set us up for Tri-Nations glory. We earned a bonus point for losing by less than seven points in the match. Although we didn't care about the lone bonus point at the time, as we were so shattered to have lost the test, it later made the difference between winning or losing the title. Interestingly, it was the first bonus point we'd earned in New Zealand since 1997.

Our team was very young and inexperienced, yet we scored three first-half tries and led 21-12 at the break. The fact that we didn't score another point, and that we didn't win the match, came down to a lack of self-belief. I was devastated because we'd come so close, but I needed to be objective.

After the match, on my way to the changing room with Allister and Gert, I told them we needed to be very careful about how we spoke to the team. There was no place for anger or blame. And after four wins and a bright start to the year, the players would be looking to us to see how we handled the defeat.

I told the guys that the reason we didn't win the test was because we'd lacked the belief that we were as good as New Zealand. I emphasised that we had the talent, the skill and the structures to beat the best. I told the players that it was time we changed our mindset. They handled it well and, even though we'd lost, there was a sense of growing confidence.

The match also earned us respect from critics in New Zealand. For the first time in years the Boks were competitive in Kiwi country, and most of them acknowledged that we had probably been unlucky to lose the match. Our performance had also unsettled the All Blacks. They'd been whacking us in our own backyard for several years, and now they'd only just escaped with a win on home ground. All of a sudden, a trip to Ellis Park didn't seem like such a fun prospect for them.

We still had the small matter of playing the Wallabies in Perth before we could turn our attention to the home leg. It was inevitable that Clyde Rathbone, by then a capped Wallaby, would be the man to score the try that condemned us to a second narrow defeat. I had had a bad feeling during the week, sensing that Clyde would produce something special. He was one of the best finishers in the game, and I knew that against his old countrymen, he'd find a little extra motivation.

George Gregan played his 100th test that night. It was a great game. The lead changed hands about seven times. We led for the last time when Gaffie du Toit scored after collecting a grubber kick to put us back into a three-point lead. It was never comfortable and, when the Wallabies put Rathbone into space, there was only one outcome. Again, I say we lost because we lacked the belief that we could win. But we picked up another bonus point, and on the flight home I said to John, 'Now we need Australia to beat the All Blacks in Sydney.'

The Wallabies and All Blacks met the following weekend, but I didn't watch the match because I was at Bishops watching my son Clinton playing rugby for his school. While I was standing on the side of the field, John sent me a text message, which read 'first part of the mission completed'. Australia had won 23-18. The Tri-Nations was up for grabs, and we had two home games ahead.

It was an amazing lift for the team and, when we gathered the next day, there was a buzz. Everyone was saying we were two wins away from becoming Tri-Nations champions. But my personal exhilaration was slightly deflated, as I had encountered for the first time the internal politics that would become part of my daily existence on the job. I'd decided on the team for the match, and when I gave it to Mr P, he said that it wasn't right. Breyton Paulse was the only black player in the starting line-up and, according to Mr P, Van Rooyen would not allow it. I'd picked Fourie du Preez to start at scrumhalf, and when Van Rooyen saw that, he insisted I start with Bolla Conradie. I argued that I'd already told both players that Fourie was going to start the match, and that it wouldn't be good for the squad to make such a blatant politically motivated change.

But Van Rooyen was adamant, and I made the switch before naming the team at the midweek press conference. I felt bad for both players. It wasn't that I didn't have faith in Bolla's ability; it was purely a rugby decision for that match on that day. Fourie was naturally upset, but I think he understood the bigger picture. Fortunately the mood in the camp was so good that we were able to put the interference behind us.

Ellis Park was electric for the game. Fans believed we could beat the All Blacks, and we were bullish. Victor Matfield returned to the team and we dominated the game, even though New Zealand led with 13 minutes remaining.

Centre Marius Joubert scored a rare hat-trick, becoming the first Bok to score three tries against the All Blacks since Ray Mordt in 1981. We controlled the game and gave one of the best performances of any team I'd coached, with a 40-26 win. It was New Zealand's second heaviest loss against the Springboks and, more importantly, the outcome of the Tri-Nations was undecided going into the final match of the series.

Back at our hotel in Sandton, the staff had laid out champagne for the team. While we toasted the victory, I asked all the players in the squad who had never beaten the All Blacks to stand up. It had been four years and eight consecutive All Black wins since the Boks' last victory. Out of the 30-odd players present, about 25 stood up. Only Os, Monty, Breyton Paulse, John Smit and Albert van den Berg had been on a winning side against New Zealand. It was staggering.

Victor Matfield had never beaten the All Blacks, and he had almost 30 test caps at that stage. Guys like Joe van Niekerk and De Wet Barry had been playing test rugby for three years and had never beaten New Zealand. I asked myself how far we had fallen as a rugby nation if a group of talented players hadn't once beaten the best team in the world.

We enjoyed the moment, and then turned our attention to Durban and the Wallabies. The match was a final. The winner would be Tri-Nations champion. The most amazing thing was that we could have finished first, second or third in the competition, depending on how the match played out. It was an all-or-nothing game.

One evening I was in my room at the Beverly Hills hotel, when the phone rang. A woman's voice at the other end of the line said, 'Mr White, would you take a call from the president?' I almost replied, 'President of what?' because I thought it was a wind-up from a mate or even a player. I played along and said, 'Sure, I'll take it.' She then informed me that the president would call in five minutes. I was confused, because it didn't sound like someone was taking the mickey.

Exactly five minutes later the phone rang, and I heard the familiar voice of President Mbeki. He said, 'I want to congratulate you for beating New Zealand, and I want to wish you all the best for the weekend. I hope you guys win the title.' That was it; the first time I'd ever had contact with the man. That was special.

Durban was frothing – the crowd was even more amped than at Ellis Park, because the match had the added edge of being a final. It was tight and tense, but Victor Matfield and Joe van Niekerk both delivered brilliant performances and were both rewarded with tries. The Wallabies led 7-3 at the break, but we took control in the third quarter, scoring 20 points to move into a comfortable 23-7 lead. But as the match wound down, Breyton and Monty both received yellow cards. We battled to hang on as Australia made a predictable late rally. Home-ground advantage had helped us, but after two narrow losses on the away leg of the Tri-Nations, the difference this time was the team's belief that they could win. They had to come from behind in both home matches, and against Australia they had to dig deep to hang on for the win. Against the All Blacks, we won it going away. Against the Wallabies, we won it with our backs to the wall.

South Africa collected only its second Tri-Nations title – I couldn't have wished for a better start to my Bok coaching career.

16

Grand Slam tour

Winning the Tri-Nations was massive for South African rugby for several reasons. Considering where we'd come from in less than nine months, it was unbelievable. It also gave South Africans something to love about the Springboks again. It would be a bit of a stretch to say that what happened in 2004 saved South African rugby, but I do wonder whether the game would have flourished if it had gone through another year of scandal and controversy at Springbok level. But as there are always scandals playing out in the media in South African rugby, it might have.

As far as I was concerned, creating a winning Bok team was a priority and, while we were far from the finished product, at least we'd restored some pride. My initial goal had been short term. With six out of eight test wins and an undefeated home record for the season, I was able to look ahead to the end-of-year tour and bring in some new players.

The fixture lists just seemed to become tougher every year, and in 2004, after a difficult first half of the year, we faced a Grand Slam tour to Britain and Ireland, with a test against Argentina tacked on at the end. While the media hyped the Grand Slam tour, I saw it slightly differently, wanting to create some opportunities for a few new players. As Bok coach, I was under pressure to select black players, which was something I'd fully bought into when I took the job.

I saw a tour with four tests as the perfect opportunity to blood some youngsters, which included several promising black players. I really hate speaking in terms of colour, because I like to see players as players, but the reality is that in some cases I was forced to view black players separately from white players. The touring party included 11 black players in the 34-man squad. And, while a player such as Boland wing Jongi Nokwe was chosen ahead of more established and possibly deserving players, the idea of the tour was to give promising non-white players a chance to experience the culture of Springbok rugby.

It didn't necessarily mean they would start matches, but rather become part of a Bok squad in order to gain an understanding about what it means to play for South Africa, and what the expectations at that level are.

They would also experience at first hand the difference between provincial and test rugby. As always, the idea was to balance opportunity with good results.

We beat Wales, but lost the second test of the tour against Ireland. So my plan to give many of the fringe players a chance in the final test against Scotland took a blow. With world champions England as our third opponents, I'd always wanted to choose my strongest team for that match. In an ideal world, we would have had two victories under our belts before England, so we could afford to treat the Scotland test as a more experimental game. But losing to Ireland changed the nature of the tour, because my honeymoon really was over this time. The media climbed into us for losing, which made future results more important than anything.

We beat Wales 38-36, but the score flattered them. We'd led 38-22 with about 14 minutes to go. Only, I thought it was about five minutes to go, because I was following the stadium clock, which didn't take stoppages into account. So I threw on a bunch of reserves, including flank Tim Dlulane and scrumhalf Michael Claassens, who made their debuts. After they took to the field, I learnt that in fact there was about 12 minutes to play. Wales came back at us with two late tries and nearly pinched a victory. After the match I made mention of the mix-up with the clock and was lambasted in the press for using that as an excuse.

It wasn't that I didn't have faith in the reserves, but Tim and Michael were very raw, and my plan was to give them a few minutes at the end of the game to get a feel for test rugby and what it was like to be part of a winning team. The idea wasn't to give them so *much* time, as I wasn't 100 per cent sure of their abilities. Also, our momentum shuddered to a halt when I made the changes. Had I kept the starting players on for six minutes more, I believe Wales would never have scored again.

But, most importantly, we won, and had another away win under our belt. The tour moved to Ireland, where I really put my foot in it. I love Ireland. I love the people; they're incredibly friendly and they're passionate about rugby. It's a great place to tour because the people engage with you and there is always a lot of banter. But at a pre-match press conference, I was suckered into a question by one of their media.

He wasn't one of their regular rugby writers; I'd never seen the man before, and haven't seen him since. This journalist asked me: 'You played Ireland in the summer, and you saw our team. How many of them do you think would be good enough to make your team?'

It seemed a straight question and I gave it little thought before answering. 'Your lock pairing is one of the best in the world, and Brian O'Driscoll picks himself in any team around the world on any given day.' And I left it at that. The next day, the headline was, 'Coach says only three Irish players good enough to make the Springbok team.' That's not how I'd said or meant it, but I was stitched up. I had also walked into it to some extent. I knew the piece would be nailed to their changing room door, and the Irish team would use it as motivation. Naturally, the next day the press wanted to push the statement further, but I blanked them.

Of course the story didn't end there. A few minutes before kick-off, I was doing an interview with one of their TV reporters on the side of the field. The crowd is pretty close to the pitch at Lansdowne Road, and the fans were verbally abusing me. If I hadn't realised the scale of my comment before, I did then.

That incident was one factor in our eventual defeat. The other was a bad piece of refereeing by Paul Honiss. We were defending our line and, after Joe van Niekerk went offside at a ruck, Honiss blew for a penalty and called John Smit aside. Honiss told him to go and talk to the players because one more penalty in the red zone would result in a yellow card. But as John huddled the players together for a chat, Irish flyhalf Ronan O'Gara took a quick tap penalty and scored without anyone laying a hand on him. I was appalled that the try was allowed. John argued with Honiss, but to no avail. The try stood and, although it was early in the game, it was just the momentum-shifter Ireland needed as a boost.

Although it was only five points, and people say it shouldn't have dictated the outcome of the match, it did. We lost by five points, and besides, the 10 to 15 minutes it took the team to regroup also cost us in the final analysis. That was a poor piece of refereeing by Honiss, and he acknowledged it some time later. But his post-game admission couldn't change the final score.

We lost 17-12, and the media pressure really cranked up. My words at the press conference were thrown in my face, of course, but more concerning was some of the negative press we received. It wasn't that the year had been a disaster, but after losing to Ireland I saw the agendas of certain journos and newspapers surface. It was unsettling.

Back at the hotel, a few Irish supporters hung around in the foyer. When they saw me, they shouted out, 'Only three players good enough to play for the Boks, hey?' I just kept walking; there was no point in engaging them after an afternoon that had likely included many celebratory pints of Guinness.

I was also very disappointed in coach Eddie O'Sullivan. He accused me of having no respect for Irish rugby because of my skewed comment. That hurt, because if any coach has a respect for the traditions of the game, and for Irish rugby, it's me. Willie John McBride, Fergus Slattery, Syd Millar and Noel Murphy are Irish legends I grew up worshipping. Coaching is hard enough without having to make it personal with your opposite number. Coaches routinely use every advantage they can find, but to put the boot in like he did, and publicly, left a bad taste. I've sparred in the press with other coaches. Wallaby coach Eddie Jones and I often had subtle digs at each other through the press, but it was never personal. We're good friends today because of that.

O'Sullivan's words gave the Irish people the impression that I had no respect for their rugby history. I saw him at the after-match function, but I didn't go out of my way to greet him. Some of his players were disrespectful as well, and passed comments when I was within earshot. That's not how professionals handle themselves. So I certainly don't exchange Christmas cards with O'Sullivan.

Hence it was with mixed emotions that we moved on to England for the third of our four tests, under increasing pressure. The team was deflated after the Irish test, and we knew that England at Twickenham would be our toughest match of the tour. I always knew it was a match we'd battle to win, but I never expected to travel there on the back of a defeat to Ireland.

As I was friendly with Clive Woodward, who'd retired after guiding England to World Cup victory the previous year, I was keen to meet up. He's an interesting guy with a great understanding of the game. But because of his association with England and the fact that it was only a year since they'd won the world title, he wasn't keen to meet before the test in case we were spotted having a drink. Can you imagine the headlines in the English tabloid press if that came out a few days before the test?

We were hammered 32-16 on the slower northern hemisphere fields, where the game centred much more on close combat, mauling and fighting for the ball on the ground. The young Boks weren't up to it. I know we'd been Tri-Nations champions earlier in the year, but in that environment we were well off the pace. That's why I said after the game that it had been men against boys. We had promising youngsters and a good group of senior players, but aside from Os, Breyton and Monty, we didn't have a lot of test-match experience.

We came off the back of the Ireland test, and I believe the players weren't mentally ready for an England side that just kept coming at them. A long season was nearing its end, and the relentless England pressure was too much for them. But, like all defeats, they learnt from it.

In the week leading up to the game there had also been a few disruptions concerning selection. I'd already endured interference with the selection of Bolla Conradie over Fourie du Preez in the Tri-Nations, and now I had another problem. My plan was to play Ashwin Willemse on the wing in the England test. He'd come off a long knee injury in time to be selected for the touring party. Before the tour I'd told Ashwin that I wanted him to play for about 60 minutes against Wales, and then a full game against Ireland, so that by the time we met England he'd be match-sharp. I wanted big wingers for the test against England, because I knew they'd use cross-field kicks as an attacking weapon. I wanted to play Ashwin and Jaque Fourie on the wings.

All went according to plan against Wales, and Ashwin was substituted after 55 minutes. Against Ireland, I emphasised to Ashwin that he needed to play a full 80 minutes so that I knew he was ready for the England game. In his usual fashion, he said, 'No problem, coach.' With the first move of the game he took a short ball coming off his wing from a Bok lineout and was tackled. He picked himself up, but sent a message to Clint Readhead that his foot 'felt funny'. Clint treated him, and all Ashwin would say was that it felt as if his laces were tied around his toes. Clint took his boot off and he seemed to be okay. He played the rest of the match.

When we arrived in England, Dr Hassan came to see me and said he was taking Ashwin for a scan of his foot. I asked, 'What do you mean, a scan of his foot?' I wasn't aware anything was wrong. When they returned, Hassan told me Ashwin had a fractured bone and would miss the rest of the tour. I called Ashwin to my room and asked him why he hadn't come off in the first few minutes against Ireland if he knew his foot was hurt. I was angry. And he said, 'Coach, you asked me to play 80 minutes against Ireland, so I did.'

People often want to know why I'm loyal to Ashwin. I'll tell you why. If you had 15 Ashwin Willemses in a team, you'd never lose a test match.

But we had to move on. So I sat with then SA Rugby chairman Tienie Lategan and president Brian van Rooyen to see whether they'd allow me to choose Jaque Fourie and Jean de Villiers as wings. That would mean I only had one black player – prop Eddie Andrews – in the starting line-up. We discussed it, and they both gave me the green light to go ahead.

We trained with that in mind and I informed the team of the selection for the test match, with Breyton Paulse on the bench. But the next day, Van Rooyen sent a message that I couldn't pick Jaque. I would need to put Breyton in the starting XV so that we'd have two black players. I argued that I couldn't do that because it would be massively unfair to Breyton. He'd know he was a political selection. I rated Breyton as a player, but it was a case of horses for courses, and for England I wanted a different player on the wing.

I'd explained my reasoning to him, and he understood the motivation. But now I had to tell him he was back in the team. He's not stupid; he knew why. I couldn't exactly convince him he'd grown three inches overnight. It stung Breyton, because the week before he'd made his 50th test appearance. He was one of the most experienced players in the team and he was being treated as a political choice – a quota player. That was tough on him *and* tough on me.

I understood the bigger picture from a political perspective, but it compromised me as a coach. I've always been honest with players, which is something they respect. I never used skin colour as a selection criterion, although that week I was forced to.

Of course Jaque Fourie was pretty angry as well. He'd thought he was playing, and suddenly he was demoted for no apparent reason. It was a mess. But I felt desperately sorry for Breyton especially. As it turned out, he had one of his weaker tests, but who can blame him? He was clearly pissed off about the way he was selected, and rightly so. The one thing about Breyton is that he's always wanted to be selected on merit and, aside from that time, I always did select him on merit. He hated the notion of being a 'quota' player, because he wasn't one. But on that day, he was made to feel like one. As it turned out, England scored a try with a cross-field kick, although it wasn't to Breyton's wing.

After the disappointment of Twickenham and the drama surrounding the build-up to the game, I finally met Woodward at his house the day after the test. We had a good long chat and I picked his brain, especially for his views on how we'd been beaten the day before. I asked him what I needed to do if I wanted to build a team capable of winning the World Cup. He didn't have one answer, but he made it clear that experience and physicality were non-negotiable.

Clive has three traits that are exceptional in my opinion: first, he thinks out of the box in the way he looks for different ways to improve himself and his teams. Second, he allows his players and coaches to express themselves, to feel in control of their roles and that they are contributing. And, last, he has an insatiable desire to be the best and to win at all costs. Those three aspects rubbed off on me the most during our friendship. He couldn't give me the exact answer as to why we'd been outplayed, but he planted seeds that I needed to nurture if I wanted to create one of the best teams in the world.

I also met up with my good friend Eddie Jones during the tour. Australia was touring Britain at the same time and, while we were in London, they were in Edinburgh preparing to face Scotland. On our day off, I flew to Edinburgh to meet with Eddie and discuss tactics against both England and Scotland. He shared some insights on the Scots and I shared insights on the English, as the following week we would swap opponents. It was great to meet, because we didn't normally get to see much of each other during the year, and I was still learning about what was required to beat these teams in their own backyards.

After the struggles in Dublin and London, we headed off to Scotland to conclude the tour. Bryan Habana had made his test debut against England off the bench, and showed me enough to believe I should start with him against the Scots. I'd called him into the Bok group during the Tri-Nations as a non-playing member, so he could soak up some of the atmosphere of being in a test environment. His seven minutes against England, which included a try, suggested he would make the transition to test rugby pretty smoothly.

We put ourselves under a lot of pressure as a team that week, as we'd never lost three games in a row. In the Tri-Nations we'd lost twice in consecutive weeks, but three successive losses would've been a train smash. I met with selector André Markgraaff to discuss the team for the weekend. I was starting to get angry with him, because we weren't really having selection meetings any more. Instead, he was dictating whom I should pick and what style of rugby we should play. Markgraaff knows rugby and may be a former Bok coach, but in 2004 he was a selector, and his role was to debate, not dictate, the make-up of teams. That was the beginning of the souring of our relationship.

I eventually put my foot down and told him he'd had his chance to coach the Springboks. Now it was my time. He was in no doubt that I wanted him to stay out of coaching, which upset him. During the previous tests on tour he'd sent me messages via Allister and Gert on when to make substitutions and what calls to make. I always ignored his suggestions, but it was an irritating habit. In Edinburgh we were on a supporters' bus when someone asked him to predict the outcome against Scotland, and he said he thought the Boks would lose. He was the convenor of selectors, for heaven's sake! He'd had a part in choosing the team, and then he told random people he thought we would lose. Crazy.

We made seven changes for the test at Murrayfield. Solly Tyibilika and Gurthro Steenkamp made their test debuts, with a recall for centre Gcobani Bobo on the bench. We played really well, winning 45-10. Habana scored two tries, and Tyibilika became the first ethnic black South African to score a try in test rugby. We even had to play with 13 men for almost 10 minutes after Bakkies and Victor were sin-binned.

Before heading home, we had a final test to play in Buenos Aires against Argentina. But there was also the IRB awards dinner on the Sunday night following the Scotland test. I was nominated in the Coach of the Year category, Schalk Burger was a nominee for Player of the Year, and the Springboks were nominated for Team of the Year.

It was a clean sweep of awards for us. It was unbelievable! Never in my wildest dreams did I imagine we'd receive the bucket full of accolades we did. I was so proud of Schalk, who was only 21. And of John Smit, whose efforts as captain were recognised with the team award.

After the awards, the squad travelled to Argentina for a test against the Pumas, which we won 39-6. Schalk, AJ Venter and Bobo stayed behind to play for the Barbarians, while Monty was released to return to Newport, his Welsh club side. Jongi Nokwe, the only player on tour who hadn't participated in a match, concerned me. I really wanted to give him a chance to play, but when he was selected it was clear that his chances were slim. So I tried to get him a game with the Barbarians during the tour.

He trained hard and was a good tourist. The Barbarians were looking for a player against the All Blacks, and I put his name forward. With Schalk, AJ and Gcobani Bobo alongside, I thought it was a good idea, but Jongi wasn't keen. I understood his apprehension. He was overseas for the first time in his life and he hardly spoke English. Then, to pack him off with a bunch of foreign players against the All Blacks was a little overwhelming for him. So I didn't push it. I took flak for not playing him, but the opportunity never presented itself, and I don't regret taking him. He learnt a lot and, although it took him a few years to gain confidence, he's now a very good player. I wouldn't be surprised if he earned a test cap soon.

A good year with some minor problems came to an end, but not before one last bout of bickering. After winning the Tri-Nations, the squad was promised healthy bonuses, which never materialised. On the end-of-year tour, the players raised the issue with manager Arthob Petersen. A compromise was reached, and they were paid something – but, sadly, not what the players had initially been promised.

17

Car trouble

When sportsmen break into the top echelon and become stars, the saying goes that their second year is always the toughest. According to popular theory, opponents have 'worked them out' and identified their weaknesses, which they're able to target and exploit to their advantage. Coaching a team is similar, but that theory didn't hold up in 2005 for one simple reason: we hadn't done anything particularly different in 2004. There was nothing much to figure out and therefore no real weaknesses to exploit.

Opponents knew what they would get from us: tough defence, good set pieces and quality phase play. They all knew we employed what the media liked to call a 'rush defence'. I never thought of it in that way. It was a defensive system designed to work to our strengths: physicality and pressure. When I got the job, Bok wings were generally small guys. To have them in a one-on-one situation with a player such as Joe Rokocoko wouldn't have worked. So I needed to find a solution to overcome that problem. The answer was to stop the ball getting to the wing by pushing from the outside in, towards the middle of the field.

My players were also never comfortable with drift defences. They simply wanted to tackle the man in front of them, so I developed a system that I called 'the umbrella'. We'd press from the outside (the wings) and ensure that, after two passes, the opposition had nowhere to go. They'd have to come back inside, where we'd have players such as Schalk Burger, Juan Smith and Bakkies Botha to hit them. It wasn't rocket science. Eddie Jones called it 'culturally sympathetic to South Africans', and he was right. Everyone knew we were doing it, but finding a way around it was not easy. It's one of the reasons we scored so many intercept tries, because opponents tried to force the last pass. Often we were called lucky for scoring so many breakaway tries, but they didn't happen by accident.

So, in my second year I wasn't that concerned about suffering second-year syndrome, because, quite simply, I wasn't hiding anything. In 2005 we played our best rugby and produced, in my opinion, some of our best performances. In 2006 we would endure a tough year, for which there were reasons that had little to do with opponents working us out and more to do with life off the field.

The fixture list in 2005 was slightly better than the one of the year before. We had an easy test against Uruguay, followed by a two-test home series against France, and then we would start the Tri-Nations at home. In all, you couldn't have asked for more in the first phase of the season.

It was a great year – at least most of it was. One reason was that, at the end of 2004, my contract was extended up to and including the 2007 World Cup. I'd simply asked about an extension on the back of winning the Tri-Nations, as I'd initially been contracted for two years. Within a few days, Brian van Rooyen and board chairman Tienie Lategan said they'd extend it for a further two years. Basically we just altered dates and numbers on the existing contract – it took a few minutes. The reason I mention this is because the following year, when I asked about extending my contract beyond 2007, the board messed me around for three months, and it ultimately turned into a huge media circus.

But 2005 was, for the most part, positive. Uruguay was never going to be a threat, and I knew I could try a few new players in a low-pressure match. The Eastern Cape city of East London hosted the test, which was significant because it is in the heart of black rugby in South Africa.

Many people believe that, prior to 1994, when South Africa became a democracy, rugby was the sole preserve of whites. That might have been true for most of the country, but in the Eastern Cape rugby thrived in the townships among the black community. Port Elizabeth also had a strong history of black rugby, and we were playing there a few weeks later, against France. But playing a test in East London was a significant step towards bringing the Springboks to a sector of society with which they might not normally have interacted.

Wing Tonderai Chavhanga made his test debut and scored a record six tries as we romped home to a 134-3 win. It was tough for the South Americans, but if you want to be the best team in the world, you have to be ruthless. At one stage Tonderai had scored about four tries, and I sent a message out to get the ball to him so he could score a few more. He's the fastest player I've ever coached – quicker than Bryan Habana – but he had so many injury problems that he would only play a handful of games in the next two years. In fact, Tonderai earned only his second test cap on the away leg of the Tri-Nations in 2007.

Scrumhalf Ricky Januarie, one of my 2002 and 2003 Under-21 players, also made his test debut that day. He played really well behind a pack that wasn't just going forward, but racing forward. His decision-making was precise and his service slick.

We broke all sorts of records: highest score by a Bok team, biggest winning margin and the most tries (21) in a match. But the media criticised the standard of the opposition. Uruguay was weak, but in the 2003 World Cup the Boks had beaten Uruguay 72-6, so I think it showed an improvement on our part. Critics failed to see how ruthless we'd been.

Tonderai was never scheduled to play against France, but then he was injured in training and missed the rest of the season, so I never had a chance to see him in action again. Other players took their chances ahead of him.

Before the French test in Durban, Professor Tim Noakes, one of the most respected sports scientists in the world, gave a presentation to the board. He urged them to give the players adequate rest if we wanted to make an effective assault on the World Cup in 2007. Initially I'd just wanted to get the Boks winning again, but after having my contract extended, I looked to the future knowing that I would be leading South Africa to France. So I sought the best medical advice to ensure that we planned with precision for the World Cup. It was a lesson I'd learnt from Clive Woodward.

The board was impressed with Noakes's presentation, which he backed up with ample medical evidence on the benefits of rest. The board members appeared to buy into the idea, promising to assist in any way they could, and tentatively agreeing to allow me to select teams with an eye to the World Cup.

In Durban we drew the test 30-all, narrowly escaping a defeat when Dimitri Yachvili hit the posts with his conversion attempt to Julien Candelon's last-minute try. It was an escape, but it wasn't a bad performance, and I felt we could have won the game. We'd led by five points with four minutes to go. Instead of slowing the game and closing it down, we'd pushed and ended up losing the ball, which led to their try. That cost us, but it was also stored in the memory bank. The result was a little wake-up call as we headed to Port Elizabeth for the second test.

The day after we arrived in PE, the news broke about the death of Dan Qeqe, a legendary rugby administrator and former player. Qeqe had been one of the icons of non-racial rugby, and a legend at the Spring Rose Club in the PE townships. Allister Coetzee had played against Spring Rose and was close to the Qeqe family. He asked if I wanted to attend the funeral, and of course I went, as did John Smit. I didn't know Dan personally, but I knew him by reputation. I'd heard stories about what a fine player he'd been (he was a hooker) and, more importantly, what an influential figure he was for rugby in the community.

Although it was a sad occasion, there was also a sense of joy as the family celebrated his life. Traditional Xhosa funerals are very different to Western burials. The family was seated in the living room of his house and mourners came and went, swapping stories and paying their respects. The thing that struck me was how popular Dan was, mainly through rugby, even though his rugby exploits had been completely unknown to me while I was growing up because of the political system of the country. It drove home how important it was to find black rugby stars.

No sooner had I returned to the hotel to carry on with preparation for the second test against France than I received a call from Mr P, telling me that I had to pick flank Solly Tyibilika for the test. I wasn't sure whether it was Mr P pushing his own agenda or whether the order came from the top, but, either way, I was unimpressed. I'd just come back from the funeral feeling very positive about the need to find black stars, and suddenly I was being told whom to pick. Again. Solly was part of the squad and he would play, but I didn't want to be told when.

The message that filtered through was that Solly was a Spring Rose man, so his inclusion in the team would be in honour of Qeqe. Mr P suggested I leave Schalk Burger out. It might have been a well-intended gesture, but in the cut-throat world of test rugby there is little place for sentiment. I told Mr P that I was not going to make an emotional decision for such an important test. I had my team in mind for this match, and Solly was not part of my plans. Burger was the IRB Player of the Year and the most important member of my team. Just like the reserve hookers were stuck behind the captain in the queue, Solly was in the unfortunate position of being stuck behind one of the best players in the world in the pecking order.

It also irritated me that, for 18 months or so, I'd exceeded the board's expectations at all levels, including transformation. Suddenly it wasn't a case of transformation, but about picking the black players *they* wanted *when* they wanted them. I had to put my foot down.

The interference had started with suggestions that perhaps I should pick this or that player, but this was the first time they'd been so blunt. I told

Mr P in no uncertain terms that it wasn't going to happen. He was unhappy with my decision, and the next day, after I'd named the team to the media, I was informed that the President's Council was calling an emergency meeting over my stance! Van Rooyen sent me a text message telling me how disappointed he was with my attitude. He was angry because I wasn't prepared to toe the line, so he decided to flex his muscles, even though he'd signed off on the team.

But Van Rooyen later claimed he'd never signed off on the team and that I must change it. When I refused, he and several members of the President's Council flew down to PE to hold a 'crisis' meeting. I was stunned. From doing everything asked of me, I was suddenly in a struggle for my job because of an essentially minor incident. But I held my ground and told Van Rooyen in person that I would not change the team for emotional reasons. I told him that if that was the way he wanted to play it, I was out of there.

Mr P called a full management meeting to discuss the situation, with everyone from the kit master to the assistant coaches present. He opened by saying that, while he was a member of the Springbok team management, he was also a board member, and hence was chairing the meeting in that capacity. He informed the management that I had indicated I was resigning, and he wanted to know where the rest of them stood. After the French test, the Springboks were scheduled to leave for Sydney and the Tri-Nations the following Thursday.

I'd spoken to my agent Craig Livingstone, and he'd advised me not to use the word 'resign' at any stage. I hadn't, but I had told Van Rooyen, 'I'm out of here.' So, when Mr P told the others I'd resigned, I interjected: 'Listen, Mr P, I want to tell you one thing and I want to make it clear. I haven't resigned. SA Rugby will have to work out how they're going to get rid of me.' I'd recently extended my contract beyond the World Cup, and knew they'd have to pay me out. That was my last bargaining chip. I didn't want to resign, but I was prepared to do so because I would no longer be undermined. There'd been a few instances the previous year, but I'd accepted them as part of the transformation process. But the situation was now out of control.

So Mr P asked the rest of management to tell him where they stood. He was basically asking them if they'd carry on without me. Mr P made it clear that he sided with SA Rugby. As our team manager, his attitude was a disappointment. He addressed the men one by one. His first target was Professor Derik Coetzee. Derik hardly let him finish the question.

'Look, let me tell you, this is the easiest decision I've ever made in my life,' he said. 'If the coach goes, I'm going back to university to lecture.'

Then Mr P asked Allister, who replied, 'If the coach goes, I'm out of here.' Then Gert, who said, 'I'm out of here too.' Dr Hassan was next. We've always had a professional relationship, but we've never been particularly close away from the game. The doc said: 'From a medical point of view, Jake is the first guy I've ever worked with who's been able to understand and listen to us, so I'm also out of here.' Then Mr P turned to physio Clint Readhead, who lost it.

'What is it about SA Rugby that they're always bloody putting the spanner in the works?' he demanded to know. 'Well, I'm also out of here.' He'd been through 2003 with Rudolf Straeuli and the Kamp Staaldraad fiasco.

Fitness coach Mark Steele said he would leave too, and so on, until Mr P got to baggage master Philip 'Flippie' Malakoane. As he asked Flippie where he stood, I jumped in. I had spoken to most of management and warned them about what might be coming, but I hadn't consulted either Flippie or media manager Rayaan Adriaanse, and I thought it was unfair to put them on the spot, as it was the first they'd heard of the situation. Both Flippie and Rayaan were employed by SA Rugby, while the rest of us were on contracts. So for them to align themselves either way would have been difficult. Mr P realised he was in a pickle, because if I left there'd be no Bok management, and this with a Tri-Nations series looming. His next words were laughable. 'Well, it's good to see the management team is sticking together.' He was basically insinuating that he was a part of the management team again and not siding with SA Rugby.

Mr P went off to tell Van Rooyen and the presidents of the outcome of the meeting. We weren't sure where we stood, and I thought I would probably be fired after the test because I'd defied the council. That notion was reinforced the day before the test, when Allister received a text message from a *Rapport* journalist. It read, 'Win or lose on Saturday, Jake is gone.'

I was philosophical about it. If I was fired, I'd have to move on; what else could I do? My contract was loaded with key performance indicators

(KPIs), which I'd exceeded. Now they were shifting the KPIs, which they couldn't really do, so at least if I was axed, they'd have to pay me out.

The night before the test I was killing time when Karl Dahl from Paarlberg BMW, who sponsored my car, called to see if I wanted to pop out to a restaurant for a quick drink. He was entertaining clients, and I promised to show my face. Karl always joked that I wouldn't get around if it wasn't for him. So, while I was having a quick beer, I asked: 'Karl, tell me, if I get fired or lose my job, do I get to keep the car for a while?' He asked what had happened, and I said, 'I'm probably out of here; I can't take this shit any more. The hierarchy is interfering.' He was shocked, his usual joking temporarily suspended. But I was serious and I'd made up my mind.

In hindsight it would be easy to say I never believed they'd fire me. But at the time I seriously thought it was my last match in charge. I never mentioned a thing to the players. They knew nothing and we prepared like we always did. But it was tough. Coaching the Springboks is hard enough without all the added pressures. People don't understand what a coach goes through. Test matches shred your nerves and take years off your life. You do the best you can, and then on the Saturday it's up to the players to do the job. Afterwards you take the criticism and get very few plaudits. In my case I had to do everything expected of me as a coach, while dealing with the other problems and protecting the players. The pressure was immense, and sometimes there seemed to be no way out. I lay in bed on that Friday night and thought my world was collapsing. Coaching the Boks was my dream, and I had been doing it well. Now it appeared to be over.

Before I left the restaurant that Friday night, I had asked Karl again how much time I'd have to give the car back. He kept a straight face as he answered, 'Just make sure it's back by Tuesday.' I think he was joking. I'll never know.

18

Madiba magic

On the morning of the test, a story that I was about to lose my job appeared in the Saturday papers. Only then did the players become aware of what was happening. The *Independent on Saturday's* front page screamed, 'I will quit, says Jake'.

The first two paragraphs read: 'On the day of the deciding test match against France, South African rugby is in turmoil again, with Jake White on the verge of resigning as Springbok coach just 16 months after taking the job. White has accused the SA Rugby Union of breach of contract and has given it an ultimatum that unless he is allowed to select his team without interference, he will quit on Monday.' Writer Dale Granger quoted Van Rooyen as saying that he would appoint a black coach if I stepped down.

It seemed that my fate was sealed. We won the test and played very well. France was never in the match, and we beat them 27-13. I thought that at least it was a nice way to end my coaching career – a series win over France and we'd maintained our unbeaten record.

But at the after-match function, it was smiles all round from the President's Council members. There wasn't any mention of the meeting Mr P had chaired and none of them cornered me for a quiet chat. Just smiles and backslaps. It was as if nothing had happened. After all the tension and angst the President's Council had put the management through, they didn't even have the guts to confront me.

On the Monday I continued with my planning for the trip to Sydney, where we were set to play against Australia in the first of two Mandela Plate matches. We were scheduled to leave on the Thursday, although I wasn't sure if I was going. There was dead silence from the men above me. The days went by and the travel arrangements were made. Still no word – not even an acknowledgement that the spat was over and that I should continue as before. Perhaps they were waiting for me to quit, as they had no reason to fire me. I returned the compliment by reciprocating the silent treatment.

I suppose the whole thing died down because they knew that the entire management would walk out if I was fired. Besides, the Boks were doing quite well, so none of the presidents wanted to be the man to propose the sacking of the coach without a concrete reason.

At the time, Markgraaff was deputy president of SARU and also head of an SA Rugby technical committee, the function of which I never understood. He wasn't my greatest fan and, along with vice-president Mike Stofile, would not have been sad to see the back of me. Van Rooyen, for all his faults, actually gave me some support. Although he had tried to force me to pick Tyibilika, he'd been acting under pressure from other sectors of the game at the time. Privately he still backed me, although he never actually said it – I just knew. Not for the last time, winning a test probably saved my job.

We arrived in Sydney 10 days before the Mandela Plate test. It was a one-off, and we'd return to South Africa for the second leg of the series at Ellis Park before the Tri-Nations started. It was quite difficult, having to travel across the Indian Ocean and eight times zones twice in such a short space of time.

In Sydney we'd decided to work the guys really hard for the first few days. A week before the match, on a Saturday, Derik conducted a particularly physical session, which absolutely drained the guys. It was all planned. *Everything* was planned, down to the exact minutes of every movement when we were on tour. We planned months in advance; I had an idea of the personnel I wanted to use, and in which games. With the make-up of my squad, I'd decided on the match 22 for the Sydney test. Hell, I'd already decided on the squad for the return match in South Africa. Obviously injury or other factors could force a change, but I informed players well in advance when they might expect action during our campaign.

As part of our overall fitness plan, we worked the players very hard at the Warringah Rugby Club. I knew we ran the risk of overdoing it, but the Tri-Nations was our main goal and we needed to use every opportunity to ensure that the right fitness work was done in advance. In the long run, the hard physical work we did in Sydney was to our benefit. But in the short term, i.e. the first leg of the Mandela Plate, it worked against us. I named a strong team, but on the night at the Telstra Stadium we were flatter than a Benoni accent.

The Aussies thumped us 30-12 and we never got off the ground. That was probably our second worst performance in my coaching tenure, but it was the result of too much physical work prior to the test. Because of the structure of rugby in South Africa, with Super 14 and Currie Cup demands on the players, you have to do what you can, when you can, as Springbok coach to prepare the players. Sometimes short-term objectives are sacrificed for longer-term success. Until there is a global season or single contracts for South African players, it'll continue to be a problem. We saw the impact of the schedule that night. I could have been easy on the players, but it would have caught up with us later.

The press climbed in again, but we deserved it for that performance. The week before the test, I'd told the *Sunday Times* that if Wallaby prop Bill Young had attended practice at Stellenbosch University for the first time and told the coaches he was a prop, they'd probably have sent him to the fourth team. I had meant it as a backhanded compliment to Young, who wasn't built like a classic South African prop, yet was so successful because he had guile. In South Africa, his physique would have immediately prejudiced coaches against him. I had clumsily tried to praise him for becoming a difficult opponent and Wallaby stalwart in spite of his non-prop-like build. Those South African quotes were twisted by the Aussie media, and received wide play during that week.

It gave the Aussies a little more motivation, but the reason we lost had little to do with the Young comment. It simply came down to a flat performance. Of course I was unhappy, but, after analysing the game, I could see we were just off the pace physically, and I knew that by the time the Wallabies arrived in Johannesburg, we'd be fully recovered and far more dangerous.

Part of my plan all along had been to give some of the fringe players a game against Australia at Ellis Park, knowing that I wanted my 'first team' to start the Tri-Nations the weekend after the Mandela Plate return test. Not for a second did it mean that I went into the match believing we couldn't win, or wanting to concede defeat. I was confident that any team I put out from my squad of 30-odd players would be good enough to beat Australia on home soil.

So, when I drew up the squad, it contained nine black players – six guys starting, and three more on the bench. I didn't even think about it in those terms, although the significance of so many black players in the team wasn't lost on me. I was proud that I was able to select those players, which was the point I'd tried to make a few weeks earlier in Port Elizabeth. I wasn't opposed to transformation, but I didn't want to be told who to pick and when.

Most of the media made a huge fuss about the racial make-up of the team, which was understandable with South Africa's history. But what I didn't enjoy was some sectors of the press insinuating that I'd decided to throw the match because of my selections. I guess their logic was that no Springbok team with nine black players could possibly beat Australia. If there weren't enough black players in a given team I was criticised, yet when I selected nine black players, the conservative elements of the press started questioning my intentions, and even my integrity. It was laughable, but also frustrating.

I called a meeting with referee Steve Walsh, as I was concerned about the impressions he might have drawn from some of the editorials. It was a sensitive meeting, as I wanted to explain to him that the Springboks would be playing to win and not to appease politicians, as had been suggested. I told Steve that if he'd read or heard that the Boks were chucking the match, it was nonsense and he should pay no attention to it. We were approaching the match just like any other test, and expected to beat Australia. He assured me it had never crossed his mind. It probably hadn't, which just shows the things we sometimes worry about in South Africa. I was addressing colour issues, whereas Walsh only saw rugby players.

It being a Mandela Plate test, the man himself attended the match. Nelson Mandela had famously worn François Pienaar's No. 6 jersey at the World Cup final in 1995 and had previously attended three Springbok matches. South Africa had won them all. We hoped we could maintain a perfect record for the great man.

Before the match, Madiba was introduced to both teams on the field, and afterwards we all walked back towards the changing rooms to make final match preparations. As we were about to file in, Madiba came up the tunnel in his golf cart. In a totally spontaneous move, he asked the driver to stop so he could speak to John and the players. His entourage of bodyguards, coupled with 22 players and the coaches, caused a bottleneck. And at the same time the Aussies were coming in from their warm-up. They had no way through all the bodies, and just stood there while Madiba addressed the Boks.

Madiba has an aura that you can't help but be touched by. The Aussie players were intimidated by his presence and by the situation. Madiba was speaking passionately to our team. It's not so much *what* he says, but *how* he says it that is important. When you hear his voice, you have to stop and listen. It's so genuine, so full of passion for life – and at that moment, for 'his boys' too – that it felt like he was part of the team. He loves being part of an occasion and the players loved having him there. I could see chests swelling with pride and determination. At the same time I looked at the faces of the Wallabies, and I sensed they were thinking: 'Oh, crikey, he's here again.' They were already beaten by the Madiba magic.

The Boks fired from the first whistle, and we played some of the best rugby of the year in the first half. We raced into a 20-3 lead after 21 minutes, and by the end of the third quarter we led 33-8. We should have had 50 points by then, but we'd wasted two or three golden opportunities. The Wallabies came back with a couple of late tries, but we won 33-20. We'd avenged Sydney, silenced critics and put ourselves in prime position for a good start to the Tri-Nations the following weekend.

19

Trouble with Markgraaff

As defending Tri-Nations champions, we had the luxury of starting with two home games. This gave us a small but vital advantage; it was up to us to use it. But as was becoming the norm, at least for me, rugby played second fiddle to off-the-field wrangling.

There was a power struggle playing out between the president, Brian van Rooyen, and the deputy president, André Markgraaff, who was also head of the SA Rugby technical committee. Although the matter didn't involve me directly, the Springboks are the flagship brand of SARU, and as such any infighting at board level, however small, has an impact on the Boks. The spat would ultimately lead to Markgraaff's resignation, and I got caught in the crossfire.

The details of the squabble centred on Van Rooyen's management style, which upset various people. I can't say whether his corporate governance skills were poor or not – all I know is that while he was president, I received decent support to do my job. He interfered occasionally, but generally I had his backing. So I wasn't unhappy with Van Rooyen, but I was with Markgraaff.

Ever since the tour to Britain and Ireland in 2004, when Markgraaff had tried to dictate to me at selection meetings and impose his coaching techniques, our relationship had soured. And he was still butting in as the Tri-Nations loomed. He would never confront me directly, instead sending messages via his acolytes to tell me how to do something. Whenever I questioned the message-bearer about why I should listen to Markgraaff, I was told that as head of the technical committee he was in charge of rugby.

I laughed it off. My contract said nothing about me reporting or answering to the head of any committee. I reported to the managing director of the company, and that was it. But André was under the impression that I had to consult him, and I never did, which bothered him. I simply didn't trust the man. He'd been in and out of South African rugby politics, aligning himself with one person one year and with another the next. He was a political survivor, and that didn't build trust.

The escalating spat between Markgraaff and Van Rooyen reached its pitch about a week before the start of the Tri-Nations. It followed a meeting in Stellenbosch between Markgraaff and some of his allies on how to oust Van Rooyen.

That same week I happened to mention to Van Rooyen that I was tired of receiving messages from Markgraaff about selection and tactics, as I didn't need to report to him. A few days later Markgraaff and I met, and I conveyed my feelings directly. He responded: 'But you're supposed to report to me, that's what the board has decided.' I told him I didn't care what the board had decided.

'My contract's quite simple. I don't deal with you, André. You're the deputy president. If you want to change the contract, that's up to you, but I deal with the managing director of the company.'

He didn't enjoy that. Markgraaff wanted to have the power, and I was not playing the game. By the time the squad arrived in Pretoria for the opening Tri-Nations test against the Wallabies, he was fuming. That week, in a selection meeting to decide on the touring squad for the away leg of the Tri-Nations, Markgraaff became rude and aggressive. He was completely out of order. He claimed to be in charge of SA Rugby and told me that if I didn't toe the line, I would be fired.

'André, you've had a chance to coach the Springboks and you wouldn't have accepted interference like this, so back off,' I told him. 'Things have changed; I would like to do it my way.' When André was coaching the Boks, he would change his team in the tunnel before the kick-off at a test match. At Griquas he would get 28 guys to warm up and tell them in the changing room who was starting. That might have worked for him and brought out the best in his players by keeping them on edge all the time, but it wasn't my style.

When I started as Bok coach, he was convenor of selectors and suggested bringing only 22 players to our first training squad in Bloemfontein. It worked, and I'll give him credit for that. All the guys who arrived knew they were in the 22, so there were no sideshows and personal battles to win places in the team. But as we went on, he tried to get me to keep players on edge by not telling them who was in or out. It didn't work for me or the players, and he became frustrated when I ignored him.

I think André felt I owed him because he was on the technical committee that had recommended me for the Bok job. Or, because he'd been fired in 1997, perhaps he was trying to vicariously complete his Bok coaching career through me. He wasn't afraid to tell people that it had been his call when the Boks did something well. I heard from many journalists that player X or Y was in the team because Markgraaff had spotted him and told me to select him. The funny thing was, when things went wrong, Markgraaff's name was never mentioned.

André loves rugby and had been good to me at times. I've mentioned our good working relationship when we were both assistants to Harry Viljoen. André genuinely wanted the Boks to do well, but I never wanted to be sucked into all his power plays. He also doesn't take 'no' very well. It's his way or no way.

Managing director Johan Prinsloo happened to be in the selection meeting as well, so when it ended I called him aside and said I would not be spoken to like that. I then met with Van Rooyen.

'I'm not prepared to be treated that way,' I told him. 'I don't care who says what – I don't report to Markgraaff. SA Rugby has a contract with me and we must stick to that.' So Van Rooyen told me to put it all in writing and promised he'd sort it out.

'List all your grievances and I'll take this up,' he said.

After the test at Loftus, Markgraaff confronted me at the team hotel. Van Rooyen had obviously had some words with him about his inter-ference. He demanded to know why Van Rooyen was on his case. 'You know why, and that's the way it is,' I responded.

So my agent Craig Livingstone and I drew up a list detailing Markgraaff's interference in tactics, attitude to selections and his constant badgering on issues relating to the Springbok team. I took the opportunity to raise other issues, such as the bonus payment for winning the Tri-Nations, and I asked for Markgraaff to be removed from his position.

And then my letter appeared in a newspaper. I didn't leak it, but Mark-graaff assumed I had. The story broke a few days before the All Black test in Cape Town, which followed the Wallabies test in Pretoria. I'd given the letter to Van Rooyen in person, so how it appeared in the press is a mystery to me. It seemed I was used as a pawn in the power struggle between Van Rooyen and Markgraaff. Soon after the details of my grievances went public, Markgraaff resigned, and Van Rooyen won that round of the battle. And I was the inadvertent messenger who had delivered the final blow to Markgraaff. SA Rugby politics can be dirty at times.

To this day, André thinks I had sold him down the river with the letter. I wasn't happy with his constant interfering, but I would never knowingly have stooped to stitching him up. But although I'd been used, I wasn't angry at the time. I was resentful towards André because this happened in a week leading up to a test match against the All Blacks. And he knew what a tough rugby assignment that was, requiring tremendous focus. He'd been in the same situation, yet I believed he was determined to undermine me and make my life as difficult as he could. I was beyond caring about his feelings at that point. We had a fallout because I drew a line in the sand and stood my ground, and he couldn't deal with it. We haven't been on speaking terms since.

In between all of this, I had test matches to prepare for. We'd come off beating the Wallabies at Ellis Park in the Mandela Plate match, and faced them at Loftus a week later, this time to begin defending our title. It was a tight match in stark contrast to the way we'd played the previous week. But the Wallabies were more acclimatised and prepared for this match. And if we were honest, the Ellis Park Mandela Plate test had not been the primary focus of their tour.

They led at the break, but our growing maturity as a team showed in the second half. We didn't panic and controlled the match, outscoring them 16-6 in the second half. Breyton scored a try, and André Pretorius landed a last-minute drop goal to settle the contest 22-16. Of personal significance for me was the fact that we'd beaten the Wallabies for a second successive week, something we'd never managed before. I knew that to bring home the World Cup we'd have to win at least three tough games in as many weeks. So, as a simulation, the following weekend's test against the All Blacks in Cape Town would be an acid test of our growth.

After all the off-field antics I wasn't feeling that great heading into the test at Newlands. It was a reasonably happy ground for the All Blacks, as they'd won their previous two tests against the Boks in Cape Town. Preparation had gone well, even though I'd been a little distracted.

When we came in off the field after the warm-up, baggage master Flippie Malakoane was in the changing room, preparing the players' jerseys. He is a very special oke. He's very loyal, and he loved being a part of the Boks. He had been with the Boks under Rudolf Straeuli, and was very experienced and excellent at his job. When you're in the changing room as a coach, you feed off the people around you, trying to get positive energy from wherever you can.

That day, as the players were about to arrive to make their final preparations, I asked Flippie, 'What do you think is going to happen today?' He never hesitated and replied, 'We will win today.' And I said, '*O ja*, Flips, you probably said the same thing to Rudolf too.' And after some consideration he smiled and said, 'Nah, I didn't. He never asked me.' His deadpan delivery made me chuckle and put me in a more positive frame of mind.

Early on in the match, Victor Matfield flattened Byron Kelleher with a tough tackle – the All Blacks claimed it was illegal. I've seen worse tackles than that on our boys go unpunished, so I wasn't too concerned about what they thought. We dominated the lineouts and held the edge at the scrum. Kelleher, who might still have been shaky, threw an intercept pass and Jean de Villiers scored our only try.

Although we led 13-0 midway through the half, New Zealand typically fought back to 13-all before Monty landed another penalty to give us the lead. He then added two more in the second half. Our defence was superb. We kept them down to a lone penalty to win 22-16, the exact score of the week before.

At that stage of my career we'd played the All Blacks three times and were 2-1 up. The game also marked a third consecutive week we'd won against two of the top teams in the world – a feat no Springbok team had achieved since Mallett's coaching days.

The away leg of the Tri-Nations would start in Perth – a good venue for the Boks against Australia. The Markgraaff issue had gone away with his resignation, and we were top of the Tri-Nations table, heading to a friendlier venue than normal. Suddenly life was good, whereas eight days earlier I'd been in a war with the deputy president of SA Rugby.

20

Uncharted territory

Perth has always been a good venue for the Boks. In the Tri-Nations, we had won there in 1998 and drawn in 2001 – and I was on both those tours. In 2004 we'd lost to a late Clyde Rathbone try, but then we'd gone on to win the Tri-Nations, so that loss had been diminished in our minds. Returning to the city didn't hold a great deal of fear for the players or me.

Also, coming off three consecutive wins against Australia and New Zealand, we were in great shape. Injuries hadn't harmed us much at all, and I thought we were playing better and better rugby. We were certainly as confident as ever. The Wallabies also didn't enjoy Perth as much as other venues. It was a long way from home for all of them, as the Western Force franchise hadn't yet been established, so it was practically an away game. From a Bok perspective, while you can never, ever write the Wallabies off, we believed it was a test we *should* win. The week after, we would play New Zealand in Dunedin – a test we believed we *could* win.

For once the build-up to the match was low-key and without incident. No emergency meetings, no political wrangling and no forced selections – just harmony. We prepared well and, as Perth is a little closer to South Africa than Sydney, there was less jet lag.

During the week all the coaches were hosted at a function at Boktown, the temporary village SA Rugby had erected for the 2003 World Cup. There are thousands of South African expats in Perth, and they really enjoyed coming out to meet us and to talk about rugby 'back home'. It was nice to meet them and also secure some support for the match.

The evening of the game was perfect, and during the warm-up Wallaby flyhalf Elton Flatley told coach Eddie Jones that his vision had suddenly blurred. He couldn't focus and wasn't feeling well. The Wallabies had to make a call, and with about 20 minutes to go, they withdrew him and called Adam Ashley-Cooper to the bench. He'd been sitting as a spectator in the stands. It caused a major backline reshuffle, with Matt Giteau having to play flyhalf, Morgan Turinui coming in at centre, and Rathbone moving from the bench to starting wing.

As expected, the Wallabies were still very good. In fact, we only won the match thanks to two long-range tries from Bryan Habana on Wallaby turnover ball. There was a bit of controversy surrounding the second try, which Monty appeared to have knocked on. But the previous year, Joe Rokocoko had scored from a knock-on and we'd lost by two points against the All Blacks. It happens, and sometimes it goes for you. It went for us that night, and we held on for a 22-19 win.

It was the Springboks' first away win over one of the four leading teams in the world since the 1999 World Cup. It felt wonderful. It's hard to believe, but it had been nearly six years since the Boks had beaten Australia, New Zealand, England or France on their patch. There was no doubt that winning those home games had given us momentum. And the fact that we'd beaten Australia and New Zealand before the Perth game meant we'd beaten top tier-one teams over three consecutive Saturdays. After Perth, we had won four in a row.

That's when people started realising we could win back-to-back Tri-Nations titles. I believe we played better in 2005 than in 2004, and we'd won the title in 2004. But our next stop was Dunedin, and Carisbrook is not the happiest hunting ground in Springbok history. But it was all on the line that week – not only the Tri-Nations title, but also the number one ranking in the world. If we beat the All Blacks, South Africa would go to the top of the IRB rankings for the first time since they were introduced. Considering that the team had been ranked seventh in the world when I took over 18 months earlier, we'd made incredible progress.

Dunedin is not a big city, but the people love their rugby. From the moment we arrived at the small airport, we were left in no doubt that we were in All Black country. Banners and posters celebrating the All Blacks were plastered all over, and when I walked down to the Octagon in the centre of town, every mannequin in every shop was wearing black. They're our greatest rivals, but you have to like the country for the way it loves rugby. I knew when the security guard at the hotel greeted me with, 'It's nice to have the Springboks back,' that he didn't mean in Dunedin. He meant 'back' as a force in world rugby.

The Springboks had not beaten the home team in Dunedin since 1921. In 2005, it was South Africa's seventh visit to the city, and we'd lost all previous encounters. We wanted to change that stat, so Henning Gericke drew up a list of all the Bok players who'd played at Carisbrook in a test and never won. We really focused on those guys; we put the match programmes up, listed their names, what their teams had been like and presented all the information to the players in a video.

Once our players understood the history, I told them that they could be the first Springbok team to win in Dunedin. They'd be the first to win back-to-back Tri-Nations, and a rare Springbok team indeed to win three consecutive tests against the All Blacks (the last time it happened was when the Boks won the last two tests in 1970 and the first test in 1976). We had beaten New Zealand at Ellis Park in 2004 and again at Newlands in 2005. Of course, the world number one ranking was on the line too. We had everything to play for in that match.

As Henning put it, the guys from the six previous teams to play in Dunedin were still in Chapter 1, but our group had the chance to become the first players in Chapter 2, by winning in the South Island city. The players understood the relevance and were stimulated by our approach.

Our presentation placed a lot of emphasis on respecting and understanding the haka, and how important it is to New Zealanders. We explained that 'Ka mate Ka mate' means ''Tis life, 'tis life, 'tis death, 'tis death', and how New Zealanders thought the haka was not the best they could've chosen, because it's about a guy who hid under the ground, and when he came out the war was over. In Maori custom, hiding under the ground was considered cowardly. We spent a lot of time explaining the haka and its tradition. And then, out of nowhere, the All Blacks changed the haka that week.

In doing so, I think the All Blacks inadvertently gained a small psychological advantage over us, as we'd prepared the players so well for *Ka mate*, and then they came with the new haka, *Kapo o Pango*. I saw the reaction on my players' faces on the field; they were confused, as they'd prepared all week to face the haka they finally understood, and now it was different!

I don't know what impact it had on our psyche, but after the match I told the players that it was a huge honour that New Zealand had chosen to unveil their new haka against the Springboks. It will go down as one of my rugby career highlights. New Zealand is one of the best rugby nations in the world, and to have them pay respect in such a way was special. It ranks right up there alongside George Gregan's 100th test, played against South Africa, and Stephen Larkham's 100th test, also against us.

Those are the events that make rugby special, and I was glad that we could be a part of those history-making occasions.

Unfortunately, despite the respect shown us with the new haka, there was nothing friendly when hostilities commenced. The game soon turned into a titanic struggle. The lead changed hands five times. Rokocoko scored from a charge-down, and then scored another after a few soft tackles. But we bounced back, Ricky Januarie at scrumhalf charging down and scoring on the stroke of halftime. Bryan Habana had scored to give us a 10-7 lead after Rokocoko's first try, but then they scored two tries in quick succession, running into a 21-10 lead.

A win looked to be slipping away until Ricky's piece of opportunism, which pulled us to within four points of the lead at halftime. We eventually put our noses in front with a Jaque Fourie try, after Ricky intercepted with 15 minutes to go. It was a slender three-point advantage, but we held the lead for the first time since the ninth minute.

Late in the first half, we'd lost Schalk to a bad cut in his mouth. It kept him off the field for the full 15 minutes he was permitted. He was playing out of his skin that night in one of his best games ever, and to lose him for 10 to 15 minutes was critical. It wasn't only the time he was off; it was the other five minutes it took for him to find his rhythm that was costly.

As the match wound down I considered putting Fourie du Preez on, but Ricky had enjoyed an outstanding evening and was still looking sharp as we entered the last 10 minutes. In hindsight I shouldn't have let sentiment get in the way and Fourie should've gone on to close out the match. He possessed a superior kicking game and could have done enough to keep the All Blacks pinned back.

The Kiwis kicked deep and Ricky fielded the ball in the right-hand corner. They pressurised him as he was trying to shift the balance to his left side so he could kick for touch, as he's left-footed. But the pressure was too intense, so he feigned left and went right. He was tackled but secured the ball, and Jean de Villiers came in to clear the ruck. Jean's touch-finder only travelled about 10 metres. Had Du Preez been on the field instead, he might have hoofed it 40 metres off either foot. Ricky had tried to run out of trouble.

From the ensuing lineout close to our try line, they drove and Keven Mealamu scored the winning try for a 31-27 victory. Had they been a further 25 to 30 metres up field, it wouldn't have happened.

The other factor in our loss was the way we'd defended the lineout. Joe van Niekerk, Schalk and Juan Smith were at the back of the line. We'd practised how we would contest that type of defensive lineout. A few minutes earlier Richie McCaw had executed a move where he'd run around the back of the line and they'd thrown the ball over the top.

In this lineout, he started the same run to the back of the lineout, and Joe followed him. But McCaw then checked and came back into his original position, where Mealamu threw to him. Joe was out of position and couldn't support Smith. Juan lost it with Joe because he could've contested the ball and at the very least disrupted their lineout. But with no support, Smith was helpless and they set up a nice drive. It showed the importance of experience, because we subsequently defended similar lineouts, and Juan Smith has become one of the best exponents at back-of-the-lineout play, because now each player understands his role. Joe had made an honest mistake that night.

As I sat there, helpless, in the coach's box, I could see the scenario unfolding even before the lineout. I didn't know exactly how it would play out, but I felt uneasy. One thing about the All Blacks is that they never make it comfortable; you're never in total command of a game. Their supporters make it even tougher in New Zealand. The All Blacks are a formidable team, which is why they were ranked as the best in the world for so long. I've never doubted we could win every time we played them, but I always knew it would be extremely tough.

Had I put Fourie du Preez on and he kicked us out of trouble, I would have looked great. But had we won the lineout, Ricky would have been man of the match and I'd have been praised for keeping him on. That's coaching for you. Piri Weepu swapped his jersey with Ricky that night. It was significant, because the All Blacks only swap jerseys with players they think are deserving of theirs.

I didn't think about it then, but the Dunedin defeat cost me more than the chance to coach a winning team in New Zealand – it cost me millions in earnings too.

My contract was structured in such a way that winning the Tri-Nations for a second time would have given me some hefty bonuses. I'm saying millions, because it would've had an impact on how much I would've been able to earn by going up to another salary scale. When I took the job, I started on much less than any other international coach had previously been paid. Nick Mallett and Rudolf Straeuli had had much bigger contracts. Mine was based on the principle of 'the better you do, the more we're going to look after you'.

But that didn't even enter my mind that night. Afterwards, All Black coach Graham Henry said some flattering things about how great it was that the Boks were 'back' and rekindling the rivalry of previous eras. It was a tough defeat to stomach, not because of anything the All Blacks did or said, but because we had come so close for a second year. Losing 31-27 was heartbreaking, but, ever the optimist, I still hoped we might win the Tri-Nations if the Aussies could beat the All Blacks in Auckland the following week.

At the after-match function I was very impressed by the way in which the New Zealanders treated their players and the respect they shared for the jersey. It was one of Tana Umaga's last matches in New Zealand, and John Graham, a former All Black, and Jock Hobbs, another former Kiwi great, thanked Tana at the reception. It was sincere and passionate. I thought how wonderful it would be if everyone in South African rugby put the game first and shared the same passion. We've got the players, but we need to have greater respect for what it means to be a Springbok. That night in Dunedin I realised there's a reason they get it right on the field – it's because they do so much extra off the field as well.

The following weekend, the Aussies raised expectations and ran the All Blacks close for a while, before losing in the end. I was back in Cape Town, shouting and screaming at the TV, hoping for an Aussie win to give us Tri-Nations victory. It was to no avail. Despite winning three out of four Tri-Nations matches, the title went to New Zealand, and we missed out on the number one ranking.

21

World Cup foundations

Despite the Boks not winning the title, I considered the Tri-Nations to have been a success. We'd won three out of four matches, which was South Africa's second best return in the competition in its 10 seasons. I was, of course, disappointed that we hadn't retained the title, but I could appreciate how much we'd grown as a team in the 20 months since I'd become coach.

By then my position as coach was entrenched until after the World Cup, which meant my planning was geared towards France 2007. When I'd come on board initially, my goal had been to restore pride to the Boks as feared opponents – to create a culture of winning again. By the end of 2004, when I knew I was in for the long haul, my attention turned to building a team with the potential to win the World Cup.

All through 2005 my belief grew that if I could keep a core group of players together for a further three years, then by the time the World Cup began we would be serious contenders. Crucial to securing the services of a central group of players was ensuring that they had contracts to keep them in the system for several more years. So, after the Tri-Nations I sat down with senior figures at SA Rugby in order to decide on a way of contracting the right players through to the end of 2007.

It is a tough business to contract players, as rugby is so abrasive on the body. Employers are understandably slow to hand out three-year contracts, as there is always the chance that players could earn salaries for months, and even years, if they sustain serious injuries and cannot play. On the other hand, players want security, knowing that they will be taken care of in the event of an injury. So it's a tough balancing act.

When I sat down with then president Brian van Rooyen and other members of the SA Rugby board, I wasn't even sure of the exact number of players I wanted to sign up. But I did know which names I wanted, though: John Smit, Schalk Burger, Victor Matfield, Bakkies Botha, Os du Randt, Fourie du Preez, Percy Montgomery and Bryan Habana were some of the players I desperately needed to keep in the system.

I submitted a list of 13 or 14 men, but members of the President's

Council, who represent the 14 provincial unions in South Africa, soon realised that the more players they could put on Springbok contracts, the better for the council's bottom line. The economic reality was that SA Rugby would subsidise the wages of their top Springboks.

It became a bit like horse-trading. If I put X forward, someone would ask me about Y and why he wasn't being considered for a contract. It was frustrating, but ultimately I wanted several key players, and if SA Rugby decided to contract more, that was fine by me. After weeks of debate we came up with a list of 33 contracted players, a number larger than I'd intended, but still better than a list of only 13 or 15 players.

The plan was structured in such a way that if a player didn't represent the Springboks within a certain time period, he would eventually fall off the list, which is what happened to guys such as De Wet Barry and Marius Joubert. It explains why, by the time the World Cup started, only 24 players were contracted to SA Rugby.

It was a fairly complicated system, as players have dual contracts in South Africa. Their provinces pay a percentage of their salaries, and SA Rugby pays them extra if they play for the Boks. Ideally SA Rugby should centrally contract all players, as they do in New Zealand, but economically it isn't feasible, considering how many professional players there are in South Africa.

During these negotiations, I was planning for an end-of-season tour, which would include Argentina, Wales and France. The Free State Cheetahs won the Currie Cup for only the second time in history, and several of their players made an impression on the selectors. We were taking a large squad over anyway, because, as ever, we were trying to strike a balance between resting key players and creating opportunities for new ones. Cheetahs' utility back Meyer Bosman, who scored the winning try in the Currie Cup final, and scrumhalf Michael Claassens both made the tour.

Argentina is one of the best places to tour, and I was looking forward to the challenge of playing the Pumas in their backyard. First stop was Buenos Aires, where the people are friendly and they eat red meat cooked over an Argentina-style braai, which makes them very popular with South Africans. But first we had a rugby game to play and, while I was happy to tour Argentina, I knew it would be a difficult match. Unfortunately the players didn't seem to realise it.

There was a strange mood in the camp at the beginning of the tour.

They were all friendly and happy among themselves, but they seemed almost too relaxed and a little blasé about turning up and beating the Pumas. I let it go during the first two training sessions of the week, which didn't look sharp. But eventually I couldn't take it any more, and I completely lost it.

'Guys,' I screamed at the team, because they were messing around, 'I'll tell you what's going to happen! You will lose on Saturday, because you think this is going to be an easy test match. Remember what I tell you today, because you all think I'm kidding.'

They were surprised by my outburst, and it had little immediate effect. But by halftime during the Argentina test, they suddenly woke up to the realisation that my words were coming true. In front of a packed Velez Sarsfield Stadium, we struggled in the first half and the Pumas led 20-16 at the break.

At halftime I was angry. 'I warned you, and you thought I was kidding!' I shouted at the team. 'I want you to look at the player on your left and the player on your right, because you're about to become the first group of Springboks to ever lose to Argentina.'

Immediately after halftime, Bolla Conradie broke around the side of the scrum, feeding Jaque Fourie, who scored under the crossbar. That shifted the momentum, and the players were much more focused after that. We ended up winning 34-23. It wasn't always pretty, but at least we scored 18 points in the second half. When the boys switched on, they had the ability to win from behind.

André Pretorius injured his ankle in the match, which ruled him out of the remainder of the tour. It meant that Bosman would have to play against Wales, even though bringing him on tour was intended to introduce him to test rugby slowly.

Jean de Villiers was involved in an unfortunate incident when he pushed wing Lucas Borges, not knowing that there was a 10-foot deep moat around the pitch. The Argentinian stumbled over the advertising hoarding and was about to plunge into the moat – an incident that could have caused serious injury – when Jean grabbed him by the ankles and hauled him back to safety.

Although it was an accident, Jean received a yellow card and was the target of hefty verbal abuse. Nevertheless, his quick reactions ultimately saved Borges from a potentially serious injury. Jean felt pretty bad about what had happened, because his intention was never to harm his opponent.

But that game concluded only the first phase of the tour. After playing the Pumas, we had a gap of two weeks before our next test against Wales. Our original plan was to give the guys a few days off in Buenos Aires after the Argentina test. However, Pumas coach Marcelo Loffreda, a good friend, suggested that we take the squad to Patagonia instead. We could have moved to Wales early, but it's a more expensive country, and Cardiff would not have been new for the players.

So we headed south to the town of Bariloche, a resort that offers skiing in winter and great golf in the region in summer. It's a stunningly beautiful place, located on the shore of Lake Nahuel Huapi, with the Andes looking down on the town from a distance. Most of the players had never seen snow before, and I told them that I didn't want to see them for the next three days. There were no planned activities and they were allowed to go out, drink local beer or wine, and let their hair down. Of course they had to remain responsible and mindful that there was still some serious rugby to come, but there were no restrictions.

My good friend Graham George and his wife were on tour and, after watching the game in Buenos Aires, they joined me in Bariloche. We played golf at some wonderful estates and visited the ski resorts. Although there was no skiing because the season had ended, there was still some snow. Every now and then I'd bump into rugby players building snowmen and having snowball fights. It may sound childish, but these were men who lived in a hot country where snow was something they only saw on TV.

One afternoon Graham and I were with a few other South Africans, enjoying a long lunch at one of the ski resorts. Naturally the lunch included quite a few beers, and a couple of bottles of very good Argentine wine. The transport we'd arranged was scheduled to leave, but we weren't concerned and decided we'd catch a taxi back to town later on. But when we left, we discovered that, because the ski season was over, these were scarce. There wasn't a taxi to be found.

In our slightly inebriated state we ambled up the road to try our luck at a hotel, but it, too, was closed for the summer. We found a lone security guard who was about to go off duty. He had a battered old Renault, and we asked him to give us a lift back to town. He wasn't that keen, but Graham eventually offered him enough money to make it worth his while.

I'm not sure it was worth *our* while, though. That drive downhill was one of the scariest journeys I've ever experienced. Allister Coetzee sat in the passenger seat, while four of us piled into the back. The old car screamed and shuddered down the hill, and it kept slipping out of gear. It was a terrifying descent, and I was convinced the end had come. But somehow we made it back into town in one piece and gratefully stumbled out of the car at our hotel.

It was an enjoyable few days off and everyone had a good time. But the serious business of winning test matches soon came into sharp focus. Wales and France awaited and, after such a good year, we were desperate to finish on a high.

We arrived in Wales without Pretorius, so the big story of the week was the inclusion of Bosman as the starting flyhalf. Having worked with him for a few weeks by then, I was convinced he had the attributes of a good test player. His size and versatility were positive attributes, while his obvious lack of experience, not only at test level but at all levels of the game, counted heavily against him.

Meyer played well, considering he'd only ever started one senior match and that he was partnered with an equally inexperienced Michael Claassens at scrumhalf. But all in all they both did well. We won the match 33-16, but we wasted so many scoring opportunities in the first half, it should have been a higher score.

Bryan Habana scored two tries, which took his tally to 12 for the season – a Springbok record. On the downside, Percy Montgomery was shown a red card when he received a second booking for a dangerous tackle on Welsh wing Shane Williams. On review the first yellow for a dangerous tackle on the same player was rescinded, which was good news, as it cleared Percy to play against France the following week.

The French leg of the tour was important, because it served as a reconnaissance mission for the Rugby World Cup. We planned our training programme and gained an understanding of the challenges that would be posed during a tour to France. I hadn't taken the team to France as senior coach, so it was a learning experience for me as well.

It was a worthwhile tour, despite our eventual defeat in the test. We played at the Stade de France in Paris, which provided the ideal opportunity to experience the atmosphere. We sat in the same changing room we would hopefully occupy two years later, and we got a feel for Paris and its rugby culture. In fact, before the game I told the team they needed to use the opportunity to stake a claim for a place in the World Cup squad. The team that started the match was largely the team that would later go to the World Cup.

Percy, Jaque Fourie, Jean de Villiers, Habana, Schalk Burger, Victor Matfield, Bakkies Botha, John Smit, CJ van der Linde and Os du Randt started that day, and all would be part of the 2007 squad. Albert van den Berg, Gary Botha and Danie Rossouw were on the bench in 2005, and all three would be part of our campaign in 2007.

France ran into a 15-0 lead after about 12 minutes, thanks to a long-range intercept try by Frederic Michalak, among other things. It was a poor start and really knocked the stuffing out of us. We tried hard to fight back, but eventually went down 26-20.

John Smit was cited for foul play after the match. He'd caught French captain Jerome Thion across the throat with an attempted tackle. It looked bad, but it hadn't been intentional. The French press went nuts, and there was talk that John would be banned for several months. I was worried because of the media hype, so I called Schalk Burger Sr, Schalk's dad, to see if he knew anyone who could help with the hearing.

While the rest of the squad returned to South Africa, John and I stayed behind for a few days to attend the hearing. Andy Marinos, SA Rugby's manager of national teams, had organised a lawyer from the Confederation of African Rugby. He was a nice bloke and spoke French, but I got the feeling he wasn't forceful enough, which is why I called Burger Sr. I wanted the best guy we could find.

Schalk knew a lawyer in London who did work for the Jordan Formula 1 team. He was unavailable at such short notice, but he put us in touch with another lawyer at another big firm. John received a six-week ban, which was pretty rough, but it could have been worse without our assertive legal council. I realised then that proper legal advice was vital, and that's why we later had some of the best lawyers on standby for hearings during the World Cup.

Accommodation provided another learning curve. On that 2005 tour, we stayed in Chantilly, a town about 40 kilometres outside Paris. We thought it would be a good venue for our preparations during the World Cup, but we quickly realised it was too far away from the city and its stadiums. Players need downtime and distractions and, while Chantilly would've been fine for a week, spending two months there during the World Cup would not have worked.

John and I returned to South Africa following some extra time during which we could dissect our season. It had been a satisfying year. With a bit more luck, we could have beaten the All Blacks in Dunedin. The only game we were never in contention for was the final test against France. What niggled at the back of my mind was that the players had been on the go for two full years. They were starting to tire. I sensed that 2006 might be tough, but I had absolutely no idea *how* tough.

PART V
THE YEAR FROM HELL
2006

22

Hung out to dry

When the 2006 schedule was proposed, I knew we were in for a tough year. But it was worse than I could have imagined, because off the field I was hit from all sides. Administrators, the media and sections of the public all had a go, and in the end I only just survived as Bok coach. The politicking behind the scenes was diabolical. I always knew that South African rugby was riddled with people who had no interest in the game, only in what they could siphon from it, but in 2006 many of them revealed their agendas openly. I never considered walking away from the job, but there were times when it didn't seem to be worth the stress and pressure on me or my family. But I loved being Bok coach, and I wasn't going to give some people the pleasure of resigning. Besides, I believed – and still do – that South Africa has the players to dominate world rugby.

The 2006 Springbok test programme was probably the most difficult ever scheduled, and as coach there was very little I could do about it. The Tri-Nations had been expanded, which meant six matches instead of four, and that included an extra one away from home. We also had two home tests against Scotland and one against France before the Tri-Nations. And then the end-of-year tour had been designed to replicate the centenary tour of the first Springboks in 1906, which meant a test against Ireland and two against England in consecutive weeks. Considering the Boks hadn't won at Twickenham since 1997, it was a real challenge. I also knew that by then I'd be resting key players in anticipation of the World Cup the following year. And all this was on the back of a Super Rugby competition that lasted two weeks longer, having been expanded from 12 to 14 teams.

Resting players is not a popular thing to do in South African rugby, because the public demands that the Springboks win every match. Of course we want to win every match as well, but the reality of professional sport is that sacrifices sometimes need to be made with an eye to the bigger picture. That doesn't mean we ever go out with the intention of losing; just that in terms of selection we might not choose our best combinations in the interest of greater goals.

But rugby issues were only part of a difficult year. Before the international season began, I'd been trying to gain some clarity on my contract, with a view to extending it beyond the World Cup. Obviously I wanted to stay in South Africa, but to do that I needed some clarity and security beyond 2007.

The media often made out that I was holding a gun to SARU's head and making unreasonable demands. But my request to re-look my contract had been on the board's agenda for three months before our first tests of the season in June.

From the beginning of 2006, through my agent Craig Livingstone, I'd requested that SARU look beyond the World Cup to let me know what their long-term plan was.

The board promised me faithfully that they would be able to give me an answer before the Springbok camp in May. But after the second test against Scotland, which was played in the middle of June, I still hadn't heard anything more.

They strung me along for months. National teams' manager Andy Marinos, under the board's instructions, told Craig, 'Look, I don't think it's going to be a problem; we just need to make sure we handle it the correct way.' So we left it at that.

But after the Scotland tests, I became slightly agitated, as we were still unbeaten at home after two and a half years, and I thought I'd done reasonably well. We had a 70 per cent win rate. We'd been transforming as a squad. We had done everything asked of us as a team. My key performance indicators had been near perfect. I was in a position of strength to negotiate whether they wanted me to stay or go. All I wanted to know was 'yes' or 'no', so that I could make alternative plans after the World Cup.

With the French test looming, I had another word with Craig, and he approached the board through Andy. News of my 'contract negotiations' leaked to some of the media, and the rumour mill geared into overdrive.

SARU did a strange thing then, and called an unscheduled press conference two days before the French test (our third of the year). An hour later, they cancelled it. That sent the media into a spin, speculating about my future and suggesting that I was holding SARU to ransom over my contract. Some reports even suggested that I'd called the presser.

In the meantime, the board had finally decided, in a meeting late that week, that my contract didn't actually fall under their jurisdiction.

This, after knowing about my request for more than three months! They decided that it was a matter for the President's Council. I was staggered. It felt like they were merely finding a cop-out so they wouldn't have to make a decision.

The thing that worried me was that the legal brains – and there are quite a few legally qualified people on the board – weren't aware of the fact that my contract wasn't under their jurisdiction. That seemed crazy, and it really scared me. President Oregan Hoskins and deputy president Koos Basson are both lawyers, and they didn't know that my contract discussions would not be decided by the board, but by the President's Council – after that length of time.

That was one problem. But there was another complication. I'd been headhunted by an agency in England to apply for the position of director of rugby with the Rugby Football Union (RFU). It added another sensitive dimension to my contract negotiations.

It happened while I was at the pre-season Bok camp in Bloemfontein and, looking back, it was very clever on the part of the RFU. They knew I was under contract and that I couldn't negotiate with anybody, as was stipulated in my contract. So all the agency asked was for me to apply. They weren't offering me anything, just making it clear that they were keen for me to throw my hat into the ring for the job.

Naturally I was flattered and somewhat interested, because my future after the World Cup was not secure. I went straight to the board and told them that I'd been asked to apply for the RFU position. I wanted my actions to be above board.

I said: 'I don't want to be unreasonable, but I've been approached about this job, and I want you to know first and not find out through someone else. It's not that I'm holding a gun to your head, but it's a good opportunity.' They seemed okay with it, even thanking me for being 'totally honest'.

Andy Marinos was also made aware of the situation. I even showed him the e-mails and a copy of the contract, which set out the job description and salary package.

I said to Andy: 'I want you, as the national teams' manager, to know that I'm not playing anybody off against anybody else. These guys approached me and said, "Would you consider it?"'

I didn't even know when the contract would commence. It wasn't stipulated in those early exchanges. It could have been post–World Cup, which would have been the only condition under which I would have taken the job. I was comfortable that I wasn't negotiating myself out of my Bok contract, because the new job would have commenced after the World Cup, once my contract with SARU had expired.

If the RFU had asked me to start the next day, I would have declined. Why would I accept the job while coaching one of the most successful teams in world rugby, a team I believed could win the World Cup? Why would I have walked away from that? It never entered my mind.

But it came back to bite me. The story that ended up in the media was that I'd been offered the RFU job, and was going to walk away as Bok coach unless SARU upped my contract. Someone had leaked that idea to the media. I was disappointed but not surprised, because it suited the board to ensure that I looked like the bad guy.

SARU then turned the whole thing against me and implied that I was holding them to ransom, and that I'd manipulated the media for my own objectives. They were saying I'd used journalist Mark Keohane to stir the pot, because a report on his website had mentioned that I had been approached by the RFU.

But Keohane knew about the RFU offer through his own contacts – he didn't hear about it from me. He also knew that SARU had to make a decision, so he kept asking questions about the matter in the routine pre-match press conference, which Marinos attended. The fact that Marinos was even there immediately got the media's tongues wagging, as it wasn't standard for the national teams' manager to attend a pre-test presser. A few journos took up the issue, asking: 'Why did you cancel the pre-France-test press conference? And Andy, why are you here on a Friday before a test match?' I just sat there and watched.

When I look back now, I was actually hung out to dry. Why on earth would I have called a press conference on a Friday to announce that my contract was not going to be renewed? It was insane.

SARU were not going to publicly acknowledge that my contract had been on their agenda for three months – or should have been – before they realised that the President's Council had to make the decision. And then, after all that, I had to go to the President's Council and explain myself. The council couldn't understand why I wanted to extend my contract, or why they had to make a decision in June 2006. They said they would decide after the World Cup. So I finally had an answer, but it had caused a huge amount of media hype and unnecessary conflict.

People have asked why I wanted to sort out my contract if it ran until the World Cup anyway, which is a fair question. But I wanted to know what SARU was thinking, because if they weren't going to keep me on, then I could start letting rugby people know that I was in the market post–World Cup.

The players also wanted to know who the coach was going to be in 2008. Remember, they'd come from a situation in South African rugby where coaches had changed so often. They wanted some indication of what might happen after the World Cup, as the identity of the coach has an effect on their livelihoods too. How do they know the next coach will pick them? How do they know if they're in his plans for the future?

I was also surprised at the resistance from SARU and the President's Council, because I hadn't even contemplated that they wouldn't want to extend my contract after the World Cup. At that stage my overall win rate was close to 70 per cent; we'd won the 2004 Tri-Nations; we were undefeated at home for two years; I'd been IRB Coach of the Year in 2004; and we'd had four guys nominated for IRB Player of the Year in 2004 and 2005. Transformation was going well, so I had little reason to doubt my credentials. Perhaps I was being naive, but it did reveal some of the agendas at headquarters.

When the RFU story emerged, sponsors' representatives from Sasol and Vodacom wanted to know what was happening. The reality is that, whether you're in business or in sport, people want an indication of what's going to happen to their contracts in two years' time. I'd had a meeting with the sponsors, and they wanted to know whether I was staying or going and what the succession plan was if I wasn't going to be around. They'd invested huge amounts of money in the Springboks and, although they weren't saying they wanted direct input, they did want to be kept abreast of what was going on.

The week after the French test, I was called to a lunch with SARU president Oregan Hoskins and the chairman of the board, Mpumelelo Tshume. We sat in a quiet little corner at the Wijnhuis restaurant in Cape Town, and they laid down the law.

They suggested that I had gone about things incorrectly to orchestrate the extension of my contract, which I thought was incredibly unfair. I must emphasise, they didn't *have* to extend it. They could have decided not to, and I would have moved on. They just didn't seem keen to make a decision either way.

It was a very uncomfortable lunch, because they asked about my connection with journalist Mark Keohane, and about why I'd used him 'to fan the fires around my contract negotiations'. The discussion got a bit heated, as I hadn't told Keohane anything; he'd put the pieces together himself. I said to them, 'Look, what are you trying to tell me?' That annoyed them, and Oregan said, 'What do you mean, *trying* to tell you?'

I could see that they thought I'd held a gun to their head and they were on the back foot.

But I was also suddenly in a weaker position after the French test, because it was the first time we'd lost at home. We had been 23-11 ahead, early in the second half, and ended up losing. After Brent Russell scored, the crowd turned around to look at the coach's box and gave me the thumbs-up. They were going mad. They were over the moon. From there on in, we went downhill.

During the game, De Wet Barry missed a tackle, and France scored. They scored again, and we lost 36-26. The same people who had given me the thumbs-up booed me on the way down to the changing room. They didn't only boo me; they flipping abused me. It was the Boks' first loss in two and a half years at home, and I got this kind of reaction at Newlands. I was shocked.

Barry had been recalled at inside centre, and we moved Wynand Olivier to outside centre because Jean de Villiers wasn't available and Jaque Fourie was injured. We had a tremendously inexperienced team against France, and the day before there had been this huge public furore over my contract.

Now I had to go and have lunch with the top brass. I thought – or perhaps hoped – that it would be a goodwill lunch. It wasn't. But the chairman of the board and the president said they still backed me. They said they were the ones fighting for me. I'll never forget what Regan said to me at that meeting: 'I can't promise you an extension on your contract, because I think that's unfair for me to do as president. It's got to go through the right channels. But I will promise you this: you will never lose your job until after the World Cup. You will stay coach until after the World Cup.'

I remembered those words well, because they were going to be said again eight months later in London.

23

The pressure mounts

Several incidents clouded the Springboks' performances over the next few months, over and above my contract negotiations saga, which in itself had a big impact on the team. I didn't fully appreciate the effect on the players at the time; it was something I only came to realise later.

One of the early problems from a rugby-playing perspective was that we lost talismanic flank Schalk Burger to a career-threatening injury. You don't just find another player with Schalk's qualities. It would be a similar problem for New Zealand if they had to replace Richie McCaw and Daniel Carter. Look at the way England struggled to replace Martin Johnson and Jonny Wilkinson. Players with their talents only come around every generation or so.

But even before losing Schalk, I had a feeling that we might be stagnating a little as a team. I don't think we played good rugby overall in 2006, and it started in the Scottish tests, where we never really went up a level in our performances.

And that was partly my fault, partly the schedule, and partly because the players were feeling the effects of a three-year cycle.

Scotland were tricky opponents first up. They were on a high. They'd come on well under coach Frank Hadden in the Six Nations. They'd also beaten England and France for the first time in years – there aren't too many teams that had accomplished that recently. So, for us, beating Scotland was the main objective; the way we played was secondary. We beat them twice in consecutive weekends to win the series, and it proved again what we were capable of. We'd beaten every major nation on home soil since 2004. But I think people had started to become a little arrogant and expected the Boks to turn up and whack Scotland on home turf.

Initially, press reports said that Scotland was going to be tough to beat, and that they might cause an upset. The week before, we had laboured to a 30-27 win over a World XV at Ellis Park, in a match riddled with penalties.

I'd be the first to agree that the Ellis Park game had been a poor spectacle, but the media read too much into this match and started writing us off against Scotland – even though we hadn't lost at home for two years.

We beat Scotland 36-16 in the first test, with many of our frontline players, such as Os du Randt, Victor Matfield, John Smit and Fourie du Preez, back in the team. The same journalists then said it was a poor Scottish team. Only a few days earlier they'd been predicting a Scottish upset. That was frustrating – I didn't think the media were being fair.

We won the second test with a slightly flattering 29-15 score and, while I admit it wasn't pretty at times, the result was good. As usual, though, it wasn't as straightforward as it seemed. I took some flak for the way we played, but wing André Snyman received most of the negative press.

We've always had small, tricky backs, but I wanted to experiment with a big, powerful guy like André. He'd done well at Leeds, and I thought it was worth giving him a go to see if he could add value. I offered him a six-month contract and asked him to come back to South Africa. He really worked hard and was a popular member of the squad. Unfortunately it didn't go André's way during the tests, and I realised that he wasn't better than the players I had been working with. I explained the situation to him, and said I didn't think I could see him in the squad at the World Cup. I made it clear I appreciated him taking the opportunity to come back, but it just hadn't worked out the way we would've liked. He took it reasonably well, considering the circumstances. I still don't feel bad about trying him out, and I think he enjoyed the chance to play for the Boks again – something he thought he'd never do after being dropped in 2003.

Although we scored five tries in the two tests, our approach was a bit conservative. It's hard to explain how the stagnation started, but the pressure of the job played a part, especially with all the off-field problems around my contract happening at the same time.

You begin to panic slightly, and you start wondering whether you're past your sell-by date. For the first time in my life I began to question my ability and decisions. Battling constant conspiracy theories also takes a toll, and eventually you start playing not to lose rather than playing to try to win.

That's not a good way to approach rugby. In your first year as coach you've got free rein and everyone backs you. When I look back now, in 2006 I probably coached a bit for survival. This approach rubs off on the players, whether you like it or not. They're not stupid, and they're also susceptible to the mood of the country via media reports.

They'd come off a gruelling Super 14, playing more games than they ever had before. They'd travelled more, and there seemed to be more injuries than before. Those were all contributing factors to our approach. But it starts from the top, and the coaching staff had to take the blame. I can't speak for Gert Smal and Allister Coetzee, my two assistant coaches, but from my perspective it was a bit of a survival approach. You just want to stay there until the World Cup.

How do you coach for survival; what's different? I don't know if you actually change anything, but there are subtle differences in your body language and in the way you talk to the team at halftime, or the way you talk to them before a game. You emphasise performance more, saying, 'C'mon boys, this is very important. We need to win this one.' You talk about this being 'the most important game'. It has an effect on the players, because they start noticing that you are in a mild panic, with doubts, and it rubs off on them.

In my first two years as coach, I was much calmer and more in control. I'd say, 'Listen, it doesn't matter; I'll take the pressure. You just go out there and play. That's why I picked you. Use the skills you have.' I still desperately wanted them to do it, but I communicated it differently. In 2006, they could see that it was a different guy standing in front of them in the changing room. The experienced players know the signs; they've seen many coaches come and go. In hindsight, it's easy for me to see it too.

During my very first week as Bok coach in 2004 in Bloemfontein, we lost seven players to injury in the first few days. But I wasn't fazed, and not once did I say, 'Oh, jeez, he's out.' Instead, my response was: 'It doesn't matter. We'll get another guy to come in and carry on.' That was because I had full faith in the replacement players; it didn't make any difference.

In my third year as coach, there was a lot of expectation to go up many levels. When we lost players to injury early in the season, it therefore became a case of, 'Oh, jeez, we've lost so-and-so. What do we do now?' Which was probably the worst thing for the team, because they could see that my attitude – instead of being carefree – was one of concern. The players knew the atmosphere wasn't the same, and it had an effect on them. I knew that when I brought a new guy in now, he'd be two years behind the player I had intended to use, and my agitation showed.

People might argue that my consistent selection policy had led to holes in my team when injury struck, because I'd not blooded enough players.

But I never doubted my selection policy, and I still don't. I think that a guy who has been there 35 times is always going to be better than a guy who comes in first time. You might have the odd exception, but the reality is that, over a long period of time, the guy who has the experience is going to win you more games. His impact on his teammates, and to an extent the psychological impact he has on the opposition, is much more meaningful in the scheme of things than the performance on any given day.

These issues were all unfolding on the practice ground and in the changing room. The French test was looming, I was embroiled in a public contract saga – and then we lost Schalk Burger.

It happened in the second test against Scotland in Port Elizabeth. Although I saw the knock he took, I didn't even know that Schalk was injured. From where I sat, it didn't look too bad, but John Smit was right next to him and was astounded that Schalk carried on playing.

The whistle went a second or two after Schalk's mistimed tackle. John carried on running, and he thought, 'Jeez, that's Schalk gone.' But he turned around and Schalk was getting up and jogging back to his mark. John was amazed. He said to me afterwards, 'It's unbelievable that the guy can get up and carry on as if everything is fine.' I'll never forget that.

We won the match, but I suspected something was not right, as Schalk hadn't had his usual impact in the second half of the game. When he changed into his number ones and walked outside, I asked him if he was okay. He replied: '*Ja*, fine. I'm going to have a beer now and relax.' His family has connections in the Eastern Cape, and he was going out with his dad and some family friends that night.

I didn't worry about it, as I assumed everything was fine. But when he came to me the next morning and said, 'Listen, I've got to tell you, I'm sore,' I realised something was wrong, because Schalk never tells people he's in pain. Never. I don't think he knows what a physio is. So when he complained of pain, I was very worried. On the aeroplane back to Cape Town, he sat behind me. He didn't move. He rested his head on the seat in front of him so he could prop his neck up. I knew something was very wrong, and he repeated, 'I can't move. I'm really sore.'

As soon as we landed, he went to the doctor. He was diagnosed with damaged vertebrae, and it was a career-threatening injury. It was a huge blow to us as a team, and an even bigger blow to him personally.

Losing Schalk was massive – he was averaging 21 tackles per test at that stage. People were raving about Richie McCaw's impact in 2006, and he was making 14 tackles per game on average. With Schalk, it's like having another half of a McCaw on the field. Losing him was a tremendous blow, although even I didn't realise the magnitude at the time.

Once I'd come to terms with the fact that he was no longer going to be part of our plans for the remainder of the year – at best – I became annoyed. I was annoyed because I knew how much we needed him, and that keeping him in the system for another season, in the year before the World Cup, would have added immense value.

If you consider that it was our second test of the season and we still had another 10 left, those were 10 lost opportunities for him to gain more test experience and to establish himself as one of the best flankers in world rugby.

I was further annoyed because I knew he could have been helped. He never wanted to play with a scrumcap and shoulder pads, although I'd tried to make him. But Schalk is such a tough guy and he sees things differently. He said that he felt too uncomfortable and got too hot in all that extra padding. Who knows whether protection would have prevented that injury; we'll never know.

I was also pissed off about the extent of the injury. I had hoped that Schalk would be off for only two weeks or so, because he's such a tough guy, but he got a second opinion and, by the time I heard about the full extent of the injury, the decision had been made to have the operation. I told my media manager that we'd better hold a press conference to announce the news of Schalk's injury, so that people could understand how serious it was. I also suspected that more such injuries could occur to the core group of Bok players if we weren't careful. I knew that Schalk's injury was a freak accident, but I had concerns for other players of a similar age who'd never had a break.

The Fourie du Preezs, Ricky Januaries, Jean de Villierses, Jaque Fouries, the Schalk Burgers, Jacques Cronjés, John Smits, Gary Bothas and Gurthro Steenkamps had all been part of that Under-21 side that had won the 2002 World Championships.

This freak accident happened in 2006. It wasn't a surprise to me, as no one had ever given those players an opportunity to develop. I'm talking about developing physically. Because of the skill levels they possessed, they played with older players from an early age. No one had ever thought to give them a break and say, 'Right, we need to invest in you over the next five years, because you're a great player.' They take better care of their players in New Zealand and England.

So, I had suspected for a while that it was just a matter of time before one or more of those players would be seriously injured. As luck would have it, it happened to the best player we had – the guy who made the biggest impact on the field. Ironically, we probably could have got through the Scottish series without him; it was during the France test and the Tri-Nations when Schalk would be missed the most.

There's no doubt in my mind that Schalk grew up with old-school rugby values, thanks to his father, who was a great player and a Springbok lock in the 1980s.

There's nothing wrong with those values. That's how I grew up as well. Schalk enjoys rugby, but he also enjoys the camaraderie. Wherever he goes, he has friends in the opposition teams. All Black flank Jerry Collins is a good friend, and other players, too, will come up to Schalk and greet him warmly. The Wallabies even tease Phil Waugh. His mates call him 'mini-Schalk', which he apparently doesn't enjoy.

The point I'm making is that Schalk has a great reputation. When he goes to Wellington, Collins and his mates will fetch him and he'll go and have a beer with their players. If he goes to France, French players arrive to take him out. It's the same in Ireland. That's how rugby used to be.

That's also just how Schalk is. I think he's probably the toughest guy I've ever coached – tough in terms of not showing any pain. In the Dunedin test against the All Blacks in 2005, he and André Pretorius collided. Schalk needed stitches in his mouth.

He went to the blood bin five minutes before halftime. When I went into the changing room to give the team talk during the break, Ricky Januarie had just scored from a charge-down kick, we were back in the test match and I wanted Schalk back on the field. But I thought we still had 10 minutes into the second half, as you're allowed 15 minutes in the blood bin.

However, as I walked into the changing-room area, the match-day doctor came to me and said, 'Schalk Burger must return to the field at the end of halftime.' I argued that Schalk still had 10 minutes of playing time before he had to return to the field. But the doctor said, 'No, if the blood replacement runs through the break, his 15 minutes are up.'

I went to the room where Bok medical man Dr Yusuf Hassan was stitching Schalk up. I said, 'Doc, he's gotta go, hey.'

The doc said, 'I'm not finished, Jake.'

'What do you mean, not finished?' I asked.

'He needs about 15 stitches outside his mouth, and at least 15 stitches inside.'

'Look, Doc,' I said, 'you've got to make a plan, pal, because he's got to go on – even if he goes on and bleeds and then comes off again. But he's got to go on, and you've got to make sure that you patch him up.'

Poor Schalk was just sitting there, and I turned to him and said, 'What do you want to do?'

He sort of mumbled something, got up, and the next thing he was in the tunnel running out onto the field. He had more than 15 stitches in his mouth, and during the second half he split the cut open even further. As I said, he's a tough bloke.

The amazing thing is that he played the whole of that second half without coming off. No more blood bins. He just wiped, wiped and wiped it off again.

At the final whistle, Jerry Collins ran up to him and swapped jerseys.

Piri Weepu swapped with Ricky Januarie and Collins swapped with Schalk. That shows you the respect the All Blacks have for Schalk in particular.

When you see that sort of thing, you understand what you have in him as a player. Admittedly, he's not the best gym-goer. True, he doesn't like stretching. Yes, he's a throwback to the amateur days. But he's only amateur in his values off the field – and I mean that in the best possible way.

When he's on the field, Schalk is as professional as you can get. And in 2006, it was a learning curve for me as a coach, because I was very hard on him; I thought that his work ethic wasn't good enough. But I've realised that maybe you have to treat Schalk a bit differently from the way you'd treat other players, because of the value he offers to the team and the way we play. This is of much greater relevance than him not stretching properly or not going to the gym and bench-pressing 180 kilograms.

But I knew he'd be an even better player if he did all those things too. And that's why I pushed him; I knew that if he could perfect the other elements, he'd be the best player in the world.

Ironically, I think Schalk's neck injury helped him come to the same realisation. Now, more than ever, he values the fact that rugby could have been taken away from him, and what a gift he has. He might never have played for South Africa again.

So we had to face France without Schalk, in addition to not having Bakkies Botha, as he'd injured himself in the Super 14 semi-final. Jaque Fourie pulled out with an injury during the week leading up to the test, and Jean de Villiers also failed a fitness test.

I decided to give Joe van Niekerk a go at openside flank, which I still think was worth a try. He did a good job, and the stats show that he got to a lot of breakdowns first, and made a lot of tackles. But, in that position, he isn't Schalk.

France had also brought their strongest possible team on tour, unlike the previous year, when they'd brought a lot of youngsters. This was a big match for them, and they rolled out the big guns in the hope of scoring a win in a one-off test.

This time they'd included giant lock and talismanic skipper Fabian Pelous, who had missed the tour in 2005. The other lock, Jerome Thion, had also missed the 2005 tour, as had flank Serge Betsen. But they were all in South Africa in 2006, with only one objective: to inflict our first home defeat since I'd become coach.

And, to compound our problems, there was the tragic death of Pieter de Villiers's brother. Pieter is a South African *boytjie* who has become one of the best props in the world, and arguably one of the best to ever play for France.

He still has a home in the Western Cape, where most of his family still live, so the death of his brother galvanised the French team. They really wanted to win for him, and for his family. Never underestimate the value of emotion in rugby.

So, here we were, playing France, with new combinations in so many positions. In retrospect, we weren't physical enough in all positions in terms of being able to take them on. Look at the backs they picked that day. Damien Traille played flyhalf. That guy's bigger than a lot of loose-forwards. With Yannick Jauzion at 12, and Florian Fritz at 13, they had a powerful set of backs. It was always going to be tough for us to physically match their backs, even though we had De Wet Barry back at centre.

Every test is tough, so I'm not trying to make excuses, because whatever team France puts out, you know you're in for a difficult afternoon. But

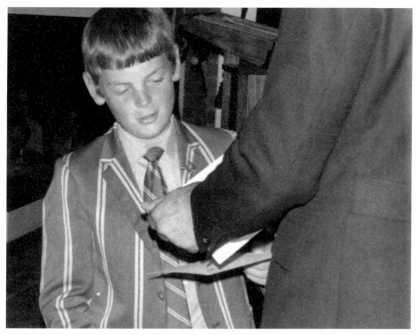

As a schoolboy at Lord Milner

First XV captain, Lord Milner, 1976

Jeppe Under-14A coach.
James Dalton is in the second row, second from right

With Debbie at my
1985 college graduation

With my brother Jon and father Johann

Enjoying South Africa's 1998 Tri-Nations victory
with Nick Mallett and Alan Solomons

Relaxing at Wentworth golf course with Gary Teichmann
and Nick Mallett during the Grand Slam tour, November 1998

The victorious Baby Boks after the
1999 Under-21 SANZAR/UAR final

With Harry Viljoen

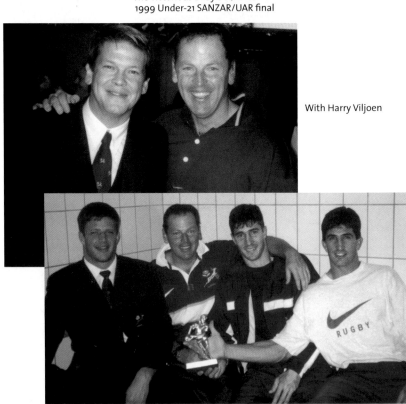

In the changing room with Bob Skinstad,
Pieter Rossouw and Henry Honiball

Celebrating the Baby Boks' victory in the
2002 IRB Under-21 World Cup with captain Clyde Rathbone

Assistant coaches Gert Smal (left) and Allister Coetzee were an
integral part of the Springbok set-up for the four years I was coach

Nelson Mandela, John Smit and me
with the Mandela Plate, 2005

The faithful Bok supporters:
Ellis Park, July 2005

Congratulations from Brian van Rooyen
after our victory over the All Blacks
at Newlands, August 2005

© Images24.co.za/Rapport/Sharief Jaffer

SARU president Oregan Hoskins (centre),
with vice-presidents Mike Stofile and Koos Basson

© Images24.co.za/Beeld/Jan Hamann

© AP Photo/Mark Baker

Andy Marinos, national teams' manager

With team physio, Clint Readhead

With Wesley and Clinton at the field
named after me at Jeppe Boys High

The Boks celebrating their victory over
the All Blacks at Rustenburg, September 2006

Percy Montgomery, Ricky Januarie and Schalk Burger congratulate
Pierre Spies on his try against England, June 2007

Coaching Ashwin Willemse, Luke Watson and Derick Hougaard,
prior to the Samoa test, June 2007

Jean de Villiers leaves the field injured during the Springboks' opening match of the 2007 Rugby World Cup

The tackle for which Schalk Burger was unfairly cited after South Africa's match against Samoa

Fourie du Preez, man of the match in the World Cup pool game against England

South Africa's outstanding lineout: Victor Matfield is lifted high

Bryan Habana on his way to scoring a
record-equalling eight tries in a World Cup

With technical advisor and good friend Eddie Jones. Eddie's
assistance during the World Cup campaign was invaluable

François Steyn evades England's
Jonny Wilkinson during the World Cup final

An injured Percy Montgomery kicks
one of four penalties during the final

Jubilation as the final whistle blows

President Thabo Mbeki, John Smit
and the Webb Ellis Trophy

Congratulating Bryan Habana

With Clinton, Wesley and Debbie
at our hotel after the World Cup final

Presenting the Webb Ellis Trophy to former president Nelson Mandela
at his residence in Houghton

The Springboks' victory parade, Cape Town

given the week I had personally endured, as well as the players we'd lost, I didn't have a great feeling about the game.

I remember strolling onto the Newlands pitch shortly before kick-off and walking over to French coach Bernard Laporte, who's a good friend of mine. I knew him before he became the French coach. We'd met when I was assistant coach to the Sharks in the Super 12, and he was coach at Stade Français. He came to see what the Sharks were up to at the time, we struck up a good rapport, and we've stayed in contact ever since. After he was appointed as French coach, I subsequently met up with him at various International Rugby Board conferences.

He struggles a bit with English, and I, of course, have almost no French. But somehow we seem to be able to understand each other through broken English.

So, on a great sunny Cape Town day, only an hour or so before kick-off, he said to me, 'Just hang in there. It'll be fine with the injuries, and don't worry about the nonsense in the press about your contract.'

He was actually staggered by the media reports about the contract saga. Clearly someone had been translating the South African newspaper reports for him.

He said, 'Look, if you want to come and coach in France, let me know. I'll organise you a French coaching job.'

When I walked back into the changing room, I realised we lived in different worlds. He was relaxed, even though he'd had a disastrous Six Nations. They'd even lost to Scotland. But you could see from his body language that he didn't have a worry in the world. He wasn't even worried about the result of that day's test match. Of course he wanted to win, but he had enough confidence in his position to know that losing was not going to cost him his job.

It made me realise how big a role such confidence played with the players. Laporte wasn't fazed. I don't think he even wore a tie. He had on an open-neck shirt with a jacket and pants. He stood there as if he was about to have a coffee or a glass of wine with some mates. I said something about the game, and he shrugged in a typically Gallic way, and said, 'Well, what must be must be. The players must get out and play today. We've done what we can for them.' I thought that was quite a different and refreshing way of approaching a test match. South African coaches have a sword hanging over their heads every Saturday.

It was a strange game, and one we somehow lost from a great position. But losing on home soil was always going to happen at some stage. You're not going to win every single game at home.

I would have preferred to approach an extended Tri-Nations with the confidence that would have come from beating France that day. I knew that we might see the return of some of our injured players for the Tri-Nations, so a little momentum gathered by beating France would have been welcome.

In this job, you have to be a realist. The home record had been great, yet it had to come to an end at some stage. But if I could have chosen a time to end our unbeaten streak, it would not have been that weekend, and simply because the SA Rugby board was not my biggest fan right then.

I would have loved it if the board and people at SARU could have understood that losing the record was inevitable. But I didn't get the feeling that they viewed it in that light at all. I felt that they had all jumped on the anti-Jake bandwagon as well. We had led 23-11, and ended up losing. I didn't coach the team to throw away a lead, and they didn't intend to lose, but on the day some things went wrong and we were punished to the full. On another day we might have got away with some of the mistakes that occurred.

Just to be clear: my request for clarity on my coaching future was still unresolved, and after the test I knew the landscape had changed. Had I won, there might have been some sympathy for me, but losing to France – and, worse, losing our cherished home record – left me in a weak position.

At that lunch with the president of SARU and the chairman of the board, I realised that we were not going to be moving forward. They were not going to make a decision. It was the same line they'd been trotting out for months: 'We'll tell you later on in the year.' I interpreted it as: 'You win the Tri-Nations, and we'll give you an extension.'

I thought to myself: Who could work in such an environment? They were buying time to see how the Boks progressed in the Tri-Nations. What sort of professional company operates on that basis? If we'd won the Tri-Nations, it would have been the second time in three years, but nothing was resolved. And then the situation really started to deteriorate.

24

A torturous tour

If someone had told me before the 2006 Tri-Nations that we'd suffer a record defeat at the hands of Australia, I'd never have believed them. In fact, I still can't quite fathom how we lost 49-0 in Brisbane. We'd had some off days as a team before, most notably in the Mandela Plate game in Sydney in 2005, and against England at Twickenham. But even though we were playing off a home loss to France, I was still pretty confident that we could grab an away win in the Tri-Nations.

Winning on the road in the southern hemisphere's premier tournament has always been difficult for South Africa. Nick Mallett's team managed it in 1998, and we won in Perth in 2005, to end a seven-year stretch between away victories. So I was under no illusions that winning away in 2006 would be tough. We also had an extra away game, due to the expansion of the tournament to six matches per team.

While that added an extra challenge, I saw it as another opportunity to win away from home and, had we not had such a blowout in Brisbane, we might have repeated the feat of the previous year by winning a game. But the fact that we came back to within two points of victory in Sydney three weeks after being thumped was probably a small achievement in itself.

The tour was beset with problems even before we left, and they became worse as the tour progressed. Injuries were obviously a factor throughout the campaign. But there was actually more going on behind the scenes that destabilised the team, particularly management issues.

We didn't have a team manager, for a start. The manager is traditionally a ceremonial position, which, if used properly, can have a very positive effect on a team. Look at Morné du Plessis with the Springboks in the 1995 World Cup, or Naas Botha with the SA Under-21s in 2002 and 2003.

I'd had my differences with the previous manager, Arthob Petersen, and when he and SARU ran into contractual differences, I can't say I was sorry to see the back of him. It was nothing major, but I didn't think he added value to the team, and I thought he sometimes overstepped his mandate. A touring rugby team is like a small army, so every member has to pull his or her weight – I don't think that was always the case with Arthob.

SARU couldn't – or wouldn't (I'm still not entirely sure which it was) – employ another manager for the away leg of the Tri-Nations tour, and it left me in a tight spot. A four-week tour to Australia and New Zealand is a long time, and a good team manager, who could've helped with media commitments and other logistical issues, would have been useful.

I wanted Naas Botha as the manager. He was a legendary Bok flyhalf and I'd successfully worked with him at Under-21 level. However, due to several factors that I'll discuss later, I wasn't allowed to have Botha on the management team.

So we went without a manager – the first ever Bok touring team who had no one in that position in a hundred years of touring. In addition, my strength and conditioning coach, Mark Steele, had signed a contract with the Sharks, as SARU would not commit to a national contract. It was another position that would remain vacant until the end of the year. In the meantime, fitness coach Professor Derik Coetzee took on that role as well.

After the defeat to France, we had nearly two weeks at home before heading to Australia. In that time, I had the awkward lunch with Hoskins and Tshume, and I also had a review meeting to assess my performance up to that point. These meetings are not unusual. At the end of every match-playing section, such as an incoming tour, or a Tri-Nations, a panel reviews me. Because of the personnel changes at SARU, I've had a different review committee every time I've had to appear at one, so I haven't had any consistency there. But although the members of the committee have tended to change, the process remains pretty much the same.

That particular review committee consisted of the president of SARU, Oregan Hoskins, the chairman of the board, Mpumelelo Tshume, SARU's human resources manager, Elna van Niekerk, national teams' manager Andy Marinos, the managing director, who at that point was Johan Prinsloo, and my personal mentor and Springbok selector, Ian McIntosh.

One of the things that came out of that meeting was that the media, and my way of handling them, needed to be reassessed. Without any discussion, the panel informed me that they'd tasked former South African cricket boss Ali Bacher to head a committee to help with media management. Bacher would work closely with the board and report to them.

I didn't really know what to make of it, but I wasn't particularly opposed to the idea, as I figured any help with the media would be welcome. Until that point I'd say I'd had a decent relationship with most of the journalists. I'd been voted as the most media-friendly sports personality by the Fourth Estate and television analysts in South Africa the year before. But after the publicity surrounding my contract, I got the feeling that there was some sharpening of the knives towards me in the press. If Bacher could help, I wasn't going to complain.

The panel asked how I'd feel about Bacher's involvement. I said: 'No problem; I buy into it.' They then told me that I needed to take a back seat with the media, to stop being so candid during media interviews. They emphasised that I needed to step back, and that SARU would 'sort out the media'. Again I didn't have a problem.

But in the next breath, the committee told me that my media manager for the Tri-Nations would be Vusi Kama. With all respect to Vusi, that was a strange decision, to say the least. Rayaan Adriaanse, who'd been doing the job, was more senior. And as far as I could tell, he had the respect of the media.

I didn't have a team manager, I was told to take a back seat with the media, and then I was given an inexperienced media manager. Their reasoning was that his skills needed to be developed by getting out of the office and touring with the team. I've got no problem with that. But, in the bigger scheme of things, they were saying my interaction with the media was a problem, and then they gave me a guy who, by their own admission, needed to 'be developed'. People more cynical than me might have seen that move as setting someone up to fail.

The committee also outlined a new set of media protocols. These guidelines stipulated that the media's attendance at Bok practices should be strictly controlled. They also emphasised that I shouldn't allow one-on-one interviews at any time, but only offer media opportunities at official press conferences. Players would be allowed to do one-on-ones at one presser per week, which had always been the case.

Oddly, they were outlining the media protocols and basically expecting me to enforce them. But surely that was the job of my media manager?

So they made up all these standard recommendations for going forward, which later came back to haunt me, because none of the review committee or SA Rugby board members were there to step in and talk to the media when the going got tough. I didn't even have a manager to take on that role.

That review committee meeting also dealt with rugby issues, such as where we could improve and where we'd gone wrong.

Despite the review committee changing personnel regularly, and despite its odd media directive, I always felt that the committee members supported me. In fact, the one thing that I enjoyed about the committee was that it had been very consistent – maybe not in terms of members, but in what they'd allowed me to build on.

I'm assigned a score on various issues, from results to transformation targets, and despite losing our first home test under my tenure, I received an 80 per cent overall score.

We'd blooded some new players, such as Wynand Olivier, who'd stepped up to test rugby smoothly. And while the committee felt I was doing well on transformation, it became clear that more needed to be done in that area.

I was told I needed to find more *ethnic* black players and bring them into the national set-up. SARU deputy president Koos Basson informed me that SARU vice-president Mike Stofile had issued a veiled warning that he could not keep on fighting against people who wanted to see more black players in the Bok team.

I said to Basson: 'Hang on, I've picked Breyton Paulse, Ashwin Willemse, Lawrence Sephaka, Tonderai Chavhanga, Gurthro Steenkamp, Ricky Januarie, Bolla Conradie, Hanyani Shimange, Solly Tyibilika, Tim Dlulane, Quinton Davids and Jongi Nokwe.'

Basson listened, and then said warningly: 'No, no. What Mr Stofile means is more ethnic black players.' I said I understood. I did point out that it was going to be difficult to find ethnic black players if there were hardly any playing in the Super 14.

At that stage, the only regular-choice black players were the Ndungane twins, Odwa and Akona, for the Sharks and Bulls respectively. Both are wings. Solly Tyibilika was in and out of the Sharks team, Lawrence Sephaka was on the fringes of the Cats (as they were known then), and Shimange was battling to get a place at the Stormers.

But I'd worked with Lawrence, Solly and Shimmy, so I wasn't concerned about selecting them again. As for finding new ethnic black players, though, there weren't a lot of guys to choose from.

The committee agreed with me. I pointed out that it was all very well putting expectations on me, but they also had to play fair and ask where the national coach was expected to find ethnic black players if they weren't coming through the provincial ranks.

They understood that. But the message was clear: We had to be more sensitive about picking ethnic black players. It was not an attack on me, and I appreciated that; but it was their mandate, which I'd bought into.

So I left for Australia feeling slightly vulnerable. I'd effectively been muzzled from speaking to the media, I had to select more black players, although no one could tell me where they were going to come from, and I had an inexperienced media officer, no team manager, and no strength and conditioning coach.

I ran into a mini-crisis literally hours after we arrived in Brisbane for our first Tri-Nations test. Vusi Kama informed the media that I was not available to speak to them. They became agitated, which I can understand, as they had pages to fill.

Although nothing of significance had happened, they still had editors to answer to and reports to file. But I wasn't allowed to speak to them; those were the rules as they'd been laid out to me.

I ran into some journalists in the hotel foyer, and they immediately started asking questions. I replied: 'I can't talk to you now; I've just landed. I can't talk to you. Those are the rules. I'll speak to you at a press conference tomorrow or the next day.'

They went berserk. They demanded to know who had made up those rules. I told them it came from the board. Then they demanded to know which board member it was. They said they were going to find out and see that that person was fired. It wasn't the last I'd hear of this, they told me; they were going to make a scene.

Rudolf Lake from *Rapport* mentioned something about having had people on the Golden Lions Board fired, and that he'd make it his mission to get the entire SA Rugby board fired.

He and other journalists then climbed on Tshume's case, saying they had 'stuff' on him – allegedly about his business operations – and that they were going to 'nail' him. They threatened that Tshume should be careful if he thought he could come in and change the way things happened at SA Rugby. If he did, he'd have a surprise coming. What could I say to that? I'm in Australia, and these guys are, understandably, angry with the board. I think I suggested that they take it up with SA Rugby.

They expressed disgust that their companies had spent a fortune to send them on tour to be close to the team and coach, and then they weren't allowed any access to either.

I stuck to the party line: 'That's what I was told. I was given that mandate from the board and from the review committee. From now on, that's the way it's going to be handled.'

In the 10 days following the French test, a lot of the rugby journalism had been very negative about my assistant coaches Gert Smal and Allister Coetzee. People were calling them 'yes-men'. The media had been critical about selection, tactics – everything. So the board wanted us coaches to take a step back and make sure we stayed out of the papers.

SA Rugby had asked me to assist with that, which I did. And from that day, from the Sunday after the French test, we went into a downward spiral in terms of press reports. My bosses' decision came back to bite me, because there was media chaos – the direct opposite of what they were trying to achieve with their new media directive.

The media began to threaten Vusi, and the poor guy, on his first Tri-Nations tour, was out of his depth. I was supposed to receive assistance with the media, and instead I was now embroiled in a mass battle – and the tour hadn't even started. In addition, the guy sent to deal with the media was being swamped, there was no team manager to speak to the press, and I was left to deal with the situation.

So I called a meeting with the media in the hotel, which technically was in breach of my mandate. But the situation was out of control, and we'd only been there a few hours. I tried to take a conciliatory tone. 'Listen chaps, we're not here to fight with you. Threatening Vusi is not going to help. The reality is, it's not Vusi. The review committee has instructed me, and it's been mandated by the board, that from now on I'll only do a couple of press conferences per week. That's the way it's going to be handled. You guys have had *carte blanche* to do what you want and say what you want. The board is tired of the negative press towards the Boks.'

I was doing what the board had instructed, blocking the journos from obtaining much access to the team, and to me. And because they couldn't get the access they wanted, they became more vocal, more vociferous and more scathing about the team. The gloves were off, and it seemed as if they were attacking us at every opportunity. At least, that's how we perceived it. I don't entirely blame the media for being pissed off, but I should have been given more protection and assistance from my employers.

Six months earlier I had been considered the most media-friendly personality in South Africa. How had it changed so suddenly? We'd played three tests and lost one, and I was effectively muzzled. It was bizarre, but it was the way it was.

25

In a tight corner

Preparations against Australia during the Tri-Nations in Brisbane went as well as can be expected under the circumstances. As you can gather, they were hardly ideal. Due to our injury problems and the fact that we'd been under-performing in terms of how we wanted to play, we selected two debutants. Looseforward Pierre Spies, selected at number 8, and wing Akona Ndungane were to be awarded their first test caps. Despite everything, I was optimistic.

I'm good mates with ex-Wallaby coach Eddie Jones, and I met him for coffee prior to the test. We chatted about rugby and kept the conversation fairly general, as he obviously still had links with the Australian camp.

But one thing he said to me was interesting. 'Jake, the Suncorp Stadium is a multiphase stadium, so it's very quick. The tempo of the game is much quicker than at any other stadium.'

He meant that it is a ground that's conducive to quick, flowing, running rugby, with as few scrums and lineouts as possible, which is exactly the way Australia like to play it. While I regard Eddie highly, I thought he was a bit off the mark with his deduction. 'Jeez, Eddy, how can you make a statement like that?' I thought. 'You already know what kind of game it's going to be between two teams playing on any given Saturday in the middle of July.' I didn't quite buy it. It's a stadium with four lines and grass.

But Eddie was spot-on. Australia played well and really sped the game up, and – it still hurts to say it – ended 49-0 winners.

No one was as hurt as the team. The players were devastated. I was devastated, and understandably the public was upset. Naturally I didn't get much sympathy from the media, and I didn't expect any either.

The way we played, we probably wouldn't have won the game. But there were a few key moments – and I was lambasted for saying this after the test – when referee Paul Honiss made some big calls that changed the flow of the game. He penalised Os du Randt for scrumming illegally when we were on the attack. It was a bad call. The score was 3-0 to Australia at that stage, and the match was still evenly balanced.

But from that penalty Australia won the lineout and scored: 10-0. Yes, we should have defended better, but we should never have been in that position. Australia should have been under pressure down the other end of the field.

Their second try came from a blatant knock-on by George Gregan. After that there was no way back into the game. The fact that we defended poorly and played as badly as I've seen any of my teams play, says it all.

Once they were two scores ahead and they could run the ball from anywhere, they grew in confidence and ran us ragged.

There's no doubt that 49-0, the second worst defeat in Bok history, was shocking. We fell so far behind we didn't even go for poles when we had some kickable opportunities. If we had taken every penalty kick for poles, maybe we would have got three, six or nine points. But the reality was, we never gave it any thought. We were so far behind, we wanted a try. By throwing the ball around wildly, we also exposed ourselves, and they scored a couple more soft tries because of our desperation.

Perhaps, in the bigger scheme of things, we should have taken those points and slowed the game down. Who knows, the statisticians might have felt losing 38-9 or something was better than 49-0, but either way it was a nightmare for us. We played poorly and were punished on the day.

In test rugby, the margins are minimal ... and at the sharp end of the international game mistakes are magnified hundreds of times. What you can get away with at lower levels of the sport, you can't get away with against teams such as Australia and New Zealand.

The French team had lost 46-3 to the All Blacks the year before (2005). In 2006, New Zealand beat them by 40 points during the end-of-year tour. Where does that come from? We beat the All Blacks 40-26 at Ellis Park in 2004, and we had been 10-0 down.

It happens when you play top teams. If they get it right and you're not on top of your game, it can get ugly quickly. In hindsight, the issues around my contract extension definitely had an effect on the team, and I take full responsibility for that.

While I still maintain it was handled poorly and never should have been played out in the public domain like it was, it affected my players and team. And as coach, I can't shy away from that.

There's no doubt in my mind that in business and in sport, external pressures have an effect on your staff. They want and need to know what's happening. My future has an effect on their futures. It's their playing careers that are at stake, and whether we like it or not, lots of money comes into it.

John Smit, Os du Randt and Percy Montgomery were three players who wanted to know whether they would be required after I'd gone. Should they stay in South Africa? Would they be offered new contracts? Then there were young guys such as Pierre Spies and Chiliboy Ralepelle, who were with the squad for the first time. The last thing they needed was this ongoing war in the media. The coach was unsettled ... he was going to England ... no, he was staying ... or he could be fired ... They'd heard all sorts of rumours, and it had to impact on them.

Dale Granger wrote in the *Cape Argus* that I had travelled to England to see the RFU the week before we left for the Tri-Nations. I hadn't even been there. At that Brisbane meeting, I said: 'Dale, people think I was at Twickenham, but I was in my office reading your paper.' He apologised.

'Your apology's accepted,' I said. 'But 90 per cent of the public still believes I went to Twickenham. You're apologising to me and I accept it, but people out there believe that I've applied for an English job. I read that story in my office at the Sports Science building.'

The team was clearly destabilised, on top of a horrendous injury run and some players struggling with form. In hindsight, we were mentally just not in a state to compete properly.

The Sunday papers in South Africa caned me. *Rapport* led with the headline, 'Jake must go', while the *Sunday Times* version was, 'Now it's the Cry-Nations as Jake blames ref'.

Former Springbok scrumhalf Divan Serfontein told *Rapport*: 'That was the worst ever performance by a Springbok team.

'It was shocking. The faster White resigns the better. He has no clue what's going on, he must do the honourable thing and pack his bags.

'Jake has his favourite players and sticks with them whether they're the best or not. You can paint your face green and sing the national anthem at full volume, but if you're not the best, then you're not the best.' It was disappointing.

The *Sunday Times*'s view was: 'Jake White committed the cardinal sin of blaming the referee, and the absence of regular starting line-up players in his analysis of why his side lost by a humiliating score.'

And Frik du Preez, a man I'd tried to involve on a mentorship basis with the Boks, also let me have it in *Rapport*: 'It's a scandal. It's never nice to lose, but to lose like that was pathetic. The players don't pick themselves, so you can't blame them. Blame the coach. If I was Jake White I would resign.'

There are so many things we copy from other countries when it comes to rugby, but one thing we don't is the code of former players and their support of the team. You never hear an All Black speak badly about another All Black, and you never see a Wallaby talking badly about another Wallaby.

I suppose those former Boks were criticising the coach, and I'm not a former Bok, but it was awful for the team. Sadly, it's the South African way. The way some former players attacked us, you'd have sworn we'd been the worst team in the world for the previous two and a half years.

It was a pathetic loss, but so many other factors were at play.

Our Springbok code of conduct, which applies to all Springboks past and present, says that players will never put their own interests above the interests of the national team. It states that they will never bring the game and their team into disgrace; they'll wear the colours with dignity and pride. Sure, we lost badly, but some help from ex-players would have been far more useful. What I've tried to inculcate with this group of players is that, when they've finished playing, they shouldn't be sucked into becoming a rent-a-quote.

It's easy when you're retired from the game to have all the answers, but when you're playing, it's far more difficult. It's not fair to have a full go at a current Springbok, as the player cannot respond or defend himself.

I'm naturally an optimistic guy, and that test, and its aftermath, had some positive spin-offs. It helped me to get to know the players better, and also to understand how they responded to real pressure for the first time since I'd been in charge.

We had been very successful for two and a half years. And while I was looking at the players, they were looking at me to see how *I* handled it.

I couldn't attend the press conferences over the next week and shout, scream and perform and blame the players. The questions came: 'Don't you think the players dropped you?' and 'Don't you think you're too loyal to this group?'

Where did this 49-0 come from? I believe it came from left field, due to the fact that, for the first time since we'd been together as a group, there was a palpable sense of insecurity.

26

Knives out
in New Zealand

One of the good things about the Tri-Nations is that there is not a lot of time to dwell on what might have been. Brisbane was over, and we had six days to prepare for the All Blacks in Wellington. Nothing I could say was going to change the Brisbane result, and all we could do as a team was prepare for a tough challenge in New Zealand.

Even if we hadn't lost in Australia, our chances of winning in New Zealand were statistically slim. Since South Africa's return to international rugby in 1992, we'd only recorded one win in New Zealand in 13 attempts. Given our result in Brisbane and the Boks' record in New Zealand, it was easy for the media to jump on the bandwagon and write us off. It was a difficult point to argue against, but I believe that every time we take the field, we have a chance of winning. I'm also a realist, though, and given the mental battering we'd just taken, we faced a mountainous task. So all we could do was prepare and be as ready as we could.

During the week leading up to the test, I felt that the media overstepped the mark and resorted to bullying tactics. They knew we hadn't won in New Zealand in nine years, and also that, given our state and history, we didn't have much going for us. So they sharpened their swords and loaded their guns, waiting for us to fail again. They fed the negative hype back home, and the team was caught in the crosshairs.

I guess some sections of the media had already fired me in their editorial pages and employed a new coach, but that didn't bother me. I still had a contract until after the Rugby World Cup in 2007, and I had the backing of my bosses – until then, at least.

But I did feel there was an agenda to oust me, especially from *Rapport*. It got back to me that one of their reporters was going around telling people that he was going to get Jake White fired. It's sad when a guy thinks he wields so much power that he makes it personal. Deep down I was concerned, but I could never say to the players that we were looking down the barrel of a gun. I was optimistic, and thought: 'We played badly; let's put it behind us. Let's move on.'

It was important how I handled myself in front of the players and management. It was about how positive I could be. The players as a group had never been in that situation. We could lie down and die if we wanted, but that's not what the public expect from a Springbok team. South Africans would've been even more annoyed if the coach and the players had lain down and given up. The great thing in rugby is that every week you have a chance to redeem yourself.

But in Wellington I was in the firing line again, this time over the selection of flank Solly Tyibilika. Solly's selection had partly been a political decision, only because I'd been directed to be sensitive to selecting more ethnic black players. We'd just come off a 49-0 loss, and Solly had been with the squad for months, and always performed well for the Boks. I had no problem selecting him, and never ever thought that he would weaken the team. He was always going to play at some stage of the tour. We'd given Pierre Spies a go the week before, and it hadn't gone well. So I thought I'd give Solly an opportunity.

It's important to understand one thing: if I'd taken Solly on tour and not played him, it would have been a slap in the face for him and clearly a political game. He'd played five Springbok test matches before then, and the team had never lost. I know he had some problems at the Lions the following year, in 2007, and didn't pitch for training, but when I worked with Solly, I was nothing but impressed.

He trained hard. He wanted to be a Springbok. He was dedicated. He had a lot of talent and his teammates enjoyed him. Solly had a few limitations, but all players do. I didn't for a minute think he'd be a liability, although some of the media implied as much after his selection. The first question at the press conference to announce the team was: 'Is your back row balanced?' I knew what was coming.

I was quizzed throughout about whether I thought Solly was the best openside available, and why I had not brought in Western Province flank Luke Watson. Now, player selection is always a matter of debate, but Watson had never been part of my squad, whereas Solly had been there for two years. I pointed this out to the reporters.

My words were: 'Watson has never been part of our squad. What message would I be sending to Solly, who is doing the job here, when I bring in another flank from home? There is also the question of relationships with players that's important. Solly has been part of our set-up for over two years.

'I also have a responsibility towards transformation, and would send out the wrong message if I ignored Solly to make room for Luke.

'We live in a country where we have to be sensitive to transformation; that is a reality.'

Dale Granger then wrote a piece in the *Cape Argus* that Solly had only been selected because he was black. That was incorrect and insulting to Solly. And the story did some damage. SA Rugby were annoyed that I'd been quoted in the media, when they'd told me to stay out of it. It was an official press conference, which I had to attend. And besides, what I said and how it was interpreted were quite different. But the bosses who read the newspapers now had more ammunition with which to nail me, and more ammunition to argue that I'd lost the plot, which was all nonsense.

I was annoyed too, because board members were staying in the same hotel while this was going on. They never came to a media conference; never even came downstairs and said to the media: 'Hang on, chaps, let's understand this. Thank God we've got a coach who understands transformation, who's bought into transformation, who's been genuine about transformation and who's prepared to give players opportunities.'

Not one of them said a word. My only recourse was to send a letter to the managing director, which was what my contract stipulated I should do if I had a grievance. There were certain channels I had to follow, so I did. I asked my agent Craig Livingstone to write to the President's Council and the board, and make it clear to them that I was following my brief. The letter was leaked to the media – not by me, of course – adding more fuel to the fire.

The contents of the letter reminded the board that I had been instructed by a review committee to be more sensitive to ethnic black player selection. I suggested that they needed to stand by me on that decision. They couldn't now renege. In addition, I wanted them to openly tell the public how they'd directed me at that meeting to select more ethnic black players.

The response was a denial by the board that the meeting had ever taken place. They basically jumped on the bandwagon and left me out to dry. Again. And while this was going on, I was trying to prepare for a test match against the number one team in the world, at a stadium where they've been virtually invincible. This also had an effect on the team, and particularly on Solly. I called him into a one-on-one meeting to ascertain his state of mind and reassure him that I had full faith in him.

'Don't worry about what they say,' I said. 'You just concentrate on your job. You've been part of our squad, and you know I have faith in you. You were always going to play, so just get on with the job.'

I then sent him out to do one-on-ones with the media. I had nothing to hide, and nor did he.

I treat players with respect. You have to be sensitive to race in our country, and as Bok coach you have an obligation to your country to help with transformation. We live in a unique situation. But, more importantly, players are human, with sensitivities and feelings like any other person.

Transformation is sensitive, and the player is often the victim. When I deal with it, I think: How would I feel if it was my son? But I was set up to fail again, because I was misquoted. The same guy who apologised for saying I had gone to Twickenham when I had actually been in Cape Town stitched me up again. And the board had dropped me as well.

The TV broadcasters came to me and said they'd run the press conference again, as they had all of it on tape. They said they could prove that I'd been misquoted. SuperSport's Kobus Wiese and Hugh Bladen were very supportive during that period. 'This is not the way it should be,' they told me. 'You didn't put it like that.'

It was too late, though. The incorrect message had gone back to South Africa. Most of the negative press was thus based on a factually incorrect story written by Granger. One of the things I realised was that the journos on tour have a huge impact on perceptions at home. All the websites pick up on one story and build on it, and it often snowballs into a huge incident based on the wrong information.

By that point I didn't know what to do, as the situation had become ridiculous, and I was pretty isolated. My media manager was out of his depth, and it seemed that whatever I said was being misquoted or interpreted in a different way to how it was intended. There was no protection. I didn't want to be written up in the media, the board certainly didn't want me to be written up in the media, but I was on my own. I didn't know which way to turn any more. You go left, you're in trouble; you go right, you're in trouble.

I kept saying to myself: 'Focus on the rugby. Focus on the rugby. If there's a God, we'll get out of this one. We just have to be positive. The players want you to be positive.'

Captain John Smit was a rock. I confided in him a lot. The poor guy had to take the pressure from the coach, on top of his own pressures following two successive defeats.

Another controversial decision was to fly Butch James over to New Zealand to replace Jaco van der Westhuyzen at flyhalf. Jaco had had a nightmare game against Australia, and we needed to make a change at flyhalf. We had no Jean de Villiers at inside centre; he was injured. Wynand Olivier was playing at 12. He was doing well, but had very little experience at test level. And with Jaco battling for form, it was adding pressure to the backs on his outside.

Although we had Meyer Bosman on tour, he had only three caps; I wanted more experience. We had Monty, who could go to 10, but I preferred to leave him at fullback. The management discussed it, and we came to the conclusion that Butchy was the right option. He had more experience, and a bit more temperament than Jaco was displaying at that time.

It was unfortunate for Jaco, who had done well for me in 2004 and 2005. It was a tough decision to make, because I'd coached Jaco as an Under-21 player. When we won the Under-21 World Cup, we beat New Zealand in the final. Their team included Rico Gear, Chris Jack, Paul Tito, Carl Hayman, Doug Howlett and Ben Blair. And Jaco was the flyhalf. He was an excellent junior flyhalf, as he was also an athlete. He could run. He could kick out of hand and for poles. So, when I became Bok coach, I was prepared to make him my flyhalf and leave him there. He was playing for Leicester in the English Premiership when I recalled him to the Springboks.

He'd left South Africa after missing selection for the 2003 Rugby World Cup and becoming disillusioned. His form at Leicester was superb, and they were trying to renew his contract when I came knocking. But Jaco chose to return to play for the Boks, and he performed well at the beginning, even though his selection was continuously questioned. But then he took a club contract in Japan, and his standard of rugby slipped.

It was only natural that his form had dipped when he stepped onto the field in test matches. He was coming off a poor standard of rugby into test rugby, and the gap eventually became too wide to bridge. In Brisbane it became obvious that we couldn't persist with him any longer.

Initially I'd thought that by continuing to select Jaco it would build his confidence, and he would eventually turn the corner. I'd compared him to Australia's Stephen Larkham in many ways. Ex-Wallaby coach Rod McQueen was always asked, 'Is Larkham a flyhalf?' He got hauled over the coals at every test match Australia lost. 'Is Larkham really a 10?'

But then Larkham dropped the match-winning kick against the Springboks in the 1999 World Cup semi-final, and today coaching videos and training manuals use him as a shining example of the modern flyhalf.

But Jaco didn't kick on in the same way. I couldn't afford to put him in a test environment, knowing full well that I was blooding him for test rugby. It was the wrong way round. He should have been blooded for test rugby at provincial level.

I sat him down and told him that the gap was getting bigger and bigger, and that he needed to make some calls on his career. It was simple.

'You're going to have to come back and play Super 14 rugby, or you're going to get left behind.'

He agreed, but was very worried about the fact that he couldn't get out of his Japanese contract. (He did play Super 14 in 2007, but at fullback, which didn't help me. I needed to see Jaco playing flyhalf week after week, in the toughest provincial competition in the world.)

So we called Butch over to Wellington. At that point, you must remember, André Pretorius was still injured. There were probably other flyhalves in the country, but not the type I wanted. So Butch was risky, but I think ultimately a good call. He did very well in the test, considering his aeroplane had landed on the Tuesday night and he had had to overcome jet lag.

Butch has the kind of attitude I like in a player. He doesn't really get nervous or too worked up. He said, 'I'll just do the best that I can. I'll get out there and play.'

The test itself was another case of ifs and maybes. We scored inside 15 seconds through a Fourie du Preez charge-down try. They countered with four Dan Carter penalties, and just before halftime we had a penalty to make it 10-12. Percy missed the kick. They counter-attacked and kicked the ball deep into our 22. Fourie du Preez tried to clear but, instead of kicking the ball out, he tried for too much distance and they counter-attacked, leading to a Piri Weepu try. Fourie had had all day to kick it out. They ended up going into the changing room 19-7 ahead, as opposed to leading only 12-10.

All of a sudden, my team talk changed from the time I left my seat, when Monty was lining up to kick, to when the halftime whistle went. It changed by 180 degrees. I was mad. Fourie is a great player, and as a coach you've hopefully given the players all the tools to perform. And then they make a basic error and miss touch? It was a mistake that cost us dearly.

But it happens. Just as I was learning lessons about myself and about how I had to act in front of the players, about how I had to make sure that I didn't let my agitation affect them, this young group of players were learning lessons as well. Fourie had never been in a similar situation and made a mistake, which he subsequently learnt from. John Smit had never lost three games in a row as captain. He had never been as under the whip as he was during the 2006 Tri-Nations. These were all things we had to learn to handle. There was no book to refer to that had these answers. It's called gaining experience.

In the second half, Carter landed two early penalties, and Breyton Paulse scored from a great cross-field kick by Du Preez. But another poor kick, this time by the recalled James, led to another New Zealand try, and effectively ended the contest.

However, it was encouraging that most people, including the media, who watched and wrote about the test (or at least the ones who understood rugby), put things in perspective. They gave us some praise – limited praise, of course – and encouragement for the way we'd played.

The score wasn't that close in the end, but there were opportunities that we never took and they did. We made some costly mistakes, although defensively we were much better than the week before. There were positives, which people wrote about, and that also helped a bit.

The reaction was better, but we were still heading to Sydney to play Australia on the back of three straight losses. We weren't out of the downward spiral. We had a bye after the Wellington test, but had to stay in Sydney, as it wasn't practical to go home. The time leading up to the Sydney test was reasonably quiet by the standards of this particular tour, although the entire squad had a big meeting with Hoskins and Prinsloo.

We also welcomed Jean de Villiers and Juan Smith back from injury.

What was also nice during that week, which I think helped a bit, was that Hoskins stayed with us in New Zealand and in Sydney. As much as the results showed we were struggling, he was there and could see how we trained. He could sense the mood himself and get a feeling for what it was like. By living with us, he saw at first hand what an impact the negativity of the media and other outside influences was having on the team. I think that gave him an appreciation for the difficulties we faced. However, it was slightly disappointing that he never came out and said, 'Listen guys, as president I can't allow this any more.' Maybe I was hoping for too much, but I wanted a public show of support.

One night Hoskins, Prinsloo and Tshume (who'd only recently been appointed) called a meeting with the entire management, which took place in a boardroom – it was like a company AGM, and everyone was allowed a say. They asked all sorts of questions. What do you do? Are you happy? They were there to listen and ask how they could help. A lot of the meeting was directed towards the way things were being run.

Tshume was new, and he wanted to know who was who. Who was the physio? Who was the doctor? What were their requirements and job descriptions? The entire management team was there: the doc, the coaches, the physio, the PR lady, the baggage master. And they said, 'Right, here's the chairman of the board, and here's the president. Let's talk. What are we going to do?'

I'm glad that people were outspoken. Everybody agreed, saying: 'Listen chaps, this is ridiculous. We're not enjoying this any more. We need help here.'

It was very positive, and I know Prinsloo told the media after the meeting that whatever Jake wants, Jake would get. It was a nice quote, but of course things didn't quite work out as simply as that.

27

Os speaks up

Os du Randt doesn't say much, but when he speaks, people tend to listen. On a Tri-Nations tour during which we were missing many key players, Os, who is a mountain of a man both physically and in stature as a player, was a vital part of keeping the squad together. He was, and remains, an absolute icon of the game. He's also the most highly regarded prop of his generation.

But before our second match against Australia in Sydney, he was more valuable for his input off the field. I was under severe pressure, John Smit was under severe pressure, and young players such as Pierre Spies and Wynand Olivier were wondering if being a Springbok was all it was cracked up to be, given the circus the tour had been up till that point.

Os quietly helped maintain the core values of being a Bok, and showed by example what it meant to play in the green and gold. He did this by unexpectedly calling a team meeting of his own accord, after the match-day 22 had been announced. No one argued or questioned it. They all just turned up on time and waited for him to address them.

He stared at his teammates and said, 'Look, the past few weeks don't matter now. What's past is past. We've got to play for each other. Don't listen to all the negative media back home. Everyone is clever after the fact. Now it's time to do it ourselves.

'We're going to show the people back home that we can win, and prove them wrong.'

It was short and simple – no histrionics or battle metaphors. No tub-thumping or rallies to war. Just a few words delivered in measured tones. It galvanised the team.

I'm not a believer in motivating people merely to prove others wrong. I don't believe it's a remedy to becoming the best side in the world. Retreating into a laager and taking an 'us and them' approach was not how I wanted to coach. As I told the players, I believed that had been one of the biggest problems with South African rugby in the past. As long as we continued to close our doors and have crisis meetings in search of answers, we were not going to be the best.

But on that day, in that situation, it was the perfect approach. Os had obviously sensed it too, because he was never a man to head-bang the wall. He spoke from the heart, and the others listened. As a player he'd been there, and his teammates looked up to him.

We didn't win that game, but we should have. We lost 20-18. We came within four minutes of victory. There was a huge warm-up area at the back of the changing room under the stadium. The rest of the team dejectedly filed into the locker room after the match, but Os went to the warm-up area.

He sat there and sobbed his eyes out. Victory had been in the Boks' hands, and it was snatched away. It showed me how much it meant to him. There was a message in there for me.

Os was 34 years old. He'd played over 70 tests, won a World Cup, two Tri-Nations titles and a Currie Cup. Yet the hurt of losing a test match had never diminished, despite all his achievements in the game. If people outside of our group could've seen him, they'd appreciate that, despite scores of 49-0, no Springbok ever goes out to lose. And even the best of them hurt.

That's why I get angry when I read things like, 'Players didn't show commitment.' Just being on the field in a test requires extraordinary commitment and tremendous sacrifice to get there.

Os didn't join us for the post-match team meeting. We had to wait for him until he'd regrouped. He would come back in his own time. Os was very emotional.

It reminded me of why, when I got the coaching job, I had wanted Os back in the squad. Seeing his face before and after the game proved to me that I'd made the right decision in putting so much faith in him. He more than repaid me over four years, but I think that week he was amazing.

When I was appointed coach, one of the first things I did was to pay a visit to Os. I asked him, 'Would you consider coming back to play rugby?' At that stage he was on the fringes of the game, unfit after a serious knee injury.

There was a lot of speculation that he only wanted to come back for the money, but I can tell you that wasn't the only motivating factor. I'm sure income played a part, but to come back after his injury went far deeper than mere rands and cents.

He replied honestly. 'I'd really like to come back and play rugby again, and I'd love to be a Springbok again.'

The one regret he'd had as a player was that he was dropped as a

Springbok and never got the chance to fight for his place in the team again. He knew people would remember him as a World Cup winner, but also as a man who was dropped from the Springbok team. That actually killed him inside. That's why, if he made a proper and committed comeback to rugby, he was so determined to get back into the Bok team.

So I said to him, 'Look, Os, I'll be honest. If you put the effort in and you show me you want to make it, I'll give you a chance.'

He did. From the time I took over as coach, Os was a rock in my team, and that week in Sydney I gained even more respect for him – if that was possible.

As if it wasn't enough that I had problems on tour, I then heard from my wife that my son Clinton had taken abuse at school because of the Springboks' performances. Clinton played scrumhalf for the Under-15B side at school, and by all accounts he'd played well that weekend. He was under the impression he was going to be promoted to the A-side.

I phoned home to find out how it had gone. My missus said he'd played really well. He was quite excited. A lot of the dads had told Debbie that it was the best they'd seen him play in a long time.

A few days later, when I phoned home again from Sydney, Debbie said Clinton was very upset. I asked why, and she said, 'He just got in the car and burst into tears.' I asked, 'What's wrong now?' and she said he'd been dropped to the C-team.

After I spoke to Clinton, I found out that he wasn't upset because he'd been demoted – he was just using it as a cover-up for something else that had happened, so I wouldn't get upset. Eventually I dragged it out of him that one of the coaches at the school, who is also a parent, had made a sarcastic comment along the lines of, 'Why doesn't your dad sort out the Springboks instead of you worrying about which team you're in?'

That pissed me off. All this little oke was trying to do was play Under-15 rugby, and his life was becoming hell. You think: Is it worth it?

I said to Debbie, 'Phone the guy. I want to talk to him.' She told me to calm down. 'I want you to phone him,' I demanded. 'Or get me his number and I'll phone him, because this is not the way he should be talking to Clinton. He mustn't make sarcastic comments to Clinton about what's happening with the Springboks. If he's got a problem, he should phone me, and I'll explain it to him.'

In the end I didn't speak to the man, because Debbie talked me out of it. It was probably a good thing, as he might have gone to the newspapers, and it would've turned into a big scene.

I always knew that something like this could happen. I was prepared if the abuse was aimed at me and, although I knew that my family would also be fair game, it still hurts when you hear about it.

When SARU appointed me, I sat down with my wife and two sons and I said: 'I've seen this before. I've been with Nick [Mallett] and Harry [Viljoen]. And when I was involved in Transvaal, I saw how it affected Kitch [Christie]. Are you prepared for it?'

They said: 'You must take the job. You must do it.' I asked Wesley and Clinton: 'Are you sure you're going to understand if they give you a hard time at school?' They assured me they would.

You know what it's like. Everything they hear from the boys at school comes from the parents. Dads will make comments about Jake White and the Springboks, and it travels via the kids back to my kids at school.

It's a very difficult and public job, and it does have an effect on your family. That story about Clinton is an isolated incident and, although I'd briefed them, it was upsetting. The reality is that when it does happen, no matter how much you've spoken about it, it still has an effect on the family. It was difficult to deal with, especially as I was halfway around the world.

I've made a point of not getting involved with my boys' rugby, because I want to avoid giving anyone ammunition against them. Remember, I was a teacher and a school coach, so I had experience with interfering fathers, and it's a pain. Having the Springbok coach interfere would be even worse.

On match days I stand behind the poles, as I always did when I was a schoolboy coach. I still do – on my own.

Standing there puts things in perspective for me. How many future Springboks are going to be playing in the Under-15Bs at Bishops, and how many future Springboks are going to be playing in the Under-11As at Western Province Prep? Maybe one Springbok in the next 20 years will come out of this group – if you're lucky.

So, if you look at it from that angle, there's no point in getting upset. I always say to the dads when I'm at a game, 'Who won the Under-11A game between Bishops and Western Province Prep five years ago?' How important is it really in the bigger scheme of things? And yet dads treat it like a test match.

I'm not saying for one moment that we should ever lose the emotion. It's nice that masters and teachers and dads all get excited and are passionately involved. But when you've been through the mill after being on top of international rugby, you see things differently on a Saturday morning, standing next to a rugby field in Newlands.

I tried to remember that in Sydney.

28

Soul-searching

While the extra week was tough, as it made the tour that much longer, it did give us a chance to regroup before our next match, and before facing a reception back in South Africa.

The management had decided to give the players some time off, so that they could forget about rugby for a few days. I told them to go to the beach, surf, to go and see the sights in Sydney and have a few beers if they wanted to. They're adults, after all.

We based ourselves in Manley, which is a nice suburb by the sea with a good beach and a short ferry ride from the centre of Sydney. It's important to stress that giving the players time off was not a spur-of-the-moment decision in response to a crisis. Springbok tours are not planned on an ad hoc basis, and touring schedules are drawn up months, even years, in advance.

We had known we would have some time to kill months before heading off on the tour. And we planned to have three days off. Sometimes South Africans believe that punishing players will make them perform more consistently, but the idea was never to make the players run hills and do extra fitness drills. Maybe it works in certain situations, but this was not one of them.

Rugby is so scientific nowadays, we had planned exactly where we needed to put in the effort and in which week we would rest. We regrouped towards the end of that week, knowing that we had eight days to prepare. Having an extra day of preparation built in also made a difference, as it gave me one more day to put all the pieces together and do some more analysis. As far as the year had gone, preparations were about as good as they'd ever been.

Although we lost the test 20-18, thanks to a Mat Rogers try four minutes from the end of the match, I thought we played really well. Considering we were 10-0 down at halftime, and taking into account our last outing in Australia three weeks earlier, it was a credit to everybody that we stood up and showed courage and guts.

The result didn't go to plan, but we did everything except win that game. I knew that the reception back home was going to be heated, and with three matches to come, including two against an All Black side in the middle of a purple patch, we had a big month ahead.

This is not an excuse, but in 13 years of touring Australasia since 1993, we'd won four matches out of 31. In 1993 we beat Australia. In 1998 we beat both Australia and New Zealand, and in 2005 we beat Australia. That's it. It's not good; it's a desperate run of results, but it does put in perspective that it is a rare occurrence to win there. The 49-0 was the big difference, though.

Travelling back for the Tri-Nations home leg in South Africa, I took comfort in the fact that Australia hadn't won on our soil since 2000, and since 1992 had only beaten us twice in South Africa. It's not like they came over every year and whacked us either.

I always kept that in the back of my mind. As easy as it was to say we lost three in a row, there are many teams that go Down Under and lose every game. In 2006, Ireland toured there and lost three matches. England lost three. The year before, the British Lions had also lost three away games. I'm not suggesting that we should accept our poor record, but we mustn't lose track of the facts either.

Our first test at home was against the All Blacks at Loftus Versfeld – a field they enjoy. And New Zealand enjoys a very good record in South Africa. I don't think Loftus is a good ground for the Springboks. There is hype about the aura of Loftus, but I don't buy it. I think Loftus is good for the Bulls, but I don't think it's a good ground for South Africa.

A lot of non-Bulls players don't enjoy it. How many players from Western Province would enjoy Loftus? They've recently been hammered there, so it has a negative impact on their psyche. The Lions don't enjoy Loftus either. Maybe some of the Free-Staters enjoyed it after winning the 2005 Currie Cup final there, but there weren't many of them in the Bok squad. Only the Bulls players enjoy playing at home. Our test results at Loftus against the All Blacks also haven't been very good.

I know the All Blacks don't enjoy Ellis Park. In fact, no one enjoys it but the Boks. But I would think the All Blacks also dislike Loftus, because the atmosphere can be intimidating. The problem is it's intimidating for some of *our* players as well.

Ideally I'd like to see one venue for the Boks. Ellis Park would be my choice, but that's out of my hands. England are very good at Twickenham, and for four years they were nearly invincible there. I believe the Boks could build the same aura at Ellis Park.

The media and public had been relatively quiet in the build-up to the Loftus test, although there was a lot of talk about the All Blacks choosing their second-choice team. The media tried to make a story about how, if we lost to their B-team, it would be an even worse defeat than the one in Brisbane. But All Black coach Graham Henry, by his own admission, said, 'There's no such thing as an A- and B-team. We have two teams that can play on any given Saturday.'

Richie McCaw and Dan Carter were selected. That made it an A-team for me. The All Blacks, under Henry, often made 13 changes to their team. But the one consistency was McCaw and Carter. If they were out, New Zealand would be weaker, but they never were.

I didn't even worry about what the media were saying. The reality was, we were playing the All Blacks, and it's always a big test match. It was at Loftus in Pretoria. The Loftus crowd is passionate about rugby – perhaps the most passionate in South Africa. An All Black test in Pretoria is as big as it gets.

I refused to buy the B-team theory. In fact, it was more of a worry. They had nothing to lose; they were on a high and very confident. If it didn't go well, they had another chance the following week in Rustenburg. We were in a four-match losing streak; all the pressure was on us.

I just tried to focus on the job at hand and on what was important for the team.

I'd brought in prop BJ Botha, SA Under-21 skipper Chiliboy Ralepelle, and scrumhalf Ruan Pienaar onto the bench from the team that lost in Australia, while Jean de Villiers made his first start of the Tri-Nations. The crowd started booing Monty late in the game. As they started, I took him off, and put Ruan Pienaar on at fullback, even though he is, firstly, a scrumhalf.

But Fourie du Preez was playing well, and Monty wasn't having his best afternoon. After the game, television pundits in particular questioned my decision to play Ruan out of position, among them Joost van der Westhuizen, who criticised me for playing him at fullback.

I found that quite odd, as Joost had played on the wing in one of his early tests against England, and he ended up becoming South Africa's greatest scrumhalf.

Joost was big, strong and quick. Exactly like Ruan. I felt we needed him on the field to give him an opportunity to play test rugby. It was no different to what had happened to Joost. Who knows, maybe Ruan will become an 89-test scrumhalf like Joost over the next decade. And then people will say, 'Thank God he was introduced into international rugby at a young age.' Just shows you how people can see things so differently.

Our preparations were disrupted, though, with the late withdrawal of Juan Smith and Joe van Niekerk, so I recalled Pierre Spies for the first time since Brisbane.

We started the test brilliantly, going 11-3 up and looking good. But then, in the 10 to 15 minutes on either side of halftime, we fell apart and they ran us ragged. I couldn't work it out. I got the feeling that we were dead on our feet. My only answer – and this is only a perception – is that the format of the tournament had drained us.

The schedule was a complete and utter disaster. We had three away games, which included hanging around for a week between the second and third matches of the away leg. We were away for five weeks. We then came home and had a three-week break before the All Blacks at Loftus, followed by two more tests – three tests in consecutive weeks.

It wasn't conducive to us finding any rhythm either. We looked exhausted in that game. It was the first time we'd lost to New Zealand in South Africa since I'd become coach. Five losses in a row, we were only one loss away from equalling the Boks' worst ever run of defeats. The All Blacks had also extended their winning streak to 15 matches, and we had another contest with this old enemy the following week in Rustenburg.

The pressure mounted. I stopped listening to and reading the media reports that week, but I subsequently learnt that the popular opinion was that I would be sacked if we didn't win at the Royal Bafokeng Stadium.

Despite the results and the problems, I still didn't feel like I was about to be fired. No one at SA Rugby had indicated to me that it would be the end of my Bok career if we didn't beat New Zealand the following week.

There might have been plots to that effect but, as far as I was concerned, I was Bok coach until after the World Cup in 2007. More importantly, though, I wanted a win. It suddenly felt like years since we'd tasted victory.

During the week leading up to the Rustenburg test, one of the most significant meetings in my career took place; maybe even one of the most significant meetings in the past 10 years of Springbok rugby.

SARU wanted to be seen to be doing something, so they called a meeting of all the former Bok coaches. It was a sort of think-tank and washout session. Hoskins and Tshume were probably a bit sick of hearing from me, and wanted some input from men who'd been where I was.

Initially there was resistance to the meeting from Rudolf Straeuli, and I think Nick Mallett, but they both attended, and I respect them for that. Harry Viljoen was there; Carel du Plessis and Ian McIntosh were also in attendance. The only ex-Bok coach who didn't come was André Markgraaff, but that was hardly a shock to me. He said he had another meeting and couldn't make it. Naas Botha also attended, as a former Bok captain.

I think it was the first time most of the former post-isolation Springbok coaches had been together in one room. I couldn't remember that ever happening in my time. The second very important thing was that, whatever doubts the president had about my capabilities, dissipated. Whatever negative things he'd heard about me as a coach, I think, disappeared after that meeting, because all those coaches said exactly what I'd been saying to him since he got the job at the beginning of the year.

'We will be inconsistent. We don't have structures in place. We worry about provincial teams first. We don't look after the players.' These were all gripes they had had as Springbok coaches, and they were concerns I'd expressed at various meetings. The former coaches spoke about three-year cycles and how the team hit the wall in its third year. They said that Hoskins and Tshume could hire any coach in the world and the situation would not change as long as the structures remained the same.

Harry Viljoen pointed out that two years earlier I'd been voted the best coach in the world by the International Rugby Board, and now we were discussing whether I was good enough to coach South Africa. He asked what had changed in 24 months.

He pointed out that we had the same players with more experience, who should be reaching their prime as a team. But we were losing. 'Why were we not competing?' he asked rhetorically. The answers were no different to when he, or Mallett, or Straeuli, were in charge.

Mallett and Straeuli concurred that structures were not conducive to supporting the coach, and that we could fix the symptom, but until we treated the causes, we'd always be stuck in this rut.

Hoskins and Tshume went away with something to think about and, while I didn't leave the meeting running and high-fiving everybody, I was pleased. Hopefully, with the input of these coaches, Tshume and Hoskins understood that I was not alone in expressing concerns about player protection and other issues.

Nick Mallett came up with ideas that he thought would be a way forward. I felt better that at least I wasn't going mad. People were seeing things the way I was seeing them. Now think about this for a second. Just about every week before a test I had some or other crisis meeting, or critical issue to contend with. What other coach in the world had so much outside pressure on him when trying to put a rugby team on the field?

And this meeting, while important, was yet another disruption in a test-match week. I was distracted in my job of preparing the team. And while Gert and Allister did a good job, they and the players noticed when I wasn't around. They knew I was fighting another fire or defending someone. It took its toll.

We had a test match to prepare for, though, and after the loss at Loftus, some decisions had to be made. Butch James had done well, having joined the tour in Wellington. But I thought André Pretorius had looked good in the last 15 minutes at Loftus. He appeared to be back to full fitness, and I was ready to give him a go.

Pierre Spies deserved another chance, but I recalled AJ Venter and Pedrie Wannenburg to team up with Spies in the back row. I wanted more bulk and more aggression.

The Loftus game worried me. As I've mentioned, we looked dead on our feet. I addressed the team one night and spelt it out for them. I told them that we had run out of numbers on defence, which was of huge concern to me, because there was nothing wrong with their fitness or their patterns.

I said I believed that it was partly an attitude problem. 'You've got to have an attitude to get back and scramble on defence. If you don't put yourself into positions to make tackles, you're not going to make them.

'I don't mind you missing tackles if you get into a position to make them. But if you're not getting into those positions when you should, then I start worrying, because I think you might be hiding.'

I was that honest with the players. I said: 'That is what disappoints me. Not the fact that they got through, but the fact that they didn't even have to work for their tries. They ran in from the halfway line and we ran out of numbers.'

The players, to their credit, never tried to give me excuses or blame someone else. They knew what I was saying to them. Considering that I was in charge of defence, I wanted to know how come we had run out of numbers on defence. I told them they were becoming lazy about getting up and putting themselves in line.

'I can read into that that people are now starting to hide, and it worries me. You can't hide here. The reality is, you need to stand up and put yourself in line. At any given time it's about how you cover for each other when you're on defence.'

They all agreed with that. And I said, 'Therefore, as a group, we're not helping each other.' The one thing you notice when the spiral's going down – like this one was – is that people tend to look out for themselves. It happens in business, too; it happens in any aspect of life. People cover themselves and only concentrate on their primary job if things are going badly. I felt this tendency had crept into our play, and understandably so.

But in rugby, unfortunately, it can't work like that. You can't worry only about protecting your own environment, such as the lineout, or scrum. You've got to make sure, in a team game, that you complement the guy next to you. Sure, you still focus on your key role, but you can't then say, 'As long as my key role is okay, I don't really care if the other guy's battling.'

And that was something we learnt about ourselves as a team in 2006. This was not the way it was supposed to be. We were, by our own code, always supposed to help each other, and always be there for each other through the difficult times. We were in the midst of difficult times, and therefore we had even more reason to go out of our way to help one another. That was the message I was trying to get through to them about defence.

I thought they showed a lot of immaturity as a group, but only because they'd never been in the same situation before. However, I must stress, no one had ever taught anyone about self-preservation in the Springbok set-up. They'd never had a coach for long enough to help them with that aspect. Usually, the way our systems work, coaches get fired and the players never have to answer to their peers or have to stand up and give reckoning in such a situation.

The coach leaves, a new guy comes in, and the player never goes through a necessary learning curve. What happened in those final two weeks of the Tri-Nations was vital, because it showed we had learnt some lessons.

At the end of the Tri-Nations, after we'd managed back-to-back wins, John Smit said: 'People won't appreciate how big those wins were for this group of players. One day when we're older, we'll look back and know how vital it was to us.'

29

Rustenburg redemption

Rustenburg was an odd choice as a test venue, but that's a story for the rugby politicians to discuss. We weren't doing cartwheels about playing the All Blacks at a venue that held no history for us, but in an odd way it worked in our favour. The ground held no history for the All Blacks either, and sending them out deep into the South African hinterland probably didn't suit them.

We'd only ever lost one home series to the All Blacks – in 1996 – and I wasn't about to become the coach that lost another. I was determined we should win this game.

The All Blacks were on a 15-match winning streak, only two short of the record held by the All Blacks of 1965–1970 and Mallett's Springbok team of 1997/98. And even though I didn't feel as if I was about to be fired, I did realise that a win wouldn't hurt my cause. There were a lot of things to play for.

All those aspects were in the mix at that test, but I didn't dwell on them.

The reality was, we prepared for that test as we would for any other test match. It was important to win it, just like it was important for us to have won in Sydney, Brisbane or Bloemfontein. We'd chatted about our defects, we'd worked on them and we'd prepared properly. Nothing was different from a 'normal' week.

Externally, the media might have been making a big thing about it, but internally it was business as usual, with the odd hiccup that occasionally plagues the build-up to a test. In 2006, though, we seemed to have a lot more of these than before.

One of the 'hiccups' in the week preceding the Rustenburg test was Fourie du Preez, who was sick with a stomach ailment. He had been one of the most consistent performers of the year, and had been named in the starting line-up. Ricky Januarie, our other scrumhalf, was sent back to his provincial team, the Lions, to play a Currie Cup match on the Friday night.

We'd picked Ruan Pienaar on the bench as reserve scrumhalf. The week before, Ruan had made his test debut off the bench, at fullback.

Fourie came to me on Friday afternoon at the captain's practice and said that he didn't feel that he could play, but he would sit on the bench. I was a little surprised and said, 'No, you're not sitting on the bench. You either play or you don't. You're not going to be half-in and half-out.'

I then asked logistics manager Mac Hendricks (who had become the unofficial team manager) to phone Ricky and put him on standby. Mac got hold of Ricky and told him to come across to Rustenburg on Saturday morning after he'd played his Currie Cup match on Friday night.

On the morning of the match I went to Fourie, and he wanted to know whether he was in or out.

I said, 'Ricky's on his way to us as I speak, so either you play or you go home.' This was not an attack on Fourie, but a decision he had to make. We were going through a tough patch as a team, and I needed my best players to front up. I had to make sure that, if he was genuine about being ill, then he wasn't going to play. If he was sick, he wasn't going to sit on the bench. Remember, match fees are paid to the entire match-day 22, as well as bonuses. If he was on the bench, he'd be paid; if he wasn't in the 22, he'd miss out on a lot of money.

I think it was a bloody wise thing I did, because he came to me a short while later and said, 'Okay, I'll play.'

I was happy Fourie was playing and clearly felt well enough to take the field, but I also felt bad for Ruan Pienaar. The day before, I had called Ruan and said, 'Listen, you're playing. Fourie's sick and Ricky's on his way home.' Ruan, whose father is ex-Springbok fullback Gysie, had already phoned his dad and told him that he was going to start.

It was disappointing for the Pienaar family, and for Gysie especially, as the 1981 Springboks who had toured New Zealand were having a reunion at the test. It was one of those tough decisions you have to make as a coach, and Ruan was desperately disappointed. Maybe I shouldn't have told him on the Friday that he'd start, but I genuinely thought Fourie was not going to play, and I wanted Ruan to be ready mentally.

Ricky also arrived, only to be told he wouldn't be part of the match 22, so there were a few disappointed guys around. But Ricky had played a Currie Cup game 18 hours earlier, so he probably wouldn't have been at the top of his game if he was required to come on.

Fourie's decision to play was an unbelievable turnaround, not only that morning, but in his season, perhaps. We ended up winning 21-20, and Fourie played very well. In fact, the next week against Australia at Ellis

Park he was man of the match after an outstanding performance. If he hadn't played in Rustenburg, he might not have got back into the team for the Australian game. He could have lost his Bok place had Ruan played and made the most of his chance.

Fourie ended up winning the SA Rugby Player of the Year award, and was nominated as one of the International Rugby Board's five players of the year.

I mention Fourie and this situation not because I didn't trust him and not because I want to make him look bad, but because it showed me that we were learning. He's a young man. When he was at high school at Affies, they won 99 per cent of their games. He played for the SA Under-21s, and they won the World Championship; he played for the Bulls, and they won far more than they lost. In his first two years with the Boks, we won more than we lost.

But, in mid-2006, we were losing. He'd never been in that situation and, on top of that, he wasn't feeling well, and he let it get the better of him. Had we been winning, maybe he would have ignored his stomach pain. I had to make a call as a coach. The easiest thing would have been to say, 'Okay, Fourie, you sit on the bench and Ruan will start.' But at the time I felt it was not the right call. I wanted to see whether Fourie could bite the bullet. And he did.

The Royal Bafokeng Stadium is a wonderful ground, a smooth and fast pitch with excellent facilities. The month before we played against the All Blacks, Manchester United had toured South Africa and played a match at the same venue. Sir Alex Ferguson had raved about the state of the pitch and the stadium in general.

There is an athletics track around the field, and at certain points the track came dangerously close to the edge of the playing area. I phoned André Watson, the national referees manager. He's massively experienced, and had refereed two World Cup finals. I told him that when we measured the field to its extremities, the tartan track was inches from the touchline. We were playing against an All Black team with explosive pace. Joe Rokocoko, Sitiveni Sivivatu and Mils Muliaina were all in the team.

I told Watson, 'It's dangerous. I want the field narrowed for safety reasons.' But I didn't want it narrowed for safety reasons at all; I wanted it narrowed so that there was less chance of them beating us with pace on the outside. The narrower the field, the less width they had to move in.

The reality was that I knew I wasn't going to get what I wanted. It was gamesmanship on my part. I got our team doctor to write a report outlining that, should any serious injuries happen if a player were tackled onto the track, we couldn't be held liable.

On Friday night the All Blacks were made aware of my complaint, and Graham Henry and his coaching staff had to go and inspect the field. He was irritated and declared: 'It's fine.'

I then made a show of reluctantly agreeing that it was safe, and signed off on the original field dimensions.

I'm convinced it helped us win, because they were unhappy about being dragged out there on a Friday night. I'd put some doubt in their minds and made them think about possible injuries. And it cast some doubt in the referee's mind too, and put more pressure on him. At test level you have to do some sly things occasionally. Every small advantage helps.

The match itself went off without any injuries, and no one was tackled onto the tartan track.

We made some good selections for that test. Pedrie Wannenburg played a huge game, Pierre Spies was excellent at openside and AJ Venter had a massive game. It was a risk to play Spies at openside, but it wasn't just about Pierre. It was about the big picture, and the fact that Schalk Burger would come back at some stage with Juan Smith. We were just trying to find a looseforward combination that would complement those absent players when I had a fully fit squad. As desperate as we were for a win, we needed to keep an eye on the future as well.

Bryan Habana also had a very good game; his best of the year. He scored an intercept try and was very good on defence and attack. I'd had a few words with Bryan. You've got to tighten the reins with him – not for any other reason than that he's young and rugby comes easy to him. He's very talented and has tons of natural pace and flair.

He hit the world stage like a superstar in his first year. But in 2006, opponents started working him out and marking him tightly, so it was always going to be a difficult season for him.

Captain John Smit played exceptionally well too. He'd been abused at Loftus the week before, which was disgraceful. It was good to see him respond with a mighty performance.

And Ruan Pienaar overcame the disappointment of missing out on starting by playing a vital role in our victory. He punted a penalty 60 metres downfield, and from the lineout we set up the drive that led to André Pretorius's match-winning penalty kick. André put that kick over with seven minutes left to play, giving us a one-point lead. I couldn't relax and there was a great deal of relief when the final whistle went.

I know many people said we deserved to win, but against the All Blacks there is no such thing as 'deserved'. We give them a great deal of respect.

But it went in our favour that Saturday. In the last move of the game, we were awarded a scrum, Pedrie picked the ball up from the base and charged. I thought he was going to pass it so that André or Ruan could kick it out. But he took contact and, had he not been in such a good body position, he could have been penalised for holding on. They would have had a penalty on the halfway line to win the match.

Thankfully it didn't happen, but it wasn't the best option by Pedrie. You've got to coach those players through times like that as well. He learnt a lesson and he got away with it, so it was easier to live with.

After the match some of the journalists were angry we'd won. I could see it in their body language, because they were hoping I'd be fired. They believed another loss would have been the final nail in my coffin. I found it disturbing that in our country, where rugby is such a popular and important sport, some people in the business of selling newspapers felt it was more important for the Springboks to lose because of an agenda they had against one man.

It was sad, but out of my hands.

And so on we went to Ellis Park, with more of a spring in our steps. We had a win, albeit a narrow one-pointer, and we were heading for our favourite ground against a Wallaby side that, historically, struggled in South Africa.

I mentioned earlier that the tournament wasn't fair because of the scheduling. The Wallabies were in the same boat, as they hadn't played for over a month, so they were rusty. We were heading into a third consecutive test. I'd love to know who signed off on the scheduling of the tournament.

I was upbeat that we could beat them; I always was. We had new belief as a group after beating the All Blacks. Much was made of the fact that their so-called B-side beat us in Pretoria, while very little was made of us beating their so-called A-side in Rustenburg. But the media actually got it right by not mentioning it, because I'd always maintained they didn't have an A- or B-team. Carter and McCaw played both tests; the other 13 positions were interchangeable.

I hoped our confidence would carry on into the Wallaby test match. And it did. I thought we played really well in that match. We never looked as if we were in trouble, and I felt we were going to win from the start. The 24-16 score line suggests a close game, and in some ways it was, but it was always ours to lose.

For once the build-up to the test was quiet. I selected JP Pietersen at fullback. I was a bit nervous about bringing him in, because he was still young and very raw. He was part of our group going into the Tri-Nations, and we always knew we wanted to see him at some stage. Results had conspired against us, but after a win it was time to throw him in.

JP wasn't outstanding, but on debut he tasted victory. He got to enjoy the feeling of beating Australia, which was exactly what we wanted for him. It's what we always wanted for all the players, but it was nice that someone on a debut test could come into a winning Bok team and experience that special feeling.

The most challenging and difficult Tri-Nations had come to an end, and we'd ended it on a high. There were times when it had been nearly unbearable, but those wins against the All Blacks and Australia reminded me of why I did the job.

Losing taught us a lot about ourselves as individuals and as a team. There would be more losses and more fires to extinguish before the year was out. But a year away from the World Cup, there was some silver lining around the dark clouds.

30

Selection posers and structural weaknesses

After the Tri-Nations I had a little time off, and it was a relief to get away from the media glare. I spent time with my family and forgot about rugby for a couple of weeks. But there wasn't much breathing space to kick back, as we had a huge end-of-year tour to prepare for. It was massive for a couple of reasons. First, it marked the centenary of the first Springbok tour to Britain and Ireland in 1906, led by Paul Roos. Second, the 2006 tour included a test against Six Nations champions Ireland, and, more significantly, two tests against England, whom we were scheduled to meet in the group phase of the 2007 World Cup.

Beating the reigning world champions in their own backyard was a priority for us, because less than a year from the tournament, we needed a psychological boost. The Boks hadn't won at Twickenham since 1997, so a win was vital.

Yet we had to weigh up all these things against the need to rest key players, with an eye to the all-important 2007 season. Given our results in the Tri-Nations, I wasn't exactly in a strong position to gain sympathy from the public, who wanted to see the Boks winning.

Planning for the tour had been going on for months, and resting players had been included in the plans ever since I got the job nearly three years earlier. Contrary to what some people might think, the planning for Bok tours is pretty detailed and well executed. There's always room for improvement, and obviously there are problems at times, but Bok tours are given a high priority – as they should.

Professor Tim Noakes was constantly telling the SARU bosses that players needed sufficient rest if we wanted to seriously contend for the world title. Ever since I'd been in charge, he'd been doing presentations and writing to SARU's top brass about player burnout and overuse injuries. Most of the time I think his observations fell on deaf ears, but in 2006 we managed to negotiate the resting of key contracted Springbok players during the Currie Cup.

Guys such as Victor Matfield, Fourie du Preez, Joe van Niekerk, John Smit, Os du Randt, Jean de Villiers, Jaque Fourie and Bryan Habana, among others, missed the Currie Cup. The idea was to rest most of them for the end-of-year tour as well.

The President's Council meets a few times a year. At their fourth-quarter meeting, team doctor Hassan gave a presentation on overuse and overuse injuries.

The council members were intrigued by the medical observations and, backed by Professor Noakes's constant badgering, they slowly bought into the idea of player rest.

There were certain tough decisions that had to be made, as one of the dilemmas we faced was that we'd come off an unsuccessful Tri-Nations campaign. It made it difficult to justify taking a 'B'-squad to Ireland and England. I'm not saying 'B' as in underrated, but a B-squad in that I would leave some of my key players at home.

But for once everyone seemed to be pulling in the same direction; the collective philosophy being that medical opinion, as well as the opinion of former Bok coaches – stemming from the Rustenburg meeting – and the coaching team agreed that we needed to think in the long term about the World Cup.

It wasn't about the past, and it wasn't entirely about the immediate future either. Fourie du Preez, Victor Matfield, Jaque Fourie, Bryan Habana, Percy Montgomery, Os du Randt, Bakkies Botha and Schalk Burger were all going to be left at home. Bakkies and Schalk were still injured, but even if they had been fit, they wouldn't have gone.

We ran the risk of not being up to par, but the feeling was that we had never really toured well at the end of the year over the last decade anyway. So it didn't seem to be such a bad thing to take some new players and test them. Therefore the planning started on the basis of who was going to stay at home, rather than whom we would take.

Captain John Smit came up for discussion. We thought we should rest him, but it would have been extremely unfair to send some raw, new players off to Lansdowne Road and Twickenham with a new captain as well. Besides, there weren't any outstanding candidates for captain if John wasn't selected. If we were going to give a youngster a chance, we needed to surround him with at least some experience and security. Without such senior players as Os, Victor, Schalk, Bakkies and Joe in the pack, we thought we couldn't take the captain out as well.

Our new strength and conditioning coach, Steve McIntyre, gave the senior guys who were left behind a training programme. He monitored them until the week of the Ireland test and only joined the tour then, as we didn't want to take the entire coaching staff and management away with no one to monitor the players who were left behind.

So Steve was around until their programme ended with us, which was at the end of the Irish week, and they then went back to their unions and trained there. The plan was always that, up to that date, we would monitor them full time at our Cape Town base.

I need to be clear here when I say 'the plan'. I don't just make a decision and then inform the board. It's all done through Andy Marinos, who is the manager of national teams. Andy is the sounding board. He'll have a flip chart in his office, and I'll draw things and discuss ideas and put arrows in and say, 'What do you think of this?' He then takes it to the board. This was something of an anomaly in my contract, as I'd initially reported to the chief executive. My contract stipulates that I deal with the managing director, but in 2006 SARU didn't have an MD.

Johan Prinsloo was only the acting MD, so he wasn't mandated to make a call. SARU then created the position of national teams' manager, and Andy was given the power to make those decisions.

According to my contract, the process still wasn't legal, but the legal department pointed out that national teams' issues had been ceded to the newly created manager. Apparently there was a clause that stipulated the MD could cede his powers to someone else.

I've nothing against Andy, but I wasn't entirely satisfied with this development, because if the pressure came on, they could always say that no one was mandated to execute certain requests. Yet, having said that, Andy, as an ex-international player and a guy who's been involved in South African rugby, has generally done a good job. But the system worked against him as well.

One of the frustrations I encountered, especially in 2006, was that Andy would take my requests to the board, and sell them to the men who hold the purse strings. Andy would do colourful presentations in PowerPoint, yet the board could just abdicate responsibility. On a few occasions they claimed, 'We didn't get the notes.' It made life tough.

But Andy had a job to do, and I continually talked to him about issues. We talked about selection, and I don't mean whether he agreed or not, but whether it could be done.

As a rugby guy, he'd say, 'Shit, are you sure?' if I approached him with an idea from left field. But when I sold him ideas about what happens in the changing room and how people see Os or Monty, it made it easier, because he'd been there as a player.

But it seemed that, between Andy and the board, or between Andy and the President's Council, the message didn't always go through clearly. And if it did, there was always a grey area about who would make the final call. In my opinion, those requests should have gone through an MD, but as we only had an acting MD, the system didn't really work.

That made 2006 even more difficult. It was an injury-laden year. It was a year in which the leadership of SARU changed – in other words, a new president and new council members. In your third year as Bok coach, you couldn't have packaged it any worse if you'd tried. As most people acknowledge, the third year is always the most difficult.

In selecting for the end-of-year tour, I used the same criteria I used every time I picked a team. I looked at the balance between youth and experience. I measured the balance between test caps and inexperience. I weighed up the balance between size and speed, skill and physical presence. I tried to ensure that the pack of forwards would be physical enough and skilful enough in the scrum, and competitive in the lineouts.

Nothing changes from week to week, even if the players do. I studied the transformation charter and my transformation requirements, and asked myself if we were being fair, whether we were giving opportunities to players from previously disadvantaged areas.

If I could tick all those boxes, then the team was balanced. For argument's sake, if I picked Breyton Paulse, Brent Russell, Ricky Januarie and André Pretorius in one backline, they might be skilful enough, and I could tick all those boxes. But they might not be physical enough on defence. So I'd complement those players with guys like Jaque Fourie and François Steyn, because they're bigger and more physical defenders.

With that in mind, I recalled Johan Ackermann, who offered physicality in the scrum. Ackermann filled an Os du Randt–type role. Os was seen as a tough guy who'd been around the block. He didn't stand back for people. We had to make sure that, in our pack, we had that sort of guy on the tour. Ackermann was initially brought in for the end-of-year tour, but after his performances I knew that, in the following year, we could use his physical presence again. AJ Venter, Bakkies Botha, Os and Ackermann are guys who are very similar – not in the way they play, but in the way they impose themselves on opposition players. All we do is make sure we have certain players who can do that, which allows guys like Pierre Spies the freedom to play his natural game. Not that Pierre doesn't have a physical presence – but he's young, and he'll become more assertive over time.

We picked the squad for its ability to physically stand up to the opposition. We knew that England was going to be as physical as they always were. We were determined not to go there and be bullied, as we'd been in the previous few years at Twickenham.

So, getting our choice of props right was essential. We decided to leave Eddie Andrews behind, as he needed to work on his strength. That created an opportunity for Deon Carstens to tour. We didn't really want to take CJ van der Linde, because he'd played a lot of rugby. But looking at the tightheads, we only had two who seemed capable of competing. If we had to start with Chiliboy Ralepelle, we had to make sure that we could surround him with at least some level of experience, strength and maturity. This is exactly what we did in the World XV game. We played CJ at tighthead, Deon at loosehead and Ackermann behind them, which gave Chiliboy a lot more confidence.

Of course selection is always difficult, and some players will miss out. Yet again the media went mad when Free State's Kabamba Floors was left out. Kabamba had played well in the Currie Cup, but he hadn't even started most of the games leading up to the semi-final and final, although, admittedly, he'd played really well in those two games.

But one of the things we've always done as a selection panel – for which I must compliment Ian McIntosh and Pieter Jooste – is to pick the team three weeks before the end of the Currie Cup or Super 14 competitions.

If you don't make your selection early, you get involved in emotional decisions. For argument's sake, if one guy scored all the points in the final, like Derick Hougaard or Willem de Waal, emotionally you'd feel compelled to take them on tour. In fact, that *was* the policy until the 2007 season, when the training squad was announced on the Saturday of the two Super 14 semi-finals.

That happened with Kabamba, and we decided, 'Well, he wasn't good enough three weeks ago and he wasn't in our planning then, so to change our minds now would be wrong.'

The squad was selected on the dynamics and balance of the team.

To pick Kabamba after the Currie Cup final would have been the wrong decision from a rugby point of view, because it would have been an emotional one. And the reaction to his omission proved how emotional it was. I received dozens of phone calls, telling me that I had to take Kabamba.

Later Pedrie Wannenburg was injured, and we didn't call up Kabamba as a replacement, because we still felt he couldn't fulfil the same role as Pedrie. I know that some people saw it as a statement by the selectors and the coach that they weren't prepared to budge, but it was purely a rugby decision, as he simply wasn't going to fit the role of the player who was injured, or fit into our original selection process.

In the past I've been blamed for taking black players on end-of-year tours and not giving them enough game time. So I was in a hell of a quandary. If I took Kabamba and didn't play him, the critics and politicians would question why he was taken at all. I'd been ticked off for that before at a review committee meeting, so for me it was a bit of a Catch-22 situation. At the same time, Kabamba had been picked to captain the SA Sevens team. I felt it would have been unfair on him if he were to sit around as the 28th member of the squad rather than play in the Dubai and George Sevens.

People might argue that it's more prestigious to be a full Springbok rather than a Sevens Bok, but in my heart I knew that he wasn't going to be in my starting team in those first two games. If Jacques Cronjé and Pierre Spies hadn't been injured in the first England test, perhaps Kabamba would not have been flown over. But that's how opportunities work in all sports. It had nothing to do with Kabamba, and everything to do with how it works in rugby for all players.

31

Managerial merry-go-round

During the Tri-Nations the team didn't have a manager, so I was determined that we wouldn't go on the end-of-year tour without one. At the meeting in Sydney, when Oregan Hoskins, Mpumelelo Tshume and Johan Prinsloo promised me that 'whatever I needed, I'd get', I assumed it meant a team manager of my choice. I was wrong.

A seemingly simple matter such as appointing a manager to the Springboks turned into a saga that would've kept Hollywood scriptwriters happy, which was in keeping with the entire year. When I was appointed Springbok coach, Arthob Petersen was appointed as manager. Having him as a member of the squad was part of the deal I had agreed to in accepting my job.

Arthob was a board member, and he was hoping to get back into the set-up for a second stint. He'd been manager under Nick Mallett, so he knew the ropes. He also enjoyed the job. The SARU hierarchy at the time, which included then president Brian van Rooyen, asked me if I had a problem with Arthob, and I said not at all.

Mr P and I generally got on well, although we had our differences. Sometimes he would interfere with team selection, which annoyed me. I'd show him the team sheet, and he would say, 'I don't think the president's going to be happy with this team.' When I asked why, he wouldn't give me an answer.

I felt this wasn't the way things should be done, and I told him so. He didn't enjoy that. He also knew that I was keen on an ex-Springbok as a manager, someone with international standing, such as Morné du Plessis, Naas Botha or HO de Villiers.

But besides that, we got on reasonably well. Arthob was very passionate about transformation and about giving black players opportunities, and you have to respect him for that. He probably tried to use his influence to manipulate team selection on occasion, but he was the manager and he showed an interest.

But when Hoskins became SARU president after a bitter battle with

Van Rooyen, he and the new board were uncomfortable with Mr P. One day early in the year, during a routine chat about the team, Hoskins said that they weren't quite sure how to handle the issue, but asked if I would have a problem if they replaced Mr P.

'No, not at all,' I replied. 'It's been well documented that I would like to bring in a manager who's a figurehead and an ex-Springbok.'

In principle, Hoskins was very happy with that. He even said he'd sort it out. They felt that Mr P was a Brian van Rooyen man, and they weren't comfortable having a guy in the system who wasn't part of their management philosophy. Andy Marinos wielded the axe. In hindsight, maybe I should have kept quiet. Maybe I should rather have backed Mr P.

Anyway, there were some contractual problems, which Mr P and SARU argued over. It didn't help my search for a new manager.

In March 2006, assistant coach Allister Coetzee phoned me from his home in Port Elizabeth and said, 'I've heard we're getting a new manager. It's a guy called Zola Yeye, who works at the SABC.' (In fact, he was eventually appointed only eight months later!)

I told Allister I had no clue about any appointments or who Yeye was, and Allister said he'd played with Yeye in the old non-white leagues back in the 1980s. I made a few enquiries and didn't find out much, other than that he worked for the SABC. I confronted Andy Marinos, and he denied that Yeye had been appointed as the new Bok manager. We'd already been through the incoming tours and Tri-Nations without a manager, despite my repeated enquiries about the position.

Andy assured me that the selection process was ongoing; he even showed me a shortlist and the candidates' CVs. Only towards the end of the search did the board make it clear to me that the position had to be filled by an ethnic black guy.

After the Tri-Nations, Andy asked me: 'How would you feel about Songezo Nayo as manager?' Songezo was the former deputy managing director of SA Rugby when Rian Oberholzer ran the show. He was a man I respected, and I thought it was a very good call. Songezo could be incredible. He knew the ins and outs, the presidents; it made perfect sense. He is liked and respected in the rugby world. The IRB knew him, and he was part of the panel that had appointed me, so I didn't have to worry about whether he thought I was good enough for the job.

SARU then conducted interviews with the candidates on the shortlist.

They underwent psychometric tests and, at the end of it, Songezo was way ahead. But then politics came into play, and the board refused to appoint him because they felt there was a conflict of interest, as he'd worked under Oberholzer. Surely they'd known that when they'd asked him to apply?

In the meantime, the Boks were due to assemble to go overseas when I received a call saying that Zola was back in contention for the manager's job. I asked Allister Coetzee: 'Is this the same guy you mentioned eight months ago?' He seemed to think it was. I asked Marinos, and he said, 'No, it's not Yeye. It's Yebe.'

I was now confused and thought it had to be someone else. But Allister was convinced it was Zola Yeye. I went back to Marinos and said, 'No, Andy, I'm hearing it's Yeye who has the job. It's the same guy I spoke to you about in March.'

It all seemed suspicious. Eight months earlier Yeye's name had cropped up, and after a difficult year and an apparent interviewing and selection process, he was back in the frame. My suspicions had nothing to do with Zola's credentials or personality; I didn't know much about him. They concerned how the process of choosing a manager had been conducted.

Our pre-tour camp ended on a Friday morning. The squad would all go home for the weekend, and reassemble on Monday before flying to London that Wednesday. On the Thursday night before we were due to fly home for the weekend, I received a call from acting MD Basil Haddad, asking me to wait at Johannesburg airport. Zola Yeye was flying in from Port Elizabeth, and SARU wanted me to meet him and introduce myself.

I said no. I was going home to see my family the next day; I wasn't going to hang around at the airport. It was also a sneaky piece of management by SARU. They'd told me that the manager would be appointed in consultation with the coach. So, if I met Yeye at the airport, they could say, 'Look, you met him; you were consulted.'

I didn't appreciate that, and I was pissed off. I suspected they had been lying to me. Eight months earlier I'd heard about Yeye and SARU denied he was going to be appointed. Now they wanted me to meet him.

I told Basil, 'I'm not going. I'm uncomfortable about meeting like this, and I don't think it's the way things should be done.' This must have got back to Hoskins and the President's Council. They were angry and implied that I was being anti-establishment.

But I wasn't; I was only against the process. Yeye had also made a lot of derogatory comments in the media about the team being *kak* during the Tri-Nations. So, as with everything, it wasn't simple. He had come out and voiced his opinions, and now they wanted me to jump for joy at his appointment and the way in which he'd been appointed.

The fact that he worked for the SABC was not perceived as a problem either. Yet, when I'd initially requested Naas Botha as manager, I was told he couldn't have the job because he worked for SuperSport, and SARU wasn't comfortable with that.

While this little spat might not seem that significant, it was the incident that really soured my relations with the President's Council. My attitude and reservations got back to the council members, and I was summoned to a meeting at the Oliver Tambo International Airport in Johannesburg on Tuesday night – the eve of our departure for a tough tour.

The meeting was held at the Airport Holiday Inn, and the entire council attended. It was terrible.

The squad and I were staying at the Montecasino Hotel in Fourways. I was instructed to be at the Holiday Inn at 7 p.m., and I arrived on time. When I walked in, I was told to wait outside the meeting room where they were all gathered. At 7:35 p.m. I was called in.

A council member asked me: 'What have you got to say for yourself?'

I replied that I had nothing to say; they had called me here. That took the wind out of their sails a bit. I think they hoped I would become confrontational.

My attitude made them angry, and they started having a go at me.

The arguments centred around the appointment of the manager. I enquired whether Zola's ties with the SABC shouldn't be an issue for them. They asked me why I cared.

'Because that was the excuse you guys used when I suggested appointing Naas,' I replied. 'Before it was made clear that the position had to be filled by an ethnic black guy.'

They told me that I wasn't helping, and that every time they came up with a proposal, I was against it. They were angry, but failed to see how the appointment of the manager was not a proposal, but a done deal that I was supposed to roll over and accept.

SARU vice-president Mike Stofile implied I was a racist. He said I didn't understand transformation. Hoskins was annoyed because he thought I didn't show him the same support he'd shown me, which he was finding difficult to accept. Tshume was there as well. He didn't say much; he just listened.

The council members were annoyed that I didn't agree with them often enough, and that I didn't follow their instructions. They even accused me of being 'a Brian van Rooyen man', saying I'd campaigned for him in the presidential elections earlier in the year. It was rubbish and, when I denied it, they accused me of lying.

It was ridiculous. The Springbok coach, on the eve of a tour, was sitting in a hotel facing nearly 20 men (who supposedly had the best interests of the game at heart), being accused of – what exactly? Disagreeing with them? Wanting a proper process to be followed?

While they had a go at me, my mind wandered. Would Graham Henry, the All Black coach, be sitting at Auckland airport on the eve of a tour, getting nailed by his senior executives? It just wouldn't happen.

This same council that was questioning my integrity hadn't followed due process over the appointment of the manager. They were the ones who criticised me on performances, but if they did something incorrectly and I refused to follow, I was out on a limb. That was the hardest meeting I'd ever had to attend.

That night, at the airport, they told me in no uncertain terms where their support started and ended. 'We don't back you, and we find it hard to support you.' I thought, 'How am I supposed to work under these conditions?'

I was also formally informed that Yeye had been appointed as manager, whether I liked it or not. He arrived at the team hotel the following morning. I'd never met him, none of the players knew him, and I think he had a good idea of my objections to the process of his appointment. It was awkward.

Allister Coetzee knew him vaguely, and tried really hard to break the ice. The players weren't happy about the situation either – not because of Zola, but about the way in which he'd been appointed. They didn't have a clue who he was.

It was tough on Zola too. I think he was very uncomfortable. It's very intimidating to walk into a Springbok team room when all the players are sitting there. I felt for the guy, because it wasn't his fault. I didn't have an axe to grind with him, although I wasn't happy with what he'd said in the press some months earlier. I didn't think he should've been so vocal about things he didn't understand.

But I was civil towards him and we had a cordial relationship, although I didn't feel I could confide in him on that tour. I don't think he quite became part of the team, but he got involved. I had the feeling that he really wanted to be part of a successful Bok team, which I respected.

So, off we went on tour with an inexperienced squad, a team manager people were slightly suspicious of, and the explicit non-backing of senior rugby administrators. Perfect.

32

100 years remembered

With the words of the President's Council still ringing in my ears, plus some negative hype surrounding Kabamba Floors's omission from the squad still bubbling over, we landed in London en route to Dublin. It was the start of a historic tour with deep significance. Paul Roos's South African team had sailed to Britain in 1906 and named themselves the 'Springbokken' on the voyage over. It was the birth of a team and – to use modern marketing terminology – a brand that is arguably the most recognisable in rugby. The All Blacks might argue otherwise, but mention the Springboks, and your immediate thought is 'rugby'.

We wanted to doff our caps in recognition of those pioneers a century earlier, but we also had an obligation to do everything possible to win the World Cup in 2007. It meant that we didn't tour with our best players. It was a decision that weighed heavily on me, as I'm a big believer in honouring and respecting history and tradition.

As desperately as I would have liked to put my best possible XV on the pitch, I knew that it wasn't practical. And in the long run it was the right decision.

We had decided to wear a replica of the 1906 kit in the test against Ireland as part of the celebrations. A green jersey with white edging and a black badge, coupled with blue socks and shorts, was what the first Boks had worn. Team sponsor Sasol also generously agreed to allow us to play without their logo on the jerseys in recognition of the 1906 tourists.

Sartorially we were set for the tour, but the coaching staff had their work cut out to get our new combinations working in time for the test against Ireland – arguably the best team in Europe at that stage.

But no sooner had we landed than the grumbling from the media began. Our team hotel in Dunboyne was about 20 kilometres outside Dublin, which meant it was a trek every day for the travelling media to get to Bok training. Also, the practice facilities at the Garda Rugby Club in Westmantown were not great, but this was not unusual for a European tour, so we just had to get on with it. This was also a part of the plan – not to mess the media around, but to ensure that we built a team spirit.

We knew we were going to be on tour for nearly five weeks, so we planned to stay outside of Dublin, away from distractions, where we could mould a unit. The players had to become comfortable with one another and form a bond.

That's why we also chose to base ourselves in Bath, rather than London, for the second week of the tour, when we decamped to England. Only in the third week did we move to London.

The build-up to the test and the team selection had actually been disrupted before we'd even left South Africa. Jaque Fourie was supposed to tour, and Bryan Habana was scheduled to rest. A lot was made of my 'interesting selections' when I put debutant Jaco Pretorius on the wing, even though he'd been playing centre for the Lions. I selected Habana at centre and played Frans Steyn, another debutant, at wing.

I don't think they were interesting at all. Basically we'd been running for 10 days with a backline that had Jean de Villiers and Jaque Fourie as centres. That experienced combination picked itself. With them in the midfield, we were comfortable selecting Bevan Fortuin at fullback for his first test, as well as Pretorius and Steyn. I didn't think it would be fair to take them on tour and then not use them, so I figured that trying them out in the first match, with some experienced players to support them, could help.

At that stage Pretorius was the most capped South African Sevens player, and he could play anywhere in the backline, except at flyhalf. It wasn't a gamble to put him on the wing at all. We had a centre combination that we didn't want to split up.

We were a bit short on wings who could finish with deadly precision, and I believed Pretorius was that type of player.

With Bevan set to start at fullback, the only jersey available to Steyn was on the wing. I thought that, as a guy who'd played mostly fullback (which is relative, as he was only 19 years old), there seemed no reason why we couldn't double him up as a winger and then let him come in at flyhalf or fullback.

Steyn was a revelation on the tour. I didn't know a great deal about him, but I'd watched him play in the Currie Cup and saw something special. I wasn't alone. I'd spoken to his coaches and his schoolmaster and asked them about his stats, such as what his time trials numbers were. I asked his conditioning coach at Grey College in Bloemfontein, South Africa's premier rugby school, about his conditioning when he was at school, and he said he'd be more than adequate as an outside back. They assured me he was really quick. That's all I needed to know.

So, before we even left for Ireland, that team had been running for 10 days. Then, two days before we departed, Jaque Fourie broke his hand. I was faced with a selection poser. The easier thing would've been to slot Wynand Olivier in at centre. He had done very well in his first Tri-Nations, and was developing into a quality test centre. But we'd already done that and knew he could do the job, so we weren't going to learn anything new. He was also struggling with a knee knock after the Currie Cup final. We weren't sure we could risk him, because we really wanted to play him against England, now that Fourie was out.

The other option was to bring Jaco Pretorius off the wing and put him at centre, where he'd been doing well for the Lions, and bring in a new wing.

The selectors and I then decided that bringing Habana in at centre might be worth a try. His speed and mobility, coupled with De Villiers's hands and skill, could potentially be an exciting combination. There was a lot of debate among the coaching staff. We liked the fact that Bryan knew the Boks' defensive patterns from a backline point of view, despite being on the wing for most of his test career. Part of his contract with the Bulls was that they had to give him some game time at outside centre.

In hindsight, maybe it was the wrong call for the Ireland test. He battled against Gordon D'Arcy and Brian O'Driscoll, who were playing some superb rugby. But at the time I didn't hesitate to give it a go. There was an opportunity to see Habana at centre, something we'd always had at the back of our minds. Both Bryan and Jean possessed pace, so with Pretorius and Steyn out wide, we were quite excited about the idea and the make-up of the backline.

What critics tended to forget was that the tour was largely experimental, with a view to the World Cup. Also, our priority was to beat England at Twickenham. They were drawn in our group at the World Cup, and South Africa hadn't won in London since 1997. It was vital for our confidence as Springboks to beat them. Not that we didn't want to beat Ireland, but it was the one match where we could really experiment.

The loose trio was also a little unbalanced. I picked Pierre Spies at number 8, with Juan Smith returning on the flank after a long injury.

Danie Rossouw was the other flank. Pierre had been outstanding in the home leg of the Tri-Nations, although at openside flank. He's such a great athlete that I wanted to see him at number 8 again.

With the three of them, I also had extra lineout options. Considering we were missing Victor Matfield and Bakkies Botha, and playing against the best lineout in the world, I needed as many options as possible.

Juan though, was a little short of gallop after having had such a long lay-off. It was inevitable. If I didn't play him, then I'd have played him in the coming weeks against England, and he'd still have been game shy.

That was the problem, and one for which there was no easy solution.

Some guys were rusty because they hadn't played much rugby. Yet, at the same time, those guys were more conditioned than they'd been in a long time, as they'd had time to do gym work and other drills. What a player lost in not playing, he gained in other areas. I said this to the review committee afterwards.

If I had that tour over again, I would have done everything the same, except I would have left a little earlier and scheduled a midweek game against one of the Irish club sides to get rid of the rust. It was a new situation for me, as I'd never taken guys on tour who'd come off a rest. Usually they were straight out of the Currie Cup into the test arena.

In 2004, when we lost to Ireland in Dublin, they had taken their players out of rugby for 10 weeks after they were beaten earlier that year in South Africa. I learnt then that their conditioning programme had made them so much better. We were heading in the right direction with resting players, but they still needed a game to find sharpness.

Before the 2006 Ireland test, something I'd said in 2004 – about only two Irish players being good enough to make the Bok team – came up at a presser. I knew it would; I was expecting it. An Irish hack surreptitiously chucked it in. I killed the moment by saying that the International Rugby Board chairman Dr Syd Millar, an Irishman, had told me that once a player had represented one country, he couldn't play for another. I therefore couldn't pick any Irish players at this point, I said. That got a laugh from the media.

Ireland was very bullish that they would win the test. And why wouldn't they have been? The first time we'd met during my time as coach, in June 2004, we had a combined 175 test caps, or thereabouts, and we beat them. Two and a half years later, they had virtually the same team as they'd had then: John Hayes, Paul O'Connell, Donnacha O'Callaghan, Malcolm

O'Kelly, David Wallace, Simon Easterby, Peter Stringer, Ronan O'Gara, Brian O'Driscoll, Gordon D'Arcy, Geordan Murphy, Shane Horgan and Girvan Dempsey were all still around. But we were a vastly different team, with different objectives as well. Only John Smit had played against Ireland in June 2004.

They were also confident because we were away from home in a stadium where the wind and weather play a huge factor. We were always going to be the underdogs at that fixture, which is probably why the Irish were bullish.

You've got to give credit for what Irish rugby has achieved. They don't have a lot of players, but they've put systems and structures in place that have made them one of the forces in world rugby. The fact that their name was being mentioned in the small group of countries that were potential world champions deserved praise.

They only have four regions, of which one, Connaught, is really a development region. Their forwards largely play together for Munster, as do their halfbacks. The rest of their backline represents Leinster.

They nurture their players; they give them tax rebates for not playing overseas when they retire. They've done everything they can to make sure that Irish rugby, in terms of the national team, is competitive, and that's why they were getting results.

On the night of the Dublin match, the weather was foul. There was a massive wind blowing down the ground. We won the toss, which was a very good toss to win on the day. Normally in rugby it doesn't matter, but that night we thought it might.

We played against the wind first. I knew with all the emotion and adrenalin in the changing room, because of the new caps and the centenary celebrations, special jersey and so on, the players would have enough energy to combat the wind. However, it went horribly wrong in the first half. I think certain players copped out of making big calls. Maybe some of the players involved thought they were going to be definite starters on tour, because of the make-up of the tour group.

We let Ireland make a good start, but we got ourselves deep in their half for a few minutes. We should have scored, but they collapsed three lineouts in a row. That's test rugby, and they scored soon after our period of pressure.

We had some more opportunities to score, but on the stroke of half-time they scored a third try. That made the gap just too wide to close in the second half. I thought that, with the wind, even if they were 10 points ahead at halftime, we could come back. But 22-3 down at the break left us with too much to do.

Murphy's Law has its origins in an Irish saying, and it came into play that day, because the wind died down in the second half. We had won a toss we thought would be really important, and we didn't get the return. There's an unwritten rule in rugby that says you make sure you use the wind in the second half.

I think the emotion of the centenary and the unique jersey played a slight role as well. We had three boys playing their first test match, which happened to be in the new jersey, and which made for an emotional moment. Bevan, Frans and Jaco had never even played in a traditional Springbok jersey, and all of a sudden they were playing in a jersey steeped in history. But I don't believe that was why we lost or started nervously.

We played against a good Irish team, with O'Gara producing a wonderful exhibition of flyhalf play in those conditions. He kicked us into corners and used the wind brilliantly. He used it better than we did.

Our flyhalf, André Pretorius, had a night he'd rather forget, but maybe that poor performance was the reason he played so well against England a few weeks later. He took stock of himself and knew he had to up his game, which he did.

I knew there would be a public reaction to the defeat, but I never thought it would be the start of a desperate tour. If we believed in what we set out to do, then it shouldn't have been a problem.

We knew we were going to give three players test caps in the important back three positions against a kicking flyhalf and a kicking scrumhalf. What do you do? Should you say, 'We can't do it because we're playing against two guys who kick well,' and wait to throw them in for their debuts against England in front of 80 000 people? The coaching staff were never in doubt about our objectives and ideas. Of course, we believed we could beat Ireland, and we didn't play well, particularly in the first half. But we never lost sight of the bigger picture, which was beating England. Unfortunately, given my problems with the President's Council, the sharks began to circle very quickly.

We took a lot of criticism in the Sunday press; some of it justified, some over the top. Most critics weren't in the know. And because they weren't part of the planning, we let it slide. We had to accept that they had an opinion, but it didn't make it right. In some ways, the former players who lambasted us actually helped make the team stronger. I could have become negative and bitter, and talked badly about Springbok legends in front of the players, but I didn't think it was the right thing to do. What I said to the players was, 'You see boys, this is how *not* to be a Springbok.'

Part of a Bok's education is teaching them that it isn't only about being a Springbok on the field. It's about being a Springbok off the field too. This means that you behave as if you are still a member of the team. The code of conduct stays with a Springbok for life, in my opinion.

It's in the difficult times that old Boks have to stand up and be counted. I continually told the players, 'Boys, as youngsters you have to appreciate that this is part of being a Bok. The expectation, the history, the records, ethos and the standards that have been set before us are not negotiable.'

But the one thing we could negotiate was whether critics were being genuine and acting in the interests of the team. And players know whether a guy is genuine when he says they were poor and they need to wake up, or whether the guy's got an agenda and he's bitter and twisted.

The players and coaches understand when they are below par; anybody who plays sport knows. If you play a good round of golf one day and you play badly the next and someone asks, 'How did you play?', you say, 'I played badly today.'

That doesn't mean that you're a worse person than you were the day before. They're Springboks. They play at that level. They understand. They're also realists. Before we even played that Irish test match, we knew we were going to be underdogs. We always knew that we had to play much better than the Irish at their home ground to beat them. We didn't.

I didn't take any positives out of the performance. But what I did see was a group of very hurt players in the changing room. You know you're dealing with the right group of players when you walk into a changing room and they are upset about losing. If they are laughing and giggling and having a beer while acting as if it's just another fixture, then you've got a problem. Then you've lost what it's all about. In that sense, it was positive.

They were as sore about losing as any experienced team I'd coached in the previous three years – perhaps even more so, as it was a game that celebrated the centenary of Bok rugby. A lot of them would've liked to have framed that jersey with a plaque displaying a winning score at Lansdowne Road. They would never play at Lansdowne Road again in that jersey. But we were going to play at Twickenham – the following week, in fact.

33

Twickenham heartbreak

You don't live in a bubble in the Springbok set-up, despite how it may appear from the outside. External pressures, media scrutiny and sponsor commitments all have an effect on the team and its morale. Defeats don't help. Especially in the first match of a tour, because the mood and camaraderie you've spent weeks building take a knock. But that's where character comes in. The group of players on the 2006 end-of-year tour displayed a lot of character.

Following the loss in Dublin, I was under the gun again. Media reports speculated about my future, and I heard through friends and contacts that certain sections of the SARU hierarchy were also gunning for me. In this environment I had to prepare the team to face the world champions in their own backyard. By this stage I'd developed a thick skin for rumours and speculation. But, that said, I did follow the press to gauge the mood.

It's easy to say you'll ignore the media, but their comments do have an effect on your well-being as a coach. I could also see patterns and agendas developing. And while it might sound like I spent hours pondering over media reports, that wasn't the case. But I did scan the headlines.

One of the themes raised was that our match against Ireland was supposed to have been a celebration of 100 years of Bok rugby, but that we'd embarrassed the Bok emblem by picking an under-strength team for such a historic game. If the game was in isolation I might have agreed, but it came at the end of our third year in a four-year cycle to the World Cup.

Weeks later, in my review committee meeting after the tour, it was suggested that maybe we (and when I say 'we', I'm referring to SARU) should have packaged the Ireland test a little better and informed the public more clearly; that, in terms of the bigger picture, we should have been clear that it was an experimental side. It was ironic, considering I had been the one out on a limb saying exactly that before the game.

There wasn't much public support from the board or the President's Council for that line of thinking before the test. I certainly didn't hear any of them coming out and saying that the Boks were looking ahead, and that this was a tour where they'd experiment – even though that's exactly what they had bought into, and endorsed, in private.

After the Irish test, a lot of words like 'shame' and 'disgrace' were bandied about in the press. I wasn't surprised. I knew there were agendas against me and I had no control over them. But, while the vitriol wasn't unexpected, it still wasn't pleasant. It wasn't pleasant personally and, with back-to-back tests against England to come, it wasn't pleasant for the team either.

It becomes difficult to remain focused and stay in tune when there are loud calls for your head. Remember, I had also left under a cloud following the informal President's Council meeting at the airport in Johannesburg, so I knew my friends were few and far between.

Nevertheless, there were young players on their first Bok tour and others who hadn't toured with me as coach, and they were looking to see how I handled the situation. In the Internet age, players are very aware of what's being said and written, and they knew what kind of pressure I was under, which in turn made them edgy.

It was hardly the dream they'd envisaged of becoming a Bok.

And those off-field pressures did have a direct influence on our on-field performances. By then, every week before a test, there was some crisis or other involving me, the team selection or something else. It had to start having an emotional effect on the team, especially on young players who'd never been exposed to that level of attention before – even if it wasn't focused on them directly. Everyone in management was very aware of the pressure on our 'new' squad, and we had to be very supportive of some of these young guys.

We started to prepare for the first England test, under mounting pressure as a squad, with even more strain on me personally. I'd maintained throughout, especially in the Tri-Nations, that I never felt as if my job was on the line, as I had a contract until the end of 2007. But that week in Bath, I began to feel insecure for the first time, due to the media speculation and bits of news dribbling back to me from South Africa.

Logic told me to forget about it and get on with my job, as I had an airtight contract. But my emotions told me to watch my back, as the agendas against me were becoming more apparent.

Grumbles about team selection against Ireland were becoming louder from high up in South African rugby circles, as far as I could tell. The plan to rest players and try out new combinations was decided on by a group. The team had been signed off not only by the president (Hoskins), but also by the two vice-presidents (Mike Stofile and Koos Basson), as well as the chairman of the board (Tshume). That was a clear indication to me that they understood what the intention and objectives of the tour were.

Although they might all have been okay with the outcome of the Ireland game, none of them communicated any support, which left me feeling increasingly isolated. And it has an effect on the way you coach. You end up coaching for survival. The more the noose is tightened, the less expressive you are as a coach.

The team feels the tension as well. If you look at how we played in our third year, we were less free and less expressive, be it on defence or attack. Obviously we had some days when we played really well, but generally I think the team felt the pressure too.

I felt like I was coaching to save my job. But what probably saved me was that I knew I had the backing of the players, as well as that of the sponsors. It didn't matter who the players were, how old they were or where they came from; I knew they genuinely felt that I'd treated them fairly and supported them. You can lose your grip on many things as a rugby coach. You can lose the support of the fans, the support of your bosses, and even that of the sponsors, but you should never lose the support of the players. When that happens, it's over for you. Their support kept me going.

How did I know the players backed me unequivocally? Simple. I was in a weak position. If any player was unhappy and wanted me out, now was the time to do it. There were opportunities for players to complain about me, and they could easily have jumped on the bandwagon. I know some were even approached to help in ousting me. Some players were asked about me openly, or in quieter corridors, yet not one said a word against me, to their credit as Springboks. It demonstrated that whatever was being said externally wasn't poisoning us from the inside. I think that pissed some people off, as they couldn't weaken us by dividing the squad.

I'm loyal to players because they're loyal to me. We might have differences and sometimes I have to make tough decisions, but they are always treated respectfully. I know for a fact that players had filled out a questionnaire provided by the South African Rugby Players Association (SARPA), which quizzed them on the Bok set-up. It was confidential, and they were encouraged to speak their minds.

There wasn't one player who'd said he was unhappy – just the opposite.

The technology was good, the coaching was good, and they were treated well. I know those forms made their way to the board and upset a few people, as it did not give them any ammunition to use against me.

That week leading up to the first England test, England's coach Andy Robinson was enduring an equally torrid time. His team had also battled in the face of a lot of injuries and loss of form to some players, and Robinson was in the firing line. For a big part of that week, a lot of the press focused on him trying to save his job and left me alone.

England had just lost at home to Argentina for the first time ever, and their team was under the whip. But it also made them dangerous, as they had their backs to the wall and were desperate for a win – as were we. The media spent a lot of time asking me what I thought of Andy's position – did I relate to it, and what did it feel like?

Robinson was down; I felt for the guy. I knew how hard it was to get out of a downward spiral. I told the press that it wasn't easy for him, with a world champion team, and that, like anything, it was a cycle. One thing rugby still maintains in the professional era is a sense of camaraderie. I knew it would be one of those games in which a lot of emotion, pride and passion would be exhibited.

I didn't know Robinson as well as some of the other coaches, but in all my dealings with him, he was hell of a friendly and very passionate about his job, and I related to that. It made it difficult, knowing that he was so close to being sacked, and that the result of the match could spell the end of his career.

For the England test, I made six changes to the side that lost to Ireland. The tour planning was such that the emphasis was on beating England. That was the most important objective of the tour, in addition to blooding some new players.

The biggest selection change I made was to recall Butch James at fly-half. It's ironic, because a lot of questions were asked on whether it was a wise decision to select him ahead of André Pretorius. The media really grilled me on the selection, yet after the test they all lambasted me for substituting Butch.

My reasoning for selecting Butch was that I thought André hadn't been defensively sound against Ireland. I didn't entirely blame him for that, as he didn't have a lot of protection in his channel that night. But we needed a more physical approach in the flyhalf channel.

England had chosen Charlie Hodgson at 10, and I was aware that he liked to play on the advantage line. I knew that if we played André, they'd get a lot more momentum than if Butch were in front of Charlie, knocking him back in the tackle.

It was a balancing act, as I also knew I was sacrificing a goal-kicker. It wasn't that Butch couldn't kick for goal, but André's record was better when it came to kicking. It was a bit of a gamble, but I knew I had André on the bench if Butch didn't work out.

I also moved Frans Steyn to fullback. He'd been one of the successes against Ireland, and I was impressed with him. It meant Bevan Fortuin missed out, but we needed a back-up goal-kicker on the field, and Steyn was better than Bevan in that department.

We also recalled Akona Ndungane on the right wing, and moved Bryan Habana back to left wing after a less than successful experiment at centre. Wynand Olivier returned to the midfield to partner Jean de Villiers.

Up front we included BJ Botha at tighthead, Johann Muller at lock, and brought in Jacques Cronjé at number 8. With Danie Rossouw and Pierre Spies on the flanks it was a big back row, which I wanted against England. For years, England had produced monster packs. I knew we had to fight fire with fire. We picked the biggest pack we could on that tour, with Johan Ackermann retaining his place at lock.

England won 23-21, but the bottom line was that it was a game we lost, as opposed to one that England had won. Still, it was a shattering loss, as we had bossed it for so much of the match, and we should've been out of sight going into the final 10 minutes.

I can honestly say we were the better team on the day. But we didn't take all our chances, and Phil Vickery scored the winning try with a few minutes to go. A lot of questions were asked about why I had substituted Butch James when we'd gone 12 points up. But let's go back a little.

Part of the team talk that I'd given after the Irish game was that I was tired of players not putting their bodies on the line. The one criticism that I was constantly nailed on was my loyalty to the players. I always deflected questions in a press conference if they related to certain players and their individual performances. Nick Mallett had hammered Gaffie du Toit and Dave von Hoesslin after a 28-0 loss in Dunedin in 1999, and they never recovered. Nick was sorry about it, and I know he would change it if he could. So I learnt a lesson from his experience.

But, after the loss to Ireland, I was angry. We hadn't played well, and not only because of inexperience. I thought we'd showed lack of commitment at times. So, before the England test, I said: 'Today I'm watching to see which of you can really put your hands up against England. If you thought Ireland was physical and climbed in, a desperate England at Twickenham will be far worse.

'If you break your leg, or your leg is hanging by a thread, you cut it off and you put it on your back and you play with one leg. You don't show those guys that you're in pain. I want to see whether or not you've got it, because this is the test that matters. We have to beat England in the World Cup, and that starts now.'

In the first minute of the game, Butch got a whack on his knee. He went to physio Clint Readhead and said, 'My knee is gone.'

He stayed on. In the 60th minute he chipped a penalty kick, which gave us a handy lead. But the ball barely made it over the crossbar, as he had no power. He couldn't put any pressure on his leg because his knee was so buggered. He hobbled back to Clint and said, 'Look, I'm telling you now – my knee's gone. I'll stay on if the coach says so, but I just want you to know if they run at me, I'm not going to be able to move left or right, and I'm worried that I might let the team down.'

Clint relayed this to me, and I immediately sent André Pretorius on. Butch had taken my team talk literally by playing for 60 minutes with a bad knee – and playing brilliantly … it was the game of his life. He went home the next day and had an operation.

In the back of my mind I always knew that if we needed to win the game with a long-range penalty, we could make a replacement and put André on. I knew François Steyn could kick the ball from miles away, so we were confident about winning, especially as Butch was playing so well.

It was never my intention to take Butch off. I got killed in the press conference for doing that, but the journalists weren't aware that he went straight to hospital after the game. He didn't even go to the changing room, but left Twickenham in an ambulance for a scan. On Sunday morning he was heavily strapped, and limped around the hotel preparing to head home.

He said to me, 'If you hadn't given that team talk, I would have come off earlier. But because you said what you did, I decided I was staying on as long as I could.'

I knew I was dealing with the right guy. He said he'd been in pain the entire game, but he stayed and stayed until he felt he was going to let the team down. He even scored a great try in the match.

Unfortunately, André wasn't at the top of his game. He made a couple of poor kicks out of hand, which put us under pressure. But we should have closed that game out anyway.

In the first half we had them under pressure, when Josh Lewsey tackled Jean de Villiers into touch inches from the try line. Had he made the pass inside to Akona, or chipped it inside to Pierre Spies, who was running unopposed with the uprights in front of him, we would have scored.

De Villiers could have sidestepped, or stopped and cut inside. The point I'm making is he knew he probably had eight options, and he didn't take any of them. In the end, he was only inches away. He backed himself. He's quicker than people think, and he thought he was going to make it. As a coach I had to back him on his decision.

The reality was, he should have passed. He knows that now. Had he passed, and had we finished the break that François Steyn made two minutes later, where they pulled him up just short of the line, we would've been 28-3 ahead at the break. This is exactly the margin by which the All Blacks had led against England at halftime two weeks before.

Jean knew he'd made a mistake, but the tackle had been great too. Jean learnt a lesson that day.

It was a game of 'ifs', and we should really have won both tests at Twickenham in 2006. Had André found touch with a late penalty, it would have driven England back into their 22-metre area, and the game might have ended differently. We could have won a lineout down there, they wouldn't have come downfield, and Vickery might not have scored. I don't believe the game would have unfolded like it did had we kicked the ball out.

But that's rugby. After the test and in the lead-up to the second test, we discussed our lack of composure in killing the game. With the Schalk Burgers, Os du Randts, Victor Matfields and Bakkies Bothas, we knew how to control a match. We didn't have that experience to fall back on at Twickenham.

The year before in Durban, when we drew 30-all with France, we learnt a lesson. We could have won the game, but only managed a draw after a late French conversion hit the upright. We learnt about killing a game from that experience, and it showed in many of the tests we played after that in 2005.

The group of players against England also learnt that lesson the hard way. People said they went into their shells and should just have kept playing the same way they had been and they'd never have lost. That's nonsense. In test rugby, when you're up with 15 or 20 minutes to go and the opposition has to score twice to win, that's when you close a game down.

You've got to keep them on the other side of the field. Why would you want to play in your own half and give them yards for nothing? That's a given in rugby. We didn't do that. We made stupid mistakes. We let them come into our half and, inevitably, they scored.

So, as a team, we spoke about that. If you look at the next test match, they took on board the lessons learnt seven days before. It showed how much they had progressed in a week.

34

Goodbye Jake?

Imagine my surprise to wake up to the news that I'd been fired. At least according to *Rapport* newspaper, which ran a front-page story under the headline, '*Koebaai* Jake'.

The piece didn't even speculate about my future; it was written as fact. According to *Rapport's* writers, I was gone, and Bulls coach Heyneke Meyer had already been approached to succeed me. The report was clearly wrong and *Rapport* damaged their credibility with that piece of journalism. But the spin-off was that the story caused a huge stir and created a great deal of angst among the players, the staff and my family. If that was their intention, then they partly succeeded.

I spoke to my wife Debbie, who was in South Africa. She had a copy of the newspaper. She was worried and was taking it quite badly. I assured her there was nothing to worry about, but I wanted some answers from Oregan Hoskins and Mpumelelo Tshume. I didn't call them, though; I figured it was their job to inform me whether the story was true or not.

The management team were very supportive and remained positive, although I knew that the article had affected them as well. The story filtered through the camp, and I could see that some of the younger players were looking increasingly bewildered by the whole situation.

It was my responsibility to equip the players with the tools that would ensure that they experienced what it was like to be part of a winning Bok team. So far on this tour, the new boys hadn't tasted victory, and now they were faced with what looked like a massive crisis. That spurred me on, because I was determined that they would experience the feeling of being in a winning Bok squad, even if it was my last role as national coach. In some ways I felt like I was letting them down as well. They were looking to me, and I couldn't afford to crack or show any weakness.

The *Rapport* story claimed that Hoskins, Tshume and vice-presidents Koos Basson and Mike Stofile had held a crisis meeting on the Friday night before the first England test. It claimed they had decided to report back to the board and the President's Council that they'd lost faith in the coach and the selectors.

I don't know whether they had met on the eve of the test or not, but what I do know is that, following the Sunday report, Hoskins and Basson scheduled a meeting with national selector Ian McIntosh and me on the Tuesday night in a London hotel. They indicated that they wanted to assure me that they knew nothing about the *Rapport* story.

But on the Monday, the Blue Bulls Rugby Union (BBRU), buckling to a rallying cry from its Old Players' Association, which was headed by Piet Uys and the great Springbok lock Frik du Preez – a frequent critic of mine in the pages of *Rapport* – called for a vote of no confidence in me as Springbok coach.

Within hours of that development, I received a call from Barend van Graan, who headed up the Bulls' professional arm, which employs all its players and coaches. He assured me that he and Bulls coach Heyneke Meyer did not support the motion of no confidence, and neither did any of the Bulls players. They distanced themselves from it, and Barend explained that the motion had come from the amateur arm of the union. I thanked him for taking the time to call, and also asked him to thank Heyneke.

The actions of the BBRU set in motion a lot of backroom politicking at SARU, which I think caught Hoskins off guard as well. He was in London, and at home the unions were gathering in an effort to oust me. We might have had our differences, but I think he was appalled at how the so-called 'custodians' of the game were behaving. It was an unprecedented attack on a Springbok coach and, by extension, the Springbok team.

Hoskins and I met alone a few hours before the full Tuesday night get-together with McIntosh and Basson. It was a constructive meeting, and we finally cleared a lot of issues that had been bugging both of us. He pointed out that I didn't always support him on some key issues, yet he had to defend me. He was pretty blunt, and said I could've been more accommodating on the issue of the team manager's appointment. I still maintained that the process hadn't been followed correctly.

Hoskins also questioned my reluctance to select Kabamba Floors in the touring squad. He felt that, due to the public outcry over his omission following the Currie Cup final, we should have reassessed the situation and included Floors in the touring squad.

I hadn't added Floors to the squad then, and I told Hoskins I wouldn't compromise on the way we selected teams. It would have been hugely unfair to bring him in on the back of public sentiment. What message would we send out then? I reminded him that our touring squads were routinely selected two weeks before the final to avoid any emotional decisions, which the late inclusion of Floors would have been.

The touring squad had been signed off two weeks before the Currie Cup final, as was the norm. All the criteria had been agreed upon and met. The board gave the thumbs up to a young team, with an opportunity for experimentation and the resting of senior players. The racial demographic of the squad was also signed off, which the executives were all very happy with. Then, when people exerted extreme pressure from outside, the board suddenly wanted to change what it had agreed to.

That was the first thing. Secondly, I told Hoskins, I didn't see how we could use Kabamba if I'd brought him along on tour, because there were many other good looseforwards in the squad. I wanted a big pack against England. With Danie Rossouw, Pedrie Wannenburg, Juan Smith, Pierre Spies and Jacques Cronjé in the running, I couldn't see how I could've used Kabamba.

But Hoskins was upset, as in his view I hadn't supported him. But once I explained my point of view, and how Kabamba's selection would have undermined the credibility of the selectors, he grudgingly agreed that perhaps I had a point. By the same token, I could have helped him at times. But the one thing I couldn't do was compromise on team selection. As it turned out, Kabamba would get his chance.

Hoskins and I concluded our meeting amicably, and then Basson and Mac joined us. Ian McIntosh was a superb coach who had guided Natal through their glory years in the 1990s, and had also been a Bok coach. He spoke from experience when he said that it was difficult enough to coach South Africa; doing so without the backing of the people who employed you was virtually impossible.

Mac knew what it was like, because when he was Bok coach in 1993/94, he said he never had the backing of rugby boss Louis Luyt. For Mac, it resulted in an acrimonious split from SARFU. He told Basson and Hoskins that he wanted to know whether we had their backing. He didn't want more meetings and promises. He wanted to be able to look them in the eye and see if they backed us or not.

They promised us that we had their support, and they also assured us that they weren't linked to the *Rapport* story. They said they would try to find out who'd misinformed *Rapport*.

Then we turned to the motion of no confidence, put forward by the BBRU. Hoskins said that the President's Council had called a meeting the following week, and there was going to be a vote on it.

I asked if it was even constitutional, and whether the motion had been seconded by anybody. No other union had seconded the Blue Bulls' motion, to their knowledge. I found that amazing.

Hoskins agreed, but said he had a huge problem on his hands. He had unions baying for my blood and the media saying I was fired, based on information passed to them from somebody on the board. 'It leaves me in a tough position as president,' Hoskins said.

I understood his problem, but I again pointed out that I was counting on the backing of the board, as well as that of the President's Council. I reminded him that, when we'd met in Cape Town after the French test, he'd given me his word that I'd be coach to the World Cup. I always had that promise at the back of my mind. So, when he started saying he had a problem with the Blue Bulls, I became uneasy. This wasn't the same guy who had guaranteed my job. I became edgy. Mac asked again, 'Do you support the coach?'

Hoskins and Basson looked sheepish, and said they found it difficult. I hadn't made selections they thought I should've made. I hadn't backed them on the appointment of the manager, and they found it difficult to support a guy who wasn't, seemingly, working with the board.

I knew I was in trouble then. They were battling to back me. I had to concentrate on winning a test, at the same time knowing that the meeting in Cape Town the following week could be the end of me if I didn't convince Hoskins and Basson to support me.

Then Mac said to them, 'This vote of no confidence. Where do you two stand on it?' They wouldn't commit. In that case, Mac said, he felt it was only fair that I be allowed to fly back and present my case to the board and the President's Council.

Basson and Hoskins liked the idea. For once we didn't have to fight about something; we all agreed. Hoskins felt comfortable with the suggestion, as he would have had to present Jake White's case otherwise. Considering how hard he found it to back me on certain issues, he couldn't have ensured that he'd represent me fairly. That was fair enough.

After that I didn't think about the issue much. I had a test match to prepare for and win. Mac said, 'Don't worry, it will be fine. Keep focusing on what you do. Go and coach the team.'

That helped, because I stopped worrying about the sideshows. I was going to focus on what I did best, and that was coaching. While all of this was going on, we had issues with team selection, especially among the looseforwards, where we had some serious injuries. It raised the Kabamba Floors issue again. Pierre Spies and Jacques Cronjé were both injured in the first England test. I needed cover. We'd lost Wannenburg before the tour, and now two other looseforwards were in doubt. So I called for Kabamba.

This happened more or less at the same time as the motion of no confidence was emerging from South Africa. Kabamba had just been named as captain of the South African Sevens team, which was due to go to Dubai. I think it was Mac who tried to contact him on the Monday, but we couldn't get hold of him. SA Rugby eventually tracked him down at home.

It was a tough call, because I was going to deny Kabamba the chance of captaining the SA Sevens team, while not being sure he'd play against England. He was to be flown to London purely as cover for Spies and Cronjé.

Juan Smith also appeared to be ready to play after sitting out the week before. We were in a situation where we had four looseforwards who might or might not be fit. To bring Kabamba over to hang around meant he'd miss the pre-Dubai training camp. If the other guys came through a fitness test, he wasn't going to play. Given all that had been going on, can you imagine how that would've looked? It would've been seen as window dressing for sure.

I was perched on a hornet's nest. We asked SA Rugby to get hold of Kabamba, and later the message came back that he didn't want to come over. I was surprised, and only later did we discover that someone – and I have a very good idea who – had contacted him and told him that he shouldn't go to London, as he was only being called up as an afterthought and used as a political pawn.

When Mac, as a selector, asked Hoskins and all the top brass who were at the hotel whether he could get Kabamba over, Mike Stofile said to Mac, 'I can't agree with that.' Mac was staggered, but not deterred. He demanded an answer on whether he could get Kabamba over. Someone had to make the call. They conferred and told Mac that the selectors had to make the decision. So Mac got hold of Kabamba and told him he was going to be a Bok.

I then burst Mac's bubble by saying that I wasn't sure Kabamba would play if the others passed a fitness test. He was angry, and said: 'You're not going to do that to me, Jake. If he comes, he plays. There are certain things we have to do.'

'What happens if these other guys pass the fitness test? How do I tell the other guy he's out and Kabamba's in?' I asked.

'Look, Jake, we've gone down this road. They told you they were un-happy about it. He's now coming. You can't *not* pick him,' Mac reiterated.

I could see his point, although the rugby coach in me said it wasn't right. But the rugby gods came to the rescue. Neither Spies nor Cronjé passed a fitness test, paving the way for Kabamba to play. It's ridiculous that you have to hope some players aren't declared fit, but that's what makes South African rugby unique.

The one who did pass was Juan Smith. It left me quite well off, because he had more experience than the other two. With Danie Rossouw fit, I had two big, strong guys in the back row, which allowed me to accommodate a guy like Kabamba, who's a very good athlete and covers a lot of ground.

Kabamba eventually arrived on the Tuesday, and Mac immediately met with him to find out more about his initial reluctance to fly over. Mac wanted to know if we were going to have a problem, and whether Kabamba really didn't want to play for South Africa. But he assured Mac that he wanted to be a Springbok, and that he was totally committed to the cause. What we'd heard had only been a rumour, which Kabamba hadn't known about until Mac got hold of him. We'd never actually heard it from the man himself.

He fitted in well from the start. The players enjoyed him. He tried hard to catch up with our calls and trained hard. He also had a couple of mates in the squad. He and Bevan Fortuin had played together at South Western Districts, and they got on quite nicely. At that point Bevan was also in the mix for the test team, so it was very positive.

Kabamba is a tough little oke. And we got the balance right. We needed him for that fixture, considering how the team was made up. Had we played him with another athletic looseforward, or had we played him in conjunction with another athletic lock, maybe he wouldn't have had the same impact. But on that day he was allowed to run freely, as the other players were basically doing all the hard yards, and it worked well.

Despite everything that was going on that week, I felt really good about the second test. We had thrown away the first test, and I was sure we had the beating of England. I suspected that they, too, knew they'd got out of jail the week before.

At the start of the year, when I had looked ahead, I felt that we would beat England. I looked at the players and knew that our only barrier was psychological, as the Boks hadn't won at Twickenham for nine years.

Ideally I wanted to win both tests, but if we lost the first one, I wanted the players to come off the field saying, 'We could have won that game.' Which is exactly what happened.

Had we been hammered, it would have been an uphill battle in the second test. But the vibe that week was electric. The players couldn't wait to play England again, because they knew they had a great chance of winning. The mood was positive, and there was a steely resolve to pull off a victory at Twickenham.

André Pretorius was the only change to the backline, as Butch James had flown home following his knee injury. André hadn't played well on tour up to that point, and he knew he needed to produce a big performance. And he did. That said a lot about his big-match temperament.

Gerrie Britz had joined the tour, and would provide lock and flank cover from the bench, while Meyer Bosman also came out and sat on the bench. We had a non-test game against a World XV the following week, and those guys were always in the mix for that fixture.

We ask someone to hand the players their match-day jerseys on the Friday before every test. It's often a former Springbok, but not always. Golfer Ernie Els and former England cricket captain Tony Greig had done the honours before. That week I broke slightly with tradition and asked SARU president Oregan Hoskins to present the jerseys to the team. I asked him because I wanted him to understand what we were going through, and to experience what it was like in the inner sanctum. It was too easy to criticise from the outside, but if I placed him in the centre, he would have a better understanding of what it was really like.

Oregan told the team he felt honoured, as the jerseys were usually handed out by a legend, and he didn't consider himself to be one. He also spoke passionately about growing up in apartheid South Africa and how, as a black man, he'd faced racial discrimination in his own country. Because of that, he used to support the All Blacks. I could understand the sentiment, but I felt that it wasn't entirely appropriate to mention it in that situation.

While some of the older players could understand where he was coming from, I don't think all the younger guys did. A guy like François Steyn, a 19-year-old boy who was about to play against England – the world champions – heard the president of SARU say he'd supported the All Blacks. That, knowing full well about all the ructions taking place off the field regarding his Springbok coach, must have left him with mixed emotions. But Oregan's words were intended to show how rugby could be a unifying force, and the power it had to play a positive role in South Africa. The Springboks were the men tasked with leading that spirit of change.

After the test, which we won, Oregan came into the changing room. I remember that I told the team – and John Smit echoed my thoughts – that Hoskins was now a legend. He was the oke who had presented the jerseys the day before we beat England at Twickenham for the first time in nine years. It went down quite well. For that day, he felt like he was a part of the Bok squad.

The match itself was tight, especially as we had to come from behind, but I always felt we were in control. Shortly before halftime, CJ van der Linde scored, which swung the momentum our way. Everyone will tell you that in rugby the 10 minutes on either side of halftime are vital. At Twickenham that day, this was certainly the case.

England had been leading comfortably on the scoreboard until CJ's try. We were in that game, but they led. When he scored, though, their belief disappeared, and we took control. People might not know this, but CJ was a 4 × 100 m athlete at Grey College in Bloemfontein. He's a real athlete. That try was as much a result of his athleticism as of his strength, and it unleashed a lot of self-belief. He scored many more tries for the Cheetahs after that. He began to appreciate that his athletic abilities were as important as his size and strength.

And the most pleasing thing about the match was that we showed composure in the final 15 minutes and killed the match off. The players showed that they'd learnt their lesson from the week before. When you look back at that second England test, the way we played in those last 35 minutes set a platform for going forward to the World Cup.

We controlled that match in everything we did: the calls we made; the composure we showed; the defensive capabilities we exhibited; the way we came back from being 11 points down. There were so many positives to come out of the second half in particular. No amount of money could buy the experience we gained, considering the pressure we were under.

John Smit deserves special credit. Put yourself in his situation. He was the most capped test captain in the history of South African rugby. He was one of the most capped Springbok rugby players of all time, and at that point the second most successful captain in terms of results.

If you consider that we seldom played against tier-two nations – we mostly played against tier-one countries – his achievements in the game are superb. Yet he seldom got the credit he deserved.

I felt for him on that tour. I think he must have been the only captain in the world who had to listen to his coach's problems when he should have been doing something else. I doubt that any other coach could knock on the captain's door and open up to him. I told John about having to fly home, about the problems I faced and about my own insecurities. He listened. And while there wasn't much he could do, he at least proved to be a great sounding board.

And then we still expected him to play brilliantly. It was probably unfair on him, but I didn't have anyone else on that tour with whom I could close the door and talk. The rest of the management were also concerned about their futures. They needed me to be their sounding board, and John was mine. The fact that, in that test match and in many others, John played well and captained astutely, said everything.

People don't understand what he went through on that particular tour, and in the Tri-Nations as well. Maybe one day he'll tell the story from his perspective in a book. The newspapers questioned his abilities all the time. Even within the SA Rugby system, people asked if he was the right man for the job. It was ludicrous.

He was groomed to be a captain. He was the Northern Transvaal Schools captain. He was Pretoria Boys High captain. He captained SA Schools. He captained the SA Under-21s. He captained the SA Under-23s. He then became the Springbok captain in the 2003 World Cup against Georgia. What more did he need to achieve to become the national captain?

He'd been groomed to take over, and yet people doubted him a lot of the time.

Being the captain of South Africa is unique. You have to be able to relate to all types of people and cultures, and help gel them into a unit. English, Afrikaans, coloured, black and white. You have to deal with all these diversities, and make them all understand that you're the leader. And then earn their respect. It's a hell of a skill.

Package all of that, and you realise that in John you're dealing with someone special, someone unique.

In 2005, when Tony Greig presented the Bok jerseys in Perth, he told us that South African sportspeople had to endure more than any other sportspeople in the world, both from an expectation and political point of view. He was right. There are no athletes in the world who have to put up with what our sportspeople have to. Besides selection and expectations, they have to live up to the standards set before them. They endure heavy criticism and live very public lives. John was at the forefront of all that. And he excelled, especially on that tour.

So he was as thrilled as I was, not only with the victory over England, but the way in which it had been achieved. I was also relieved. I didn't believe the result would have a huge impact on whether I kept my job or not; I still wasn't sure where I stood. But I knew the trip back to South Africa would be easier now that we'd beaten England in London for the first time in years. And we'd beaten them with a team that we knew would be even stronger when we had all our resources at our disposal.

At the after-match function, I chatted to Andy Robinson. He was very kind, respectful and humble. He said to me, 'Well done. I'm going through a difficult time, but you probably needed this one more than I did.'

I could relate. He knew that the heat was on. But, like me, he probably felt that he had a secure contract and the backing of his bosses. Obviously that had changed, as Andy lost his job soon after. And I still had the small matter of a vote of no confidence to face.

35

Council sessions

People have often asked if there were times during 2006 when I was tempted to pack it in and walk away from the job. Was it really worth it? Were the good times still outweighing the bad?

There's no simple answer to those questions. When things went badly, the job was extremely testing and frayed my emotions. My mood fluctuated on an hourly basis at times, and towards the end of the year it became worse. This was because I didn't feel I had much backing from anyone at the top. Oregan Hoskins was probably on my side, but not unconditionally, while the President's Council had many men who wanted to see the back of me.

My feeling of isolation was never more evident than at the post-match function after the first England test, which we lost. As is the tradition, Hoskins, as SARU president, made a speech. He congratulated Andy Robinson, captain Martin Corry and the rest of the England team on their victory. That was fine. But he started his speech by referring to the Springboks' *annus horribilis*. It was a slap in the face for me, but even more so for the players who'd just bled for the Springboks.

It wasn't intended as an insult to our team, but it hurt deeply. Your own president publicly proclaiming the year to be a disaster – that cut to the bone.

John Smit had to follow him to the podium. After congratulating the England team, he said in a slightly sarcastic tone that he had enjoyed the 'fantastic support' the Springbok team had received from the board. For John to do that suggests that he was incensed by Oregan's comments. I really don't think Regan meant them in a hurtful way, but he's intelligent enough to know better. That's part of the reason why I asked him to hand out the jerseys the following week.

This brings me back to the question of my job. Yes, for fleeting moments I did think about walking away from it. But that's all they were: fleeting moments. By the end of 2006 I knew I had the skill to continue doing the job, and through all the adversity we'd faced I also knew I had the players to be successful.

I think there was a feeling that Jake White might resign after being summoned back to South Africa in the middle of a tour. But by the time I boarded the aircraft to South Africa I was feeling pretty bullish, and was determined to look those President's Council guys in the eye and have my say. I wasn't afraid of being fired. I knew the difficulties we'd faced at every turn during the year. And while I'd made some mistakes, I believed various people who were driving their own agendas against me had compounded them.

I was ready to face my critics and happy to address them. I'd also heard that the sponsors had got together because they were extremely unhappy with the BBRU for proposing a motion of no confidence in me, and with the President's Council for endorsing the motion by summoning me home. I was buoyed by that news.

The sponsors did not approve of the way I was being treated. They wanted to know if the newspaper reports had any truth to them. Sasol chief executive Trevor Munday had sent me a couple of text messages after the *Rapport* story emerged. One of them said that he was baffled and suspected 'real mischief'. He suggested that I ask for an urgent meeting with Regan Hoskins and any other board member who was in the country. And that's what I did.

That was followed by an encouraging message, signifying his anger at the way things were happening, and wishing me strength on the road ahead.

I heard that some big shots from Vodacom, Sasol, Ford and Canterbury had got together to discuss the problem. They let the board and the President's Council know that they weren't happy with the way things were being done.

Johann Rupert, a great supporter of mine, met with various people behind the scenes to lobby for me too. He's the man behind Vodacom and wields a lot of power in South African business. He invited some people to his farm – people who were central to a decision on ousting me or not. It was the weekend the Boks beat England, and Johann discussed the issues with them. I don't know what was said but, knowing Johann, it was probably frank.

I'll probably never really know how much the sponsors' and Johann Rupert's interventions were responsible for helping me keep my job, as a lot of it happened behind the scenes. But I suspect they weren't insignificant.

Johann is a man I look up to, and I confided in him before the

President's Council meeting and discussed my best course of action. I asked him how I should handle the situation. His advice: 'Just acknowledge that you've made mistakes, Jake. It's going to leave a better taste as well.'

I had made some mistakes, so I probably would've admitted to that anyway, but his advice crystallised my thinking. I flew out of London on a Tuesday night and landed in Cape Town at 6.30 a.m. on the Wednesday morning. The meeting was to be held at the Woodstock Holiday Inn.

I went home to see my family and have a quick shower. I arrived at the hotel at 9 a.m., knowing that the meeting was scheduled for 10 a.m. As I'd arrived early, I was already there as various union presidents started arriving. When they passed me, I felt a bit like a naughty schoolboy waiting outside the headmaster's office to be called in.

A lot of the men greeted and congratulated me on the previous weekend's win. It felt odd. These were the same guys who'd told me they didn't back me the night before we left on tour, and now they were saying 'well done'.

As 10 a.m. came and went, I waited and waited.

National referees manager André Watson went into the meeting to deliver his annual report. Television broadcaster SuperSport, represented by Gert Roets, followed him to discuss programming and the format of the 2007 Currie Cup competition. They had just flown me over from London as a matter of urgency. Yet instead of being the first item on the agenda, I must have been the tenth.

I passed the time chatting to a couple of journalists who were there to report on whether I'd be axed or not. It was pleasant enough, but I was guarded about what I told them. They seemed pretty supportive, although they may just have said the right words to be polite.

Eventually I was told to go upstairs. As I walked into the room, I saw the presidents were voting by a show of hands. They had clearly been voting on the motion of no confidence – before I had even had a chance to address them!

I was quickly ushered out of the room, told to stand outside and wait to be called. It was after 1 p.m. I'd flown back at a cost of R55 000, I was tired, and they couldn't even do me the courtesy of letting me speak first. It was staggering when I later reflected on what had happened. But at the time I was so used to their arrogance and the kind of treatment they meted out, I hardly gave it a second thought.

Interestingly, Boland president Jackie Abrahams was standing in the hallway, as he was abstaining from the vote. I asked him why he was waiting outside the boardroom and why he wasn't voting. And he replied, 'Sometimes you know it's not the right thing to do.' He wasn't saying he was with me, but he clearly wasn't voting against me either. I later heard he had been one of the men entertained at Rupert's farm a few days earlier.

Eventually I was called in to face my accusers and supporters. They sat around a U-shaped table and I was sat down in the middle of it. I wasn't informed of the outcome of the vote at that time, but I was later told that five of the fourteen unions had voted against me.

Hoskins was the first to address me, explaining that I was there because some of the unions were concerned about the state of Springbok rugby and wanted to talk to me directly. The presidents from every union would have the chance to quiz me, and I would have the right of response. Hoskins urged everyone to use the opportunity to ask me questions.

I was grilled for two hours. Some questions were good, others rather ridiculous, but I was ready. It soon became clear that most of the presidents were basing their questions on what they'd read in the papers.

'Explain your choice of captain. In two tests you've ended a match with an all-white team. Why? And why did you hold a gun to SARU's head about taking an overseas coaching contract? Why are you picking players out of position?' That was their line of questioning.

Ironically, Valke president Rauties Rautenbach had told me that morning that their coach was moving flank Sean Plaatjies to hooker, and they couldn't wait to see how it would work out. Obviously experimenting with positional changes was fine, as long as it didn't happen in the Bok team. The Valke president didn't call his provincial coach in and say: 'You're playing Plaatjies out of position. Why?' Instead he thought it was a great piece of coaching and selection. Yet when the national coach did the same, he was criticised.

I did concede that I'd made some mistakes. I also pointed out that it was easy for them to sit on the other side of the table and tell me how I should coach because none of them had ever been in my shoes. I told them I was frustrated, as many of them had never coached a team before, so they'd never had to sit through a selection meeting with all the criteria I had to contend with.

They'd never had to face the media to explain how selection worked.

During the session, I got the feeling that a lot of their questions came straight from various newspaper editorials.

They even questioned whether John Smit was the right man for the captaincy. The newspapers had been beating that drum all year. I would have expected the members of the President's Council to at least back their Springbok captain. One person said: 'I go to a lot of pubs and restaurants, and people there ask me about the captain.' What can you say to that? At times their ignorance seemed almost laughable, but their interrogation was bloody nerve-wracking as well.

I approached it like a court session, except that I was guilty until proven innocent and not the other way round. I don't think anybody deserves to be treated in such a way, let alone the coach of a national team.

They grilled me on why Bryan Habana had been selected at centre against Ireland. I pointed out that he had played at centre for the SA Under-21s, and was a man with exceptional talent who could play just about anywhere in the backline. I told them that I'd moved him from centre to wing for the Springboks, and he was a great success. None of them had questioned my decision then. But when I played him at centre against Ireland and it went badly, they all jumped up to criticise. I told them they should be consistent.

They wanted to know why Jaco Pretorius had played wing when he'd done well at centre for the Lions. I explained that Wynand Olivier, Marius Joubert, Jaque Fourie and Jean de Villiers could all play at 13. I needed to see another wing in action, because the position worried me. Habana could play wing; I knew that. I wanted to see how Pretorius would do on the wing.

I pointed out that in order to be fair to a guy like Jaco, I had to pick him in a position where he might make the World Cup squad. I knew if all my centres were fit, there was no way he would make it in the midfield. I also emphasised that I'd just picked Danie Rossouw at number 8 against England, and he'd been man of the match. His performance was lauded in the English and South African press. He had played out of position too.

But they didn't fully appreciate my opinion, because they didn't want to see my side. They'd read in the newspapers that Habana had played out of position, and that he and the team had fared badly. It had nothing to do with how well or badly Habana had actually played. I got the feeling they just wanted me to admit to making mistakes.

I thought it was terribly unfair of them to query selection and individual player choices. I'm sure as presidents they didn't agree with every choice their provincial coaches made in terms of selection. If they didn't agree with their own coaches 100 per cent of the time, how, then, could they expect me as national coach to always please them?

I didn't go into the meeting with a belligerent attitude; I knew I was treading on thin ice. I wasn't about to attack them. I just answered their questions and gave my opinion, but I also made it clear that it wasn't for them to tell me how to do my job, as none of them had ever been in my situation.

I was honest with them, which didn't always help me. I don't play political games very well. I said, 'Listen, of course I've made mistakes. Not everything I've done has worked. Not every call I've made has been right.'

They questioned the make-up of my 24 contracted Springboks and why they would need contracts until after the World Cup. The irony was a lot of unions sign up their players for three to five years with the blessing of the president. But contracting players nationally was now an issue for these presidents.

I'd like to believe that when I left the meeting, the message I had conveyed was that 'Jake White is only human. He didn't come here with guns blazing. Some of the things he said actually made sense.' I don't know if I succeeded.

But I left with a tentative backing until the World Cup, which came as a huge relief.

I flew back to England that night to complete the tour with the team. Our last game was against a World XV in a match without test status.

We won comfortably, and Chiliboy Ralepelle had the honour of becoming the first black Springbok captain. It ended my toughest year on a rather nice note. We were set for 2007 and the World Cup.

PART VI

THE GUTS
AND THE GLORY
2007

36

Welcome back, Jake, we've cleared your desk

After a difficult 2006, I returned to work after a short Christmas holiday with the family. On our first 'proper' family vacation in a while, we went skiing in Austria and visited London. On my return to South Africa, I felt calm, relaxed and ready to face the year. It was, after all, a World Cup year and, having survived the axe at the end of 2006, I was feeling bullish about the season ahead.

I left home on a beautiful summer morning and arrived at work feeling chipper and good about the world. Not even thinking about the President's Council could dampen my mood. My optimism lasted about five minutes.

The lift to the fifth floor of the Sports Science building opened to SA Rugby's offices. I greeted a few people and strolled towards my corner office, which had a great view of Newlands cricket ground. But, as I approached, my PA, Carla van der Merwe, intercepted me. Apparently it wasn't my office any more. Newly appointed managing director Jonathan Stones had been moved in there instead.

I had been shunted to a new space, a pokey little room with no windows that was completely inadequate. It didn't even have a phone connection. My things had been packed into boxes and dumped there. No one had even had the courtesy to inform me of the new arrangement, let alone ask my opinion. Welcome back to the most important job in South African rugby!

My anger wasn't directed at Stones; it wasn't his fault. I was just irritated at the sloppy way it had been done. I spent most of my time out of the office, and Stones didn't, so it was logical that he should benefit from a well-equipped office in a pleasant environment. But the lack of courtesy in removing me from my office without communicating with me beforehand seemed to typify the way in which SA Rugby operated.

However, I wasn't going to fight over an office on the first day of a new year; it wasn't worth the stress. What would be the point of kicking up a fuss anyway? So I got on with work instead.

SA Rugby made a big splash about the establishment of a technical committee, to be formed under the chairmanship of the vice-president, Mike Stofile. The committee would meet with the franchise coaches and the national coach at least once a month during the Super 14 to discuss the state of the game. As I write this, the Super 14 has ended two months ago and I still haven't met the committee. I'm not sure what this committee is supposed to achieve and I'm not unhappy about the lack of progress, as I have my doubts whether it will be helpful. But I did arrange personal meetings with the various franchise coaches, and we held conference calls from time to time.

South Africa enjoyed a fantastic Super 14 season during 2007, and in the case of the Bulls and the Sharks, excellent Super 14 tournaments, which culminated in a historic final in Durban. Throughout the season, the coaches and I worked really well together and they accommodated my player requests whenever they could. Watching our teams and key players doing so well in a World Cup year made for an enjoyable few months.

Schalk Burger came back from his career-threatening injury without any further problems, which was a huge relief. Other key players such as John Smit, Victor Matfield, Bakkies Botha and Percy Montgomery were all in great form. But the one aspect that bothered me was the lack of transformation in the Super 14. I was under pressure to find black players for the Boks, but it was a hard task when very few black players were given opportunities in the competition. Politicians love to throw numbers around, but you have to be fair to players as well, and if they do not have the skills and experience, they cannot rise to the challenge in a test match.

I knew the issue would only intensify in a World Cup year, and that the bosses would be under pressure to find black players. And I'd be under even more pressure. But transformation just wasn't happening in the Super 14. During interviews I tried to highlight the lack of black players, and a few journalists drove home the point in their copy, but mostly my concerns fell on deaf ears. Even the top brass at SA Rugby did nothing to 'encourage' the franchises to select more black players. It was well documented that there were fewer black players in the 2007 Super 14 than in any previous season, which was a real problem in a World Cup year.

I knew there would be pressure when I had to select the first squad of the season, but I never imagined the extent. Considering that there had been near silence throughout the Super 14, I was lulled into believing that, for once, politics was taking a back seat to rugby.

The selectors and I decided to name a squad of 43 to 47 players towards the end of the Super 14 in May. The final 30 men for the World Cup squad would be chosen from that group. We knew more or less who we wanted, but a few positions were still up for grabs. We also had five consecutive test matches straight after the Super 14 final to consider, so we needed a bigger squad in order to rotate players.

We reckoned that one South African team would probably reach the Super 14 semi-finals, and perhaps the final. But in the end two of our teams went all the way, which cut down our preparation time and also increased the chance of injuries. So, in retrospect, a large squad turned out to be a prudent decision.

As I explained earlier, we chose squads well in advance, as we didn't want to make emotional decisions based on individual performances in a final. I wanted to announce the squad on the final weekend of round-robin matches in order to eliminate any chance of emotional calls for player X over player Y.

But then a request came through from the Bulls and the Sharks to delay the naming of the team. I wasn't keen, but the Sharks were concerned that the announcement would have an effect on the players who didn't make the squad. The Bulls had seconded the request. And given my rocky relationship with the latter, especially after they'd proposed a motion of no confidence in me six months earlier, I agreed to the delay. There was no reason to be hard-arsed about it.

The Bulls won their final pool match by 90 points to earn a home semi-final. The Sharks also had a home semi, so the possibility of an all–South African final was very real. It was great for the South African game, but difficult for the national team in some ways. Then again, I'd rather have players with the confidence of a Super 14 win at Bok camp!

Stones, national teams' manager Andy Marinos and I, along with the selectors, agreed that the team would be announced after the semi-finals – with no more delays. During the week in the run-up to the matches we finalised the 44-man squad, and convenor Pieter Jooste presented it to Regan Hoskins. The president spoke to whomever he speaks to about such matters and the squad was signed off without any problems. We were ready to go.

And then I got wind that there was a push to include Western Province and Stormers flank Luke Watson in the team. I couldn't believe it was possible, especially as some members of the President's Council, Hoskins included, had told me they didn't think Watson was good enough to make the squad.

But on the Monday evening of the week of the squad announcement, I received a call. I was told that I had to fly to Johannesburg early the next day, along with selectors Pieter Jooste and Ian McIntosh, to meet with certain board members. It was the beginning of a very traumatic month.

37

Number 46

If I had a rand for every word written about my relationship – or lack thereof – with Luke Watson, I would be a very wealthy man. A small rainforest has been destroyed in the provision of newspaper pages detailing our supposed feud. Most of the stories are completely inaccurate, for the simple reason that we have never had a relationship, and we still don't. I've never rated him as a test-quality flank, and nothing has changed.

Articles have been written about my supposed feud with Luke's father Cheeky and my objections to his political stance, which somehow made me biased against Luke. Nonsense. I've met Cheeky once, and until he started criticising me in the press, I had absolutely nothing against him. Actually, I still have very little against him; he's entitled to his opinions and he's not the first father of a player to be angry with me about issues pertaining to his son. He won't be the last either.

Cheeky was an anti-apartheid activist who refused to play 'whites-only' rugby in the 1970s and early 1980s. He bravely went against the system and played multiracial rugby. I've heard he was a great player who might have been good enough to make it at Springbok level, but I never saw him play myself. I know as much about Cheeky as what I've read in the press, which I always take with a pinch of salt, given what I've seen written about me in newspapers on occasion.

My views on the Watson family's political past are completely ambivalent, as I've never been a political person. I'm sure that what Cheeky and his brothers did was the right thing for them, and you have to respect their decision. But suggestions that their political views somehow prejudiced me against Luke are completely preposterous.

Luke went to Grey High in Port Elizabeth and captained every rugby team he played in. He represented SA Schools, SA Under-19s and SA Under-21s. He had every opportunity in the game, unlike his father, so when I read quotes or heard people saying that he'd suffered while growing up, I have to admit, I found that difficult to stomach. As a rugby player it doesn't appear as if he was left wanting as a child. Ashwin Willemse and Ricky Januarie are two of many South African players who persevered through real obstacles while growing up, in a way I don't think Luke did. It made me angry when I heard about Luke's 'suffering' and his complex background, because I had interacted with players who seemed to be dealing with much worse.

In my view, Luke Watson was a decent, hard-working flank, but he couldn't add anything to the Springboks. I didn't rate him as a player – it was that simple.

But let's backtrack a bit to the early part of the 2007 international season. Before the Bok training squad was decided, about midway through the Super 14, I was asked to attend a meeting with Brian Biebuyck, my lawyer at the time. He asked me to meet with him at his home the next day and bring my agent Craig Livingstone, as he had 'something important' to propose.

Craig briefed me that Brian also had the Watsons on his client list, and suggested that in light of the rather public campaign to include Luke in Bok selections at the time, the meeting might be about that.

On arrival, Brian and I chatted about a few legal issues, including my contract and whether there was a possibility of extending it beyond the World Cup. But I was there at his request, so we didn't linger on the topic. After a short while, Brian said, 'Listen guys, I've been asked to meet with you on behalf of the Watson family.'

Confused, I asked him what he meant. He explained that he did a lot of work for the family through the various brothers (Luke's uncles), and that one of them had asked him to relay a message. Brian was at pains to establish that he was only the messenger, and that we shouldn't shoot him.

He pulled out a document listing nine points. I can't remember each of the points verbatim, and he gave neither Craig nor me a copy of the document. The opening preamble of the note included statements such as 'Luke will be picked for the Bok squad', and 'Luke will play a test', and 'Luke will go to the World Cup'. They were listed like a set of demands, stating that, in return for my cooperation, the Watsons could ensure that I would work in South African rugby beyond the 2007 World Cup.

It went on in that fashion, until we got to point number nine, which warned that if I did not agree to these 'terms', I would not coach the team to the World Cup. I was stunned. The Watson family had drawn up a document paving the way forward for Springbok rugby for the rest of the year. Who the hell did they think they were?

Brian then mentioned something about the power of 'knowing to-morrow's news today'. He said that a story would break in the press the next day about a so-called third force that ran rugby in South Africa, to which I would be linked. He also warned me that I was being watched and that my phone calls were being monitored. It made no sense, and I told Brian that it was sounding bizarrely like a Mafia movie.

I turned to Craig and asked him what we should do, as on the one hand it seemed ridiculous, and on the other a little scary. I was Bok rugby coach, and suddenly a clandestine 'offer I couldn't refuse' was being put on the table by the family of a slightly above-average rugby player. Yet I was becoming increasingly aware that Luke – or his family – was extremely well-connected politically, and appeared to have the backing of some powerful people in government and in rugby.

This was a serious threat, with the ultimatum 'pick Luke or lose your job'. I took a step back for some serious reflection. I thought of how things were said to have been done in the old days of South African rugby, when certain players might have been members of the Broederbond, which meant they may have received the inside track over other players when Springbok teams were selected. I came to the conclusion that I probably wasn't the first coach to feel this underhand sort of pressure – rightly or wrongly.

It crossed my mind that perhaps I could kill the media and public speculation on the 'Watson case' once and for all by accepting these 'terms' and getting on with the job. I wondered whether my clashes with politicians and rugby bosses on quotas and selections would lessen if I picked one 'approved' player. If it meant I could go to the World Cup with 29 out of the 30 players on my wish list, then perhaps the 'terms' were worth considering.

I told Brian I needed to think about the matter. Craig and I went for lunch and discussed the meeting. He suggested that maybe I should accept the terms, reasoning that Luke wasn't the worst player in the world and that I could get by with him in the squad. Hopefully it would also take away all the negativity and buy me some goodwill with the powers that be.

By the end of our lunch I'd decided to take the deal so that I could move on and coach the team without any more interference. I wasn't happy, knowing I was compromising on my selections, but I figured it was a fair trade-off in order for a stab at winning the World Cup. Craig phoned Brian the next day to tell him that I was prepared to take the deal, only to be told that the Watsons had backed down. Their list of ultimatums no longer applied. Seemingly they had got cold feet and called the deal off.

I'll never know why the Watsons changed their minds, but my guess is that they'd tried to pressurise SA Rugby in the same way, and met some resistance. At some point they probably realised that they might not come out of it looking very good.

I was relieved that the deal was off, because I'd felt extremely uneasy about it in the first place. But I was also slightly annoyed, because it meant that the Watson issue was likely to continue. We'd had a chance to end it and the moment had passed, so I was adamant that I wasn't going to select him at any later point. That was the theory anyway; in reality it was a lot more complicated.

After presenting Hoskins with the 44 names that would comprise the first Bok training squad of the season, I was satisfied with its make-up. All the role-players seemed to be in agreement, and for once we all seemed to be pulling in the same direction, to the benefit of South African rugby. But then I received a call instructing me to fly to Johannesburg on the Tuesday before the semi-finals. Together with the selectors, I would meet several President's Council members at Oliver Tambo airport. They wanted to quiz us on our 'thinking' behind the squad selection.

I was sceptical and smelt a rat. Until that point the squad had been given the green light, but suddenly I was being asked to clarify my 'thinking'. It was odd at best. But I boarded the aircraft as instructed.

The meeting started pretty cordially, and there were smiles and a bit of verbal jousting. Stones, Marinos, Hoskins, Mpumelelo Tshume, Mike Stofile and, strangely, team manager Zola Yeye were all attending. I was surprised to see Zola, as he had nothing to do with selection. Hoskins said that the reasons for the meeting were, first, to understand our selection criteria and, second, to ensure that when the names were announced, we wouldn't all speak at cross purposes. I gathered then that we were there to align our stories. Odd.

Also strange was being forced to go through our selection policies again, especially since Hoskins and Tshume had always been in the loop. Once we'd gone through our selection criteria, our policy, our plans, how we'd built on our selections of the previous three years and what we looked for in each player, the real point of the meeting started to emerge.

Yeye confronted Jooste and Ian Mac, accusing them of being my 'yes-men'. He blamed them for the make-up of the squad. It was a bolt out of the blue, but at least it gave us an idea of where the meeting was headed. He accused Jooste and Mac of 'rolling over' whenever I rejected their recommendations. At one stage he even questioned Jooste: 'How's your conscience when you get out of bed in the morning?' Jooste was angry, because he's a proud coloured man and a former non-racial player who has a superb history in the game. Jooste shot back, 'My conscience is very clear that we make rugby decisions and not political decisions.' Zola didn't have a retort, but the meeting had become strained.

Then the name of Odwa Ndungane came up. Zola demanded to know why he wasn't in the squad. I must stress that I have no problem with people having opinions on selection; it's part of living in a multiracial, rugby-mad country. But I was contractually allowed to choose my teams and was supposed to have the final say on selection. There were always going to be disagreements, but as the coach I had the right to make the calls. Yet as far as most of the men at that meeting were concerned, this was not the case. They had political agendas they were determined to see implemented.

Zola said he'd had a meeting with the Ndungane family, and that Odwa had been almost suicidal after being left out of the Sharks team the week after he'd scored the winning try against the Crusaders. I said I had no say in Sharks team selections, and pointed out that none of the President's Council had called a meeting with the Sharks to interfere with *their* selections when they didn't pick Odwa.

Zola demanded to know on what grounds Odwa hadn't been selected for the Bok squad, and I replied, 'He's too slow.' I said I also believed his twin brother Akona was too slow, but that, thanks to a good Super 14 run and the fact that he'd been part of the Bok set-up, I was prepared to work with him. That's why we'd included Tonderai Chavhanga in the squad – he possessed pure speed.

They quizzed me about why Odwa hadn't been selected ahead of Ashwin Willemse, who had been injured for almost 18 months. I've explained my reasons for picking Ashwin, and while I appreciate that he'd lost some pace, he's an athlete, big and strong, with the heart of a lion.

Yeye laughed and said this was rugby, not athletics; we didn't need athletes. That in itself is a ludicrous statement and in my view shows a complete lack of understanding of the modern game. I was angry now, as I was entering into a debate with the team manager about athletes versus rugby players – a complete waste of time. But it was clear they wanted Odwa in the squad.

They didn't want Bob Skinstad either. Bob had returned after two years' retirement to play a crucial role for the Sharks in the Super 14, and was a revelation. With his experience and skills, it would have been stupid not to include him in the training squad. But they didn't want him, and they didn't want Ashwin or Tonderai either.

Then Luke Watson came up.

Tshume asked me what the story was regarding Luke Watson. I said, 'What story? In my opinion he's not good enough and he never will be.' But I saw what they were angling for with Watson and Ndungane. Tshume said, 'We would like to see both their names in the squad.' It wasn't exactly an order, but it was clear that they weren't going to let it go.

'Excuse me,' I said to Tshume, 'but are you saying we must put them in the squad? Will you tell these players that you've added them? I'm not clear exactly what you're saying.'

Tshume got defensive: 'We're not saying you have to put them in; we're saying we'd like you to consider them.' This was completely bonkers. We'd considered the squad carefully and they hadn't made the cut. That was it.

The meeting ended without resolving anything. It was clear that Tshume and Yeye, in particular, didn't care about selection criteria or our judgement. They had an agenda to get Odwa and Watson into the team, which was the only reason they'd called the meeting.

I flew back to Cape Town with Pieter and we discussed it on the aeroplane. 'Pieter, on principle I don't think we should put those players in,' I said. 'I think it's disgusting that we're being treated like this.' Pieter suggested I calm down and forget about it for the night, and we decided to talk about it in the morning. The next day he called me.

'Jake, politically it's the right thing to include Odwa. But politically it's wrong to include Watson,' he suggested.

I could live with that. So Pieter went back to the presidency and told them that we'd include Odwa. They enquired about Watson, and he said that we'd take Odwa to the camp in Bloemfontein, but we weren't taking

Watson. Hoskins was non-committal, and we didn't hear another word. It was Wednesday; the squad was being made public on Saturday.

Hoskins called me privately and asked if I wouldn't just add Watson's name to the squad. He was feeling the political pressure, with a special squeeze on Watson's inclusion. He made a suggestion. 'Invite him to the training camp and then you can leave him out when you make team selections.' I was amazed. 'Come on, Regan, if he's not good enough, why should I take him to the camp in the first place?' I asked. 'It's not fair on me, on him or on the other players.' It was ludicrous.

We heard nothing more about the squad over the next few days. I assumed that they'd tried to force our hand but that we'd conceded on Odwa, and that would be the end of the story. How wrong I was.

The televised announcement of the training squad was scheduled to take place immediately after the Durban semi-final, live from the Absa Stadium. The actual recording had been done a few hours earlier, in the bowels of the stadium, with Hoskins and team manager Zola Yeye present. I didn't travel to Durban, as I didn't want another confrontation with board members over the make-up of the squad. But Jooste was there, and about an hour before the pre-recording of the squad, he sent me a text message saying that trouble was brewing. Tshume and others had confronted him on the Watson issue. They wanted him back in the team.

I sent a text message back to him, saying, 'I'm not prepared to accept it, and I'm not prepared to go down that road.' Pieter was in the firing line, and Ian Mac then called me. He was upset. He said that Tshume and Hoskins were screaming and shouting and demanding that Watson's name be included. They were very emotional, according to Mac. I stuck to my guns, and said to Mac, 'It doesn't matter: we said we would pick Odwa because it was the right thing politically, and they've signed off on the team. I'm not prepared to back down on Watson; he's not good enough.'

At 16:30 I received another text message from Jooste, saying, 'You won't believe it. They've announced the team on a pre-recording, and Watson's name was read out.' They had handwritten his name at the bottom of the pre-typed 45-man squad.

The broadcast went out at 7 p.m. that evening, which is when I saw it for the first time. I was livid.

Luke Watson had summarily been made squad member number 46.

38

Doing a deal

I was in shock. I'd watched the delayed live broadcast from my couch at home, still hoping that what Pieter had told me wasn't true. But, sure enough, the last name the president read out was 'Luke Watson'. Contractually I had the final say on the make-up of the squad, and I could fight this, but I knew that it wasn't going to be enough to stop the hierarchy at SA Rugby pushing through its own agenda. I had been forced into a corner where my only options were to accept their decision or quit. And I think that most of them were hoping I would fall on my sword.

But quitting never crossed my mind. I'd worked too damn hard with a squad of players that, to my mind, had become a formidable unit. I wasn't going to let someone else come in at the last minute and piggyback on my sweat and tears and take this team to the World Cup. For once, however, I wasn't alone, as the media immediately smelt a rat. The Watson support seemed to vanish when a few sports journalists figured out what had transpired. Hoskins and the rest of the SA Rugby hierarchy took a pounding for the way in which they'd added Luke's name.

Pieter Jooste and I both received phone calls that weekend, querying the events surrounding Watson's selection, and neither of us lied. We told the press that we hadn't selected him, and it was left to Hoskins, in particular, to front up – and, boy, did he have a tough time!

Popular Johannesburg morning radio host – and former Irish rugby player – John Robbie interviewed Hoskins on the Monday morning. He absolutely tied the president in knots for his role in overriding the selection panel. Here is an extract from that interview:

REGAN HOSKINS: Hello, John.

JOHN ROBBIE: Is it true that Jake did not pick Watson, and you guys did?

HOSKINS: Yes.

ROBBIE: Doesn't that make a mockery of the whole idea of having a selection panel?

HOSKINS: I have just spoken to your sister station in Cape Town, Cape Talk, and he [the presenter] totally disagrees with you.

ROBBIE: Well, I don't care about that, Regan; doesn't it make a mockery of having a selection panel?

HOSKINS: John, of course you are entitled to your opinion, but I don't agree with you.

ROBBIE: So why do you have a selection panel if they don't select the team?

HOSKINS: John, obviously you know … It's an unprecedented move, and it's not something that I would like to see happen again.

ROBBIE: Why not?

HOSKINS: Because, as you said, the coaches and the selectors are there to do their job, but we believe here that we have a situation that is not tenable. We have a player who was a Super 14 player of the year in 2006. He has played well enough in 2007 to warrant selection to the training camp, has not been selected, and we have done what we did.

ROBBIE: But Bradley Barrett has had a fantastic season. Derick Hougaard has just scored points, he has taken the Bulls in the most magnificent way. Should we put them in, Regan?

HOSKINS: No.

ROBBIE: Why not?

HOSKINS: Were they the Super 14 players of the year last year?

ROBBIE: But that was last year, Regan.

HOSKINS: Yes, but Luke Watson has had a fantastic Super 14 season in 2007, John.

ROBBIE: But it's the principle, Regan, surely. Every single rugby fan in this country believes he can pick a better team and a better squad than the coach. I mean, that's what sport is … [Interjection] … hang on a second …

HOSKINS: Have you solicited the rugby people's view on this matter?

ROBBIE: But that's irrelevant, Regan.

HOSKINS: You just referred to that fact, John.

ROBBIE: Yes, but everybody thinks they can pick a squad.

HOSKINS: No, not everybody, we are talking about popular opinion, John.

ROBBIE: But are you therefore saying that popular opinion selects the squad?

HOSKINS: No, no, no. I am saying at times, popular opinion is correct.

ROBBIE: But then why not have a vote for a team? Why not do away with selectors? We can use the Internet and vote the team in, Regan.

HOSKINS: Well, look, John, you have heard what our situation is, and what more do you want me to say?

ROBBIE: I mean, I would like you to stand up ... I mean how can you say, Regan, that you don't want the situation to happen again? You have basically said that it's unprecedented, that you have agreed with me that this goes against the whole principle of having a selection committee, and yet you are still justifying it. I can't believe it.

HOSKINS: Okay, what more do you want me to say, John Robbie?

ROBBIE: Well, what are you going to do to Jake White now, if Luke Watson, having got into this squad, performs badly? If he is disruptive to the squad, if for whatever reason, surely now Jake White cannot be accountable for the performance of a team that hasn't been selected by himself?

HOSKINS: What do you think we are going to do to Jake White?

ROBBIE: Well, I am amazed that Jake White hasn't resigned. I mean, you've basically said to Jake White, you coach a side and you select a side, and then you are responsible for the side. But now what you have basically said is that you are not good enough to do it. We are going to ... we know more about rugby than you do.

HOSKINS: No.

ROBBIE: That's basically what you are saying, Regan, isn't it?

HOSKINS: John, this is a training squad for this team of 45 or 46 players, a training squad.

ROBBIE: Yes, a Springbok training squad.

HOSKINS: It is not the team itself, for number one.

ROBBIE: But forgive me, Regan, but Jake White is responsible for training the Springbok team, is he not? But he's not responsible enough to have his squad selected by him?

HOSKINS: As a principle, yes, I agree with you.

ROBBIE: So you have gone against principle?

HOSKINS: Yes.

ROBBIE: Why?

HOSKINS: But I have just told you, and I am not going to repeat what I said to you earlier on. And the reason is that we think that the player Luke Watson is good enough to be in the training squad. We believe that the coach and the two national selectors are wrong. We believe that it's time that the player was given an opportunity to be in the training squad, and we stand by that.

ROBBIE: Okay, so you have gone against principle now. Is this not a
    dangerous precedent, Regan?
HOSKINS: It is.

While Hoskins was trying to put out fires, I spoke to my lawyer and
drafted a letter expressing my unhappiness with what had occurred
in Durban. I didn't make any threats or demands, but I wanted my
unhappiness recorded in proper legal terms so that I had ammunition if
I ever needed it. My letter stated that I demanded an answer about why
Watson's name had summarily been added, as I was supposed to have the
final say over the selection of the Springbok team – a point that was
detailed in my contract. I'm still waiting for an answer.

But during this fallout there was a test season to prepare for. I was
scheduled to fly to Bloemfontein to start the camp, without any of my
Sharks and Bulls players, who were up against each other in the Super 14
final that coming Saturday. I knew that it was going to be a difficult few
weeks with Watson in the camp, simply because we would both know he
hadn't been selected. Given that I'd never selected him in my three years
in charge, he had to know that I didn't rate him as a player. I had publicly
mentioned this several times. We had been forced on each other, and we'd
have to deal with it. But I was adamant that I would not single him out for
any special attention, for example by not addressing him in a one-on-one
situation. There were going to be 46 players attending the camp, and
I would treat them all the same.

Of course, thanks to Watson's presence, the media scrum at the camp
was unwavering. In the week of a historic all–South African Super 14 final,
the bosses at SA Rugby had somehow created a situation that took all the
attention *off* the rugby field and *onto* a player and the Bok coach. A movie
director couldn't have made it up.

While all this was going on, SA Rugby instructed me to travel to Durban
for the Super 14 final that weekend. They wanted me to meet with
Hoskins, Tshume and other members of the board to discuss the Watson
situation.

A small group of players arrived in Bloemfontein. I greeted them in the
team room and pointed out that, although I hadn't selected him, Watson
was there. I gave my assurance that he would be treated fairly. I said that
I have two sons, and that I wouldn't want either of them to be treated
unfairly over a situation that might not have been of their making.

We settled into routine training and fitness assessments, but it soon became clear that there was an agenda to promote Watson's profile. The *Star*'s Kevin McCallum wrote a piece about Watson having bench-pressed 140 kilograms on his first day at the Bok camp. I was in a meeting with Hoskins when media manager Vusi Kama came in. He told us that Cheeky Watson had called the *Star* to complain about the story, as Luke had actually bench-pressed 160 kilograms, and not 140 kilograms.

The *Star*, following standard protocol, wanted the Springboks to confirm the numbers, so they could run a correction. Vusi suggested we send out a press release with the correct numbers for Watson. It was completely ludicrous. As a rule we'd never released this information to the press. Why on earth should we start now?

I appealed to Hoskins with logic: 'Regan, if we issued a press release every single time the media gets something wrong, we'd be sending several out per day.' Regan agreed and told Vusi to ignore it. But Mike Stofile called Vusi and told him to go ahead and send out a press release. He did, stating that McCallum was wrong and that Luke had, in fact, bench-pressed 160 kilograms.

Hoskins was livid that Vusi had ignored him. I was angry too, as it showed the powerful forces at work behind Watson's inclusion. But it also had the effect of polarising him from the rest of the squad, a situation which had developed naturally in players already irritated by the special attention he was receiving.

The training squad was released for the weekend and sent home, while I headed to Durban for yet another meeting with board members – and, of course, the Super 14 final. Sadly, the rugby component on the agenda was of secondary importance.

Hoskins brokered the Friday night meeting between Tshume and me, but we got nowhere. He was adamant that Watson should play, and naturally I was quite against the idea, especially after what had happened. Tshume told me I should play Watson and give him a chance, and once I'd seen what he could do, then I'd be free to keep him or drop him. He said that if Watson was given a chance and I still didn't rate him, then they would back me if I dropped him.

I agreed to a deal in which Watson would play against Samoa, which was our third test of the season, following two against England. I wasn't happy about it, but I made the deal. It was another miserable meeting with SA Rugby.

I'd scheduled another meeting in Durban for the Sunday morning, with managing director Jonathan Stones, as well as Tshume, Hoskins and Stofile. It was to discuss the letter my lawyer had sent in the immediate aftermath of Watson's selection. I wanted clarity on the way forward, and had asked for a reply by Friday 18 May, the day before the Super 14 final. My deadline having passed, I was counting on the meeting for answers.

Only Stones and Hoskins attended the meeting; the rest flew off, citing various reasons for not being able to attend. Contractually I report to the managing director anyway, so we carried on without Tshume, Stofile and Koos Basson. We ironed out some kinks and decided on a course of action for the remainder of the season, with guarantees of no further interference after Watson was given his chance.

The Bulls famously won the Super 14 final, with Bryan Habana scoring the winning try in the final minute. I had been a little concerned about the tension of the occasion and what it might do to the harmony in the Springbok camp, but I also knew that the value of two of our sides playing in a big final in a World Cup year would override any other concerns.

To their eternal credit, the Bulls players were so gracious in victory that, if anything, the 46-man squad seemed closer than ever when they all assembled on the Monday morning in Bloemfontein. It would have a big impact on the rest of our season.

39

A tough week

The season hadn't even started properly from a Springbok perspective and the Watson saga was taking its toll. But I had a job to do: before the Tri-Nations started, I had to prepare for two tests against England, as well as a one-off against Samoa. The season had been planned down to the smallest detail, and we had virtually decided that our top 15 to 20 players would not travel on the away leg of the Tri-Nations.

With the added pressure of the Super 14 semi-finals and a final for most of the players in the squad, a six-week break before the World Cup started in September was essential, and the only time it could be slotted in was during the Tri-Nations. It wasn't ideal, but with the demands of making an assault on the World Cup, something had to give.

England and Samoa would both be in our pool at the World Cup later in the year, so victories over these teams were important from a psychological point of view. I knew England would travel to South Africa with a much weaker team, but a series win over the current world champions, irrespective of who wore the white jersey on the day, was a non-negotiable part of the planning. I intended using my best teams for the England tests, and then to give some fringe players a chance against Samoa and on the away leg of the Tri-Nations. We had a plan for the senior players, and it was on track.

The guys tolerated Watson's presence at the camp, but it was awkward. I heard that many Sharks players, in particular, didn't have a lot of time for him. Some of them told me they had been happy to see the back of him when he went to Western Province. Watson had also been very outspoken in a *Sports Illustrated* article a few months earlier, offering strong views on his chances of selection as a Bok and his thoughts on me as a coach. He'd voiced opinions about the ethos of Bok rugby and had made comments about John Smit in another interview. A lot of this didn't sit well with some of the senior players.

Other players who hadn't had any dealings with him knew only that he'd been added to the squad in a most surreal way, which wasn't easy to swallow in a competitive environment. It affected the team dynamic, and if I'd had a weaker captain, or a more inadequate set of senior players, our season might have imploded into bickering and infighting. But the core players knew where they stood with me, and Watson's presence was seen as little more than a necessary irritation.

Another aspect linked to his inclusion – and the small yet steadfast support he was getting from those pushing for his selection – was that it made me doubt myself. I have shortcomings like any normal person, but I do not usually suffer self-doubt. With people constantly telling me how good Watson was, I started to wonder if perhaps I'd lost the plot and missed some vital aspect of his playing ability.

I became so conflicted that I eventually called all the Super 14 coaches – with the exception of Stormers coach Kobus van der Merwe – to ask if they would have selected Watson if they'd been in my position. I omitted Van der Merwe because he selected Watson every week and had made him team captain, so his answer was obvious.

To a man, the other Super 14 coaches all said no. Their responses confirmed my own opinion on Watson's abilities as a Springbok player, and I cast my doubts aside for good. But I still had to contend with his presence and the deal I'd made to play him against Samoa.

England arrived with an under-strength team, and then endured a torrid wave of gastro that swept through their camp, so they really struggled. We put them away 58-10 in the first test in Bloemfontein, and then won 55-22 a week later in Pretoria. I didn't care that they weren't at full strength – we hammered them in both tests. And after winning the second test at Twickenham six months earlier, we'd suddenly won three matches against the reigning world champions. To my mind, that was significant. The senior Bok players all looked good, considering that most of them had smashed each other in an intense Super 14 final only seven days before running out together against England.

In reality we'd only had four days to prepare for the first test, and it was amazing to see how the guys worked together. I've often been criticised for being overly consistent in selections, but when it came down to it, the Bulls and the Sharks had done the same in the Super 14. They were South Africa's two most experienced teams; they had the two most experienced captains. They had the best lineouts and the best scrums, and defensively they were the top two teams. And I don't necessarily mean in terms of points conceded, but in defending well when they had to.

These were all things the media praised when reporting on the Super 14, yet they hammered me for the very same when it came to the Springbok team. I raise the point because I believe we saw the true value of having a well-settled and experienced team that week. The Boks were tired and emotionally drained after an intense final, yet they trained well during the week and produced a high-quality performance at the weekend. It augured well for the rest of the season.

I could sense that something special was happening in the squad despite the Watson sideshow. Scrumhalf Fourie du Preez, one of my key players, had been injured in the Super 14 final, and missed the incoming tours. In fact, he would miss the entire international season until a week before the World Cup. But Ruan Pienaar emerged as a wonderful understudy in a similar mould, and I had the combative nature of Ricky Januarie to rely on too.

After the second test, Bryan Habana suffered a knee injury, but fortunately it wasn't too serious and wouldn't keep him out of the World Cup. I kept my fingers crossed that the injury gods would be kind to me in 2007.

Once we'd despatched England, it was a one-off test against Samoa at Ellis Park. It was a test we thought we should win, so we decided to give a few other players a chance to stake a claim for a World Cup place. It was also the test for which I would pick Watson, and consequently one of the most difficult weeks of my life.

I'd only agreed to play him in the hope of having an easier time of it in terms of political interference for the remainder of the year, but it grated on me. As the week approached I felt increasingly uneasy, as it went against everything I believed in. There was little I could do, though, and I decided to prepare as normal.

However, some of the players had a different take on the situation that week. Several players, whom I won't name, finally confronted their unhappiness with the Watson situation and told me they didn't want him to be given the traditional Springbok initiation. Others said that they wanted nothing to do with a Bok team that included Watson; a few said they would prefer to be out of the match 22 on the day he played.

They didn't have an issue with me; they were simply expressing their feelings. I was sympathetic, as they had all earned their Bok places, and as far as they, and I, were concerned, Watson hadn't. But he was there and he would play, I informed the players. I also told them, 'I can't force you to initiate him, but if you're real Springboks, you should conduct yourselves like real Springboks. In some ways you actually *have* to initiate him, because individually you're not bigger than Springbok rugby. Watson will become a Bok, and it's up to each of you how you handle it.'

It cut me up, because I felt exactly as the players did. But I had become mixed up in the murky world of SA Rugby politics, so I could only appeal to them as Springbok ambassadors. I sensed the pressure, as the situation was threatening to undo a very strong team ethos.

The media hype was incredible too, considering that Watson was one of two players earning his first test cap. Sharks centre Waylon Murray was also set to make his Springbok debut, but he hardly warranted a mention in the press. The politicians should have celebrated Murray's selection as a man of colour, as I'd been under constant pressure to select black players, yet when he was chosen – entirely on merit – there were no congratulations from either rugby or government politicians, only talk of Watson. South Africa is a very strange country sometimes.

I was upset, and on the Thursday evening before the test I went out for a few drinks with some friends to take my mind off my rugby problems. While out, I received a friendly call from journalist Kevin McCallum, who suggested I join him for a beer at a bar near the team hotel. I was given a lift, and joined Kevin and a few other journos, who had been hosted earlier for drinks by team manager Zola Yeye. As I walked in, Cape Town journalist Adnaan Mohammed, who at the time worked for *Die Son*, a tabloid that specialises in sensationalism, told me, 'The Boks had better fucking win on the weekend.'

It was all I needed after the pressures of the week. I turned to him and said: 'You know what? I'm so tired of okes like you talking shit all the time. And by the way, while I've got your ear, I didn't appreciate the article you guys wrote about John Smit and his wife.' Some time before, his newspaper had published an article alleging a relationship between Smit's wife and Luke Watson.

Mohammed said he wasn't the journalist who had written the article, but as far as I was concerned he was representing his newspaper, and I vented my anger at him. I told him I was sick and tired of their tabloid sensationalism and negativity. I know I shouldn't have become so angry or attacked him in public, but I'm only human, and in that particular week I'd had enough.

'I'll give you a story,' I raged on. 'You can write a headline story, 'cause what I'll do is punch you and knock you out. That's what I'll do, so that you can have a story.' By then McCallum had come to my side and said, 'No, no, no, Jake. Don't do that; he *will* write it.' I said, 'Well, it doesn't matter; I'll give him a story. Then he can have a headline saying that he's been beaten up, 'cause then it's all factual and it's not just made up.'

But Kevin led me away and calmed me down. I sat with him and some colleagues, but I was only in the bar for an hour or so. During that time several people came up and wished me the best. I eventually called Allister Coetzee and asked him to drop by to collect me, which he did. It was the last I saw of Adnaan that night.

When I woke up the next day, I had a text message on my phone from a friend, asking, 'What the hell have you done?' I had no idea what he was referring to, so I called and asked what was going on. My friend said a story had broken saying that I'd beaten up a journalist in a bar in Sandton.

It turned out that Mohammed had been punched by a third party after I'd left the bar. Initially it was reported that I had hit him. Then a later version suggested that my 'bodyguard' had assaulted him. I've never had a bodyguard, and I was long gone by the time Mohammed claimed he was assaulted, so I have no idea what happened. But our public spat linked me to the incident, and I was hauled into a disciplinary hearing.

SA Rugby, under the auspices of legal manager Christo Ferreira, conducted a full investigation. I was interviewed, along with other key witnesses to the event. After all the press reports and front-page stories, my name was cleared, which didn't come as a surprise. I was only guilty of exchanging heated words with a journalist, and I certainly wouldn't be the first rugby coach to have done that. But the incident added to an already stressful week.

On the training field I did everything I would have done in a normal test-match week, especially as far as tactical preparation was concerned. The press were watching closely to see if there was any animosity between Watson and me, but I treated him the same as everyone else and coached him the way I did all the other players. I addressed him on rugby issues, and asked technical advisor Rassie Erasmus to have a one-on-one session with him to explain exactly what we were aiming for on the afternoon of the test.

We didn't change our game plan and Watson had to fit in with our style of play. At Western Province he is allowed much more freedom, but as Bok coach I take a different approach, and it was up to him to adapt. I did my job as professionally as I could, but after doing training and video sessions, when my only focus was on rugby, I couldn't help feeling that he seemed like a spy in the camp. It was a difficult emotion to deal with. The trust of the group had been compromised, and it heaped more pressure on me.

There should have been a huge amount of excitement, as Bob Skinstad was playing his first test in nearly four years, as was flyhalf Derick Hougaard. But instead the happy occasion was subdued, despite the fact that we won 35-8.

Watson was injured early in the second half. Many journalists wrote that I would have substituted him then anyway, but that wasn't the case. During the match I only thought about the rugby game we needed to win. Watson was going to stay on, but after taking a big hit he told Doc Hassan that his ribs were sore. The doc sent the message back that Watson needed to come off. I wanted him to stay on; I really did. Why would I create a situation where my bosses could say, 'You weren't fair to him and you took him off after 50 minutes'? But he was injured and had to come off.

He hadn't played well, and most of the media wrote to that effect in their reports. But to be fair, he wouldn't be the first player on test debut not to have had his best game. In my experience, it's difficult for any newcomer. The feedback I've had from players in that situation is that they've often blocked out their entire debut test because they were so overwhelmed by emotion. Watson didn't have a particularly good day, though, which justified my opinion that he wasn't better than other potential players, such as Kabamba Floors, who already had a test cap. The fact that Luke had been so outspoken and openly critical of me wouldn't have influenced my decision to pick him if he was a Jonah Lomu.

As tradition dictates, a Springbok capping ceremony would follow the match at the team hotel. Both Watson and Murray were entitled to invite whomever they wanted. Waylon had 16 people present, including his mother and various friends. Luke went in for his capping alone, while his father Cheeky sat in the foyer having coffee with Mike Stofile. After all these strings had been pulled to have Luke selected, it was as if it didn't matter. When one of the players saw Cheeky and Stofile drinking coffee

150 metres from where the capping ceremony was taking place, he came over to me and asked what was happening. I was equally confused and didn't have an answer.

But it was over – Watson had his cap and I could get on with trying to win a World Cup. And he was never initiated, as far as I know.

40

The final countdown

With the political sideshows almost all out of the way, I could get on with the final preparations for the World Cup. England was duly beaten, Samoa had been seen off and we were in good shape to begin the Tri-Nations.

I knew that we were going to take a weakened squad on the away leg, and thus it was important to win our home matches with the so-called 'first team'. That would be the bulk of the team playing the big matches at the World Cup.

There had been a lot of speculation in the press that we'd been hiding aspects of our game against England and Samoa, which was not really the case. We were trying new things, but nothing revolutionary. We had a pattern of play that we weren't about to deviate from a couple of months before the World Cup. We only wanted to gain momentum by beating England, as it would mean a win against the world champions. Secret tactics were not part of the equation. England had dominated us at Twickenham for the last nine seasons, and we'd broken that hoodoo the previous year. We knew that, psychologically, we had to win the series at home.

A win meant more confidence going into the World Cup. Winning was everything. It had nothing to do with what we'd hide or show. We figured that if our game plan worked, they would be powerless to stop it the next time we met on 14 September at the World Cup. If we showed our hand and they couldn't cope, it would be a massive mental blow to them – and that is exactly what happened in those two tests.

After the Samoa match, we'd decided to cut the squad to 30 players from the original 45 (plus one). With all the consecutive games the guys had played, we just couldn't take them on the away leg of the Tri-Nations. With a couple of exceptions, they'd all played five huge Saturdays in a row. And there were two more big ones to come, so that meant seven consecutive weeks of hard Super 14 and test rugby.

The players that were cut were released to play Currie Cup, so they would stay match-sharp for the away leg of the Tri-Nations. Pieter Jooste, Ian McIntosh and I had discussed the potential make-up of the touring party before the Tri-Nations had even begun. We knew it would be a sensitive issue, so we didn't communicate it publicly. But Pieter raised the question: If we ended up winning the first two games of the Tri-Nations, would it mean we'd want our best team on the job, so we could try to win the tournament?

My view was that it didn't matter. We couldn't expect the guys to play seven Saturdays, have a week off, and then tour New Zealand and Australia – and ask them to be fresh for the World Cup. The initial plan was to send 19 'A'-team players to a training camp in Poland, while we took the 'B' squad to the Tri-Nations (and I only make this distinction for ease of understanding. I don't view any Springbok team I coach as an A or a B team. They are all Boks.)

We'd heard reports from teams who had used the cryotherapy facilities in Poland, and who swore by them. Irish captain Brian O'Driscoll only had positive things to say about the experience. It's a way to help the body recover quickly by applying extreme cold to destroy damaged tissue in the body.

We planned to send the players to Poland for about 10 days. We heard Scotland and Italy were also booked to visit the facility. It was cheap compared with staying in a hotel in South Africa, and I planned to book the guys on economy seats via London, to really make it a hardcore 'in the forests of Poland' kind of experience.

I went to see Professor Tim Noakes for his opinion. 'Listen, Jake, with all due respect,' he said, 'there's no scientific proof that cryotherapy works. It's a thing that works on players psychologically, so they think they can recover.' I'm a great admirer of Noakes and he's always supported me, so when I heard his views, I canned the idea immediately. Noakes suggested that spending more time at home with family would probably be more beneficial. And in the long run he was right, as players such as Os du Randt really struggle with touring for long periods.

The point I'm driving home is that those players – John Smit, Victor Matfield, Bryan Habana, Bakkies Botha, Os du Randt, Fourie du Preez, Schalk Burger, Juan Smith, Jaque Fourie and Percy Montgomery, among others – were never going to go on the Tri-Nations tour. The selection committee had made that decision as part of our bigger plan.

At that stage, before the Tri-Nations started, not even the players knew, as I wanted them to stay focused on the rugby. If they knew they weren't going on the away leg, it might have changed their attitude negatively. As far as they were concerned it was business as usual – play the home leg of the Tri-Nations and then prepare for the away leg. Of course they would also lose out on two match fees, and I didn't want them worrying about how this might affect their income. Fortunately, these players were not motivated by money and, when the time came, I explained that their returns would come if they did well at the World Cup.

We started the Tri-Nations against Australia in Cape Town, and it was one of the most intense matches I've been involved with. The collisions were huge, and the Aussies probably gave their best performance against us in South Africa in the four seasons I'd been in charge. But our guys were up for it that day too, even if it took two of Frans Steyn's drop-goals to seal the win. He wasn't under instruction; he just read the play and went for it – and it came off. A few weeks before he'd fluffed a conversion kick and missed a couple of drop-goal attempts in the Super 14 final.

I went up to him after the game and put my arm around him. 'You see, you cut your teeth at that level [Super 14], and now you nail two drop-kicks in a test match,' I said. 'That's experience and you're learning from it.' And he replied: 'Winning test matches, I suppose, is much bigger than any provincial game.'

But before the game I had been embroiled in more front-page news stories about my attempts to meet with President Thabo Mbeki. During the Luke Watson selection saga, SA Rugby's inner circle occasionally hinted that his selection had been at the request of the president. I didn't buy it, but I figured that if people were saying it was a request from the head of the country, then I wanted to chat to him to find out why.

I used some of my contacts, and a friend of a friend who is connected to the presidency agreed to try to set up a meeting for me. A little while later I was told that President Mbeki was happy to meet with me. My contact would arrange the meeting, and the president's office would set a time and select a venue. In my mind, the meeting was arranged and I was keen to go through with it.

A few days later, I received a call from the president's office. The meeting was on, but in terms of protocol the sports minister had to be present. I said that was fine, but I made it clear that even if the sports minister was there, I would speak my mind. It was no use having a meeting and not being able to use the opportunity to say what I thought.

I wanted to tell the president that I was tired of people ordering me to do things while implying that the instructions came from him. I wanted to know what he wanted. In addition, I wanted to know if he *did* want me to select Luke Watson. Through the sports portfolio committee, I'd heard that the ANC demands this and the ANC demands that. As leader of the ANC and the country, the president could have told me directly what he wanted. Of course I was willing to listen to him and help where I could.

I was happy to say all this with the sports minister present.

I relayed my thoughts to my contact, and the feedback was that I should go ahead: the president would allow me to speak freely. I mentioned that I preferred to keep our meeting under wraps for the time being, which wasn't a problem for them. In fact, we agreed that secrecy might be the best option, although the sports minister, Makhenkesi Stofile, had to be informed due to protocol. I knew news of the meeting might be leaked to his brother Mike, SARU's deputy president and no big supporter of mine.

And unfortunately news of the impending meeting did leak out. I'm not sure how, but one day I received a call from SA Rugby board member Viwe Qeqa. She asked me why I wanted to meet with the president of the country, and instructed me to attend a meeting with her and Oregan Hoskins after the Samoan test. It was at our Sandton hotel, and the players waited for me in the team room, while I met with Qeqa and Hoskins in a nearby conference room.

It wasn't so much a meeting as the issuing of an order. I was told that I could not see President Mbeki. Qeqa and Hoskins were defensive, saying that it was against SA Rugby protocol for me to meet with the president of the country. Actually, I've checked, and I can't find this clause anywhere in the SARU constitution or in my contract. I was told it would be viewed in a bad light if the national coach went to see the president without following the correct protocol. But it would only look bad if they were uncomfortable with the meeting, and I knew why they would be. They did not want me to tell the president of the interference I endured and how his name had been used to back their plans. They didn't want him hearing those things.

I said that as coach of the Springboks, and as a South African citizen, I was surely allowed to meet with the president if he felt it important enough to meet with me. Regan concluded our discussion by saying that I would receive a formal letter warning me of the consequences of going ahead with the meeting.

I was supposed to meet President Mbeki the day before the Aussie test at his Cape Town residence, Tuynhuis. I was in a quandary, because it would be a huge insult to the leader of the country if, after requesting the meeting, I suddenly pulled out.

I duly received the letter via Andy Marinos, stating that if I went ahead with the meeting, my actions would be seen in a dim light and disciplinary action would be taken. A few months from the World Cup, I knew what that meant. I called my man at the presidency and informed him of the situation. I said I didn't know how to proceed, as I didn't want to offend President Mbeki, but I was under threat of losing my job. It had been made clear to me that if I attended the meeting, I would be in breach of my contract, as I would be 'bringing the game into disrepute'.

I was told not to worry, and that we would try to arrange a visit some other time. Naturally the story ended up in the newspapers, and I was asked why I wanted to meet with the president. I kept my mouth shut. I knew SARU were waiting for me to say the wrong thing so they could hold me in breach of contract.

Ultimately I never met President Mbeki privately, although he met the team prior to the Rugby World Cup, and joined us on the eve of the tournament final. We never had that heart-to-heart discussion. However, when he met us again before the World Cup final, he told me I was welcome to 'pop in for tea' any time. I might still take him up on it.

While all this was going on, I had the minor matter of the Tri-Nations to prepare for. After victory against Australia, we faced the All Blacks in Durban the following week. Final preparations were also being made for the away leg of the Tri-Nations. I planned to inform the bulk of the players after the match that they wouldn't be going on tour and that the squad was going to look vastly different.

One of the blows we suffered at Newlands was an injury to skipper John Smit, who pulled a hamstring. It was his 41st consecutive test as captain, all under my coaching, and it was his 46th consecutive test match. It was a blow before the All Black test. Little did I know that it would kick-start a sequence of four captains in four weeks.

In Durban, we started well against the All Blacks, as we had done the previous week against Australia. But as the game wore on, we grew increasingly tired. And when they threw on their replacements with 15 minutes to go, the momentum of the match shifted, and they ran out winners by

26 points to 21. I had suspected it would happen, as the players were jaded. After the Super 14 semi-finals and final, I could see their performances starting to dip. They were in need of rest, and the final 11 minutes of that match, in which New Zealand scored two tries, were due to fatigue as much as anything else.

Frans Steyn came on as a replacement for Butch James at flyhalf, and dropped a crucial pass, which led to Richie McCaw's try. It brought the All Blacks back into the game. But that wasn't the reason we lost, and I wasn't angry with Frans. The week before he had been the hero with two drop-goals, and that week many fans perceived him to be the villain. I told him afterwards, 'There's a reason it's called test rugby. It's made to test you physically and mentally.'

After the game I sat the guys down in the changing room. 'Some guys aren't going on the tour,' I began. 'In fact, most of you aren't going on the tour. I want you to understand something. I never want you to experience again what you are feeling now. It's not just about losing the game; when they went up a gear, you couldn't keep up. And the reason is because you're not fit enough yet. You need time off to get your bodies in even better shape so that we can win the World Cup.

'We've got to make a promise to each other that this will never happen again. If we lose, it won't be because we ran out of steam.' And they understood. I could see it was the right time to say this, too. The players were hurting because they'd lost, but they also understood it had nothing to do with whether they had wanted to win or not. They realised their tanks were empty.

'You're going to stay at home now, and you're going to be pushed hard. And you're really going to have to show that you want to get through the pain barrier, because this is the final push to the World Cup.'

There were still about 10 World Cup places up for grabs, but I didn't have to convey that message to those going on the away leg of the Tri-Nations. The players knew. And we got exactly what we wanted out of that tour. Bismarck du Plessis came on tour and made it into the final squad. So did Bobby Skinstad, Wikus van Heerden, Johann Muller, Wynand Olivier, JP Pietersen and Ruan Pienaar. We didn't win a test, but it was a very productive away leg from a team perspective.

Of course, there was a huge media outcry about our squad in Australia and New Zealand, but for once I had the backing of SARU. The way the media carried on was over the top. The Aussies said the team was an insult. I faced a press barrage when we arrived in Sydney, but I wasn't intimidated. I threw it back at them and said, 'What if we beat you? Then what will you say?'

I also told them: 'You've got short memories, chaps. You've just finished the Cricket World Cup, which you won. But before the tournament, you played a one-day series against New Zealand and you left five of your top players at home, and lost. No one even thinks about that. It's unheard of that an Australian cricket side would lose to New Zealand, but they did. They knew there was a much bigger picture.'

I found it quite odd that a sporting nation like Australia would point fingers after they had done exactly the same thing in a different sport. I reiterated that most of my so-called 'B' squad had played in the Super 14 final. If I'd selected the team straight after that game, I would probably have been praised for selecting in-form players.

I have to praise John Smit for his take on the whole 'B'-side issue. He reminded me that I must never talk about a B side when referring to the team. He said that when you become a Springbok, you're a Springbok. And there's no such thing as an A or B Springbok. He made that clear to me, the rest of the team and the management. Some guys dream their whole life of wearing a Springbok jersey and being in a Springbok touring group, so if we, as management, or the media refer to the B team, it is an insult.

I understood that the media used this term to differentiate between players, but we never considered ourselves a B team during the away leg of the tournament. We were the Springboks on tour, representing the country. Jannie du Plessis and his brother Bismarck both became Springboks on that tour. They didn't view themselves as lesser or more deserving Springboks, nor should they have done. Both were in the final squad for the World Cup final three months later. Take Bismarck as an example. He can become one of the greatest Boks of all time, and we won't say he started his test career as a B Springbok, will we?

I'll be honest. I knew that the tour would be tough, especially against New Zealand. I didn't know what type of team they'd pick, because if we lost to Australia, New Zealand were practically assured of the title, so they might pull in a lot of their star players. But it didn't matter who they chose, because winning in New Zealand was something the

Boks hadn't managed since 1998. It was something I'd never achieved as Bok coach.

But I had a funny feeling that the team I'd put together had enough to win the game against Australia: Johan Ackermann, Albert van den Berg, Johann Muller, Wikus van Heerden, Bob Skinstad and Jacques Cronjé gave me a lot of physicality and speed to contain the Wallabies. Skinstad also captained the team.

We raced into a 17-0 lead after 17 minutes, but ultimately lost the game 25-17. The team simply didn't believe it *could* win. I'd already been through that in my first season as Bok coach, and now, with a largely new group of players, we went through it again. At one point they were asking themselves how they'd managed to be in such a strong position, and then they faltered. Derick Hougaard missed a few kickable penalties, which would have put us three scores ahead and possibly taken the wind out of their sails. But we made other silly mistakes that allowed Australia to come back into the game, too.

A week later, in Christchurch, we had our fourth captain in as many matches. Johann Muller led the team, doing a good job both on and off the field. We hung in and were 6-9 down, with about 17 minutes to play. But I never got the feeling we were going to win. We were scrambling and floundering as they put us under more and more pressure. I kept thinking that if we got a lucky break or a kick through, we could cause an upset. But because we were so defensive, we couldn't score easily.

If I had all my experienced players in that game and they were 6-9 down with 15 minutes to play, I would have backed them to win. But these players were a bit like the squad I'd started with in 2004. When we'd lost in Christchurch in that year, with Howlett scoring in the death, it was only because we didn't believe we could win. It had nothing to do with lack of ability or with them being better than us. This new group playing on the away leg were exactly the same. They were inexperienced, fighting for their lives and desperate to go to the World Cup.

Deep down, I suppose every guy was trying hard to make an impression individually. They had lost Bob to injury against Australia, they had lost John Smit as their captain, as well as Victor, who also wasn't on the tour. In those four weeks, they'd gone from a group with a large core of senior players to being on their own in the Antipodes. They did very well and I'm proud of them, as they'd fought hard. New Zealand obliterated us in the final 10 minutes to run out 33-6 winners, but that score wasn't a reflection of the match at all.

I enjoyed the tour immensely, as it was nice to work with some different players. Their energy levels were unbelievable. They really wanted to achieve, they practised hard and were completely motivated. We'd been a bit spoilt with the experience of the group we'd left behind, but this lot was shouting and running around with childlike enthusiasm during training. I enjoyed it from that point of view, but I didn't enjoy losing those two games, because we came so close.

My biggest regret as Bok coach is that I never beat the All Blacks in New Zealand. I remember talking to Morné du Plessis about it, and he said Kitch Christie had expressed the same regret. Kitch never lost a test as coach and guided the Boks to the 1995 World Cup title, but he'd wanted a crack against the All Blacks on their own turf. For a South African, that's the ultimate goal besides winning the World Cup.

Kitch stayed on in the hope of coaching the Boks against New Zealand in 1996, but then he became ill and had to resign before the season kicked off. I was tempted to consider staying on as Bok coach after the 2007 World Cup – just to have one more crack at beating the All Blacks on their home turf.

41

The dream team

With the Tri-Nations out of the way, the World Cup was coming into sharp focus. It was probably my last assignment as Springbok coach, and it was the biggest challenge I'd faced. In my mind I had pretty much cemented my decision not to stay on, despite media speculation that I might seek a few extra years as Bok coach.

I was emotionally and physically drained by the job, but mentally I'd prepared for one great push at the World Cup. I couldn't see myself coaching the Boks beyond 2007, although I was scheduled to lead the team in a one-off test against Wales after the tournament.

The 19 players left behind had worked hard in a training camp in Cape Town. They were in great physical shape by the time I returned with the squad. What was left was to add 11 names to the list for the Rugby World Cup.

I met with selectors Pieter Jooste and Ian McIntosh to decide on our final 30 for the tournament. It was a tough meeting. There are unlucky players whenever a squad is selected, and the group for the World Cup was no different. Players such as Lions number 8 Jacques Cronjé didn't make it, for instance. Sharks hooker Bismarck du Plessis also didn't make the cut at that stage.

But we didn't let emotion get in the way of selection. When the squad was finally announced, there was disbelief among the public that it had gone so smoothly. Usually when a Springbok squad is announced, there is some sort of political backlash. But this time there was none. I think the realisation was finally kicking in that I had been genuine about transformation; that over the years I had searched for my 30 best players, while being sensitive to South Africa's unique political history. So, when the team was named, no one could say I had not tried to find black players over my four seasons in charge. When I named six black players in the squad, everyone knew they were there firmly on merit.

The other factor was that the President's Council, through national teams' manager Andy Marinos, had been given an overview of my way of thinking for at least two years. As selectors, we had provided Andy with a list of 35 names six months prior to the naming of the final squad. There were no surprises for the council.

For as long as Marinos had been in the job, he and I had met regularly to discuss various scenarios. If I selected a certain player, then I'd have to select another player to complement him, and Marinos was fully aware of these combinations. He sent data packs to the President's Council and updated them on my plans, which is why I was annoyed when I was asked to explain my selections at various times. If they'd bothered to read what was given to them, they might have been better informed.

But when we settled on the final 30, and Pieter took the names to Regan Hoskins, there were no objections or requests for players to be picked for political reasons. Peace had broken out in South African rugby. It was an unfamiliar feeling but a huge relief, nevertheless.

But this was South African rugby after all, so nothing went as smoothly as I'd hoped. Admittedly, the next bump in the road had nothing to do with politics, though. Technical advisor Rassie Erasmus, a valuable member of the staff since the beginning of the international season, had applied for and was awarded the post of Stormers coach for 2008. The job encompassed the role of rugby director at Western Province. Rassie's appointment was confirmed about a week before the World Cup squad was made public, and he informed me that he wouldn't be able to go to France.

Completely unaware of Rassie's pending decision to take the Stormers job, I'd asked SA Rugby promotions manager Anne-Lee Murray to get hold of Eddie Jones. I wanted her to gauge Eddie's interest in spending a few sessions with the Boks, en route to joining English club Saracens on a full-time basis. I reckoned that even if his schedule allowed for only two sessions at our training base in Cape Town, he'd add value because of his vast coaching experience.

Eddie was flying to London via Cape Town. He told Anne-Lee he would be 'delighted' to pop in for a few days. Initially he said he could stay for about a week, but on arrival he told me Saracens had agreed to let him stay longer if I wanted his continued help. In that week I saw how much value Eddie added. He took existing ideas we had and put a different spin on them. It was a fresh approach, and I could see the guys responding to him very positively.

Of course, it came as a complete surprise that Erasmus was negotiating with Western Province. So, when he came to tell me he'd been appointed and didn't think he could go to the World Cup as planned, I was annoyed. My irritation wasn't directed at him specifically, because I realised the Western Province and Stormers job was a great opportunity professionally. I was angry because, when I looked around for possible candidates to take his place, there were no obvious South African replacements.

Rassie had done a lot of planning with us over the months and had added a lot of value. He's a hard-working guy who expends a lot of energy on the rugby field as well. We needed him at that point, as everybody associated with the team was in need of stimulation. I'd left him at home with the team while we were overseas on the Tri-Nations tour, and he did a lot of technical analysis for us, which had worked well with the players. So, when he dropped the bombshell, I was in a pickle. It is not easy to find someone of his calibre, especially five weeks before the World Cup.

But, quite fortuitously, Eddie was with us. So, after pondering for a few days, I said to Eddie, 'How would you feel about staying on until the end of the World Cup?' He didn't hesitate with his reply: 'I'd love to, Jake.' He was genuinely excited, because he thought South Africa had a chance to win the World Cup, and he saw a good opportunity to be involved with a potential world champion team.

So we put the wheels in motion. I had a meeting with Marinos and Jonathan Stones, and asked them to employ Eddie on a short-term contract. Eddie spoke to chief executive Mark Sinderbury at Saracens and explained the situation. Saracens was very accommodating, while Stones and Marinos said they would need board approval for the appointment.

There was some resistance to employing an Australian coach, although I never learnt who the anti-Eddie people were. After some persuading, Stones eventually received the 'okay' to employ Eddie, and a huge weight lifted off my shoulders. Most of the board seemed to realise he was a good appointment, and I'm glad common sense prevailed.

Eddie brought many things to the team, but for me the most important asset was that he had the experience of coaching a team in a World Cup final. Okay, he never won the cup, but he knew about the pressures of the tournament. And other than Os du Randt, no one in our set-up had that kind of experience, so Eddie's role was vital.

South Africans aren't very good at learning from people who've been there before. So it wasn't just about Eddie saying, 'Run deeper, go wider and maybe run this play.' It was that he offered me insights that you can only gain from experience. He'd been a drop-kick away from being a World Cup–winning coach, and he wanted another shot at it.

He built my confidence, and that was great for me. After all my battles and selection issues, it was good to have an outsider who was able to take an objective view. Sometimes he'd tell me to relax, because he'd gone through similar situations too. At other times he'd reaffirm what I'd been thinking or doing. It was a great comfort.

Importantly, he got on well with my management team. If our management structure had been full of people with their own agendas, it might have been a difficult appointment. But Allister and Gert, in particular, warmed to Eddie and welcomed him into the team. They learnt from him, and he gained insights from them.

So we had our 30 players, with John Smit as captain. And we had the management team that I'd requested. We were set to go. But then we suffered another blow and lost our key number 8, Pierre Spies. Our training camp had moved to Durban, and Pierre wasn't feeling well while there. When he started coughing up blood, he headed to Doc Hassan to explain his symptoms.

The doc was concerned and sent Pierre for a series of tests, which revealed blood clots in his lungs. He was ordered to stop playing all contact sport and to start taking a course of blood-thinning drugs – his World Cup was over. It was a huge blow to Pierre, the team and the country, and for weeks there were differing medical opinions about his prospects. But clearly something was wrong, and SA Rugby made the decision that he wouldn't play. If there was even the smallest chance he could have played, I would have taken him to France without thinking twice.

Pierre is a very religious man and he was philosophical about what had happened. He kept saying to the rest of us: 'It's in the Big Man's hands. I can't do anything about it, as there's a bigger picture here.' He really believed it was out of his control, which seemed to give him the necessary strength to get through the ordeal.

Pierre was devastated not to be a part of the World Cup, but he was with us in spirit all the way. Before our Pool A match against England, he sent a video message that had been recorded on camera by Jean de Villiers on the day Pierre had left us in Durban. Ironically, De Villiers was later ruled out of the tournament too, after the opening match against Samoa.

On the video, Pierre said, 'John, you're a great captain. And the senior players, you must play and lead well. It's going to be tough, but you guys are good enough to win. Don't ever take it for granted – look at me. You never know when it can be taken away.' Watching that video was an emotional moment for the team. But it triggered something within them.

As a coach you have to try to be philosophical about injuries, as you can't control the uncontrollable. It was a freak occurrence that happened to Pierre, and the injury that ruled De Villiers out a few weeks later was equally unfortunate. It's stressful and upsetting, but rugby is a tough sport. You have to move on and try to make the best of a bad situation.

I replaced Pierre with hooker Bismarck du Plessis, which raised some eyebrows. The one area of our squad that had bothered me, and that caused a lot of wrangling in our selection meetings, was the position of hooker. Along with scrumhalf, it's the one position where you need an absolute specialist. In John Smit and Gary Botha we had two very fine players, and I was confident that the position was covered. After all, prop BJ Botha had played SA Under-21 hooker, and could provide emergency cover if we needed to wait for someone to fly out in the event of John or Gary being injured.

But when Pierre was ruled out, with John still overcoming a hamstring injury, I saw it as an opportunity to bring Bismarck in as insurance. Our first two pool games were vital. We had matches against Samoa and then England, and I had to be sure that nothing would go wrong. When John pulled out of our warm-up game against Namibia with a twinge of the same hamstring, I started to realise the value of having a third hooker.

We had two warm-up tests against Namibia and Scotland, and a match against Irish provincial side Connacht, as part of our final preparations for the World Cup tournament. It was a chance to try a few moves, to gain some momentum and build team confidence.

Bismarck was an official back-up player when the original squad was named, and he was always scheduled to go on the pre–World Cup tour so that he could continue team preparations in case he was needed. But by the time the tour departed, he was an official member of the World Cup squad.

Initially the Namibia game at Newlands was not going to be a fully fledged test, but Namibia requested this status, as they were playing in the World Cup. The IRB agreed, which afforded us the opportunity to give Percy Montgomery and Os du Randt a proper send-off in their last appearance for the Boks in South Africa.

It was a very nice gesture from SA Rugby. Too many times we've let this calibre of players go out the back door with a lot of negativity. Sponsors Vodacom and Sasol went out of their way to make the game feel special for them, and SA Rugby followed suit. It's important to look after those kind of guys.

In terms of a result, we won 105-13. People said it was a mismatch. But when I saw how well Namibia played in the World Cup against Ireland, and how no other teams – France, Ireland, Argentina – managed to score 100 points against them in the tournament, it provided perspective on how well we'd played against them. Monty scored a record 35 points and we scored 15 tries. We were in a good frame of mind when we travelled to Ireland.

We struggled against Connacht, winning 18-3, but I'd suspected we would. Players were holding back for the World Cup, because they didn't want to get injured. It wasn't a test match; it was a sort of midweek fixture in front of about 5 000 people in a really open ground. Players wanted to be part of it, but didn't want to suffer an injury two weeks before the World Cup.

And I don't want to sound like I'm whinging, but we had a local Irish referee who wasn't going to allow the game to become one-sided. We had our chances in the beginning and we never took them. But reflecting on the match at the World Cup, I realised how beneficial that sort of game had been. The Tonga World Cup game in Lens was almost identical to the Connacht match, and we won.

By the time we met Scotland at Murrayfield, we put on a very good performance. The defence was watertight, we controlled the tempo and dominated all the collisions, despite being warned that Scotland was bigger and stronger than ever before. It gave our team an understanding of how we'd developed physically. Scotland's newfound size and strength had been talked up, but in the physical exchange there was no contest. We came out of that game even better off, knowing that, physically, we could take on anybody. Scotland was fresh from smashing Ireland, so it was a great boost for us. It took us to a new dimension to see how much we'd developed by leaving players at home to prepare for these sort of test matches.

Back in South Africa, Sasol set the tone for the World Cup with a great send-off banquet. We were ready. A World Cup win was the one thing left to tick off the list.

42

Bonjour,
Rugby World Cup

I had butterflies in my stomach on the day we left for Paris and the Rugby World Cup. We had been building towards this moment for years, yet considering all the angst and tribulations along the way, I found it hard to grasp that the implausible had finally come true.

As the aeroplane took off from OR Tambo International Airport in Johannesburg, I breathed a sigh of relief. I was *actually* on my way to the World Cup. I know that sounds like a childish reaction from a national coach, but I had my reasons. Top of the list was relief that I'd finally been given the opportunity to go to the World Cup. As part of Nick Mallett's coaching team in 1997, I'd been promised a place at the World Cup in 1999, which never happened. I was part of Harry Viljoen's Bok staff in 2001, and never made it to the 2003 tournament. And throughout my own tenure as Bok coach, France 2007 had hung by a thread at times. It was only once I'd boarded the aircraft, taken off my number ones and donned the Springbok travelling kit that it hit me – I was on my way. Politicians, the President's Council and other naysayers could do little now. I was more determined than ever that we should win.

I didn't give the team any tub-thumping speeches, as we'd worked towards winning the Webb Ellis Trophy for nearly four years. Every player knew his role. There was no need to make the moment bigger than it was; everyone was well aware of the magnitude of the next six weeks. We were as fit, self-assured and prepared as we could be. I genuinely felt supremely confident, as I knew that, on any given day, this group of players could beat any team in the world. We just had to make sure we had those days in the next month and a half.

Our arrival in France was actually a low-key affair. We slipped into Paris almost unnoticed, participated in a few media briefings and hit the ground running. The opening game was between hosts France and Argentina, so all the hype was focused on that match. As we were playing Samoa two days later at the Parc des Princes, we got on with things at our training base in the eastern Paris suburb of Noisy le Grand. The locals made us feel very welcome. They painted the walls of the clubhouse in traditional Ndebele murals, and put up 'Go Bokke' signs around the Alain Mimoun pitch, where we trained. It was an excellent facility.

We had great police escorts. The guy in charge of our cavalcade had shepherded France in the 1998 Football World Cup. We figured it was a good omen, as Les Bleus had gone on to win that tournament on home soil.

For the opening ceremony and match, we were offered 28 tickets to attend as guests of multinational company Steinhoff, who had forked out a lot of money for a corporate suite at the Stade de France. They were only using the suite for the Springbok matches, but had to rent it for the entire tournament, and thus we were offered the seats for the opening match. We were thrilled, but there were only 28 places, and our group consisted of 47 people. So we decided that the match 22 for the Samoa game and the coaching staff would attend the opening game.

At the World Cup in 2003, the players didn't attend the Sydney opening ceremony because they were based thousands of kilometres away in Perth. They said they'd felt isolated from the World Cup for much of the opening stages. For this reason, John Smit came to me in Paris with an alternative plan.

'It would be really nice if all the players could go to the opening game,' he said. 'Leaving the other eight guys behind isn't conducive to team spirit, and it would be a bad start to the tournament.'

John suggested that the management stay behind instead. He felt attending the events would allow the players to feel the impact of the opening match as a group. I agreed wholeheartedly. Former Springbok promotions manager Anne-Lee Murray, now working for the IRB, pulled some strings and organised two more tickets.

John deserves credit for the decision, because he knew how useful that night could be. The players would understand the enormity of what they were about to embark on. Feeling the vibe would be a bonus. And for our game at the same stadium against England a week later, the players wouldn't be overawed, as they would have sat in the stands and felt what it was like to be part of the crowd. It was a blessing in disguise that we managed to get those tickets. I watched the game with the rest of team management at our hotel.

It was a key match for South Africa. Before the start of the tournament, popular opinion suggested that the winner of Pool D would play the winner of our pool in the semi-finals. France was expected to top Pool D, and either South Africa or England to win Pool A. Of course we always believed we could win our pool, so it was about who we'd meet in the semi-finals. I didn't consider the possibility of not making the last four. Before the game, members of the press had asked which team I favoured to win the opening match, and I'd predicted Argentina. But I didn't say that I still backed France to win the group. I suspected that Ireland, the third big team in the group, would later beat the Pumas, and France would top the group on a points difference.

The opening match was always going to be tough for France, as the Pumas had beaten them in four of the last five games they'd played. Opening-match nerves would be a big factor for the French, and with practically the entire Argentinian squad playing their club rugby in France, it meant they would be comfortable in the stadium as underdogs.

We all know what happened – Argentina won 17-12, throwing the World Cup wide open before it had even really begun. My players returned to the hotel in Montparnasse, all revved up by the occasion. I could see the outing had been very useful. Forty-eight hours later we played Samoa, and I'd picked my strongest possible team. It was not only important to win, but to lay down a marker five days before our England game.

I knew that Samoa would be physical and fast, but they weren't an unknown quantity. We'd beaten them earlier in the year with a very experimental side, so there was no doubt it was a game we should win. I'd spent quite a lot of time analysing Samoa and had gone to watch them play against Harlequins in London. Prior to the World Cup, while we were in Scotland, Gert Smal, Allister Coetzee and Eddie Jones also watched Samoa play Sale Sharks. They had three warm-up games against club sides and we watched all of them. We knew what we could expect from Samoa.

I was slightly surprised by the first 25 minutes of that match – not by the way they played, but by the way *we* played. We led 9-0 early on, but they bounced back with a try and I could see our players were slightly distracted. It was because of the one factor we hadn't anticipated – something we would experience in all our matches, aside from the England game: how much the crowd got behind the underdogs. With every little thing that went against the underdogs on the field, the crowd gave the 'better, more experienced' team a real roasting. It was a new experience for the Boks to play against a team like Samoa and encounter 45 000 people screaming for the opposition. No wonder the players were slightly rattled.

Before the game, I was more nervous than I'd imagined. World Cup pressure is something else. Every game is massive regardless of who you're playing against. One slip and your whole tournament can nosedive. There is no 'next week' at the World Cup.

But the team settled down and scored a couple of tries before halftime, and then ran away to a 59-7 win, with some excellent tries in the second half. The thing that pleased me most was that we only conceded one try, and it came from a slipped tackle, caused by a mistake and not a break-down of our defensive system. Ultimately Samoa may have had a poor World Cup, but that opening 20 minutes was the most physical rugby we encountered in the entire tournament – perhaps the entire season.

We suffered a big blow when centre Jean de Villiers came off clutching his shoulder. It didn't look good, and I feared the worst. My fears were confirmed when Doc Hassan diagnosed a torn bicep, which scans cor-roborated. Jean was gutted. He'd overcome a rib injury to make it to the tournament, only to be ruled out in the first game. In 2003, he missed the tournament when he damaged his shoulder in a warm-up game after he'd been selected for the squad. Now he was out again.

Despite the win, the changing room was gloomy, as the guys knew Jean was in trouble. It hits home when you walk in and see a player with tears of frustration streaming down his face. Jean knew his World Cup was over. His bicep had snapped in a fairly innocuous tackle. Jean's dad saw me outside and asked if he could go in. I happily obliged. In hindsight it may not have been the most helpful decision, as Jean and his dad both became very emotional. He'd gone through so much to make it to the World Cup after missing the last one, and now his dream was in tatters. The players were hell of a supportive, but nobody really knew what to say.

But rugby doesn't allow for sentimentality, and we were forced to move on. We had six more matches to play. In one way our team could be con-sidered fortunate. We'd battled so much adversity in our four years together that we probably knew how to absorb a bitter blow better than most. But then we were dealt another one. More than 40 hours after the Samoan game, we were told Schalk Burger had been cited for a dangerous tackle. I was annoyed, as the so-called 'dangerous tackle' had happened in front of the ref, and he hadn't thought it serious enough to warrant more than a talking-to and a penalty. Schalk had been going for the ball and had accidentally caught his opponent.

There were six citings in the opening round of matches. Worryingly, five came from Pool A. I was concerned about a possible bias against our group, but of course that couldn't be easily proven. I saw far worse incidents occur in the opening round of games in other pools, yet all the disciplinary action seemed to involve Pool A.

Because Schalk's citing came so late (there was a 48-hour citing window, and we were informed after 46 hours), we had to make hasty arrangements to obtain legal counsel. The IRB was obliged to provide all the details and evidence of the infringement on a DVD. In this case, they should have addressed the DVD to team manager Zola Yeye, but instead it had been addressed to me. We never even thought to check at the hotel concierge under my name. After some frantic phone calls, the IRB eventually confirmed that they'd addressed the DVD to me. I was livid about the incompetency all round. When we finally watched the footage, we couldn't understand why Schalk had been cited. It seemed obvious that there was no malice or intent when his arm caught Junior Polu.

Johann Rupert arranged for John McCochran QC to represent Schalk. He flew in from London on a commercial aircraft – not on Johann's private jet, as was reported. Johann had merely made his jet available if required. McCochran had very little time to prepare, but based on the briefing he'd received, he was convinced that Schalk would escape any form of sanction.

The disciplinary panel took a long time to make their decision. They called us in at about 1 a.m. to tell us that Schalk had been suspended for four weeks – effectively four matches. I was distraught. It would rule Schalk out until the semi-finals, if we progressed that far. We'd just lost Jean de Villiers, and now we would effectively lose Schalk. After he'd had more time to study the evidence, McCochran thought we had a case for appeal. He built a case in the early hours of the morning and sent a message to the IRB that we wanted to appeal the decision.

The IRB responded that they would have to form a committee for the appeal, which would take time. We politely told them to get lost. An appeal was part of the process, and it had to be scheduled as soon as possible. They quickly assembled a new disciplinary panel. But before we could go on, there was the practical matter of getting McCochran some new clothes. He'd packed nothing, expecting to be in and out of Paris in a day.

When our QC had arrived at the first hearing, he felt as if the verdict had been decided before the proceedings had even started. But at the second hearing the mood seemed more equitable, and the committee was prepared to examine the facts. At one point McCochran felt that the whole issue might have been scrapped if a way could be found to avoid embarrassing the IRB. If one committee suspended Schalk for a month and another overturned the ruling completely, it would have sent out a mixed message. So they changed the wording from a 'dangerous' tackle to a 'reckless' tackle and halved his sentence.

Because we were at the end of the process, we had to accept the outcome. But I wasn't happy, because Schalk had done nothing wrong. Thinking back, the citing process seemed flawed throughout the tournament. I can think of three or four incidents in certain games that were not cited, yet identical incidents occurred in other games and those players were cited. I found that odd. An American player got five weeks for a spear tackle; the Georgians got one or two weeks for the same thing. Drew Mitchell from Australia spear-tackled a player and was never even cited. New Zealander Carl Hayman punched a guy twice and earned a yellow card but no citing ... The problem was that there didn't seem to be a clear rule. Some guys would be yellow-carded but not cited; others would receive a yellow card and be cited.

But we had to move on. Schalk would be back for our final group match against the USA in Montpellier. Until then, we'd have to continue without him.

Schalk was ruled out of the England clash, our crucial Pool A decider in my opinion. Regardless of what people said, it wasn't ideal. England were the world champions in spite of their recent indifferent form, which counted for nothing when we ran out against them. They had limitations, but I knew they were capable of producing some big games, and their form later in the tournament proved it. England had a physical pack of forwards and, despite our recent good form against them, this was the World Cup. All that mattered was the next 80 minutes.

We weren't sure whether Jonny Wilkinson, England's star flyhalf, would play. Stories were circulating that he could, would, should play. We weren't convinced by any of the speculation; it could have been England playing mind games. This was knockout rugby – it was a very stressful week. With all respect to the other teams in the group, I always knew that the England game would define who won the group and had an 'easier' quarter-final. Our other consideration was that, as a team, we'd decided on our plan of action: win seven games and win the World Cup. We wouldn't think of defeat.

Adding to the stress, Frans Steyn had to move to centre to cover for Jean, which wasn't in the original plan. He'd been set to play wing, as I knew England would pepper us with high balls. And at that stage, Frans seemed better equipped than JP Pietersen. But there you go: JP took his chance against England and ended up being one of our most consistent performers in the tournament.

When Wilkinson was finally ruled out of the game, it did help us a bit. England picked Andy Farrell at flyhalf and, although he probably has great strengths, a kicking game isn't one of them. England would be much more direct with him at outside half. From our perspective, it probably meant JP would not be bombarded with high kicks, and Frans Steyn would be able to handle the physical confrontation posed by Farrell.

It was a 9 p.m. kick-off, so the match day dragged. The players tend to stay up late the night before so that they can sleep until nearly lunchtime on match day. That wipes out some of the dead time. The rest of the day is long, though.

Arriving at the ground, I felt confident. We'd known about this fixture for more than two years, and now the moment was upon us. From the word go, we looked sharp. When Juan Smith scored after a sniping break by Fourie du Preez, we moved into a 10-0 lead and assumed control of the match. Smith's try also had the effect of silencing the large English crowd in the stadium. England were never in the game after that, and we ended up scoring two more tries on our way to a 36-0 win.

I thought we had the game sewn up at 50 minutes. Prior to that, they hadn't asked any questions of us defensively and, with half an hour to go, they didn't have enough time to come back, even if we stopped playing. Defensively we were too switched on for them. While we didn't do much but tackle in the last quarter, we completely controlled the match and shut it down with ease.

When the final whistle blew, I felt relief with a capital R. When England had smashed us at Twickenham in 2004, I told the team it would never happen again. We had to become more physical and more abrasive. The relief didn't only stem from the result, but from the way we'd turned the baby team of 2004 into one that could physically smash the world champions. We'd pushed them in the lineout drives; we'd tackled them backwards and never took a step back. We could have scored two or three more tries if we'd made the right pass at certain times. But it was a controlled performance. We probably didn't scrum as well as we could have, but not because they were stronger. We had a few technical issues we worked on and improved during the tournament, and by the end of the campaign we were scrumming superbly.

I was certainly surprised by how poorly England played on the night, and they admitted it, too. I could see how disjointed they were, having lost their flyhalf (Wilkinson) and their reserve flyhalf (Olly Barkley) in the same week, and captain Phil Vickery was also suspended. They tried to alternate Mike Catt and Farrell as flyhalves, and it just didn't work. England had endured a miserable week, and while I felt no sympathy for them at the time, winning being the only thing on my mind, in hindsight you had to feel for them. No team could have coped well with the disruptions they'd suffered. They were vulnerable and encountered a team hell-bent on beating them. It wasn't a happy cocktail for England, but it was a brilliant one for us.

I'd always said that winning our first two pool matches was key to winning the group. Thus, for our match against Tonga the following week, we'd decided to pick those players who hadn't already played, and I informed the squad about the team in the changing room after the England game. The decision was made before we even played England.

On the day after we beat England, Tonga threw us a curveball by beating Samoa, to suddenly emerge as the dark horse in the group. I was a little concerned and wondered if we needed our frontline players. But I quickly dismissed the idea. I couldn't exactly tell the fringe players that, because Tonga had beaten Samoa, they were no longer going to play. It would have been an emotional move, and I always tried to be unemotional about selection issues. We had planned to give the rest of the players a chance in week three, but now it happened to be against the team who lay second in the group, which caught us by surprise.

When the final whistle blew in the England game, I genuinely believed we had accomplished our goal of topping the group. Sure, we still had Tonga and the USA to play, but Tonga hadn't beaten Samoa in seven years, and had lost 50-3 against them prior to the World Cup. So, when they won in Montpellier, it came as a surprise. But if Samoa had beaten Tonga and we'd somehow lost to the Tongans, we'd still have topped the group, as we'd beaten both England and Samoa.

The Tonga match, played in Lens, was a cracking game for neutral spectators, but it was a bit too close for our liking. I should put some things in perspective, though. We should have been 21-3 up at halftime, instead of 7-3. Ashwin Willemse had dropped the ball over the try line, trying to hang onto a poor pass from Wynand Olivier. CJ van der Linde had three men on his outside close to the try line, but he tried to go on his own and was stopped short, while JP was held up in the left-hand corner. The contest should have been over at the break.

André Pretorius also missed four pretty simple kicks at goal. Let's assume we only converted two of those try-scoring chances and only two of the four penalties. We could have been 25-3 up. There is no way in the world Tonga could have come back from 25-3 down. It was our own sloppiness that kept them in the game, and I was extremely angry at halftime. I had a strong bench and could've sent them all on from the start of the second half, but I decided not to.

I said to the players during the break, 'You guys got yourselves into this mess; you must get yourselves out of it. I can make all the changes I want, but you guys must show me you're good enough to get out of the hole you've dug.' I left it to them to decide how the match would unfold.

I went up to my seat in the stands and thought that surely after that they would produce results. I was hoping they'd take on board what I'd just said. A few minutes into the second half, Tonga scored. I lost it completely. This was ridiculous. But aside from being angry, I was strangely sympathetic to what was happening with the players. Just after Tonga scored and the Boks were gathered behind the poles, I scrutinised the players' faces. I could tell they were feeling slightly bewildered. They were looking around and at each other as if to say, 'What happens now?' I realised that somebody had to make a decision, as they weren't capable of it. I left my seat and walked to the side of the field – something I never usually do during a game – and took control. Usually if I want to make substitutions I talk to logistics manager Mac Hendricks over the radio, and instruct him to warm up the players. I also inform him when I want them to take the field. This time I went straight to the substitutes' bench, looked at the players and pointed at them.

'You, you, you, you and you,' I barked. 'On. Now!' John Smit later said he'd never seen that happen before. I was seething; we needed leadership and direction. And with players such as John and Percy on the bench, there was no time to waste in getting them on.

I could see the players on the field were feeling responsible for this development. For the first two weeks, the 'other' players had done so well, and now here they were, and they were struggling. Understandably, it was playing on their minds. That's why I say I had some sympathy for them, because I knew they weren't having an easy time of it. They needed help, and I had to make a decision for them.

Bob Skinstad was captain that day, and while my move may suggest that I was upset with his leadership, this wasn't the case. I'd just realised that there was a wide gap between the leadership in one group and the guidance in the other, and we needed to address it at that moment. In the next 10 minutes, we scored three tries and ran into a 27-10 lead.

But once we were in this commanding position, we lost reserves Bryan Habana and Frans Steyn to yellow cards. It left us with 13 men, and two men down in the backline, which allowed Tonga to come back strongly. I'd never been in a position of having only five backline players on the pitch. This is when we learnt a few things, too.

After they scored, we kicked off to their right-hand side. But Habana, our left wing, was off the field, as was our inside centre, Steyn. Big mistake. We chased up but couldn't put them under pressure, and when they ran the ball there was no one at home. They kicked ahead, and Monty at full-back was stretched to the limit. He was caught out and they scored again.

Looking back, I should have issued the instruction to kick off to their left, and JP to stay back while the forwards chased up. At least we would have had an extra man back. Or we should have let the looseforward on the left wing chase, but instead all the forwards went to the right-hand side, and suddenly we were under pressure. The kick to their right had been part of the plan before the game, but I should have been flexible and changed it. I learnt from my mistake. The players did too. And in our preparation for subsequent matches, we discussed that incident at length.

Tonga came back, but we won 30-25. Some reports suggested that we got out of jail, but, as I've pointed out, that match should never have been in the balance. Tonga played well, make no mistake. But I'd choose to play Tonga every day of the week for the rest of my life if it meant topping our pool at the World Cup. If we'd kept 15 men on the field, we would likely have won by 40 points. But the job was done; Pool A was secured, with one more game to come.

43

The business end

Victory over Tonga meant a quarter-final against either Wales or Fiji, who had a crunch meeting in Pool B the day before we would play our final group match against the USA in Montpellier. After seeing off the Tongans, I could turn my attention to a last-eight match – with all respect to the American team.

We knew we weren't likely to lose to the USA, but I wanted to select a strong team to ensure that the players had one more game before the knockout stages commenced. Schalk Burger's suspension was over, so he would play, but the bulk of the team comprised players who had beaten England.

Yet again our week's preparation was disrupted. Forty-six hours after the Tonga match, we received word that Frans Steyn was being cited for allegedly biting an opponent – a serious offence, with suspensions of 12 months not uncommon. It wasn't the first time during the World Cup that I was stunned.

My first response was to get an honest answer out of Frans. 'Did you bite the Tongan player?' I asked. 'No coach, I never did,' he replied. That was good enough for me. We'd heard a few rumours after the match, 'something about biting', but in the post-match press conference the allegation was dismissed and we were informed that nothing untoward had happened.

After hearing the rumours, I took the cautious step of double-checking with the IRB disciplinary representative at the match (he monitors the game on television and isn't the citing commissioner) to see if any complaints had been made. There were none by the Tongans, so I left it at that.

However, as events unfolded it became clear what had happened. During the match, Frans and the Tongan wing Joseph Vaka had been involved in a clash, and Vaka screamed, 'He bit me!' The citing commissioner, Jean-Claude Legendre, heard the remarks on TV and decided to cite Frans, although there was no video evidence of the alleged incident. He planned to use the testimony of the Tongan player as evidence at the hearing, even though Tonga had apparently already dismissed the claim during the post-match interviews.

When Legendre notified the South African team, Frans was shocked, but adamant that he was innocent. Biting is a serious allegation that can taint a player's career, which is why we were determined to clear his name.

Australian judicial officer Terry Willis was chairing the hearing. This was the same man who had handed Schalk Burger a four-match ban, which didn't augur well, even though we didn't think we had any real cause for concern. In the interim, Tonga had tried to play the incident down. A rumour even circulated that they had issued an official retraction of Vaka's allegation, but I never saw it.

We had moved to Montpellier and Tonga were in Paris, so the hearing was conducted via a video link-up. Frans, team manager Zola Yeye, lawyer Nick Usiskin and I were present for South Africa, while Tonga brought their assistant coach Ellis Meachen, team doctor Lisiate Ulufonua and Vaka, who had been asked to testify. Willis represented the IRB, along with an independent doctor asked to verify any medical evidence submitted.

Another representative from the IRB asked Tonga to present their side of the story. Meachen replied that, as he spoke the best English, he'd be talking on behalf of Vaka. He added that the Tongans were confused as to why they were in a hearing after they'd already retracted any allegations of biting. Willis jumped in: 'What do you mean, you've retracted it?' Meachen replied: 'We've been trying to get hold of you to say that after reassessing what happened, we can't be sure it was a bite. We're not certain it wasn't a boot or something.' This didn't go down well with Willis. He was angry about the seriousness of the allegation and the slur on Frans's reputation, and he pointed this out to Tonga. Willis intoned: 'Are you all aware of what you're saying here?'

Meachen then said he wanted to double-check with Vaka about the alleged mark on his hand. They had a chat in Tongan, and Vaka confirmed that he didn't think it was a bite after all. 'But why did he say he was bitten?' asked an understandably irritated Willis. The Tongans consulted again, and the answer was that Vaka had been concerned he'd be sent off for his role in the altercation, so he had claimed he'd been bitten to divert attention.

From what I could gather, Vaka had already been issued two warnings for running into situations he had no business being involved in, so he'd made a spur-of-the-moment plan, as he knew the ref was already irritated with him. Frans received a yellow card at the time, I think for a high tackle.

The case was dismissed almost instantly. Willis wouldn't go ahead, as no evidence of a bite existed. Still, the incident was disrupting our preparations, although Frans trained the entire week. I escorted him to training straight after the hearing, saying, 'You never bit anybody, so let's go to practice. You're not going to be found guilty.'

What annoyed me most about the incident is that these things actually count against you. Whether you're guilty or not, it creates the perception that you're a dirty team. You start developing a tag you don't need and certainly don't want. Ever since I'd been in charge of the Boks, the one thing we'd worked hard on was cleaning up our act. John Smit deserves a lot of credit for that too. There had been some pretty embarrassing incidents in 2002 and 2003, so having a player accused of biting at the World Cup was very damaging to our reputation.

That's why, before Willis closed the hearing, Usiskin confirmed the status.

'Can I just stress that [dismissing the complaint] therefore means there is no black mark against this player's name?' he asked. 'We don't want a statement saying there was no evidence to prove he bit another player. We want it made clear that he *never* bit another player.' I don't think the IRB worded it quite as emphatically as we'd wanted, but I'll say it here: Frans Steyn never bit Joseph Vaka.

The USA game was very physical and they played pretty well, despite the fact that we won 64-15. Their Zimbabwean-born wing Taku Ngwenya scored a great try when he beat Habana on the outside after cleverly making him stop. It was later judged to be the try of the tournament, and I guess that beating the best wing in the world made him a worthy winner.

The only sour note was losing tighthead prop BJ Botha to a freak knee injury. As the ball rolled out of a ruck, BJ dived onto it and someone dived onto him. His knee was caught awkwardly and the ligaments went. That kind of situation happens all the time in rugby, but this time his leg was caught at the wrong angle. It was the end of his tournament and yet another blow for the team.

From Montpellier we moved directly to Marseille to prepare for the quarter-final. Instead of Wales, we were up against Fiji, who'd caused the biggest upset of the tournament by beating the Six Nations giants 34-30 in their crunch Pool B match. It was one of the great games of the tournament. We had watched it as a team, fully expecting Wales to win. The players really enjoyed the match, and many were quite excited about playing Fiji, knowing that it was going to be a different contest to the challenge of playing Wales.

In the interim, we called up prop Jannie du Plessis from South Africa. He'd toured with the Boks on the away leg of the Tri-Nations and had done very well. He's a good scrummager and, although his mobility was perhaps not of the same calibre as BJ's, he offered other strengths. CJ van der Linde would move to the first-choice tighthead. He and BJ had been vying for the position for a year, and it was hard to choose between them. So at least my choices were now simplified. That is, until CJ went down in a heap during our first training session in Marseille.

It was a freak occurrence. We were trying to do some lineout drives and driving from broken play, as the plan against Fiji was to keep it tight. We therefore had to be very accurate with our ball control in ruck and maul situations. Johann Muller was in the defensive team for the drill and CJ was on the side of the maul. Muller came in from the side and hit CJ with immense force on his leg – shoulder to knee. CJ went down hard.

I felt sick to my stomach. CJ immediately said it was probably a serious injury. I was angry with myself for calling the drill. It's like a car crash: you keep playing it over and over in your head, wondering why you turned left instead of right, or pondering the fact that if you'd left two minutes later, the accident might not have happened. I couldn't blame Muller. I'd called the drill and it was a contact session. He was doing his job, and I couldn't expect him to ease off. But it had happened, so we had to try to manage the problem. Losing two tighthead props in the space of 48 hours was a serious setback. Du Plessis wasn't scheduled to arrive from South Africa until the Thursday, and the match was on the Sunday.

We sent CJ for a scan and returned to the hotel. John Smit came to my room, angry. 'That was the worst training session we've had in four years!' he shouted. 'I didn't enjoy the drill; it reminded me of how the Boks were in 2003.' He asked me why I'd decided to run that play at the practice. 'We've been together for so many years; we can't do any more now. The last thing we need is for you to start panicking about whether we can do a certain move or not,' he continued. 'We've got three weeks left and you can't start coaching us again. You've coached us for four years. If we can't maul now, we're never going to be able to do it.' He was right, of course.

Such moments remind me why John is such a fine leader. We have a great relationship, and it's the trust between us that made him feel comfortable to speak his mind so openly that day. In my mind, I tried to find justification for practising the move. We'd won the ball at the back of a lineout against the USA and couldn't score. At the time, I'd said to myself, 'If we can't score off a back-of-a-lineout drive against America, then we need to work on it and be more accurate.' But that wasn't right, because I knew the players could perfect the move. Just because it hadn't worked in *one* lineout didn't mean we were incapable. It was my mistake, and I won't make it again. One of the most important aspects of being a coach is ensuring you always feel in control. Not in an autocratic way, but the players want stability and a solid plan. They don't want plans that had worked in the past changed.

The good news, though, was that CJ's scan showed 'only bruising' on the knee. The specialists felt he might even be ready for the match against Fiji, although he would be monitored for the remainder of the week before a final call would be made on the eve of the match.

The rest of the build-up was pretty normal. Fiji received a lot of attention as the underdogs in the game. On the Thursday, the Boks' day off, I took a break from rugby and enjoyed a relaxed seafood lunch. An Australian started chatting to me at the restaurant; I never found out his name. He didn't know who I was either, which made it even better. He had come over from Spain to watch Australia play England, the day before our Fiji game, and was incredibly funny. We had a few beers and a good laugh. It took nearly an hour to walk back to the hotel, and I saw Marseille's scenic coastline for the first time. It reminded me a lot of the Camps Bay coastline in Cape Town. We had been touring for over a month, and it was pleasant not to be transported in a team bus for a change.

Pierre Spies arrived in Marseille late in the week, and the guys really appreciated the show of support. Some of the players felt it would be appropriate for him to hand out the match jerseys for the Fiji game, and I agreed. There was only one snag: I'd already asked someone else to do the honours.

As mentioned earlier, it is standard practice for former Boks to hand out match jerseys, but for the quarter-finals I'd lined up somebody a little different for the job. I'd asked respected journalist and radio broadcaster Andy Colquhoun, who had single-handedly resurrected the SA Rugby annual in 1999, after two years of stagnation. The annual is a comprehensive record documenting South African player and match statistics at every level of the game, and Andy's personal commitment to getting the job done over the years has been immense. It seemed an appropriate opportunity to change the routine by asking a man whose life's work will forever record the players' achievements.

Andy had initially declined, saying that he wasn't a Springbok. But I'd pushed on, and his final answer was that he felt greatly honoured, but would do it only if I gauged the opinions of the senior players on having a member of the media present their jerseys. I did that, and players including John Smit and Victor Matfield had no problem with the idea.

Naturally, Pierre's unexpected arrival meant we had to change tack. The senior players decided that, as an original member of the squad, Pierre was the right man for the job before such an important game. I didn't disagree. So, a little embarrassed, I explained the development to Andy. In his usual gracious manner, he agreed that as part of the 'family', Pierre was the appropriate choice.

On paper we should have beaten Fiji easily, but this was a World Cup quarter-final, and they had nothing to lose. And what seemed a sure thing on paper had already been upended a few times that weekend. Watching England upset Australia 12-10, and then to see France stun the world by beating the All Blacks 20-18, sounded warning bells to any world-class team. I was very aware of the potential dangers of our game against the minnows from the Pacific Islands. We'd already had a tough match against Tonga, and Samoa had provided a very physical encounter. At least we knew Fiji wasn't going to try to beat us at our own game; they would try to run us ragged.

Van der Linde was ruled out, so Du Plessis came in, with Gurthro Steenkamp on the bench. The plan was simply to starve the Fijians of the ball and to keep it tight. But the best-laid plans sometimes don't take into account the organic nature of a rugby game. Once the players were out on the field they became a bit loose and careless, swept up in the incredible atmosphere of the Stade Vélodrome. They started trying to beat Fiji at their own game, particularly in the second half. They were suckered into a running contest for about 20 minutes.

Early on, we stuck to the game plan. As if to prove the point of our conversation earlier in the week, John opted for a kick to the corner when we had a sure three points from a penalty. From the lineout drive – quite similar to the maul we'd messed up in practice that week – John scored a try. We had already scored a try previously through Jaque Fourie, which had also started from a lineout.

We led 13-3 at the break, and after halftime JP Pietersen scored our third try, which put us into a 20-6 lead. We seemed to have the game under control. Fiji were even reduced to 14 men, following a yellow card for centre Seru Rabeni. And that's when our game became loose and they pounced. First, wing Vilimoni Delasau scored a great solo try. And then, minutes later, giant wing Sireli Bobo went in almost from the restart.

It was suddenly 20-20, and a crowd predominantly favouring the underdogs was ferocious in their disdain for the Boks. You could almost feel the antagonism from the stands. Standing under the poles, John called the players together to get some control back in the team. He told his men to remember the look in the eyes of the Aussies and Kiwis when they were knocked out the day before, and said he didn't want to see *that* look in any of their eyes. It was time for the boys to step up. There were 20 minutes left to play.

From the kick-off, we managed to stay in their half of the field and earned a penalty, which Monty slotted. Moments later, it took a massive tackle by JP to stop lock Ifereimi Rawaqa from scoring. Somehow JP had turned him over as he reached to score in the corner. It was a big moment, for sure, but with around 18 minutes to play, I don't buy the much-vaunted theory that the tackle won us the match. But it was a significant moment and it seemed to deflate the Fijians. John sent a message to the players to stop messing around and to slow the game down. This is exactly what they did, playing for field position in the closing stages. It seemed so much easier when we controlled the game. Juan Smith and Butch James scored additional tries, and we ultimately won 37-20. Our lineout was dominant and should've been even more so, but they got away with a lot of skew throws, which put pressure on us. But Fiji deserved all the plaudits they received for contributing massively to the tournament and the quarter-final specifically.

I was relieved to be in the last four, a stage further than the Boks had managed in 2003. New Zealand and Australia were out, and our semi-final opponent would be either Argentina or Scotland – teams we respected but didn't fear.

The Pumas duly beat Scotland to make it an all–southern hemisphere semi-final. England, almost unbelievably, made it into the last four, where they were slotted to meet France in an epic northern hemisphere battle. After we'd hammered England in the pool matches, I wouldn't have wagered much money on this outcome.

A slight disruption during this time occurred when SA Rugby advertised the job of Springbok coach a few days before the Fiji match. The closing date for applications was 19 October, the day before the World Cup final. It was insensitive in the extreme, but it didn't completely surprise me. They had done worse things in the past four years.

Nevertheless, it was a distraction. Assistant coaches Allister Coetzee and Gert Smal were suddenly caught in the bizarre situation of having to think about applying for my job while working with me in a crunch phase of the tournament. Gert didn't apply, but Allister told me he was considering throwing his name in the hat. I told him to go for it; I wouldn't take it personally. I've never objected to someone trying to further his career. I would have done the same. But the timing was shocking, as Allister suddenly had to think about putting a CV together while still performing his World Cup duties. If SA Rugby had stopped to think about their actions for a moment, they might have realised how silly their decision was.

Back on the field, we had to prepare for a tough match against the unbeaten Pumas. It was the last hurdle we had to clear to make it to the final. We were the only unbeaten teams left in the tournament, as both France and England had lost pool matches.

A semi-final is incredibly tough. To get that close and then miss out on a chance of playing for the ultimate prize is probably worse than losing in the final. I didn't want to stumble at this stage, and the players were even more desperate to avoid a defeat. It was a huge Sunday match that followed the Saturday semi, giving us one day less to prepare and recover for the following week's final – should we win. But at that stage of the tournament we were living only for the day.

After the helter-skelter rugby we'd played against Fiji at times, I sensed it would be a different game against the Pumas. They were a more direct team. They built their game on powerful set pieces, on the accurate boot of flyhalf Juan Hernandez and the flair of inside centre Felipe Contepomi. It was a style we would have no problem countering, although it was clear we'd be facing a barrage of high balls and lots of pick-up-and-goes around the fringes of the rucks.

I decided to bring Bob Skinstad onto the bench over Wikus van Heerden – a tough decision, as Wikus had been a rock of stability during Burger's suspension.

But I went for Bob because of Argentina's kicking game. They would be turning us around a lot, and I figured that someone of Bob's athletic ability would be able to fall back and support Monty and the wings later in the game. I called Wikus in to explain my decision to him. He had been part of the success story against England and had played off the bench against Fiji in the quarters, and suddenly he was being 'dropped' for the semis. I say that in inverted commas, because it was simply a 'horses for courses' selection, and he knew that. Wikus's dad had been a Springbok, so he understood more than most the relevance of the Bok ethos: the team came first. He wasn't happy about it, but he accepted that ultimately my call was going to benefit the team.

The match itself didn't vary from what we'd expected, although some observers said the Boks had kicked less than expected. I don't think they did. The boys just coped with the opposition's kicks well, and put them under more pressure they'd probably been in during the entire tournament. Some of the Argentinian kicking was ordinary, and in the loose and the lineout we had the edge. They only dominated us in the scrums, but over the rest of the park we were superior. We scored three of our tries from turnovers because of the pressure we applied.

I had a good chuckle when I read the English media, who criticised us for 'only' scoring from turnovers. Is punishing the mistakes you pressurise your opponents into making not a worthy way of scoring points? Defence wins World Cups, not only because it stops other teams from scoring, but because it puts the opposition under pressure when they have the ball. Pressure leads to poor decision-making and, ultimately, mistakes. It's then up to your team to make the opponents pay for those errors.

Against the Pumas we enforced pressure ruthlessly. Habana scored two tries, to equal All Black great Jonah Lomu's record of eight tries in a tournament, as we won 37-13. The Argentinians probably had more possession, but our boys took their chances. It was the efficient kind of performance we needed, because it set us up perfectly for the World Cup final. Unbelievably, it was to be a rematch against England.

As an interesting aside, Ernie Els won the World Matchplay title for a record seventh time that afternoon at Wentworth, England. Before I got changed for our match, I had phoned Ernie's dad Neels to pass on my congratulations to Ernie. He handed the phone to his son, who told me he was about to get on his private jet to fly to Paris for the game. So I invited him to the team hotel afterwards.

After the game, Ernie dropped by to meet the boys. He was obviously very happy that we had won. To win the World Match title, Ernie had had to beat Angel Cabrera, which he did, 6 and 4. We had both beaten Argentinian opposition that day.

44

Preparing for history

We had spent four seasons planning, preparing and visualising the Webb Ellis Trophy. It would take just 80 minutes to finish the job. Gert, Allister, John and I had all endured times when pocketing our pride seemed the only way forward. We were determined not to stumble at the final hurdle.

It has often been mentioned that winning the World Cup requires the ability to handle tremendous pressure, but no events earlier in the tournament came close to preparing us for the atmosphere from Monday 15 October 2007 onwards. Supporters were hanging around in the foyer of our hotel in Paris's Bercy suburb, hoping to spot their favourite players and coaches. Players were besieged with photo and autograph requests wherever they went, and treated like celebrities instead of sportsmen. It was difficult to focus, because the media scrutiny was also cranked up several levels. It was largely the South African media that had been interested in us until that point. When France and England were still in the tournament, Argentina had become the underdog darlings, and we were probably the fourth most popular team as far as the media were concerned.

But all that changed for the final. France and Argentina were out, and we were suddenly favoured to beat England. The journalistic scrum rivalled any I've seen on the field. The players, who had been carefully managed throughout the tournament, instantly felt the intensity of the week. It wasn't something they'd ever experienced, or a situation we could have adequately prepared them for.

Media and fans aside, it was a strange week. The tournament had passed so quickly up till that point, yet the last week dragged. John Smit told the media, 'Every day felt like 36 hours,' and he was right. Eddie Jones was a huge help on a personal level during that time. I always knew his experience of having been in a World Cup final would be vital, but his moral support was invaluable too.

The final week was all about handling the pressure and the magnitude of the event. Drawing on his experience as Australia's coach in the 2003 final against England, Eddie kept reminding me, 'They [the players] need to hear your voice, Jake. It's about *what* you say and how *much* you say.

They draw confidence from what you say and from your body language.'
So, although I delegated to my coaching staff, I did a lot of the talking in
the last week. In retrospect, a good thing.

An earlier conversation with Eddie often played on my mind during
that week. When I'd initially asked for his assistance as technical coach at
the World Cup, he'd asked me a question.

'Can you turn silver into gold, mate?' Eddie had quipped. He was only
half joking, but now that we were on the brink of fulfilling a dream, I had
another reason to avoid disappointment. I didn't want Eddie to leave a
World Cup with another silver medal.

It hit me how big this really was at the midweek media conference to
announce the team for the final. It was the biggest media conference I'd
ever attended; it was unbelievable. There were journalists from around the
globe, a dozen TV crews and hundreds of newspaper and radio people.

The starting XV also attended the conference, and it was good for
them to observe how big the occasion really was. I remember looking at
some of the guys and seeing how bewildered they seemed by the level of
interest. They were used to the media, but this went way beyond the norm.
JP Pietersen told me afterwards that he hadn't felt any nerves until he
attended the presser and saw the cameras and microphones. The magnitude
of what was to come hit him then. Here was a young man from a fairly
small town, but despite having been through the entire tournament, this
shook him.

The only player who didn't seem wracked with pre-match nerves was
Frans Steyn. He runs around the practice field and dropkicks; he's like a
kid on a playground. As a 20-year-old, he didn't seem to grasp the enormity
and significance of what we'd achieved by making the final. And bless him
for it. I hope he stays that way for the rest of his career, because it's a rare
player who is able to put his head down without nerves getting the better
of him.

We didn't change our patterns in the build-up to the week at all. We had
Monday and Thursday off as usual, trained hard on Tuesday and Wednesday,
and had the captain's run on Friday.

I've always emphasised experience, size and consistency in selection.
So, when I assembled the players to announce the team for the World Cup
final, it was with immense pride that I pointed out that they were also
the most capped Bok team of all time. The players had 668 caps between

them. My plan may have suffered some knocks along the way, but perhaps I got it right after all. We weren't in the final by fluke. We'd qualified because we had had a plan and doggedly stuck to it, and in the face of unbelievable resistance.

As I named the team, I was thrilled to be able to say, 'Locks, Victor and Bakkies, the best lock pairing in the world, and the most capped in Bok history.' Or, 'Hooker, John Smit, the most capped captain in Bok history.' I introduced our loosehead prop as, 'Os du Randt, previous World Cup winner and most capped prop in South African history.'

As I read out the names, I had something to highlight about each player's contribution to rugby in South Africa. This was a confident group, but I wanted further motivation for those players about just *how* good they were. Monty was the most capped Bok fullback and a record points-scorer. In fact, he was the leading points-scorer at the World Cup. Bryan Habana was the best finisher in rugby, and Fourie du Preez the best number 9. Schalk Burger: former IRB Player of the Year, and Juan Smith, an unsung hero. I said to them, 'Listen to what you have. Look at the player next to you; he's the best in the world. You will probably never play with a group of players as talented as this again. Make sure you remember that.'

At this point I have to mention the unsung heroes of the Bok squad: those eight players who never made the match-day 22. Our success in the World Cup was always dependent on the attitude of those eight. If there are eight bitter or unhappy players, it can derail a campaign. Throughout the tournament, it came down to how they were managed, how honest we were with them, how much a part of the match 22 they felt, how they were looked after physically and contributed to training sessions.

I'd often thanked those eight guys for their contributions. I was open with them about why they were not selected, and I kept them on their toes by running moves. As coaching staff we ensured that we ran the same plays with different sets of players. It kept everyone sharp, and made those who weren't selected feel they were contributing in the real way they were.

Gary Botha is a great example of the perfect team player. He started the year as number two hooker behind John, and by the end of the World Cup he was behind Bismarck du Plessis in the pecking order. That was tough on him, but you don't become a hooker unless you're a tough person. His positive approach summed up the attitudes of the other unlucky seven. Gary had been my number two hooker when the World Cup squad was named, as he was such a team man. Circumstances changed, but Gary's attitude didn't.

Wikus van Heerden was the same. He was in and out of the side. Ricky Januarie had been our number one scrumhalf choice in 2005, but had slipped to number three in 2007. Yet he remained positive. I believe I've shown consistency in four years as a coach, because Ricky knows I left him out based purely on a rugby decision. Fourie du Preez had moved to number one scrumhalf and Ricky had dropped down the pecking order. He handled himself brilliantly. Wayne Julies, Akona Ndungane, Bob Skinstad, Gurthro Steenkamp, Ricky, Gary, Albert van den Berg and Ashwin Willemse – the eight who missed out on the final have my greatest respect.

Our training session on the Tuesday evening was superb. The guys were really focused and went through the drills with great accuracy. Seeing how in tune they were helped settle some of my nerves. Before training, we'd had a technical session to establish our approach to the game. We decided that we wanted to split up England's pack by dividing our forwards at kick-offs or by using short lineouts. We also wanted to stretch them with some of our players who possessed greater athletic ability, which had worked in the 36-0 match.

We knew Jonny Wilkinson would play a huge role in the game; the tactical kicking on our back three had to be more accurate than it had been in our first encounter. So we paid extra attention to reading his moves and to players falling back in support. It may seem obvious, but good discipline was vital, which I re-emphasised to the players. We couldn't afford to play too much rugby in our half and give away penalties. We eventually conceded only five penalties in the final – our lowest in the tournament.

It was slightly odd preparing for a match against England for the second time in five weeks. I never expected to play them again as Bok coach. After the pool game they had had the deflated look of a side heading home. I'd watched them closely in the media mixed-zone session after that game, and they appeared to be on the brink of collapse. When we later climbed into our bus, I noticed the England team bus was parked next to ours. It looked like a morgue. I never thought England had it in them to win four consecutive games and claw their way into the final. But I respect how they fought back. It was a great achievement.

I never spoke to any of England's players about how they'd managed to pull themselves up, but Eddie knows Andy Farrell fairly well. He told Eddie that the senior players had taken over, deciding to go back to what had worked for them in 2003. That's the value of experience in a team; something I always banged on about myself. In 2011, the bulk of the 2007 Springbok team could be at the World Cup in New Zealand. If they are, South Africa will have a huge advantage over the other teams.

We obviously realised that the England team we were playing in the final wouldn't be the side we'd met 36 days earlier. How did we feel about England as an opposing team? There were both positive and negative aspects involved. The positive was that we'd played them five times in less than a year, so we knew the strengths and weaknesses of their game. There was some concern over complacency, but also a sense of relief because we were playing a team we knew well. If we'd been scheduled to play France, we wouldn't have known what to expect. And with a side like New Zealand, we knew we could easily concede two tries in two minutes and find ourselves in a hole. England weren't likely to spring any surprises or run us ragged.

During the week, there was the added distraction of a meeting with SA Rugby managing director Jonathan Stones about my future. I didn't hide how dissatisfied I was with their timing when they advertised for my job, and Stones admitted that the matter had not been handled very well. He also pointed out that I had waived my right regarding negotiations. Actually, my contract stipulated that neither party could negotiate with each other until the contract had expired. It was odd, I know, so both parties agreed to waive that clause. I was under the impression that this allowed *them* the opportunity to negotiate with *me*, but not with *other* potential candidates. They saw it differently – hence the advert inviting applications for my job. I always assumed my performance would be reviewed after the World Cup and I'd make a decision on the way forward at that point. It didn't bother me, though. I didn't reapply, as my contract stated that I had an option to renew, so reapplying wasn't necessary. SA Rugby's decision to advertise the job seemed an assumption on their part that I wouldn't be interested.

Honestly, though, it didn't matter. I told Stones I didn't think I could work with most of the SA Rugby crowd any more anyway. My only interest was in winning the World Cup. I'd worry about the future afterwards. I didn't have time for speculation and angst over my future career.

So I focused on preparing the players for the biggest game of their lives. On Wednesday evening, we had our team dinner. Instead of a fancy Parisian restaurant or a scenic boat meal on the Seine, we accepted an invitation for dinner at a neighbourhood steakhouse. The Noisy le Grande community had invited us to their suburb. We had enjoyed our last training session in Noisy earlier in the day, and they really laid it on that night. We had a great time. People wished us well for the final, and we handed out signed jerseys and photographs. A big chapter of our World Cup adventure had come to an end.

Thursday is our day off if we're playing on a Saturday or Sunday. It was no different in the week of the final. My mates Graham George and John Kruger had arrived in Paris, and I joined them for lunch in a lovely French restaurant. The owner of the establishment took good care of us. Like any self-respecting Frenchman, he said he was behind the Springboks and he wanted us to beat England on French soil. It was a long lunch. After the pressures of the week, it was a good release before the inevitable tension that would follow. We had a few beers, and the owner soon insisted on bringing out the champagne. I needed that day in order to take my mind off rugby temporarily and socialise with my friends.

Some members of the management team visited the Moulin Rouge on the Thursday evening. Derik Coetzee said it was his best evening out in a while. The players stayed at the hotel and focused. They watched DVDs of England that Willie Maree had cut, studying their opponents' strengths and weaknesses. Tension was intensifying as the week crawled on.

On Friday morning, I really started to feel the pressure. As much as you try to switch off, it's impossible – you look out the window or flick through TV news channels, and there it is. Green-and-gold or white-and-red-clad fans were clogging Parisian cafes and Metro carriages already. Massive numbers of English supporters arriving from across the channel cranked up the tension a few more notches.

That evening we took the bus to Stade de France for the captain's run, which went without a hitch. Afterwards, team psychologist Henning Gericke had a session with the players at the stadium. He spoke about being composed and confident. The message was short and concise: bring your four years together in this game.

Henning had played video clips on the bus all week en route to our two Noisy training sessions and to the captain's run. There were messages of support from office workers wearing replica Bok jerseys, from traffic cops, petrol pump attendants and cheering school cricket teams. Clips of our tries and game highlights also featured. Producer Tex Texeira of sports broadcaster SuperSport had put the clips together, filming SuperSport staff and enthusiastic South Africans from all walks of life. It reinforced what a win meant to people back home, and how the Boks' performance that weekend would define a nation. The boys loved it, and those clips played a big role in our mental preparation. They needed to know how much support they had back in South Africa.

That afternoon, my wife Debbie and boys Clinton and Wesley arrived in Paris. The flights had been booked well in advance, but I'd promised the boys they could come over *only* if we made the final. I can imagine their whoops and shouts of delight in Cape Town when the final whistle in that semi-final signalled we were through to the final. I enjoyed having my family around, but they understood there was a job to be done, so they went sightseeing while I finished up with the team. Graham took the boys to watch the bronze-medal match between France and Argentina at Parc des Princes on the Friday. I was pleased they could experience a little more World Cup atmosphere than our one game in Stade de France.

I watched the third-place match with Allister in my room. I couldn't believe the result. Argentina had an excellent game, winning 34-10, which put into perspective how well *we* had played against the Pumas in the semi-final. I suddenly felt much more optimistic going into the final.

45

World champions

I didn't sleep well on the night before the final. Various scenarios and drills were running through my head endlessly. I wanted the match to come quickly; the waiting was killing me. We were completely prepared as a team, but there are things you can't prepare for in a final. You arrive at a World Cup; you're away from home. As much as you talk about and believe in winning the tournament, when teams fall by the wayside around you, you realise that pressure affects everyone differently.

It was 20 October 2007, the World Cup final. I'd been aware of the final date for nearly two years, and I'd often visualised what it would be like on the day. Now there were around 12 hours until the 9 p.m. kickoff. We'd left nothing to chance and couldn't do any more. We simply had to wait.

The weather was perfect – a crisp, clear Parisian autumn day. No rain was forecast, which helped. A final played in rain on a heavy field would have suited England. It was a good omen.

South African president Thabo Mbeki had arrived in Paris the previous evening, and he wanted to meet the team before the match. The meeting was scheduled for 4 p.m. at the team hotel, just five hours before kickoff. It wasn't an ideal time for nervous players, but I obliged. The president had supported us before we left South Africa by saying we should 'forget about politics and bring the cup home'.

Common sense dictates that sporting schedules should not be interfered with before a big game, so we'd considered the implications of changing the players' routine. Despite what people may say, the World Cup final is not just another game. If we had an afternoon kickoff, we normally had our walk-through in the mornings, but for a late-evening match, we have it a bit later. But I eventually realised that worrying about team protocol was of limited use on the day. We hadn't been in a final before, so while superstitions and science were factors, this was a unique situation. Eventually we reached a happy medium by having our pre-match walk-through immediately after our meeting with the president.

President Mbeki was inspirational. He said that he'd flown out from

South Africa to collect the trophy. The players were anxious, which the president seemed to sense, so he didn't speak for long. He made sure his few words counted.

I had spent the entire morning pacing and seeking re-affirmation. I would ask Gert, or Allister, or Eddie, 'What do you think, how will we do?' I had a lot of nervous energy, and Eddie eventually said, 'Jake, the players cannot be better prepared. They cannot have a better understanding of what they have to do on the field. They cannot be better off athletically, so stop worrying.' We had 30 fit and healthy players without one niggle, and Eddie reminded me of how rare this was. 'That's an incredible thing,' he said. 'It's not like we're carrying a guy who is a fifty-fifty call.' He was right.

We had lost players to injuries before and during the tournament, but not one of our squad was nursing a strain or a bump for the final. Maybe luck was on our side.

I decided to do something different before the match, something I hadn't done since my first test in charge in Bloemfontein in 2004. I wrote a personal letter to every man in the match 22. It was a short, handwritten note, which I handed out at the walk-through after the meeting with President Mbeki.

I hadn't prepared letters for the whole team in nearly four years, although I usually did it for new caps in the team. I'd say how proud I was, and what I expected of them as a Springbok. I pointed out how proud their family would be and, in the case of Pierre Spies, how proud his late father, a former Springbok, would've been if he could've seen him.

I'd spent several hours writing to each player about what made him special, my view on why he was there, and what I hoped he'd achieve. I also thanked each one for their contribution to our success, for the sacrifices they'd made and for the pleasure they had given me as a coach.

For instance, I praised John Smit for his fine leadership, and told him, 'Today people back home who've criticised you will understand what you've meant to this team, and understand what you have achieved.'

With Monty, I acknowledged how he'd been a role model to the team, and how important he'd been to the World Cup campaign. I handed out the notes, ensuring the players had a few hours to think about what I'd written. I didn't want to hand out the notes on the bus en route to the stadium, as it would have been too emotional. I'd warned the guys of the emotion and hype that surrounded the final – we didn't need to add to it.

The players went to pack their kitbags and then regrouped in the team room. Following some last-minute technical talk, we watched a message from Madiba. He'd sent a DVD with his former head of security, Rory Steyn, who'd brought it to Paris personally.

Madiba's message was typically short and to the point, but very powerful. He told us how proud he and South Africa were of the Springboks, and how our achievements had provided an opportunity for the nation. He thanked John and the management; he thanked everyone in the squad for what they'd already achieved. In his unique way, he said the result was meaningless, as we'd done enough to make everyone proud. Obviously it was the right thing to say, but I knew it was also what he had to say in order to calm the players' nerves.

Those were the last words to the group before we boarded the bus.

Bus rides to games are usually quiet, as the players listen to their iPods and enter their own headspace. Cutting out noise hones the other senses. Of course, you can't help but notice the fans as you approach the ground. They wave and cheer with their painted faces, flags and posters, urging you on. Or they jeer if they support the opposition! It's a huge inspiration to see those die-hard fans, knowing how some have spent their life savings to fly over and support their team.

During the World Cup, we played a very evocative song, called 'Ons vir jou Suid-Afrika' by Bok van Blerk and Robbie Wessels, over the sound system in the bus. Three minutes long, the song was usually played just before we arrived at the stadium, and repeated until everyone had disembarked. The lyrics talk about the love South Africans have for their country and about what makes it so special.

When we arrived, the players went to the changing room, while I was roped into a brief TV interview. I met referee Alain Rolland on the field and we chatted informally. He wished us luck for the game. We discussed when he would come into the changing room to check the players' studs and address the front rows.

Eddie, John and I checked the wind and weather to see if there were any conditions we hadn't expected. Everything seemed normal. John and I decided that if we won the toss, we'd kick off and immediately put ourselves in English territory. We moved into the bowels of the stadium, where John and English captain Phil Vickery tossed the coin under Rolland's supervision. England won the toss, but said they'd only inform us of their decision half an hour before kickoff. The gamesmanship had begun. They eventually decided to kick off, and we started the game the same way we had in the pool match. It was a good omen, and probably a bit of a psychological boost.

During the warm-up we went through our usual drills and rituals. The warm-up is planned during the week and we don't change anything at the last minute. I took a defence drill and talked to the players, reminding them of alignment, communication and concentration. I wanted them to be extra aware of being switched on defensively.

Observing the players, I could tell they were definitely tense. But there was an air of determination and purpose, and they seemed to be channelling their energy positively.

I called the players together for a final chat. 'The most important thing tonight is that I want you to be brave,' I said. 'That means brave when you play, brave in the decisions you make, brave in the way you react, brave in having a go. Don't be scared to try something and to make a decision. Trust yourself.'

I was reminded of something Professor Noakes had said. 'Some athletes go to the Olympics to make the finals. Others go to win gold. And there's a huge difference in the mindset.' That was our slogan as we'd left the hotel: we hadn't come to make the finals; we'd come to win gold.

There were six minutes to kickoff. The players returned to the changing room, and Rolland entered to check the boots. John took over and spoke briefly to the team. I went around and wished every player well. Some players shake hands, some hug me; it depends on the person. I came face to face with Frans Steyn, who normally gives me a traditional handshake. This time, when he extended his hand, he gave me the two-fingered Grey College handshake. Grey is South Africa's most famous rugby school, having produced more than 50 Springboks. I don't know exactly what his gesture meant. Perhaps he was indicating that he was treating this match like a top rugby school game, or that, in his view, I was an honorary Grey man. Either way, it was a special gesture.

I was both nervous and excited as I made my way to my seat. I kept saying to myself, there's nothing more you can do now. But it plays on your mind: what could happen; what should happen ... You've run the scenarios so many times that you can't even think about them any more. The moment had arrived.

The players lined up in the tunnel, and that compelling tournament music swelled out. It was a great choice by the IRB; I'd love to buy a copy of the CD. John Smit's face was a picture of concentration, and I saw a similar calm determination on the faces of Victor, Os, Bakkies, Bryan, JP, Monty as the camera panned down the line of players ... They looked as if they were in a trance, which is exactly where I wanted them to be. As the music reached a crescendo, Eddie turned to me and said, 'This is what it's about, mate.' I'll remember that moment, when the two teams walked onto the pitch, when I'm an old man. The feeling was indescribable.

For some reason, John was not carrying 'Bokkie', our team mascot. I heard later that Bokkie had been forgotten at the hotel. The previous game's man of the match was responsible for bringing Bokkie to the ground, and in this case it had been Os du Randt. Superstitious types might read something into this, but a man can surely be excused when emotions get in the way before his last test for the Springboks. A police rider was quickly despatched to the team hotel, and by halftime Bokkie was in place next to the flagstick on the halfway line.

As the anthems played, I thought about the fans in South Africa and how they were feeling. I remembered the mood in 1995, and if this was anything similar, the country would be going nuts. Some of the players from the World Cup–winning team of 1995 had handed out the match jerseys. It was time to start a new chapter in South African rugby.

The opening exchanges in the match were as expected, with big collisions and heavy defence. But I could tell from early on that we seemed more composed and stronger in the contact situations. It was a promising start. Monty landed a penalty in the seventh minute, and Wilkinson replied with a great kick from the touchline. They had slightly more possession, but we looked sharper with the ball and unruffled on defence.

Monty landed a second penalty in the 16th minute, and a few minutes later he was caught awkwardly and stayed down. I was concerned. He hardly ever stays down. He stood up and ran off with a limp. We had the upper hand in the next 10 minutes, and came close to scoring a few times. But Jason Robinson made a good tackle on Butch James to stop a try, and Steyn failed to spot an open Jaque Fourie on his shoulder after breaking through a gap.

In the 33rd minute, physio Clint Readhead finally made it onto the field to treat Monty. Clint radioed back to Doc Hassan that it looked pretty serious. Monty's right knee was badly injured. The doctor, usually conservative in his approach, told Clint to 'strap him tight' in order to give the knee stability. Clint asked Monty if he felt well enough to stay on. Monty never hesitated. Once he was strapped, he landed a third penalty before halftime, and then a fourth in the second half. It was incredibly brave play. He kicked 100 per cent of his goals that night with a torn meniscus and sprained ligaments. He was suffering pain and in severe discomfort, but nevertheless gave a near perfect performance for 60 minutes, virtually on one leg. After the final, he was ruled out for 10 weeks.

My seat was in a good position, but you're in the middle of the VIP area, so it's like being in a fishbowl. People often stared when I shouted and screamed into my microphone, but my only concern was getting my messages through to the field. When I spoke to Clint, Doc Hassan or Derik Coetzee, they had to put their hand up to indicate they'd executed my command. It's the only time I became a control freak. I wanted to see them talking to the player and passing on an instruction. Somebody asked me afterwards if they were comfortable seats. I replied, 'When you're winning, they're comfortable. If you're losing, the edges stick into you.'

When the halftime whistle blew, we were 9-3 up, but we'd had some good try-scoring chances towards the end of the half that we didn't convert. During the break, the same routine applied. Gert spoke, Allister spoke, Eddie spoke. Then I called the players together and had a long chat. My message was, 'We've got to score first in the second half.' (We didn't.) 'And, secondly, there are only 40 minutes left and we have a six-point lead. What more do you guys want? You're not even feeling tired yet.' I reminded them that they had laid the foundations in the first half, and they should build on them in the second. I also said, 'Guys, just understand they're not going to give you the World Cup. You're going to have to win it.'

Early in the second half, Steyn slipped a tackle on Mathew Tait, who then beat Monty. Victor Matfield managed to pull him down inches short of the line. But they recycled the ball and went left, where wing Mark Cueto dived for the corner. Danie Rossouw managed to lay a hand on him, and it was enough. The video replay clearly showed that Cueto's foot had made contact with the touchline before he grounded the ball. The try was staved off because of a defensive drill we'd worked on previously and had practised again in the week before the final. Danie had run a shadow line behind the first line of defence. Had he pushed into the front line, we wouldn't have stopped that try. We're talking fingertips, but they're all that mattered.

England received a penalty and closed the gap to three points, but it was the last time they looked like scoring. Monty added his fourth penalty in the 48th minute, and from then on we controlled the match. England had more of the ball, but found no way through our defence. I'd often said to Steyn that he would land the winning kick in the World Cup final, but he didn't believe me. Perhaps he didn't land the winning kick, but he landed the one that put us two scores ahead – a penalty from 48 metres – on the hour.

I know this sounds arrogant, but I knew, at that moment, that we had won the game. England had hit us with everything they had, and we had handled it all comfortably. The only way they looked likely to score was through field position, and they weren't enjoying any.

Our scrum was rock solid, we were winning all the collisions, and the lineout was brilliant. We stole seven of their balls and never lost one of our own lineouts. Victor and John, in particular, were outstanding. We even lost John to the blood bin in the 73rd minute, and Bismarck had to execute a crucial throw-in about 10 metres from our own try line. Victor barked out the code, looked the English in the eye and took the ball. It was a pleasure to watch. Bismarck had handled the pressure superbly well.

In some matches you get the feeling that things are going your way, and I don't mean referee calls. It's the way the ball bounces favourably or the opposition fumbles a pass. In the second half, John was penalised for supposedly playing Cueto off the ball. The replays showed clearly that Cueto had run into him. But from the lineout, which they fed, England turned the ball over. I thought to myself, 'Things are panning out for us tonight.'

With about five minutes to go, we were awarded another penalty. It was on the halfway line, and I thought we should kick for poles. I screamed the orders, but the players decided to kick for the corner instead. They wanted to keep the ball and kill the game by starving England of possession as the clock ticked down. During the week, in a meeting with the senior players, we had run through many scenarios. What would we do if we were 10 points ahead in the first half? Or if we were 10 points down? Did we have a tactic if we trailed by less than one point with a few minutes to play? We ran through many possible scenarios. One of them was: What if we're leading by one or two points, and we have a penalty with about five minutes to play?

At our meeting, half the players had indicated that they would go for poles, and the other half had said kicking for touch was the solution. We then debated their reasons. Some guys didn't favour the going-for-goal option because, if we missed and the ball didn't go dead, the opposition could counter-attack and score. They favoured keeping the ball, knowing that our lineout was superior, and winding the clock down. It had been a long debate, with every detail analysed. I'd favoured kicking for poles, but there wasn't a definitive answer.

With the clock ticking, I screamed at Derik to take the kicking tee onto the field. But before he could act, Monty kicked the ball into touch. John was still in the blood bin, but the senior players had decided that they could kill the game for the last four or five minutes in England's half. They didn't do it as convincingly as I would have liked, and England moved back into our half. When Monty kicked for touch, I thought, 'They made the decision, and now they have to show their worth.'

Earlier in the tournament we'd practised a move on the training pitch, where Juan Smith attacked the flyhalf channel from a scrum. I didn't like the move and told them not to use it, as there was the possibility of an interception or the referee penalising Juan for breaking off the scrum early. They'd called the move themselves at training. Afterwards, in his quiet way, John came to me and said, 'They need a bit of leeway, so that if they see opportunities on the field, they feel able to call them.' This was one of those moments.

The boys kept the ball for about two and a half minutes, and then turned it over. A scrum was awarded to England, but the Boks had eaten up 150 seconds, effectively sealing the win in their decision not to go for poles. Once we had won the ball back, there were only seconds until the end.

I stood up and shook hands with the coaching staff, and started making my way down to the field. The scoreboard read 15-6 to South Africa. Rolland sounded the final whistle, and the stadium erupted. The Webb Ellis Trophy was ours.

Players were charging around and whooping, and I hugged many of them. I wanted to greet John to shout, 'Well done!', but I didn't see him immediately in all the mayhem. I believe certain captains are born to lift the Webb Ellis Trophy: David Kirk, Nick Farr-Jones, François Pienaar, John Eales, Martin Johnson ... There's a certain kind of captain who hoists that cup, and I always pictured John as one of them.

People often ask if John and I butt heads, and we sometimes do have differing views. John is not a 'yes-man' kind of captain. We get along well, but he doesn't say, 'Yes, coach, no coach, three bags full, coach.' He picks appropriate times to speak his mind. That was something I've always appreciated.

Ashwin Willemse was the craziest player that night. He ran and jumped on me. He was unbelievably ecstatic. I was standing there, thinking, 'Can you believe what's happening here? How do I take it all in?'

I had my emotions under control until I saw Ricky Januarie and Wayne Julies approaching. My feelings just took over and I started sobbing on Ricky's shoulder. I suppose those two players summed up the win for me: they'd been youngsters in the Under-21 squads I'd coached – Wayne in 1999, and Ricky in 2002 and 2003. They had won an under-21 World Cup with me. They were probably the most influential guys in the Bok team, because they *had* to be positive. In the country we live in, they are probably the benchmark of whether I've achieved or not. To see them shouting and screaming and celebrating the moment pushed me over the edge.

Everyone felt tremendous relief, too. Emotions had been pent up for a long time, and now the pressure valve had been released. A stage was erected for the trophy presentation, and England went first. They were gracious. I later heard that Mike Catt had approached Frans Steyn and said, 'Well done, young man. You're going to be a superstar in a few years' time. Enjoy the moment.' That was a great compliment coming from Catt, who's done it all in the game.

The players walked up to receive their medals. The coaches were at the back of the line, and Eddie moved out of the way for me. 'You go first, mate,' he said. I refused, and told him to go in front. Eddie has often tried to stay in the background, but I wanted him to feel an integral part of the South African history that he had helped shape. He deserved his gold medal.

Funnily enough, when Eddie was asked in a press conference if he wanted to exact revenge on England for denying Australia a gold medal in the 2003 Rugby World Cup, he gave a typical Eddie response. 'It's not about revenge against England,' he said, 'but I might throw my silver medal away!' Maybe he has.

On the field I greeted Dr Syd Millar, chairman of the IRB, and received my gold medal. Other dignitaries were cordial too, but it hit me just how special it was to win this trophy when I stood in front of President Mbeki. He congratulated me and thanked me for what we'd done for the country. A few minutes later, he was hoisted onto the shoulders of the players, clutching the Webb Ellis Trophy. What a symbolic moment for South Africa!

Not every country is lucky enough to win a World Cup. Very few get to do it twice. The challenge now is to correct whatever mistakes we had made after 1995 – not only in rugby, but in South Africa. We've got another chance as a nation, and we should ensure we don't repeat the same mistakes.

I accompanied the players on a lap of honour, enjoying the moment. My family was in the stands, and I was extremely proud that my boys were there to share the euphoria. It was a long evening, and after many hours of press obligations, which included official photographs of each player with his medal in the changing room, we headed back to the hotel.

Family and friends of the squad were waiting in the lobby. I carried the World Cup inside and went straight over to show it to my wife and boys. More photos were taken, and then we went into the team room to celebrate. Sasol had laid on a huge party with plenty of champagne. Chairman Peter Cox, a Pretoria Boys High old boy, was particularly proud of John Smit, who had been head boy of his school.

Johann Rupert also invited the squad for a drink in another room of the hotel. He presented the players and some of the coaching staff with Cartier watches in commemoration of the World Cup final. I thanked him for all the assistance he'd given the team behind the scenes, as well as for the support he'd given me personally.

We eventually called it a night at 3:30 a.m. Debbie and the boys were staying across the road. My youngest son, Wesley, asked, 'Can I sleep with you tonight, Dad?' And I said, 'Sure.' It had been a long day and his head hit the pillow immediately. A lot of people asked how I slept that night. I must be honest – I didn't really get a good night's sleep. My little boy was restless, so he kicked me, or he wanted hugs and that sort of thing. I may not have slept for long, but I slept more peacefully that night than I had in four years!

Epilogue

At the annual International Rugby Board's awards ceremony 24 hours after the World Cup final, the Springboks made a clean sweep of the major categories for the second time since I'd become coach.

Bryan Habana won the coveted Player of the Year title for his brilliant try-scoring feats throughout the year. Not only did he equal Jonah Lomu's record of eight tries in a single World Cup tournament, he scored a season record of 13 tries for the Boks. He also scored eight tries for the Bulls in the Super 14, including the match-winning touchdown in the final against the Sharks.

I was fortunate to claim the Coach of the Year award for a second time. In 2007, with 13 victories from 16 tests, including the Webb Ellis Trophy for the Boks, I was honoured again.

Most importantly, the Springboks won the Team of the Year prize, emulating our 2004 achievement. John Smit had the honour of collecting the trophy for the second time in his career.

We knew our victory in France had made South Africans proud, but we were bowled over by the frenzied welcome we received on landing in Johannesburg. Over 10 000 people descended on OR Tambo airport to cheer us on. After a couple of days off, we embarked on a nationwide celebratory tour.

The warmth and fantastic support we received in Pretoria, Johannesburg, Soweto, Bloemfontein, Port Elizabeth, Durban and Cape Town will remain with me forever. Dancing and cheering multiracial crowds certainly suggested that people don't care what a team looks like as long as it is winning. It was amazing to see what a World Cup win could do for the country. I hope SARU builds on this.

Transformation is vital, and must continue, but a victorious national team is the most powerful aspect in growing the game in all communities.

After SA Rugby sent out a statement saying that I hadn't applied for the post of Springbok coach, I decided it was the final straw and called a media conference. I explained that I was disappointed with the way they'd handled the issue, as, according to my contract, I wasn't required to reapply, and I informed the world that I wouldn't stay on beyond my contract period.

I wish the future Springbok coach luck – he's going to need it.

Jake White's test record as Bok coach (correct at 20 October 2007)	
Played	53
Won	35
Drawn	1
Lost	17
Winning ratio	66%

Index

Abrahams, Jackie 253
Ackermann, Johan 216, 217, 236, 290
Adams, Bennie 92
Adriaanse, Rayaan 131, 177
ANC 286
Andrews, Eddie 122, 217
Andrews, Mark 41, 46, 72
apartheid 18, 246, 263
Ashley-Cooper, Adam 143

Bacher, Ali 176–177
Badenhorst, Skipper 67
Bannister, Roger 91
Barkley, Olly 305
Barnard, Pat 84, 88, 89
Barrett, Bradley 271
Barry, De Wet 64, 105, 115, 150, 164, 172
Basson, Koos 161, 178, 234, 240–241, 242, 243, 275
Beckworth, Mr 31
Bernard, Roland 84, 90
Betsen, Serge 172
Biebuyck, Brian 264–266
Bladen, Hugh 189
Blair, Ben 66, 190
Bobo, Gcobani 124–125
Bobo, Sireli 314
Boden, Warren 23
Borges, Lucas 151
Bornman, Neels 21
Bosch, Fanie 36
Bosman, Meyer 150, 153, 190, 246
Botha, Bakkies 106, 108, 124, 126, 149, 154, 172, 214, 216, 228, 238, 260, 284, 320, 329
Botha, BJ 201, 236, 296, 310–311

Botha, Gary 84, 88, 154, 169, 296, 320–321
Botha, Naas 88–89, 92, 112, 175, 176, 203, 219, 222
Braid, Daniel 89
Brink, Stephen 72
Britz, Gerrie 246
Britz, Schalk 84
Broderick, John 18
Brooke, Robin 52
Brophy, Peter 30
Broun, Alex 40
Brown, Grant 12, 14
Brown, Mark 12
Brown, Ryan 12
Burger, Schalk 56, 90, 91, 92–93, 124–125, 126, 129, 146, 149, 154, 165, 168–172, 210, 214, 238, 260, 284, 301–303, 308, 309, 316, 320
Burger, Schalk Sr 154, 170
Burke, Matt 48
Burn, Michael 79

Cabrera, Angel 317
Candelon, Julien 128
Canterbury 251
Cape Argus 184, 188
Carstens, Deon 217
Carter, Daniel 89, 165, 191, 192, 201, 211
Catt, Mike 305, 333
Chavhanga, Tonderai 127–128, 178, 267, 268
Christie, Kitch 197, 291
Claassens, Michael 118, 150, 153
Coetzee, Allister 81, 82, 99–100, 104, 109, 111,

113, 124, 128, 131, 153, 167, 180, 204, 220, 221, 223, 280, 295, 300, 315, 318, 324, 326, 330
Coetzee, Derik 83, 93, 104, 131, 134, 176, 323, 330, 332
Coetzee, Eduard 67
Coetzee, Hans 21
Collard, Jack 31–32
Collins, Jerry 170, 171
Colquhoun, Andy 312–313
Conradie, Bolla 115, 121, 151, 178
Contepomi, Felipe 315
Corry, Martin 250
Cowan, Jimmy 89
Cox, Peter 334
Croft, David 66
Cronjé, Jacques 90, 91, 169, 218, 236, 242, 244, 245, 290, 292
Cueto, Mark 330, 331
Cullen, Christian 49
Curren, Kevin 102

Dahl, Karl 132
Dalton, James 22, 25, 26–28, 31, 46, 53, 57
D'Arcy, Gordon 227, 229
Davids, Quinton 113, 178
De Beer, Jannie 51
De Kock, Len 20
Delasau, Vilimoni 314
Dempsey, Girvan 229
De Villiers, HO 219
De Villiers, Jean 84, 90, 122, 142, 146, 151, 154, 164, 169, 172, 190, 192, 201, 214, 226,

227, 236, 238, 254,
295, 296, 301, 302, 304
De Villiers, Peter 100
De Villiers, Pieter 172
De Waal, Willem 217
Dlulane, Tim 118, 178
Dobson, John 39–40, 41
Dunning, Matt 66
Du Plessis, Bismarck 288,
289, 292, 296, 320, 331
Du Plessis, Carel 40,
41–42, 203
Du Plessis, Jannie 289,
311, 313
Du Plessis, Morné 98, 175,
219, 291
Du Preez, Fourie 2, 90,
91, 115, 121, 146,
147, 149, 166, 169,
191–192, 201,
207–209, 214, 278,
284, 304, 320, 321
Du Preez, Frik 184, 241
Du Randt, Os 41, 102–103,
106, 115, 121, 149,
154, 166, 182, 184,
194–196, 214, 216,
238, 284, 294, 296,
320, 329
Du Toit, Apies 20
Du Toit, Gaffie 108,
114, 236

Eales, John 333
Easterby, Simon 229
Els, Ernie 246, 316–317
Els, Neels 317
End Conscription Campaign
18
Engelbrecht, Johan 34
Erasmus, Rassie 46,
280, 293–294

Farrell, Andy 304, 305, 322
Farr-Jones, Nick 333
Ferguson, Sir Alex 209
Ferguson, Dr Mark 87

Ferreira, Christo 280
Fitzpatrick, Sean 89, 102
Flatley, Elton 143
Floors, Kabamba 217–218,
225, 241–242,
244–245, 281
Flynn, Corey 89
Ford 251
Fortuin, Bevan 226, 230,
236, 245
Fourie, Jaque 121, 122, 146,
151, 154, 164, 169,
172, 214, 216, 226,
227, 254, 284, 314, 329
Friedman, Bernard 12–13
Fritz, Florian 172
Fyvie, Wayne 23, 71, 72

Garvey, Adrian 46
Gear, Rico 66, 190
George, Graham 152, 323,
324
Gerber, Danie 51
Gericke, Henning 104,
144–145, 323
Gilfillan, Gordon 90
Gillingham, Joe 72
Giteau, Matt 143
Goodwin, Timmy 87
Grace, Mark 19
Graham, John 148
Granger, Dale 133, 184,
188, 189
Gregan, George 44, 114,
145, 183
Greig, Tony 246, 249

Habana, Bryan 56, 123,
124, 127, 144, 146,
149, 153, 154, 210,
214, 226, 227, 236,
254, 275, 278, 284,
307, 310, 316, 320,
329, 335
Haddad, Basil 221
Hadden, Frank 165
Hall, Allan 30

Hart, John 102
Hassan, Dr Yusuf 104, 121,
131, 171, 214, 281,
295, 301, 330
Hayes, John 228
Hayman, Carl 66, 67,
190, 303
Hazell, Andy 65
Henderson, Grant 67
Hendricks, Mac 208, 306
Henry, Graham 77–78, 148,
201, 210, 223
Hernandez, Juan 315
Heymans, Cedric 66
Hills, Willie 63
Hinckley, Grant 25
Hobbs, Jock 148
Hodgson, Charlie 236
Honiball, Henry 46, 48, 49,
50–51, 57, 58, 69
Honiss, Paul 119, 182
Horan, Tim 55
Horgan, Shane 229
Hoskins, Oregan 2, 79,
161, 163–164, 176,
192–193, 203–204,
219–220, 221, 223,
233, 240–243, 244,
246–247, 250, 251,
253, 261–262, 266,
268–269, 270–273,
274, 275, 286, 293
Hougaard, Derick 91, 92,
217, 271, 281, 290
Howlett, Doug 66, 113,
190, 290
Human, Wylie 64
Hurter, Marius 103
Hutton, John 30

Independent on Saturday 133

Jack, Chris 66, 67, 190
Jack, Makhaya 99
James, Butch 190, 191, 192,
204, 235–238, 246,
288, 314, 329

Januarie, Ricky 90, 91, 127, 146, 147, 169, 170, 171, 178, 207, 208, 216, 263, 278, 321, 333
Jauzion, Yannick 172
Jenkins, Neil 78
Johnson, Martin 165, 333
Jones, Eddie 98, 120, 123, 126, 143, 182, 293, 294–295, 300, 318–319, 322
Jooste, Pieter 217, 261, 262, 267, 268, 269, 270, 283–284, 292, 293, 326, 327, 329, 330, 333–334
Jordaan, Jorrie 8
Joubert, André 41–42, 69
Joubert, Marius 115, 150, 254
Joubert, Rudy 34, 100
Joubert, Swys 20
Julies, Wayne 321, 333

Kama, Vusi 177, 179, 180, 274
Kampfmann, Gunter 19
Kamp Staaldraad 84, 97, 102, 131
Kefu, Steve 66
Kelleher, Byron 142
Kempson, Robbie 46
Keohane, Mark 162, 164
Kirk, David 333
Kiss, Les 79
Koen, Louis 75
Krige, Corné 103
Kruger, John 323

Labuschagne, Jannes 113
Laharrague, Julien 66
Laing, Dean 19
Lake, Rudolf 179
Lane, Tim 79–80
Laporte, Bernard 173
Lardner, Craig 99

Larkham, Stephen 55, 145, 191
Lategan, Tienie 122, 127
Lauaki, Sione 89
Legendre, Jean-Claude 308–309
Le Roux, Ollie 57, 72
Lewsey, Josh 238
Livingstone, Craig 89, 130, 140, 160, 188, 264–266
Loffreda, Marcelo 152
Lomu, Jonah 49, 281, 316, 335
Louw, Hottie 113
Ludeke, Frans 35, 55, 86–87
Luyt, Louis 40, 242

Maka, Isitolo 52
Malakoane, Philip 'Flippie' 131, 141–142
Malan, Avril 34
Mallett, Nick 36, 39–40, 41–45, 46, 47, 49–51, 52–54, 55, 56–57, 58, 59–60, 74, 76, 81, 100, 110, 142, 147, 175, 197, 203–204, 207, 219, 236, 298
Manana, Thando 77
Mandela, Nelson 18, 136–137, 327
Maree, Willie 323
Marinos, Andy 154, 160, 161, 162, 176, 215–216, 220, 221, 261, 266, 287, 292–293, 294
Markgraaff, André 39, 74, 76, 77, 79, 80, 97–98, 100, 104, 113, 123–124, 134, 138–141, 142, 203
Martens, Hentie 23
Matfield, Victor 63, 108, 112–113, 115, 116, 124, 142, 149, 154, 166, 214, 228, 238,

260, 284, 290, 313, 320, 329, 330, 331
Mbeki, Thabo 116, 285–287, 325–326, 334
McAlister, Luke 89
McAllister, Roy 34–35
McBride, Willie John 120
McCallum, Kevin 274, 279–280
McCaw, Richie 147, 165, 169, 201, 211, 288
McCochran, John 302–303
McDonald, Barry 66
McFarland, Norman 11
McFarland, Steve 11
McIntosh, Ian 55, 69–70, 176, 203, 217, 241, 242–243, 244–245, 262, 267, 269, 283, 292
McIntyre, Steve 215
McQueen, Rod 108, 191
Meachen, Ellis 309
Mealamu, Keven 146–147
Meyer, Heyneke 60, 97–98, 240, 241
Mhani, Dumisani 97
Michalak, Frederic 154
Millar, Syd 120, 228, 334
Mills, Justin 25
Mitchell, Drew 303
Mitchell, Neil 18
Mohammed, Adnaan 279–280
Montgomery, Percy 42, 46, 88, 103, 108, 109, 112, 115, 116, 121, 124, 142, 144, 149, 153, 154, 184, 190, 191–192, 201, 214, 216, 260, 284, 296–297, 307, 314, 316, 320, 326, 329–330, 331, 332
Mordt, Ray 115
Morkel, Dave 19
Moss, James 18
Moyle, Brent 5, 22

Muir, Dick 50
Muliaina, Mils 209
Muller, Hennie 18
Muller, Johann 236, 288, 290, 311
Muller, Pieter 48, 49, 54–55, 57, 72
Munday, Trevor 251
Murphy, Geordan 229
Murphy, Noel 120
Murray, Anne-Lee 293, 299
Murray, Waylon 279, 281

Nayo, Songezo 220–221
Ndungane, Akona 178, 182, 236, 238, 267, 321
Ndungane, Odwa 178, 267–269
Nel, JP 90
Ngwenya, Taku 310
Nichol, Rob 99
Noakes, Prof. Tim 128, 213, 214, 284, 328
Nokwe, Jongi 117, 124–125, 178
Noon, Jamie 65
Normand, Grazer 32

Oberholzer, Rian 41, 45, 63, 65, 69, 75, 78, 81, 83, 90, 97, 220, 221
O'Callaghan, Donnacha 228
O'Connell, Paul 228
O'Driscoll, Brian 77, 119, 227, 229, 284
O'Gara, Ronan 119, 229, 230
O'Kelly, Malcolm 228–229
Olivier, Wynand 164, 178, 190, 194, 227, 236, 254, 288, 306
O'Sullivan, Eddie 120
Otto, Krynauw 46, 52, 53

Paulse, Breyton 115, 116, 121, 122, 178, 192, 216
Pelous, Fabian 172

Pelser, Pa 20
Petersen, Arthob 97, 98, 99, 100, 101, 111, 115, 125, 129–131, 133, 175, 219–220
Pickford, Nigel 24
Pienaar, François 54, 136, 333
Pienaar, Gysie 208
Pienaar, Ruan 201–202, 207, 208–209, 210–211, 278, 288
Pietersen, JP 212, 288, 304, 306, 307, 314, 319, 329
Pitcairn, Dave 21, 22
Pitt, Clifford 13–14
Pitt, Daniela 1
Pitt, Des 13–14
Plaatjies, Sean 253
Polu, Junior 302
Ponissi, Frank 79
Pretorius, André 64, 67, 151, 153, 170, 191, 204, 211, 216, 230, 235–236, 237–238, 246, 306
Pretorius, Jaco 226, 227, 230, 254
Prinsloo, Johan 86, 87, 140, 176, 192, 193, 215, 219
Pusey, David 66

Qeqa, Viwe 286
Qeqe, Dan 128–129
Quail, David 5, 21

Rabeni, Seru 314
Ralepelle, Chiliboy 184, 201, 217, 255
Rapport 131, 179, 184, 186, 240, 241, 242, 251
Rathbone, Clyde 5, 84, 90, 98, 114, 143
Raubenheimer, Sean 25
Rautenbach, Faan 105
Rautenbach, Rauties 253
Rawaqa, Ifereimi 314

Readhead, Clint 85–86, 93, 104, 121, 131, 237, 330
Reece-Edwards, Hugh 69–70, 71, 72, 79
Retief, Dan 59
Robbie, John 270–273
Robinson, Andy 235, 249, 250
Robinson, Jason 329
Roets, Gert 87, 252
Roets, Johan 64, 66, 67
Rogers, Mat 199
Rokocoko, Joe 89, 126, 144, 146, 209
Rolland, Alain 2, 327, 328, 332
Roos, Paul 213, 225
Rosenberg, Wilf 31
Rossouw, Chris 72
Rossouw, Danie 154, 228, 236, 242, 245, 254, 330–331
Rossouw, Pieter 46, 48, 49, 57
Rupert, Johann 251–252, 253, 302, 334
Russell, Brent 107, 164, 216
Ryan, Dale 27

SABC 220, 222
Sanderson, Alex 65
Sasol 163, 225, 251, 297, 334
Sauls, Eric 63, 64, 65, 67, 68
Scheepers, Kevin 41
Sephaka, Lawrence 36, 67, 178
Serfontein, Divan 184
Servat, William 66
Sharpe, Nathan 65, 66
Shelley, Noel 29–31
Sheridan, Andrew 65
Shimange, Hanyani 67, 105, 178
Sinclair, Des 31
Sinderbury, Mark 294

Sivivatu, Sitiveni 209

Skinstad, Bob 53, 54, 55, 56–57, 58, 59, 63, 80, 103, 268, 281, 288, 290, 307, 316, 321

Skrela, David 66

Slade, John 72

Slattery, Fergus 120

Smal, Gert 99, 104, 109, 111, 113, 124, 131, 167, 180, 204, 295, 300, 315, 318, 326, 330

Small, James 41, 44, 51

Smit, John 28, 36, 63, 64, 65, 67, 71, 90, 103–104, 106, 111, 112, 114, 115, 119, 124, 129, 136, 149, 154, 155, 166, 168, 169, 184, 189, 192, 194, 206, 210, 214, 229, 247, 248–249, 250, 254, 260, 276, 279, 284, 287, 289, 290, 295, 296, 299, 306–307, 310, 311, 313, 314, 318, 320, 326, 327–328, 329, 331, 332–333, 334, 335

Smith, Franco 49, 51

Smith, Juan 90, 105, 126, 146–147, 192, 202, 210, 227, 228, 242, 244, 245, 284, 304, 314, 320, 332

Smith, Wayne 92

Snyman, André 46, 49, 166

Snyman, Dawie 64

Solomons, Alan 42–43, 44, 46, 48, 50, 53, 55, 56–57, 59–60, 70, 81

Son, Die 279

South African Players Association (SARPA) 234

Southey, Tim 41

Sowerby, Shaun 71

Spencer, Carlos 49

Spies, Pierre 182, 184, 187, 194, 202, 204, 210, 217, 218, 227–228, 236, 238, 242, 244, 245, 295–296, 312–313, 326

Sports Illustrated 276

Sprong, Geoff 32

Star 274

Steele, Mark 104, 131, 176

Steenkamp, Gurthro 124, 169, 178, 313, 321

Steyn, François 216, 226, 230–231, 236, 237, 247, 285, 288, 304, 307, 308–310, 319, 328, 329, 331, 333

Steyn, Rory 327

Stofile, Makhenkesi 286

Stofile, Mike 134, 178, 222, 234, 240, 244, 260, 266, 274, 275, 281, 286

Stones, Jonathan 259, 261, 266, 275, 294, 322

Straeuli, Rudolf 72, 73, 75, 76, 78–79, 83, 97, 103, 131, 141, 142, 147, 203

Stringer, Peter 229

Sunday Independent 1

Sunday Times 135, 184

SuperSport 69, 87, 189, 222, 252, 324

Sutton, Reg 17

Swart, François 'Swys' 89, 90, 91

Swart, Justin 42, 72

Tait, Mathew 330

Taylor, Dummy 6

Teichmann, Gary 46, 48, 49–50, 51, 52–53, 54, 57, 58, 59, 69

Terblanche, Stefan 46, 47

Texeira, Tex 87, 324

Thion, Jerome 154, 172

Thomas, Arwel 78

Thomas, Corris 99

Tito, Paul 65, 66, 190

Traille, Damien 66, 172

Tshume, Mpumelelo 163, 176, 179, 193, 203–204, 219, 223, 234, 240, 266, 268, 269, 273, 274–275

Tuitupou, Sam 89

Turinui, Morgan 143

Tyibilika, Solly 124, 129, 134, 178, 187–188

Ulufonua, Lisiate 309

Umaga, Tana 148

Usiskin, Nick 309, 310

Uys, Piet 241

Vaka, Joseph 308–310

Van Blerk, Bok 327

Van den Berg, Albert 113, 115, 154, 290, 321

Van der Linde, CJ 154, 217, 247, 306, 311–312, 313

Van der Merwe, Carla 259

Van der Merwe, Johan 22

Van der Merwe, Kobus 78, 277

Van der Valk, Rob 56

Van der Wath, Jed 23, 29

Van der Westhuizen, Joost 44, 46, 48, 49, 50, 53, 55, 103, 201–202

Van der Westhuyzen, Jaco 64, 103, 190–191

Van Graan, Barend 241

Van Heerden, Wikus 288, 290, 316, 321

Van Niekerk, Elna 105–106, 176

Van Niekerk, Joe 115, 116, 119, 146–147, 172, 202, 214

Van Rooyen, Brian 97, 98, 101, 111–112, 115, 122, 127, 130, 131,

133, 134, 138–139, 140, 149, 219, 220, 223
Van Rooyen, Thabu 111
Van Straaten, Braam 75
Van Wyk, Eugene 59
Van Zyl, Brian 75
Venter, AJ 78, 124–125, 204, 210, 216
Venter, André 46, 48, 56–57, 58, 60, 107
Vermeulen, Elvis 66
Verster, Frans 52
Vickerman, Dan 65
Vickery, Phil 236, 238, 305, 328
Viljoen, Harry 55, 74–76, 77–78, 79–81, 82, 83, 103, 140, 197, 203, 298
Vodacom 163, 251, 297
Von Hoesslin, Dave 236
Vos, André 80, 103

Wallace, David 229
Walsh, Steve 136
Wannenburg, Pedrie 90, 204, 210, 211, 218, 242, 244
Warner, Warren 23

Watson, André 209, 252
Watson, Cheeky 263, 274, 281
Watson, Luke 187–188, 261–262, 263–266, 268–269, 270–275, 276–277, 278–279, 280–282, 285–286
Watson-Smith, Butch 80–81
Waugh, Phil 66, 170
Weepu, Piri 147, 171, 191
Weir, Darryl 30
Welsh, Frikkie 66
Wernars, Gerry 15
Wessels, Robbie 327
Westerduin, Johan [father] 6–7, 10
White, Clinton [son] 33, 40, 101, 114, 196–197, 324, 334
White, Debbie [wife] 5, 7, 17–18, 20, 33, 40, 59, 101, 102, 196, 240, 324, 334
White, Dennis [stepfather] 7, 10, 14
White, Jon [brother] 6, 7, 14, 33

White, Rose [mother] 6–7, 10, 11, 14
White, Wesley [son] 40, 101, 197, 324, 334
Wiese, Kobus 189
Wilkinson, Jonny 165, 303, 304, 305, 321, 329
Willemse, Ashwin 84–87, 90, 105, 121–122, 178, 263, 267–268, 306, 321, 333
Williams, Chester 97, 100
Williams, John 87
Williams, Shane 153
Willis, Terry 309–310
Wilson, Jeff 49
Winter, Russell 25
Wiso, Temba 64
Woodcock, Tony 89
Woodward, Bryce 89
Woodward, Clive 78, 98, 120, 123, 128

Yachvili, Dimitri 128
Yeye, Zola 220, 221–222, 223–224, 266–268, 269, 279, 302, 309
Young, Bill 135

Do you have any comments, suggestions or
feedback about this book or any other Zebra Press titles?
Contact us at **talkback@zebrapress.co.za**